Complete Bulgarian

Michael Holman
and
Mira Kovatcheva

For UK order enquiries: please contact Bookpoint Ltd, 130 Milton Park, Abingdon, Oxon OX14 4SB. Telephone: +44 (0) 1235 827720. Fax: +44 (0) 1235 400454. Lines are open 09.00–17.00, Monday to Saturday, with a 24-hour message answering service. Details about our titles and how to order are available at www.teachyourself.co.uk

For USA order enquiries: please contact McGraw-Hill Customer Services, PO Box 545, Blacklick, OH 43004-0545, USA. Telephone: 1-800-722-4726. Fax: 1-614-755-5645.

For Canada order enquiries: please contact McGraw-Hill Ryerson Ltd, 300 Water St, Whitby, Ontario L1N 9B6, Canada. Telephone: 905 430 5000. Fax: 905 430 5020.

Long renowned as the authoritative source for self-guided learning – with more than 50 million copies sold worldwide – the Teach Yourself series includes over 500 titles in the fields of languages, crafts, hobbies, business, computing and education.

British Library Cataloguing in Publication Data: a catalogue record for this title is available from the British Library.

Library of Congress Catalog Card Number: on file.

First published in UK 1993 as *Teach Yourself Bulgarian* by Hodder Education, part of Hachette UK, 338 Euston Road, London NW1 3BH.

First published in US 1993 by The McGraw-Hill Companies, Inc.

This edition published 2011.

The Teach Yourself name is a registered trade mark of Hodder Headline.

Copyright © 1993, 2003, 2009, 2011 Michael Holman and Mira Kovatcheva

Typeset by MPS Limited, a Macmillan Company.
Printed in Great Britain for Hodder Education, part of Hachette UK, 338 Euston Road, London NW1 3BH, by CPI Group (UK) Ltd, Croydon, CR0 4YY.

The publisher has used its best endeavours to ensure that the URLs for external websites referred to in this book are correct and active at the time of going to press. However, the publisher and the author have no responsibility for the websites and can make no guarantee that a site will remain live or that the content will remain relevant, decent or appropriate.

Hachette UK's policy is to use papers that are natural, renewable and recyclable products and made from wood grown in sustainable forests. The logging and manufacturing processes are expected to conform to the environmental regulations of the country of origin.

Impression number   10 9 8 7 6 5 4
Year   2017

Complete Bulgarian

Contents

Credits

Front cover: © Maksim Bukovski – Fotolia.com

Back cover and pack: © Jakub Semeniuk/iStockphoto.com, © Royalty-Free/Corbis, © agencyby/iStockphoto.com, © Andy Cook/iStockphoto.com, © Christopher Ewing/iStockphoto.com, © zebicho–Fotolia.com, © Geoffrey Holman/iStockphoto.com, © Photodisc/Getty Images, © James C. Pruitt/iStockphoto.com, © Mohamed Saber – Fotolia.com

Acknowledgements

It would be impossible to thank all our relatives and friends and also colleagues, past and present, who have helped us directly or indirectly with this book. We would, however, like to single out for special mention Christo Stamenov and Vladimir Filipov, both lecturers at Sofia University, who assisted us greatly in the later stages of our work on the first edition of *Teach Yourself Bulgarian*. To everyone who has written to thank us for the book and to make suggestions for its improvement, we are grateful beyond measure. The responsibility for outstanding imperfections in this new edition, however, remains firmly with us.

Meet the authors

Professor Michael Holman

I spent my academic career at the University of Leeds, where I am now Emeritus Professor of Russian and Slavonic Studies. I am of mixed Russian and English parentage and have been married to Bulgarian-born Dorothea since 1965.

Bulgaria has played a hugely important part in my academic and personal life. Shortly after taking up my appointment at Leeds, I added the study of Bulgarian language and literature to the undergraduate course. In 1968 I set up what was then a ground-breaking undergraduate exchange with Sofia University. Mira Kovatcheva, my co-author for *Complete Bulgarian*, first came to Leeds on the exchange in 1972. She returned as Bulgarian Lector in 1989 making it possible for me to realize my long-held ambition to co-author a modern, learner-friendly but academically sound Bulgarian language coursebook. Published by Hodder & Stoughton as *Teach Yourself Bulgarian* in 1993, it went into its third revised edition in 2009 and has sold nearly 40,000 copies worldwide.

I love going to Bulgaria and since 1965 have made regular visits to Sofia and beyond, initiating and participating in numerous projects of academic cooperation. In addition to teaching Bulgarian for more than 30 years, I have also tried my hand at translating works of Bulgarian literature into English. For my contribution to Anglo-Bulgarian cultural interchange, in 1995 Sofia University awarded me an honorary Doctorate. This was sandwiched between the award of the Order of Cyril and Methodius in 1987 and the Order of Stara Planina in 2000.

Dr Mira Kovatcheva

I am currently Associate Professor in the Department of English and American Studies at the University of Sofia. My interests originally focused on English historical linguistics and English–Bulgarian contrastive studies. Between 1989 and 1992, however, I was fortunate to be seconded to Leeds University to teach on the Bulgarian programme run by Michael Holman. This period coincided with the fall of communism and a heightened interest in the languages of the former communist countries, including Bulgaria. Hodder & Stoughton were seeking to expand their *Teach Yourself* language courses and swiftly signed up Michael and me to write a user-friendly Bulgarian language course for English speakers. Thus was born our Bulgarian–English authorial tandem, which, in 1993, led to the publication of *Teach Yourself Bulgarian*.

Fired by my Leeds experience, I extended my interests to Bulgarian as a second language and languages in contact. Since 1994 I have been oral examiner for Bulgarian at the British Embassy in Sofia. My self-instruction course for advanced learners, *Bulgarian: Beyond the First Steps*, was published in 2005. In 2007, together with Christine Milner, another former Leeds student, I authored an English–Bulgarian pocket phrasebook, which, like *Teach Yourself Bulgarian*, has proved very popular.

If I owe my success as teacher and author to any one thing, it is to my awareness of the similarities and the crucial differences between English and Bulgarian. This enables me to grade explanations according to difficulty and make learning Bulgarian both easy and enjoyable.

Only got a minute?

Especially for English speakers, Bulgarian is probably the easiest of the Slavic languages to learn. Its structure has many similarities with English: the endings of nouns only change from singular to plural and the order of words in sentences often follows an English pattern. Moreover, as with English, Bulgarian has a definite article. But instead of placing an equivalent of *the* before the noun, you attach it to the end. So while the word for *(a) menu* is **МЕНЮ́**, *the menu* is **МЕНЮ́ТО**.

Pronunciation, too, is straightforward. Individual letters generally retain a constant pronunciation and do not have the quirky fickleness of English. The vowels are short, pure and clear. The consonants too present few problems. And although some combinations of sounds may initially test the tongue trained on an exclusively English diet – as in the name of the small town of **Koprivshtitsa** (**КОПРИ́ВЩИЦА** in Cyrillic), for example – practice, as always, makes perfect!

In choosing *Complete Bulgarian*, you will be taking the Cyrillic bull by the horns, but you will find this easier than you think. The alphabet is very logical, extremely efficient and well adapted to rendering the sounds of Bulgarian. Many of its 30 letters look much the same as English letters and the remainder are so strikingly different, they soon fix themselves in the memory. Have a look again at **Щ** (English SHT) and **Ю** (English YOO) in the examples we have just given you.

To give you a quick start, we use lots of well-known place names and common international words such as *Berlin* and *espresso* (**БЕРЛИ́Н**, **ЕСПРЕ́СО** in Cyrillic). You will be following thousands who have successfully learnt Bulgarian spelling this way. We will be there to guide you at every turn as you move on to master the pronunciation, the vocabulary and the grammar.

5 Only got five minutes?

Bulgarian belongs to the south Slavic subgrouping of the Slavic languages and is spoken by some 10 million people worldwide. Closely related to Macedonian and Serbian, Bulgarian was the first ever language to use Cyrillic, now primarily associated with Russian. Bulgaria was also the first country in the European Union to use Cyrillic.

The Cyrillic alphabet, Bulgaria's pride and joy, traces its origin way back to the 9th century and takes its name from St Cyril, Apostle of the Slavs. It is an original combination of Roman and Greek letters – with a few extra ones ingeniously added to render the specific sounds of Bulgarian. It is not difficult to learn. Capital and small letters differ little and of its 30 letters, six: **A, E, K, M, O** and **T** are the same as in English. A further six look the same, but are pronounced differently. Among these so-called 'false friends' **H, P** and **C** masquerade as English N, R and S. Some Cyrillic letters differ only slightly in shape from their English counterparts like **Б** for B, for example. Still others look like English letters turned the wrong way round. **И**, the backwards N, is actually I while **Я**, the mirror image of R stands for two sounds: **YA**. The remainder, like **Ж, Ф, Ц** and **Ю**, are so strikingly different that you will soon learn to recognize them. It is in the Cyrillic alphabet that much of the immediate challenge and attraction of Bulgarian lies. It also makes the language fun to learn. Even now you should be ready to decipher **РЕСТОРÁНТ, БАР, МЕТРÓ**, and even **АМÉРИКА**. Easy! This is what we call 'instant Bulgarian'. It will make you feel more at home in what initially seems an alien linguistic and cultural environment.

Learning Bulgarian is made easier by the fact that, over the centuries, it has 'borrowed' thousands of words from other languages – French, German, Italian and especially in the last 20 years, from English. A few of these 'borrowings', such as **СÝПЕР** (sooper) *super*, **ЧÁО!** (chao!) *bye!* and **МЕРСИ́** (mersee) – one of the Bulgarian words for *thank you* – remain much as in the original language. Most, however, take on some Bulgarian characteristics to help them 'go native'. Nouns adopt one of three genders: masculine, feminine or neuter, depending on the final sound. So the Bulgarian for *email* **ЍМЕЙЛ** (eemeyl) is masculine and its plural is **ЍМЕЙЛИ** (eemeyli). Verbs (doing words) also get squeezed into an accepted verb pattern, usually one of the more common ones, slightly changing the ending of the English verb. So *I am printing* is **ПРИНТЍРАМ** (printeeram). The 'borrowed' words will also be slightly camouflaged by the way they are pronounced in Bulgarian, but listen carefully and you'll soon learn to recognize them. The disguise is only skin deep!

Two further related characteristics of Bulgarian make it one of the easiest Slavic languages for the English speaker to learn. First, along with Macedonian, and just like English, it has lost almost all those complicated inflectional endings still found in nouns and adjectives in Polish, Russian and Serbian, for example. Second, the order of words in the sentence is very similar to that of English.

However, it is often the ways in which one language differs from another that make it interesting for the learner. Bulgarian has plenty to offer you here – apart from the alphabet! – particularly in the verb. First, it has a system of verbal aspects, which allows any action to be seen either as completed (perfective) or as continuing (a process rather than an event – imperfective). Also, it lacks an infinitive and often omits the personal pronouns. So, *I love to travel* is **ОБЍЧАМ ДА ПЪТУ́ВАМ** (obeecham da puttoovam) literally *(I) love that (I) travel*. Most interesting of all, however, is the parallel verb system, which allows the speaker – or writer – to show whether s/he was a witness to the events being recounted or is merely relating things second hand. But enough technicalities about the language, what about the course and its authors?

This is a practical, topic-based course for people who want to understand, read and write the Bulgarian language, but who, above all, want to *communicate* with Bulgarians in their language. It has been created by two specialists, one English and one Bulgarian, who have been working in tandem for more than 20 years. Our selection and presentation of the carefully graded material combine not only knowledge of the theory, but also many years teaching Bulgarian to English speakers.

There couldn't be a better time to learn Bulgarian. Bulgaria is now a full member of the EU and is open to the world. Moreover, more and more people are learning Bulgarian, so you won't be alone in your undertaking. You will conquer the alphabet in a few hours and will be well on your way to grasping the key to the language and culture of the Bulgarian people.

Congratulations and good luck!

Introduction

Welcome to *Complete Bulgarian*. This is a full, balanced course for beginners in spoken and written Bulgarian. It has been designed for self-tuition, but may also be used for study with a teacher. It aims to teach you to understand and use the contemporary language in a variety of typical, everyday situations. Above all, it is functional, enabling you to communicate and interact, using the language for well-defined, practical purposes. Although the course is intended primarily for people with no knowledge of the language, you will also find it useful if you want to brush up or extend some previous knowledge.

The course is divided into 20 carefully graded and interlocking units. Each unit is devoted to a particular topic or situation and each successive unit builds naturally on material covered in previous units. The first half of the book, up to the end of Unit 9, is a basic grammatical and thematic 'survival kit'. The emphasis here is on the present tense and on immediate situations you may well find yourself in on a visit to Bulgaria. From Unit 10 on, you progress to less immediate, but no less important matters. You will learn to ask about future events, inquiring about the weather, for example, or putting together a plan for the days ahead. You will also learn how to talk about things that happened in the past, how to make complaints and both give and understand directions. And as your vocabulary and grammatical knowledge increase, you will be able to make more use of the tables and lists in the Appendix at the back of the book.

We have divided each unit into distinct but interrelated sections. An initial Dialogue is followed by a 'Quick vocabulary' with the new words and phrases set out in the order in which they occur and a few short questions in Bulgarian based on the Dialogue. Then, up to Unit 11, comes a section **Doing things the Bulgarian way** with cultural background information primarily for first-time visitors to the country. This is followed by useful phrases relevant to the theme of the unit and worth learning by heart. Then come grammatical explanations – all proceeding naturally from the new words and constructions used in the Dialogue – followed by a set of Exercises. There are lots of them, varied, practical, with all the answers in the back – so you can test yourself and see how you are doing. Every so often within this set of Exercises you will find an additional 'Quick vocab' with a short list of new words and phrases.

After these Exercises there is always a second Dialogue. Its aim is to give you a sense of achievement, for it is based on words, phrases and grammatical structures already familiar to you but used here in a different context. In this way, the introduction of a few new words and phrases comes naturally and takes you another step forward. As you work through each unit you will feel supported by our careful explanation of grammatical points, word usages and linguistic practices, every so often summarized in the **Insight** boxes. We have rounded off each unit with a further extensive set of Exercises designed to help you test your progress.

In the dialogues, we have tried to concentrate on the activities of a limited number of characters, both English and Bulgarian speakers, whose paths cross in Bulgaria one year in May. First, there is Michael Johnson, a man of entrepreneurial disposition from Chelmsford, UK. Mr Johnson is in Sofia for the first time and has wisely learnt some Bulgarian in preparation for his visit. He is on a two-week business trip, establishing contacts, especially with Boyan Antonov, director of a Sofia-based advertising agency. You will also meet members of Mr Antonov's staff: Nadya, his hard-working secretary, Nikolai Dimitrov, a junior colleague, and Milena Marinova, a photographer. (Particularly keep an eye on Nikolai and Milena . . .) Then there is a married couple from Manchester, Victoria and George Collins. Victoria is an interpreter and George is a teacher. They too are visiting Bulgaria, but not for the first time. Victoria speaks Bulgarian well. Nevena Petkova is a hotel receptionist. (Nevena doesn't miss a trick and is worth keeping an eye on too!) There are other characters as well taking part in a variety of situations and locations, from Sofia in the west to Plovdiv in the south and on to Varna and the Black Sea in the east.

How best to use this course

Before starting Unit 1, you will need carefully to work through the sections on the alphabet and pronunciation. Look, too, at the section on pronunciation and spelling at the beginning of the Appendix. Despite the different script, you will soon find that there are many Bulgarian words you recognize, both in their written form and when you hear them on the recording that accompanies *Complete Bulgarian*.

◄) CD1, TR 1

Dialogues or other sections marked with ◄) are included on the recording. Do make full use of it. As you listen to the native speakers, imitate their pronunciation and your own pronunciation will improve. New technologies allow you to listen to recordings anywhere any time, so use every possible opportunity. Repeat the words and phrases as often as possible so as to get your tongue round the foreign sounds. Before going on to a new unit, listen again to the dialogues recorded from the previous unit. The more you listen and the more you speak, the better you'll be!

Learning techniques obviously vary and you will probably need to experiment a little before adopting the procedure that suits you best. However, since each unit follows the same pattern, you might find the following procedure worth trying for a start.

Dialogue

Don't skip the English introduction at the beginning of each dialogue. It will establish the context for you. If you have the recording, listen to the whole Dialogue and see how much you understand.

Now work through the Dialogue, listening to the recording and reading aloud as you go. This will do wonders to boost your confidence. The vocabulary after the Dialogue gives you the meaning of all new words and key phrases. If you find this initial vocabulary doesn't list a word you cannot understand, turn to the Bulgarian–English vocabulary at the back of the book. (Do learn the alphabetical order of the Bulgarian letters right away – it will save you hours of dictionary searching later on.) For numerals and prepositions, the best place to look is the Appendix. If you are searching for the Bulgarian equivalent of an English word, there is the English–Bulgarian vocabulary. It contains most of the words used in the different units.

Having memorized as much of the vocab as you can, listen to the recording again, following the text of the Dialogue in the book.

Questions

Trying to answer the questions that follow the Dialogue is a first step towards using the new language creatively. The questions don't just test your understanding, they show you how the words can be rearranged to achieve a different function. Read the questions out loud and then provide the most suitable phrase from the Dialogue for an answer.

Background information

For a little light relief and insight into some interesting cultural and linguistic practices, have a look at the sections marked **Doing things the Bulgarian way**.

How do you say it?

This section lists the most frequently used phrases in a given situation. Not all the words and phrases will have appeared in the Dialogue, but they will all be relevant to the topic of the unit. Try to memorize as many as possible.

Grammar

This section gives you the key to understanding the structure of the language and demands careful study. In some units, this section is longer than in others. Always, however, the grammatical explanations refer to material used in the Dialogue. The usage should, therefore, already be familiar to you. And since many of the examples used in the Grammar section are taken from the Dialogue, this should help further to consolidate your knowledge. If there are some words introduced for the first time in the Grammar section, their English translation is given either immediately after the word or in a nearby

'Quick vocab'. Don't miss the opportunity to learn these too – they are sure to appear again later!

Exercises

Once you feel you have a reasonable understanding of the material, test your knowledge by working through the Exercises. We have designed them not only to be communicatively useful but also to help you master the relevant grammatical structures. Practice is a vital part of the learning process, so try to do them all! The answers in the Key at the back of the book will give you an idea of how you are doing.

Another small step forward

Move on to the second Dialogue when you feel you are ready. First, read the Dialogue out loud and listen to the recording without reference to the vocabulary. Then look at the vocabulary, in which we have again listed the new words and phrases in the order they occur, and work through this second Dialogue as you worked through the first one.

Test yourself

You will now be ready to take the second set of Exercises in your stride. Most of these exercises focus on the content of the second Dialogue and on the topical phrases in the 'How do you say it?' section.

Now can you . . . ?

Each unit always ends up with a number of self-checking questions to enable you to test your progress. If you are uncertain about any aspect of your answers, listen again to all the recorded material of the unit you have just been working on. If you do not have the recording, read through the dialogues aloud, making sure that you have understood everything this time.

Good luck, and remember, *practice makes perfect* or, as the Bulgarians might say, **повторéнието е мáйка на знáнието** (lit. *the repetition is mother of the learning*).

Abbreviations

Abbreviations used in this book are: adj = adjective, f = feminine, m = masculine, lit. = literally, n = neuter, nn = noun, p. = page, pl = plural, sing = singular, vb = verb, T = true, F = false.

Alphabet and pronunciation

The 30 letters of the Cyrillic alphabet may at first seem a bit of a barrier, but they are not difficult to master. The alphabet is logical and well adapted to rendering the sounds of Bulgarian. It is also very economical, one Bulgarian letter often replacing a combination of letters in English. In standard educated speech, each individual letter is usually clearly pronounced – what you see is what you say!

The letters can be conveniently divided into three manageable, easy-to-learn groups. They are:

1 letters that look the same in Bulgarian and English
2 letters that look different
3 letters that look the same, but are, in fact, pronounced very differently. These are the 'false friends' that can, initially at least, cause the greatest difficulty.

Look at the alphabet table on the following pages and see if you can decide which letters fall into which group.

Bulgarian has six simple vowels: **А, Е, И, О, У, Ъ** – one more than English – and two letters, **Ю** and **Я**, that really stand for a consonant plus a vowel – **й** + **у** and **й** + **а**, respectively.

The Bulgarian alphabet 🔊 CD 1, TR 2

Printed letters		Written letters	
capital	small*	capital	small
А	а	*A*	*a*
Б	б	*Б*	*б*
В	в (ʋ)	*В*	*в*
Г	г (ɡ)	*Г*	*г*
Д	д (g)	*Д*	*g*
Е	е	*Е*	*e*
Ж	ж	*Ж*	*ж*
З	з	*З*	*з*
И	и (u)	*И*	*и*
Й	й (ŭ)	*Й*	*й*
К	к	*К*	*к*
Л	л (ʌ)	*Л*	*л*
М	м	*М*	*м*
Н	н	*Н*	*н*
О	о	*О*	*o*
П	п (n)	*П*	*n*
Р	р	*Р*	*p*
С	с	*С*	*c*
Т	т (m)	*Т*	*m*
У	у	*У*	*y*
Ф	ф	*Ф*	*ф*
Х	х	*Х*	*x*
Ц	ц (ц)	*Ц*	*ц*
Ч	ч	*Ч*	*ч*
Ш	ш (ш)	*Ш*	*ш*
Щ	щ (щ)	*Щ*	*щ*
Ъ	ъ	*Ъ*	*ъ*
**	ь	**	*ь*
Ю	ю	*Ю*	*ю*
Я	я	*Я*	*я*

Approximate English sound		Bulgarian example	English meaning
a	as in 'art' (but shorter)	**Á**на	*Anna*
b	as in 'book'	**банá**н	*banana*
v	as in 'vice'	**вод**á	*water*
g	as in 'good'	**год**ина	*year*
d	as in 'dot'	**д**áта	*date*
e	as in 'elephant'	**é**сен	*autumn*
s	as in 'pleasure'	**жен**á	*woman*
z	as in 'zigzag'	**зи**ма	*winter*
i	as in 'inch'	**и**ме	*name*
y	as in 'yes'	**й**óга	*yoga*
k	as in 'king'	**ка**к	*how*
l	as in 'label'	**легл**ó	*bed*
m	as in 'man'	**м**áлък	*small*
n	as in 'not'	**нов**инá	*news*
o	as in 'offer'	**ó**коло	*about*
p	as in 'pet'	**пá**пка	*folder*
r	as in 'rat'	**ресто**рáнт	*restaurant*
s	as in 'sister'	**сестр**á	*sister*
t	as in 'tent'	**тó**рта	*cake*
oo	as in 'foot'	**ý**тре	*tomorrow*
f	as in 'fifteen'	**фа**кс	*fax*
h	as in 'horrid'	**хý**бав	*nice*
ts	as in 'fits'	**цв**éте	*flower*
ch	as in 'church'	**ча**дър	*umbrella*
sh	as in 'ship'	**шá**пка	*hat*
sht	as in 'fishtail'	**щá**стие	*happiness*
u	as in 'curtain' (but shorter)	**ъ**гъл	*corner*
y	as in 'York'	**асансьó**р	*lift, elevator*
you	as in 'youth' (but shorter)	**ю**ли	*July*
ya	as in 'yarn' (but shorter)	**я**года	*strawberry*

* The letters in brackets in the second column frequently replace their small printed counterparts in printed texts and public notices.
** The letter **ь** *never* comes at the beginning of a word, so it is not used as a capital.

Pronouncing Bulgarian

The English sounds you see in the table are only very rough guides to correct Bulgarian pronunciation. Listening to native speakers and copying them is the best way to get things right, so do make full use of the recording. Try listening now to the pronunciation guide on the recording. To begin with you might find it helpful to put a rule beneath the lines with the individual letters and words as you listen and repeat. Pay special attention to the precise shape of the letters not found in the English alphabet. Later you can just listen, trying to write the individual initial letters as the words are read out. And do practise the sounds by reading the full words out loud.

Stress

You will notice that in each word of more than one syllable, for example **юли** *July*, **годи́на** *year* and **ресторáнт** *restaurant*, we have put an accent above one of the vowels. We have also put an accent above the vowel in words of one syllable when they are stressed. We have done this to help your pronunciation. Although Bulgarians don't mark the stress when they write, when they speak they pronounce one syllable in every word more distinctly than the rest. (You probably noticed this as you listened to the recording.) This is the 'stressed' syllable. As you can see, the stress can fall on any syllable, just as in English. And, again as in English, if you stress the wrong syllable, the word will sound very odd, sometimes even incomprehensible. On the rare occasions when a word has two stresses, we have marked this too. So when you learn a new word, make sure you note which syllable is stressed.

You will come across some additional notes on pronunciation both as you proceed through the course and at the beginning of the Appendix, but for now it will be enough if you note the following points:

1 Unlike the vowels in English, the Bulgarian vowels don't differ in length. (They are all a little longer than the English short vowels and a little shorter than the English long vowels.)
2 The sound of the Bulgarian letter **р** is always rolled, 'r-r-r', as the Scots pronounce Brenda and Bruce.

3 The sound of the Bulgarian **x** is not found in standard English. It is very like the Scottish **ch** in lo**ch** and is pronounced nearer the front of the mouth than the English letter **h**.

4 There is no equivalent English letter for **ъ**. We do almost have the sound, however, in a slightly longer version in the **u** in c**u**rtain and f**u**r or in the letter **e**, when read quickly but clearly in the word th**e**, for example. (Read aloud the last part of this sentence from the word 'or', and you will get the **ъ** in 'the' about right.)

Writing Bulgarian

There are four things to note when writing Bulgarian:

- While there is very little difference between the capital and small letters in the printed script, the printed and the handwritten letters differ considerably. You will, however, come across longhand letters, more rounded in form, used in printed texts alongside their more angular printed counterparts. These are the letters in brackets in the pronunciation table, given earlier in this section. (You will find examples under 4 below and in the brochure extract given towards the end of Unit 11.)

- Compared with English, both in the printed and handwritten forms, Bulgarian has fewer letters that extend above and below the line. It is important to observe the relative height of the letters.

- When you write the letters **л**, **м** and **я** in longhand, you must make sure you begin the letters with a little hook:

$$\mathcal{\lambda} \qquad \mathcal{M} \qquad \mathcal{Я}$$

This makes it impossible to join them to a preceding **o**.

- In general, Bulgarian avoids double consonants, even in foreign words. For example, Mr and Mrs Collins play a large part in this book and their surname is written **Ко́линс**. Note too that it is written with a final **с**, not a **з**. More about this in the note on pronunciation in the Appendix! Now it's time for a little practice.

Trying out what you have learnt

🔊 CD1, TR 3

To help you recognize the letters and to practise your pronunciation, here are some 'international' words – many of them names – written out in their Bulgarian spelling, with some of them spoken on the recording. We have given both their printed and handwritten forms and have arranged the words in the three different groups mentioned earlier. You should have little difficulty in identifying their English equivalents. Check whether you've got them right by looking up the Key to the alphabet and pronunciation at the back of the book. You might also try writing out the words yourself. Watch the height of your letters!

1 Letters that look the same in Bulgarian and English (at least in their printed form, but see 4 below):

A	Аля́ска	*Аляска*	адре́с	*адрес*
E	Есто́ния	*Естония*	еспре́со	*еспресо*
К	Кана́да	*Канада*	кре́дит	*кредит*
М	Мила́но	*Милано*	мину́та	*минута*
О	Ота́ва	*Отава*	омле́т	*омлет*
Т	Те́ксас	*Тексас*	телефо́н	*телефон*

Insight

The handwritten forms of the Bulgarian letters **к** and **м** differ slightly from the English, while the Bulgarian handwritten **т** is completely different and confusingly resembles an English m.

2 Letters that look different:

Б	Берли́н	*Берлин*	бар	*бар*
Г	Гла́згоу	*Глазгоу*	гара́ж	*гараж*

Д	Дако́та	*Дакота*	во́дка	*водка*
Ж	Жене́ва	*Женева*	жу́ри	*жури*
З	Замбе́зи	*Замбези*	Аризо́на	*Аризона*
И	Истанбу́л	*Истанбул*	И́ндия	*Индия*
Й	Йорк	*Йорк*	Майо́рка	*Майорка*
Л	Ло́ндон	*Лондон*	Балка́н	*Балкан*
П	Пана́ма	*Панама*	поли́ция	*полиция*
Ф	Фра́нкфурт	*Франкфурт*	Со́фия	*София*
Ц	Цю́рих	*Цюрих*	Доне́цк	*Донецк*
Ч	Чад	*Чад*	Чъ́рчил	*Чърчил*
Ш	Ше́филд	*Шефилд*	шоу-би́знес	*шоу-бизнес*
Щ	Щу́тгарт	*Щутгарт*	Бу́дапеща	*Будапеща*
Ъ	Ъ́пдайк	*Ъпдайк*	Бълга́рия	*България*
Ь	шофьо́р	*шофьор*	синьо́ра	*синьора*
Ю	Ю́кон	*Юкон*	Лийдс юна́йтед	*Лийдс юнайтед*
Я	Я́лта	*Ялта*	я́нки	*янки*

3 Letters that look the same, but are pronounced differently ('false friends'):

В	Вие́на	*Виена*	Ви́виан	*Вивиан*
Н	Нами́бия	*Намибия*	Ва́рна	*Варна*
Р	Ри́чард	*Ричард*	Йо́ркшир	*Йоркшир*
С	Сина́тра	*Синатра*	А́мстердам	*Амстердам*
У	Унга́рия	*Унгария*	Ли́върпул	*Ливерпул*
Х	Хайд парк	*Хайд парк*	Саха́ра	*Сахара*

You will notice that the Bulgarian pronunciation of names and 'international' words differs slightly from the English. Sometimes, too, a different syllable is stressed, **телефо́н** and **паспо́рт**, for example. And do remember that Bulgarians say **Со́фия** (*Sófia*, not *Sophía*!)

And talking of 'international words', it has to be said that Cyrillic is increasingly under siege from the Latin script. Both scripts are increasingly used side by side. This is particularly the case in business, commerce and communication technology. The Bulgarian mobile phone system, for example, is called GSM (**джиесе́м**), email addresses can only be given in Latin script and the word 'email' itself has only recently settled with **и́мейл** as an accepted Cyrillic equivalent.

4 Here, side by side, are some words written using both the angular and the more rounded, longhand letters. All the words appear in the previous lists. See if you can recognize them:

адре́с/адре́с, еспре́со/еспре́со, телефо́н/телефо́н, кре́дит/ кре́дит, Ота́ва/Ота́ва, гара́ж/гара́ж, мину́та/мину́та, Доне́цк/Доне́цк, шоу-би́знес/шоу-би́знес, Бу́дапеща/ Бу́дапеща, Ви́виан/Ви́виан, А́мстердам/А́мстердам.

Doing things the Bulgarian way

Saying *yes* and *no* – a vital word of warning

Another form of communication is non-verbal communication and it is very important in Bulgaria. In most European countries, you nod your head to say 'yes' and shake it to say 'no'. In Bulgaria, certainly among speakers less affected by contact with other languages, a shake of the head – actually more a rocking of the head from side to side – often accompanies *yes* (да), while a reverse nod – usually starting with a brisk, dismissive, upward movement of the head – accompanies *no* (не).

Whether you are buying an ice cream, booking an excursion or doing a deal, listening carefully, interpreting the head movements correctly and making them correctly yourself will make all the difference to your negotiations! Have fun and start practising straightaway.

Exercises

Here are some reading exercises for you to practise what you have learnt so far about the alphabet.

1 Read the following place names matching the names in English with their Bulgarian equivalents. (In this exercise each English letter is replaced by a single Bulgarian letter.)

a	America	**i**	Лóндон
b	Amsterdam	**ii**	Сахáра
c	Arizona	**iii**	Фрáнкфурт
d	Balkan	**iv**	Амéрика
e	Berlin	**v**	Аризóна
f	Frankfurt	**vi**	Плóвдив
g	London	**vii**	Рúла
h	Plovdiv	**viii**	Вóлга
i	Rila	**ix**	Вáрна
j	Sahara	**x**	Балкáн
k	Varna	**xi**	Берлúн
l	Volga	**xii**	Áмстердам

2 Do the same with this list. You might need to replace certain combinations of English letters by a single Bulgarian letter. (Remember that Bulgarian rarely uses double letters!)

a	Charing Cross	**i**	Виéна
b	Chelmsford	**ii**	Ю́кон
c	Donetsk	**iii**	Чéлмсфорд
d	Shell	**iv**	Ню Йорк
e	Shetland	**v**	Чáринг крос
f	Stuttgart	**vi**	Шéтланд
g	Vienna	**vii**	Донéцк
h	Yalta	**viii**	Шел
i	New York	**ix**	Щу́тгарт
j	Yukon	**x**	Я́лта

3 Here, concentrate on the sound; read the Bulgarian and identify the English equivalent.

....

Insight

Sometimes one English letter needs two letters in Bulgarian and vice-versa.

....

a	Лийдс	**i**	Woody Allen
b	Джéнифър Лóпец	**ii**	Beatles
c	Хéлзинки	**iii**	Helsinki

d Ли́върпул	**iv** Oxford
e Джеймс Бонд	**v** Liverpool
f Португа́лия	**vi** James Bond
g Че́лси	**vii** Scotland
h О́ксфорд	**viii** Leeds
i Би́йтълс	**ix** Chelsea
j У́ди А́лън	**x** France
k Ко́рнуол	**xi** Geneva
l Гла́згоу	**xii** Cambridge
m Жене́ва	**xiii** Cornwall
n Шотла́ндия	**xiv** Jennifer Lopez
o Ке́ймбридж	**xv** Glasgow
p Фра́нция	**xvi** Portugal

4 If you rang the following numbers, what service would you expect to answer? Read the Bulgarian words out loud!

201	БИ́ЗНЕС КЛУБ	205	БАР
202	РЕСТОРА́НТ	206	ТАКСИ́
203	РЕЦЕ́ПЦИЯ	207	ИНФОРМА́ЦИЯ
204	ФИ́ТНЕС ЦЕ́НТЪР	166	ПОЛИ́ЦИЯ

Test yourself

1 What are the names of (**a**) the pizzeria, (**b**) the restaurant, (**c**) the hotel and (**d**) the café on the following notices?

a ПИЦАРИ́Я «МИЛА́НО»   **c** ХОТЕ́Л «ШЕ́РАТОН»
b РЕСТОРА́НТ «МОСКВА́»   **d** КАФЕ́ «ОРИЕ́НТ»

2 When does your plane take off if you are flying to:

a Milan
b Geneva
c Frankfurt
d Paris
e Berlin
f Zurich
g Budapest?

Цю́рих _____	15.40
Бу́дапеща _____	16.10
Фра́нкфурт ____	16.35
Жене́ва _____	17.05
Мила́но _____	17.25
Пари́ж _____	18.05
Берли́н _____	18.30

3 Michael Johnson has to sign the register at the hotel – in Bulgarian, of course – filling in his name and home address. Try writing out what he entered in Bulgarian longhand:

И́ме:	Майкъл Джонсън	*Michael Johnson*
Адре́с:	4, Маунт Драйв	*4, Mount Drive*
	Челмсфорд	*Chelmsford*
	Есекс	*Essex*
	Англия	*England*
	CM2 7AE	*CM2 7AE*

He also needs to send his Sofia address to his wife, so she can try to address the envelope in Cyrillic. Have a go in longhand yourself!

Майкъл Джонсън	*Michael Johnson*
апартаме́нт 8	*Apartment 8*
хоте́л «Роди́на»	*Rodina Hotel*
1000 Со́фия	*Sofia 1000*
Бълга́рия	*Bulgaria*

Now write your own name and address in Cyrillic. Think of the sounds in the English words, not the individual letters! In actual fact, the Bulgarians are better at deciphering the English script than we are the Bulgarian, so you can get away with addressing your letters in English.

Now can you:

- identify the Cyrillic letters with the same sound value as the English ones?
- identify the Cyrillic letters that look the same as English letters but stand for different sounds?
- remember and write the Cyrillic letters with no English equivalents?

1

Здраве́йте! Как се ка́звате?
Hello! What's your name?

In this unit you will learn:

- How to say *hello*
- How to give your name and nationality
- How to say *please* and *thank you*
- How to say *yes* and *no* in answer to *is there?* and *are there?*

Michael Johnson, a businessman, arrives from London at his hotel in Sofia. When he enters the vestibule he is greeted by the doorman with the words **Заповя́дайте, мо́ля!** meaning, here: *Welcome, do come in, please.* (**Мо́ля** can also mean *I beg your pardon* and *Don't mention it.*)

You will often hear **заповя́дайте** and **мо́ля** in Bulgaria, used separately and together with a variety of meanings. They are always polite and welcoming words. Together with the two words for *thank you* – **Благодаря́** and **Мерси́** (*merci* – as in the French!) and the word for *there isn't/aren't* (*any*) **ня́ма** – they are what for you will probably be the five most important words in the Bulgarian language.

Dialogue 1

🔊 **CD 1, TR 4–5**

Michael goes up to the reception desk and is greeted by the receptionist, Nevena Petkova.

Невéна Петкóва	Дóбър ден!
Мáйкъл Джóнсън	Здравéйте! Ѝма ли свобóдна стáя?
Невéна Петкóва	(*Nodding.**) Не, нѝма.
Мáйкъл Джóнсън	Ѝма ли свобóден апартамéнт?
Невéна Петкóва	(*Shaking her head.**) Да, ѝма. Турѝст ли сте?
Мáйкъл Джóнсън	Не, не съм турѝст. Бизнесмéн съм.
Невéна Петкóва	Ѝме?
Мáйкъл Джóнсън	Мóля?
Невéна Петкóва	Как се кáзвате?
Мáйкъл Джóнсън	Кáзвам се Мáйкъл Джóнсън.
Невéна Петкóва	Англичáнин ли сте?
Мáйкъл Джóнсън	Да, англичáнин съм.
Невéна Петкóва	Паспóрта, мóля.
Мáйкъл Джóнсън	Заповѝдайте!
Невéна Петкóва	Благодарѝ!
Мáйкъл Джóнсън	Мóля!

*If this confuses you, look back to the vital word of warning in the 'Alphabet and pronunciation' section at the beginning of this book.

QUICK VOCAB

Дóбър ден!	*Good morning/afternoon.*
Здравéйте!	*Hello!*
Ѝма ли свобóдна стáя?	*Is there a room free?*
Не, нѝма.	*No, there isn't.*
свобóден апартамéнт	*a free apartment*
Да, ѝма.	*Yes, there is.*
Турѝст ли сте?	*Are you a tourist?*
Не, не съм турѝст.	*No, I'm not a tourist.*
Бизнесмéн съм.	*I'm a businessman.*
ѝме	*name*
Мóля?	*(I beg your) Pardon?*
Как се кáзвате?	*What is your name?*
Кáзвам се . . .	*My name is . . .*
Англичáнин ли сте?	*Are you English?*
Да, англичáнин съм.	*Yes, I am (English).*
Паспóрта, мóля.	*Your (the) passport, please.*
Заповѝдайте!	*Here you are/There you go.*
Благодарѝ!	*Thank you.*
Мóля!	*Not at all/Don't mention it/ My pleasure.*

1 Questions

Before answering these questions, listen to the recording again (if you have it), once without looking at the dialogue and once following the text as you listen. It would also be a good idea to read aloud the questions before you answer them.

You'll find all the answers in the Dialogue – except to **1c**! The answers are also in the Key at the back of the book.

a Има ли свобо́ден апартаме́нт?
b Има ли свобо́дна ста́я?
c Как се ка́звате? (Give your own name.)

2 True or false?

Write out correct versions of the false statements. Michael Johnson says:

a Англича́нин съм.   **b** Тури́ст съм.   **c** Бизнесме́н съм.

Doing things the Bulgarian way

Greetings

The most frequently heard greeting, and the one to use on formal occasions when addressing people you do not know, is **до́бър ден!** Literally translated it means *Good day*. You can say **до́бър ден!** at any time of the day except the early morning, when you should use **добро́ у́тро!** *Good morning*, and the evening, when you say **до́бър ве́чер!** *Good evening*.

Здраве́й! and **Здраве́йте!** are rather less formal and are used when you would say *Hello* or *Hi!* in English. Literally the words both mean *May you be healthy*. **Здраве́й!** is a singular form and **здраве́йте!** is a plural. You say **здраве́й!** to a friend or someone you know well. When greeting more than one person or someone you know less well you use **здраве́йте!** (Plural is always polite!) You might also use **здраве́йте!** (instead of the more official **до́бър ден!**) when addressing someone you know well but whom you still address with the polite, formal form. Both **здраве́й!** and **здраве́йте!** can be used at any time of the day or night.

You will notice that the only difference between **здравéй!** and **здравéйте!** is the addition of the two letters **-те** to the greeting you use when meeting a friend. In fact, these two letters distinguish the plural (formal) from the singular (familiar) forms. They are found on the end of other 'polite', 'non-familiar' forms too. You will notice them, for example, on the end of the word **Заповя́дайте!** used by Michael Johnson when he gives Nevena Petkova his passport. (If Michael knew Nevena better, he would say **Заповя́дай!** without the letters **-те**.) You will also see them on the end of the words used by Nevena when she asks Michael his name: Как се ка́зва**те**? and inquires whether he is English: Англича́нин ли с**те**?

How do you say it?

- Asking somebody's name, and giving yours

Как се ка́звате?	*What is your name?*
Ка́звам се Ма́йкъл Джо́нсън.	*My name is Michael Johnson.*
Ка́звам се Неве́на Петко́ва.	*My name is Nevena Petkova.*

- Greeting people at different times of the day

Здраве́йте!	*Hello!* (polite or more than one person)
Здраве́й!	*Hello!* (informal, one person)
Добро́ у́тро!/До́бър ден!	*Good morning.*
До́бър ден!	*Good afternoon.*
До́бър ве́чер!	*Good evening.*

- Saying *please*, *thank you* and *(I beg your) pardon?*

Мо́ля!	*Please; don't mention it; not at all!*
Мо́ля?	*(I beg your) pardon?*
Благодаря́/Мерси́.	*Thank you.*

- Welcoming someone or extending an invitation

Заповя́дай!/Заповя́дайте!	*Won't you please . . .?; here you are; there you go!*

4

- Answering *yes* or *no* to *is there?* and *are there?*

Йма ли свобо́дна ста́я?	*Is there a room free?*
Да, и́ма.	*Yes, there is.*
Йма ли свобо́ден апартаме́нт?	*Is there a free apartment?*
Не, ня́ма.	*No, there isn't.*

- Confirming your nationality

Англича́нин/англича́нка ли сте?	*Are you English?*
Да, англича́нин/англича́нка съм.	*Yes, I am English.*
Америка́нец/америка́нка ли сте?	*Are you American?*
Да, америка́нец/америка́нка съм.	*Yes, I am American.*
Кана́дец/кана́дка ли сте?	*Are you Canadian?*
Да, кана́дец/кана́дка съм.	*Yes, I am Canadian.*

Grammar

1 Things as *he, she* and *it*: gender

All words naming things, whether living or not, are referred to as *he, she* or *it* in Bulgarian. This means that all naming words, also called nouns, belong to one of three groups or genders: masculine, feminine or neuter. It is not difficult to recognize them:

masculine nouns usually end in a consonant or **-й**
feminine nouns usually end in **-а** or **-я**
neuter nouns usually end in **-о**, **-е** or sometimes **-и**
words of foreign origin ending in **-и**, **-у** and **-ю** are also neuter.

Masculine			
америка́нец	*an American man*	англича́нин	*an Englishman*
апартаме́нт	*a flat*	бъ́лгарин	*a Bulgarian man*
ден	*a day*	музе́й	*a museum*
мъж	*a man*	тури́ст	*a tourist*
Feminine			
америка́нка	*an American woman*	англича́нка	*an English woman*
бъ́лгарка	*a Bulgarian woman*	ста́я	*a room*
жена́	*a woman*		

Neuter			
кафе́	a coffee, a café	море́	a sea
меню́	a menu	такси́	a taxi
писмо́	a letter	у́тро	a morning

2 Adjectives

Describing words that tell you about a thing's qualities are called adjectives. Adjectives acquire similar endings to the nouns: consonants for masculine adjectives, **-a** for feminine ones and **-o** for neuter. You can see this in the expressions **до́бър ден, свобо́дна ста́я, добро́ у́тро**. This repetition of endings often seems to create semi-rhyming groups of words, especially in the feminine and the neuter. Here are some examples:

Masculine	до́бър англича́нин	a good Englishman	свобо́ден ден	a free day
Feminine	добра́ бъ́лгарка	a good Bulgarian woman	свобо́дна ста́я	a free room
Neuter	добро́ у́тро	good morning	свобо́дно мя́сто	a free place

Many adjectives – like those in the box – have an 'extra' vowel (**ъ** or **e**) in their masculine form. This vowel is 'lost' in the feminine, neuter and plural forms. To help you, in this course we list all such adjectives with both the masculine and feminine forms.

3 Свобо́ден съм *I am free*

Also, an expression like '*I am free*' will change depending on whether a man or a woman is speaking. Michael Johnson will say of himself:

свобо́ден съм.   *I am free.*

Whereas Nevena will say:

свобо́дна съм.

And you would say of them:

Неве́на е свобо́дна.   *Nevena is free.*
Ма́йкъл Джо́нсън е свобо́ден.   *Michael Johnson is free.*

6

A good-looking (but immodest) man might say of himself **хýбав съм**, while a good-looking (and equally immodest) woman would say of herself **хýбава съм**. **Хýбав** represents the majority of other adjectives that do not lose a vowel.

4 Англичáнин ли сте? *Are you English?*

To ask questions that require answers *yes* or *no* you need to add **ли** immediately after the word, or group of words, to which your question is directed:

Англичáнин **ли** сте?	*Are you English?*
Да, англичáнин съм.	*Yes, I am English.*
Не, не съм англичáнин.	*No, I am not English.*
Турúст **ли** сте?	*Are you a tourist?*
Да, турúст съм.	*Yes, I am a tourist.*
Не, не съм турúст.	*No, I am not a tourist.*

··

Insight

By moving **ли** from one word to another you can shift the emphasis of your question. In English, you do this by changing your intonation.

Мáйкъл **в Сóфия** ли е?	*Is Michael **in Sofia**?*
Мáйкъл ли е в Сóфия?	*Is **Michael** in Sofia?*

··

5 Úма and нями *There is and there is not*

The Bulgarian equivalent of both *there is* and *there are* is **úма**. The negative *there is not* and *there are not* is simply **нями**:

Úма свобóдна стáя.	*There is a room free.*
Нями свобóдна стáя.	*There isn't a room free.*
В Лóндон **úма** рекá.	*There is a river in London.*
В Сóфия **нями** рекá.	*There isn't a river in Sofia.*

And if you want to ask a question you again add **ли**:

Úма **ли** свобóдна стáя?	*Is there a room free?*
Да, úма.	*Yes, there is.*
Úма **ли** рекá в Лóндон?	*Is there a river in London?*
Да, úма.	*Yes, there is.*

6 Не съм – saying *not*

The negative word in Bulgarian is **не**. It is normally placed immediately before the verb:

Не съм бъ́лгарин.	*I'm not a Bulgarian.*
Англича́нин съм.	*I'm an Englishman.*
Не съм бъ́лгарка.	*I'm not a Bulgarian.*
Англича́нка съм.	*I'm an English woman.*

Не is never stressed when followed immediately by a verb. Here **Не съм** is read as one word with emphasis on **съм**.

Exercises

◀) CD 1, TR 6

1 Read the following 'international' words out loud in Bulgarian. This will help your pronunciation and build up your vocabulary.

a	аге́нция	i	шо́у	q	фи́рма
b	адре́с	j	му́зика	r	фу́тбол
c	аспири́н	k	календа́р	s	шофьо́р
d	ба́нка	l	пробле́м	t	при́нтер
e	би́знес	m	со́да	u	о́фис
f	би́ра	n	спорт	v	факс
g	во́дка	o	то́ник	w	ви́део
h	компю́тър	p	тури́ст	x	ксе́рокс

Which words are feminine and which are masculine or neuter?

2 How would you say *hello!* (**здраве́й!** or **здраве́йте!**) to:

a	a good friend?	e	a little boy?
b	your parents?	f	a little girl?
c	your boss?	g	a group of students?
d	a shop assistant?		

◀) CD 1, TR 7

3 How would you greet the hotel porter at the times shown in the pictures?

6 a.m.   2 p.m.

a (Добро́ у́тро *or* до́бър ден?)   **c** (Добро́ у́тро *or* до́бър ден?)

10 a.m.   7 p.m.

b (Добро́ у́тро *or* до́бър ден?)   **d** (До́бър ден *or* до́бър ве́чер?)

4 Match the questions and answers. If you don't recognize a word, look it up in the Bulgarian–English vocabulary at the end of the book.

i	Америка́нка ли сте?	**a**	Не, не съм бъ́лгарин, англича́нин съм.
ii	Бъ́лгарка ли сте?	**b**	Да, англича́нка съм.
iii	Бъ́лгарин ли сте?	**c**	Да, англича́нин съм.
iv	Англича́нин ли сте?	**d**	Не, не съм америка́нец, англича́нин съм.
v	Америка́нец ли сте?	**e**	Не, не съм бъ́лгарка, англича́нка съм.
vi	Англича́нка ли сте?	**f**	Да, америка́нка съм.

5 Answer the following questions with yes or no (**Да, и́ма** or **Не, ня́ма**):

a И́ма ли кафе́?   Да, _____

b И́ма ли то́ник?   Да, _____

c И́ма ли со́да?   Не, _____

d Ѝма ли джин? (*gin*)   Не, _____

e Ѝма ли такси?   Да, _____

f Ѝма ли бѝра?   Не, _____

6 Repeat the dialogue, which inquires whether there is any mineral water, using the following:

a уѝски   *whisky*   **c** лимонáда   *lemonade*

b бѝра   *beer*   **d** чай   *tea*

Сáндра	Ѝма ли минерáлна вода́?
Николáй	Да, заповя́дайте.
Сáндра	Благодаря́!

7 Make your choice of drink following this model:

Боя́н	Джин илѝ (*or*) вóдка?
Кен	Джин, мóля.
Невéна	Вóдка, мóля.

a Боя́н   Уѝски илѝ   **c** Джон   Капучѝно илѝ
                  джин?   еспрéсо?

   Кен   _____   (*espresso*)

   Невéна   _____   Виктóрия   _____

                                 Боя́н   _____

b Боя́н   Бѝра илѝ   **d** Виктóрия   Кафé илѝ чай?
                  Кóка-Кóла?   Джон   _____

   Кен   _____   Невéна   _____

   Виктóрия   _____

8 First, read aloud and then say in English who is admiring what or whom. Remember that **хýбав** can mean many things – *beautiful, fine, good-looking, lovely, nice, pretty*. Think up other English words meaning *nice* that are appropriate to the object.

a Мáйкъл Джóнсън   Хýбав хотéл!

b Невéна   Хýбав мъж!

c Джýли   Хýбаво морé!

d Сáндра   Хýбава бѝра!

e Трéйси   Хýбаво ѝме!

f Кен   Хýбава бъ́лгарка!

Now, using **хубав**, **хубава** or **хубаво**, express your own satisfaction with your room, your apartment or the lovely Bulgarian wine (бългaрско вино):

g _____ стая!
h _____ апартамент!
i _____ бългaрско вино!

Another small step forward

🔊 **CD 1, TR 8–9**

Dialogue 2 В ресторанта *In the restaurant*

The word ресторант is used here with an ending equivalent to *the* in English just like паспорта in Dialogue 1. You will learn more in Units 3 and 4.

Read aloud the following conversation where words and phrases you have already come across are used in a different situation:

Майкъл Джонсън	Добър вечер!
Сервитьор	Добър вечер! Заповядайте! Тук има свободно място.
Майкъл Джонсън	Благодаря! Хубав ресторант! Има ли музика тук?
Сервитьор	Не, няма. Съжалявам.
Майкъл Джонсън	Много добре! Много хубав ресторант.
Сервитьор	Благодаря! Турист ли сте?
Майкъл Джонсън	Не, бизнесмен съм. Уиски, моля.
Сервитьор	Сода?
Майкъл Джонсън	Не, мерси. Минерална вода, моля.

сервитьор	*waiter*
тук	*here*
място	*seat; place*
хубав (хубава, хубаво)	*nice, good-looking, lovely, beautiful*
съжалявам	*I'm sorry*
много добре	*very good/fine*

QUICK VOCAB

Test yourself

1 To see how well you have understood Dialogue 2, answer these questions in English:

  a What time of day is it?
  b Is there a place free?
  c Why does Michael Johnson like the restaurant?
  d Is Mr Johnson a tourist?
  e What does he order?

2 Complete the sentences:

  a Има _____ водка?
  b _____, няма.
  c _____ ли чай?
  d Заповядайте! – _____!
  e Не _____ шофьор, бизнесмен _____.
  f Има _____ проблем? – Не, _____.

3 Which sports are listed here?

  a футбол   **d** тенис   **g** хокей
  b голф   **e** баскетбол   **h** крикет
  c бокс   **f** поло   **i** бейзбол

Now can you:
- vary your greetings:

  a according to time of day?
  b depending on how familiar you are with the person you are addressing?

- say *please* and *thank you?*
- recognize feminine, masculine and neuter nouns and adjectives?
- say *there is/there are* and *there isn't/there aren't?*
- make clear you are either English or American? (Don't forget you are male or female too!)
- understand if you are asked what your name is?

2

Как сте? Ймате ли време?

How are you? Do you have a moment?

In this unit you will learn:

- How to ask simple questions using **как?** *how?* and **кога?** *when?*
- Expressions with **ймам** *have* and **нямам** *have not*
- How to respond to **какво́ е това́?** *what is this?* and **как сте?** *how are you?*

Dialogue 1

🔊 **CD 1, TR 10–11**

Boyan Antonov, manager of an advertising agency in Sofia, calls in at the office to see Nadya, his secretary.

Анто́нов	Здраве́й, На́дя.
На́дя	До́бър ден, господи́н Анто́нов!
Анто́нов	Как си днес?
На́дя	Благодаря́, добре́ съм. А Ви́е как сте?
Анто́нов	И аз съм добре́. Не́що но́во?
На́дя	Ни́що.
Анто́нов	А какво́ е това́?
На́дя	А, да. Това́ е но́ва брошу́ра от господи́н Джо́нсън.
Анто́нов	Кога́ присти́га той?

Надя	Днес. Самолéт от Лóндон имá в сéдем часá.
Антóнов	Мнóго добрé. Тук ли са Николáй и Милéна?
Надя	Тя е тук, но той днес не é на рáбота.
Антóнов	Нищо. Товá е всичко засегá.
Надя	Имате ли врéме за еднó кафé?
Антóнов	Съжалявам, сегá нямам врéме. Днес имам мнóго рáбота.
Надя	Довиждане, господин Антóнов! Приятна рáбота!
Антóнов	Благодаря, Надя! Довиждане и лек ден!

ЛЕТИЩЕ СОФИЯ
SOFIA AIRPORT

господин Антóнов	*Mr Antonov*
Как си днес?	*How are you today?* (familiar)
Благодаря.	*Thank you.*
И аз съм добрé.	*I'm fine too.*
Добрé съм.	*I'm fine.*
А Вие как сте?	*And how are you?* (formal)
Нéщо нóво?	*Anything new?*
Нищо.	*Nothing./Never mind.*
А каквó е товá?	*And what is this?*
Товá е нóва брошýра	*This is a new brochure*
от	*from*
Когá пристига той?	*When is he arriving/ does he arrive?*
Самолéт от Лóндон имá в сéдем часá	*There is a plane from London at seven o'clock.*
Тук ли са Николáй и Милéна?	*Are Nikolai and Milena here?*
Тя е тук, но той днес не é на рáбота.	*She's here but he's not in (at work) today.*
Товá е всичко засегá.	*That's all for now.*
Имате ли врéме за еднó кафé?	*Have you time for a coffee?*
сегá нямам врéме.	*I haven't time now.*
Имам мнóго рáбота.	*I have a lot of work.*
Довиждане.	*Goodbye.*

1 Questions

Looking back to the dialogue, try to answer these questions instead of Nadya:

a Здравей, Надя. Как си днес? Добре ли си?
b Има ли нещо ново?
c (*Picking up a brochure*) Какво е това?
d Кога има самолет от Лондон?
e Днес ли пристига господин Джонсън?

2 True or false?

Write out correct versions of the false statements:

a Надя не é добре.
b Това е брошура от господин Джонсън.
c Николай не é тук.
d Господин Антонов има време за кафе.
e Господин Антонов няма много работа.

. . . .

Doing things the Bulgarian way

Mr, Mrs and Miss

The traditional Bulgarian equivalents of the English *Mr* and *Mrs* are **господин** (masculine) and **госпожа** (feminine).

When written, **господин** is abbreviated to **г-н** and **госпожа** to **г-жа**. The word for an unmarried woman, **госпожица** (*Miss*), has no abbreviation.

When you address someone without using their surname, you use the words **господин**, **госпожа** and **госпожица** in their special address forms: **господине**, **госпожо** (note the stress change) and **госпожице**. So you say:

Добър вечер, **господине**!	*Good evening.* (to Mr)
Довиждане, **госпожо**!	*Goodbye.* (to Mrs)
Здравейте, **госпожице**!	*Hello.* (to Miss)

When a surname is used, the special address form is obligatory with the Bulgarian word for *Miss*, so you say: **Здравéйте, госпóжице Петкóва!** *Hello, Miss Petkova.* For *Mrs*, you can either say **госпожá** or **госпóжо Борúсова**, but for *Mr* with a surname, the special form is never used, so you can only say: **Дóбър вéчер, господúн Антóнов!** *Good evening, Mr Antonov.*

Bulgarian does not yet have the equivalent of *Ms*.

Surnames

Masculine surnames usually end in **-ов** or **-ев**, while feminine surnames usually end in **-ова** or **-ева**. Thus Mr Antonov's wife is called **г-жá Антóнова**, while Nevena Petkova's father is **г-н Петкóв**. The stress in feminine surnames is not necessarily on the **о** or **е** preceding the **в**. So, although you do say Петкóва, for example, you have to say Антóнова, Борúсова, Ковáчева and Стáнева.

How do you say it?

- Asking someone how they are and saying how you are

Как си?/Как сте?	*How are you?*
Добрé съм.	*I'm fine/good.*
И аз съм добрé.	*I'm fine/good too.*

- Asking *What is this?* and answering *This is . . .* or *This is not . . .*

Каквó е товá?	*What is this?*
Товá е календáр.	*This is a calendar.*
Товá не é писмó.	*This is not a letter.*

- Asking *When?*

Когá пристúга г-н Джóнсън?	*When does Mr Johnson arrive?*
Когá úма самолéт от Лóндон?	*When is there a plane from London?*

- Saying *Goodbye*

  Довиждане!   *Goodbye.*

◀) **CD 1, TR 12**

- Expressing good wishes on parting

  Приятен/хубав/лек ден!   *Have a good/nice day.*
  Приятна работа!   *Have a good day*
                                 (at work).

  Приятна почивка!   *Have a good rest.*
  Приятен уикенд!   *Have a nice weekend.*
  Всичко хубаво!/Всичко добро!   *All the best.*

- Expressing regret

  Съжалявам.   *I'm sorry.*

Grammar

1 Един and English *a*

Normally, no equivalent of the English indefinite article *a* or *an* is necessary in Bulgarian. Compare:

Това е имейл.	*This is an email.*
Това е хотел.	*This is an hotel.*
Тук има ресторант.	*There is a restaurant here.*
Аз съм англичанин.	*I'm an Englishman.*

However, when the English *a* means *one*, *a certain* or *a single*, you need to use the Bulgarian word for *one* – **един**. **Един** is a counting word, a numeral. It is also an adjective and has different forms for the masculine, feminine and neuter.

Masculine	един	*one*	един имейл	*one email*
	англичанин	*Englishman*		
Feminine	една бира	*one beer*	една стая	*one room*
Neuter	едно кафе	*one coffee*	едно място	*one place*
	едно писмо	*one letter*		

2 *I, you, he/she/it, we, you* and *they*

Bulgarian has almost the equivalents of the English words for these
subject pronouns, but there are two small differences. First, the
Bulgarian **аз** *I* is written with a small letter and, second, Bulgarian
has two different words for *you*: **ти** for the singular, familiar form
and **ви́е** for the plural. Moreover, when addressing just one person
in the polite, formal mode, Bulgarians use the plural form and, when
writing, spell it with a capital letter: **Ви́е.**

Singular		Plural	
аз	*I*	**ни́е**	*we*
ти	*you*	**ви́е/Ви́е**	*you*
той	*he*		
тя	*she*	**те**	*they*
то	*it*		

3 Съм *I am* and the verb *to be*

In Bulgarian, verbs, or action words, have no neutral or basic
form corresponding to the English infinitive. There are, therefore,

no equivalents of the English 'dictionary' forms *to be* or *to have*. Instead, in Bulgarian dictionaries, verbs are listed in the *I* form (1st person singular) *I am*, *I have*, etc.

Here are all the forms of **съм** in the present tense:

(аз)	съм	*I am*	(ние)	сме	*we are*
(ти)	си	*you are*	(вие)	сте	*you are*
(той)	е	*he is*			
(тя)	е	*she is*	(те)	са*	*they are*
(то)	е	*it is*	*pronounced (**те съ**)		

You have already come across **е** in the question какво́ **е** това́? and the answer това́ **е** брошу́ра. Here are some more examples illustrating all forms of **съм**, including some negated forms:

Аз съм в Со́фия.	*I am in Sofia.*
Ти си тук.	*You are here.*
Джон не é в Ло́ндон.	*John is not in London.*
На́дя е добре́.	*Nadya is well.*
Ни́е сме добре́.	*We are well.*
Ви́е сте тук.	*You are here.*
Те не cá тук.	*They are not here.*

The usage of the Bulgarian equivalent of *to be* differs from the English in two important ways:

(*a*) the negative marker **не** always comes before the verb. (Note that the usually unstressed forms of **съм** always carry the stress after **не**.)

(*b*) when the subject noun or pronoun (e.g. **Джон, аз**) is omitted, you cannot begin the sentence with any of the forms of **съм**. This means that the order of words changes so that the different forms of **съм** come second after some other introductory word or group of words.

Compare the above examples (where subject nouns/pronouns are used) with:

	В Со́фия съм.	*I am in Sofia.*
or	Не съм в Со́фия.	*I am not in Sofia.*

Добре́ е.	*(Nadya/she/he) is well.*	
Тук са.	*They are here.*	

4 Ймам/ня́мам *I have* and *I have not*

One unusual feature of Bulgarian is that the negative of **и́мам**
(*to have*) is not formed by placing **не** before the verb. Instead, a
different verb is used: **ня́мам** (*not to have*). Otherwise, as you can
see in this table and in the following examples, the two verbs have
identical endings.

аз	и́мам/ня́мам	*I have/haven't*	ни́е и́маме/ ня́маме	*we have/ haven't*
ти	и́маш/ня́маш	*you have/ haven't*	ви́е и́мате/ ня́мате	*you have/ haven't*
той	и́ма/ня́ма	*he has/hasn't*	те и́мат/ня́мат	*they have/haven't*
тя	и́ма/ня́ма	*she has/hasn't*		

Ймам мно́го ра́бота днес.	*I have a lot of work today.*
Ймаш писмо́ от Ло́ндон.	*You have a letter from London.*
Г-н Анто́нов ня́ма факс.	*Mr Antonov does not have a fax.*
На́дя ня́ма мно́го ра́бота.	*Nadya does not have much work.*
Ни́е ня́маме вре́ме за кафе́.	*We don't have time for coffee.*
Ви́е и́мате ли вре́ме за кафе́?	*Do you have time for coffee?*
Те и́мат мно́го ра́бота днес.	*They have a lot of work today.*

The verbs **присти́гам** *to arrive*, **съжаля́вам** *to be sorry* and **ка́звам
се** *to be called* also follow the pattern of **и́мам**:

Г-н Джо́нсън присти́га в се́дем часа́.	*Mr Johnson arrives at seven o'clock.*
Съжаля́ваме, но ня́маме вре́ме.	*We are sorry, but we have no time.*
Как се ка́зваш?	*What is your name?*

In Bulgarian, there are three basic verb patterns. This one is called the **а**-pattern, because all the endings are preceded by **а**. (You'll find out more in Unit 4.)

5 Asking questions

как?	*how?*	**Как са те?**	*How are they?*
какво́?	*what?*	**Какво́ е това́?**	*What is this?*
кога́?	*when?*	**Кога́ присти́гаш?**	*When do you arrive?*
къде́?	*where?*	**Къде́ е той?**	*Where is he?*

6 Counting to ten

CD 1, TR 13

0	ну́ла		
1	едно́	6	шест
2	две	7	се́дем
3	три	8	о́сем
4	че́тири	9	де́вет
5	пет	10	де́сет

7 И *and, also* and *too*

The little word **и** can have all these meanings in Bulgarian. Normally, it is used to join two or more similar things and simply means *and*, as in:

Никола́й **и** Миле́на са на ра́бота.	*Nikolai* ***and*** *Milena are at work.*

Sometimes though, you'll find it used for emphasis to mean *also* and *too*:

И аз съм добре́.	*I'm fine too.*

The word **а** can also mean *and*, but only when there is an element of contrast implied:

Той е добре́. А Ви́е как сте?	*He is fine. And* (*But*) *how about you?*
Тя е тук. А те са в Ло́ндон.	*She is here. And* (*But*) *they are in London.*

Exercises

1 Replace the personal names with the correct subject pronoun – той, тя or те:

a Къде́ е госпожа́ Джо́нсън?

b Господи́н Анто́нов е добре́.

c Как е господи́н Джо́нсън?

d Къде́ са Марк и Виоле́та?

e Неве́на е в хоте́л «Роди́на».

f Господи́н Анто́нов и́ма ра́бота.

g Тук ли са Никола́й и Миле́на?

2 Read the following dialogues out loud completing them according to the model:

Тури́ст	Аз съм Пол Те́йлър.
Неве́на	Мо́ля? Как се ка́звате?
Тури́ст	Ка́звам се Пол Те́йлър.

Insight

Note that **мо́ля?** here is used to mean *I beg your pardon*.

(**тури́стка** = *tourist* (woman); **тури́сти** = *tourists*)

a

Тури́стка	Аз съм Джу́ли Дже́ймсън.
Неве́на	Мо́ля? Как се ка́звате?
Тури́стка	_____

b

Дете́ (*child*)	Аз съм То́ни.
Неве́на	Мо́ля? Как се ка́зваш?
Дете́	_____

c

Анто́нов	Аз съм Боя́н Анто́нов.
Неве́на	Мо́ля? Как се ка́звате?
Анто́нов	_____

d

Тури́сти	Ни́е сме господи́н и госпожа́ Ко́линс.
Неве́на	Мо́ля? Как се ка́звате?
Тури́сти	_____

3 In the previous exercise, you asked questions in the singular and plural, as well as in the plural of formal speech. Bearing in mind the distinction between familiar and formal forms, ask the following people their names:

a a little girl
b an elderly lady
c a young couple

4 You are staying in room number 7. Nevena has rung through from reception. Read the following dialogue and then answer instead of Mrs Collins giving your own name and room number:

Невéна	Вíе ли сте г-жá Джóнсън?
г-жá Кóлинс	Не, аз съм г-жá Кóлинс.
Невéна	Вíе в стáя дéсет ли сте?
г-жá Кóлинс	Не, аз съм в стáя нóмер óсем.

5 Look at the following signs at the stop (**спúрка**) for the tram (**трамвáй**) and the trolleybus (**тролéй**):

СПИРКА Трамвай № 1   **СПИРКА Тролей № 3**

Now read the words on the signs, changing the number (**нóмер**) for the tram to 2, 5, 6 and 8 and the trolleybus to 1, 4, 7 and 9.

6 Ask questions to which the following could be answers, using either **как?** or **каквó?** (Don't forget to change from **аз** to **ти** and **нíе** to **вíе!**)

Model: Товá е автобýс (*bus*).   (Каквó е товá?)
         Аз съм добрé.   (Как си ти?/Как сте Вíе?)

a Товá е таксú.
b Тя е добрé.
c Те са добрé.
d Товá е музéй (m).

e Добрé съм.
f Товá е тролéй (m).
g Нíе сме добрé.
h Товá е фúтнес цéнтър (*fitness centre*).

7 To test your knowledge of the question words **къде?** *where?* and **кога́?** *when?*, read out loud, matching the questions and answers:

i	Къде́ е той?	**a**	Той присти́га в три часа́.
ii	Кога́ и́ма самоле́т от Ло́ндон?	**b**	Той е в Со́фия.
iii	Кога́ присти́га той?	**c**	Че́лмсфорд е в А́нглия.
iv	Къде́ са те?	**d**	Самоле́т от Ло́ндон и́ма в се́дем часа́.
v	Къде́ е Че́лмсфорд?	**e**	Те са в Шотла́ндия (*Scotland*).

8 Using the model that follows, ask for the places **a–e** in Sofia. Reply each time saying it is *over there*:

Тури́ст	Това́ ли е хоте́л «Пли́ска»?	*Is this the Pliska Hotel?*
Бъ́лгарин	Не, хоте́л «Пли́ска» е там.	*No, the Pliska Hotel is over there.*

a рестора́нт «Криста́л»
b булева́рд Ле́вски (*Levski Boulevard*)
c Центра́лна по́ща (*the Central Post Office*)
d хоте́л «Хе́мус»
e у́лица Рако́вски (*Rakovski Street*)

9 Complete the answers with **и́мам** or **ня́мам**:

a И́мате ли резерва́ция (*reservation*), госпожа́ Ко́линс?
Не, _____.
b И́мате ли мно́го бага́ж (*baggage*), госпо́жо?
Да, _____.
c И́мате ли но́ва ка́рта (*map*), господи́н Джо́нсън?
Не, _____.
d И́мате ли биле́т, госпо́жице?
Да, _____.
e И́мате ли ка́мера (*camcorder*), господи́не?
Да, _____.

🔊 **CD 1, TR 14**

10 Mr Johnson wants to post a letter. He asks a passer-by: **Мо́ля, къде́ и́ма по́ща** (*post office*)? What would you say if you wanted to find:

24

ресторáнт   тоалéтна
бáнка   пóща
телефóн   фи́тнес цéнтър

a

b

c

d

e

f

Another small step forward

◄)) CD 1, TR 15–16

Dialogue 2 На информáцията *At the information desk*

Insight

Here, too, the word информáция appears as информáцията with the ending corresponding to *the* in English. You will learn more in Units 3 and 4.

Michael Johnson is asking the woman at the information desk the way to Vitosha Boulevard. Together they examine this map of Sofia. Read their conversation out loud. It is not essential that you understand every word, but you should find all the new words in the vocabulary after the dialogue in the order they occur.

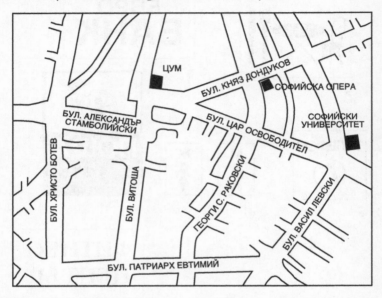

Ма́йкъл Джо́нсън	До́бър ден! Мо́ля, къде́ е булева́рд Ви́тоша?
Служи́телка	Булева́рд Ви́тоша не е́ бли́зо. Ймате ли ка́рта?
Ма́йкъл Джо́нсън	Не, ня́мам.
Служи́телка	Запови́дайте, това́ е ка́рта на Со́фия. Булева́рд Ви́тоша е бли́зо до хоте́л «Шѐратон».
Ма́йкъл Джо́нсън	Йма ли трамва́й до булева́рд Ви́тоша?
Служи́телка	Да, трамва́й но́мер едно́ и трамва́й но́мер се́дем.
Ма́йкъл Джо́нсън	А какво́ е това́ тук?
Служи́телка	Това́ е голя́м търго́вски це́нтър с мно́го магази́ни. Ка́зва се ЦУМ.
Ма́йкъл Джо́нсън	Благодаря́ мно́го. Ймам о́ще еди́н въпро́с.
Служи́телка	Каже́те!

Ма́йкъл Джо́нсън	Кога́ и́ма автобу́с за Бо́ровец?
Служи́телка	В о́сем часа́.
Ма́йкъл Джо́нсън	Кога́ присти́га той в Бо́ровец?
Служи́телка	В Бо́ровец присти́га в де́сет часа́.
Ма́йкъл Джо́нсън	Благодаря́. Това́ е вси́чко. Дови́ждане!
Служи́телка	Дови́ждане. Лек ден!

служи́телка	*counter assistant* (woman), *clerk*
бли́зо	*near*
ка́рта на	*a map of*
до	*to; near to*
голя́м	*big*
магази́ни	*stores, shops*
търгó́вски цé́нтър	*shopping mall*
мнó́го	*a lot, very* (*much*)
ó́ще еди́н	*one more*
въпрó́с	*question*
кажé́те!	*yes, I'm listening* (lit. *say!*)
за	*for; to*

Test yourself

1 To see how well you have understood Dialogue 2, identify the true statements and correct any false ones:

a Булева́рд Ви́тоша е бли́зо.

b Г-н Джó́нсън и́ма ка́рта на Сó́фия.

c Хоте́л «Шé́ратон» е бли́зо до булева́рд Ви́тоша.

d Ня́ма трамва́й до булева́рд Ви́тоша.

e Г-н Джó́нсън и́ма ó́ще еди́н въпрó́с.

f И́ма автобу́с за Бó́ровец в о́сем часа́.

g Той (the word for *bus*, remember, is masculine!) присти́га в Бó́ровец в де́вет часа́.

2 Complete the answers, using the correct forms of **съм**:

a Ви́е англича́нин ли сте?
Да, аз . . . англича́нин, а той . . . шотла́ндец (*Scot*).

b Ви́е англича́нка ли сте?

Да, аз . . . англича́нка, а тя . . . шотла́ндка (*Scotswoman*).

c Ти америка́нец ли си?

Да, аз . . . америка́нец, а той . . . бъ́лгарин.

d Ви́е от Ма́нчестър ли сте?

Ни́е . . . от Ма́нчестър, а те . . . от Ли́йдс.

e Ви́е от Ло́ндон ли сте?

Аз . . . от Ло́ндон, а тя . . . от Гла́згоу.

3 How would you say:

  a That's all.

  b I have one more question.

  c Goodbye! Have a nice day!

Now can you:

- ask *What is this?* and answer *This is . . . ?*
- ask *How are you? When?* and *Where?*
- use the expressions *I have* and *I don't have*?
- address someone as *Mr, Mrs* or *Miss*?
- be sure what form of good wishes to use on parting?
- say *I'm sorry*?
- count from 1 to 10?

3

Какъ́в сте? Каква́ сте?

Who are you? What is your job?

In this unit you will learn:

- How to ask people where they come from and what they do
- How to tell people where you come from and what you do
- How to give your nationality and marital status

Dialogue 1

🔊 **CD 1, TR 17–18**

Nevena is now asking Mrs Collins, who has just arrived at the hotel and is wishing to register, some formal – and less formal – questions about herself and her family.

Невéна	Откъдé сте?
г-жá Кóлинс	От Мáнчестър.
Невéна	Такá, от Áнглия. Знáчи сте англичáнка. А профéсията Ви?
г-жá Кóлинс	Преводáчка.
Невéна	Омъ́жена ли сте?
г-жá Кóлинс	Да, омъ́жена съм.
Невéна	Ѝмате ли децá?
г-жá Кóлинс	Да, ѝмам еднó детé.
Невéна	Мъжъ́т Ви и детéто Ви тук ли са?
г-жá Кóлинс	Синъ́т ми е в Áнглия, но мъжъ́т ми е тук.
Невéна	Каквá е профéсията му?
г-жá Кóлинс	Той е учѝтел.
Невéна	За пъ́рви път ли сте в Бълга́рия?

г-жá Кóлинс	Не, не съм за първи път тук. Познáвам странáта ви добрé.
Невéна	Товá е мнóго интерéсно. А познáвате ли Марк Дéйвис?
г-жá Кóлинс	Не. Какъв е той?
Невéна	Журналúст. Той също познáва Бългáрия мнóго добрé.
г-жá Кóлинс	Англичáнин ли е?
Невéна	Не, америкáнец. Жéнен е за бългáрка. Той и женá му Виолéта са тук сегá.

QUICK VOCAB

Откъдé сте?	*Where are you from?*
От Мáнчестър.	*From Manchester.*
Такá, от Áнглия.	*Right, from England.*
Знáчи сте англичáнка.	*So* (lit. *it means*) *you're English.*
А профéсията Ви?	*And your profession/occupation?*
преводáчка	*a translator/interpreter* (woman)
Омъжена ли сте?	*Are you married?* (asking a woman)
Да, омъжена съм.	*Yes, I am* (*married*).
Úмате ли децá?	*Have you* (*any*) *children?*
Да, úмам еднó детé.	*Yes, I have one child.*
Мъжът Ви и детéто Ви тук ли са?	*Are your husband and your child here?*
Синът ми е в Áнглия, но мъжът ми е тук.	*My son is in England, but my husband is here.*
Каквá е профéсията му?	*What is his profession?*
Той е учúтел.	*He's a teacher.*
За първи път ли сте в Бългáрия?	*Are you in Bulgaria for the first time?*
Познáвам странáта ви добрé.	*I know your country well.*
Товá е мнóго интерéсно.	*That's very interesting.*
А познáвате ли Марк Дéйвис?	*And do you know Mark Davies?*
Какъв е той?	*What does he do for a job?*
журналúст	*journalist*
Той също познáва Бългáрия мнóго добрé.	*He also knows Bulgaria very well.*
Жéнен е за бългáрка.	*He's married to a Bulgarian.*
Той и женá му Виолéта са тук сегá.	*He and his wife Violeta are here now.*

1 Questions

a Откъде́ е г-жа́ Ко́линс?

b Каква́ профе́сия и́ма г-жа́ Ко́линс?

c Омъ́жена ли е г-жа́ Ко́линс?

d Тя и́ма ли деца́?

e Какъ́в е г-н Ко́линс?

f Добре́ ли позна́ва Бълга́рия г-жа́ Ко́линс?

2 True or false?

Say which of the following statements are true and which are false. Rewrite the false ones:

a Госпожа́ Ко́линс е от Ли́върпул.

b Госпожа́ Ко́линс ня́ма деца́.

c Господи́н Ко́линс е учи́тел.

d Господи́н и госпожа́ Ко́линс и́мат еди́н син.

e Госпожа́ Ко́линс е за пъ́рви пъ́т в Бълга́рия.

f Госпожа́ Ко́линс не позна́ва Марк Де́йвис и жена́ му.

....

Doing things the Bulgarian way

Married or *single*? **же́нен/нежéнен** and **омъ́жена/неомъ́жена**

In Bulgarian, there are two different words for *married*. When referring to a man who is married, you say **той е же́нен** (from **жена́** *wife, woman* – lit. *he is wifed*). If he is single, you say **той не é же́нен**. When referring to a woman who is married, you say **тя е омъ́жена** (lit. *she is husbanded*). If she is single, you say **тя не é омъ́жена**.

The words **же́нен** and **омъ́жена** are also used when filling in forms asking for your marital status. Here, however, if you are unmarried, you should join up the words (as in English!) and put either **нежéнен** if you are a man or **неомъ́жена** if you are a woman. If you are divorced, you will enter **разве́ден** or **разве́дена** (lit. *separated*).

You will notice that the words have the appropriate feminine or masculine endings: **-a** for the woman and a consonant for the man. Thus, if you are a woman and are married, in official documents, for example, you will enter **омъ́жена** and if you are a man and married **жéнен**. In everyday speech, however, you will find that a married woman will say of herself **жéнена съм**.

For a man		For a woman	
аз съм/не съм		аз съм/не съм	
ти си/не си	**жéнен**	ти си/не си	**омъ́жена**
той е/не é		тя е/не é	**(жéнена)**
Ви́е стé/не стé		Ви́е стé/не стé	

Remember that the **не** is not emphasized. As the stress marks show, the emphasis is placed on the forms of **съм**.

АЗ НЕ СЪМ ЖÉНЕН

СПОРТ

ОМЪ́ЖЕНА СЪМ

Still on the subject of masculine and feminine, you will notice that many naming words for women, especially for nationalities and professions, have **-ка** on the end. Often the **-ка** is simply added to the corresponding masculine noun:

студéнт *student* (male)   студéнт**ка** *student* (female)
учи́тел *teacher* (male)   учи́тел**ка** *teacher* (female)

Words ending in **-ец** or **-ин** drop these letters before adding **-ка**:

	male	female
a Bulgarian	бъ́лгар**ин**	бъ́лгар**ка**
an American	америка́**нец**	америка́**нка**
a Canadian	кана́д**ец**	кана́д**ка**

How do you say it?

- Asking where someone is from and saying where you are from

Откъде́ си? От Ма́нчестър съм.	*Where are you from?*
	I'm from Manchester.
Откъде́ сте? Аз съм	*Where are you from?*
от Гла́згоу.	*I'm from Glasgow.*

- Asking someone what job they do (see also Grammar section 5 in Unit 4)

Каква́ профе́сия и́мате?/Каква́ е профе́сията Ви? or simply

Какъ́в сте?/Каква́ сте?   *What is your job?*

- And answering

For a man

Аз съм учи́тел/Учи́тел съм.	*I'm a teacher.*
Аз съм ле́кар/Ле́кар съм.	*I'm a doctor.*
Аз съм преводач/	*I'm a translator/interpreter.*
Преводач съм.	
Аз съм сервитьо́р/	*I'm a waiter.*
Сервитьо́р съм.	

For a woman

Аз съм учи́телка/	*I'm a teacher.*
Учи́телка съм.	
Аз съм ле́карка/Ле́карка съм.	*I'm a doctor.*
Аз съм преводачка/	*I'm a translator/*
Преводачка съм.	*interpreter.*
Аз съм секрета́рка/	*I'm a secretary.*
Секрета́рка съм.	

- Saying whether you are married or not

For a man

Же́нен ли си/сте?	*Are you married?*
Да, же́нен съм.	*Yes, I am married.*
Не, не съ́м же́нен.	*No, I'm not married.*
Не, разве́ден съм.	*No, I'm divorced.*

For a woman

Омъ́жена ли си/сте?	Are you married?
Да, омъ́жена съм.	Yes, I am married.
Не, не съм омъ́жена.	No, I am not married.
Не, разве́дена съм.	No, I'm divorced.

◄» CD 1, TR 19

• Referring to your family

With definite article*:

детéто ми	my child
мъжъ́т ми	my husband
синъ́т ми	my son

Without definite article*:

бáба ми	my grandmother
бащá ми	my father
брат ми	my brother
братовчéд(ка) ми	my cousin
дъщеря́ ми	my daughter
дя́до ми	my grandfather
женá ми	my wife
мáйка ми	my mother
сестрá ми	my sister

*See Grammar sections 2 and 3 below.

Grammar

1 Какъ́в? каквá?

These are the masculine and feminine forms of the question word **каквó?** *what?* You already know **каквó** from **каквó е товá?** *what is that?* where the neuter form is being used in a question. When you want to find out more about specific persons or things you have to use **какъ́в** for a masculine word, **каквá** for a feminine one and **каквó** for a neuter.

When you use **какъ́в** (or **каквá** or **каквó**) you are essentially asking what someone or something is like. However, depending on the situation, the simple question **Какъ́в е Мáйкъл Джóнсън?** may have at least three possible meanings:

What is Michael Johnson like?
What does Michael Johnson do for a job?
What is Michael Johnson's nationality?

Possible answers might be:

Той е висóк и хýбав.	*He is tall and handsome.*
Той е бизнесмéн.	*He is a businessman.*
Той е англичáнин.	*He is an Englishman.*

The context will tell you which is the most suitable.

2 -ът, -та, -то *the*

The difference between *a man* and *the man*, *a country* and *the country*, *a child* and *the child* is expressed in Bulgarian in the following way:

Masculine	мъж	becomes	мъжъ́т
Feminine	странá	becomes	странáта
Neuter	детé	becomes	детéто

From this you can see that the Bulgarian equivalent of the English definite article *the* is added to the end of the word. And, since all naming words (nouns) in Bulgarian have a masculine, feminine or neuter ending, there are also masculine (**-ът**), feminine (**-та**) and neuter (**-то**) forms of the definite article.

Most masculine nouns add -ът (pronounced -ъ, without the т)

Хотéлът е блúзо.	*The hotel is nearby.*
Апартамéнтът е голя́м.	*The flat is big.*
Клýбът е до пóщата.	*The club is next to the post office.*

However, almost all nouns ending in **-тел** or **-ар** (the equivalent of **-er** in English) add **-ят**, and all masculine nouns ending in **-й** first drop the **-й** and then add **-ят**:

учú**тел**	*teacher*	учú**телят**	*the teacher*
лé**кар**	*doctor*	лé**карят**	*the doctor*
музéй	*museum*	музéят	*the museum*
трамвáй	*tram*	трамвáят	*the tram*
тролéй	*trolleybus*	тролéят	*the trolleybus*
чай	*tea*	чáят	*the tea*

Feminine nouns add -та

Ста́ята е свобо́дна.   *The room is free.*

Ба́нката и́ма нов телефо́н.   *The bank has a new telephone (number).*

Профе́сията Ви е интере́сна.   *Your profession is interesting.*

Neuter nouns add -то

Дете́то е голя́мо.   *The child is big.*

Кафе́то е ху́баво.   *The coffee is nice.*

Свобо́дно ли е мя́стото?   *Is the seat free?*

3 Ми and Ви (or ви) *My and your*

In the dialogue, you met one of the ways of saying *my* and *your* in Bulgarian. These are short form possessive pronouns:

мъжъ́т **ми**	*my husband*
мъжъ́т **Ви**	*your husband* (polite)
дете́то **Ви**	*your child* (polite)
синъ́т **ми**	*my son*

You will notice that **ми**, the word for *my*, and **Ви** *your*, come after the noun and that the noun has first to be made definite by adding the article.

Insight

It is very important to remember that, as an exception to the general rule, with most words for relatives the noun has to be used *without* the definite article. (There is a list earlier in this unit.)

You will learn other, longer and less conversational, ways of saying *my*, *your*, etc. in later units, but, for the time being, here is a full list of all the short form possessive pronouns used with the word **апартаме́нт** *flat*:

апартаме́нтът **ми**	*my flat*	апартаме́нтът **ни**	*our flat*
апартаме́нтът **ти**	*your flat*	апартаме́нтът **ви/Ви**	*your flat*
апартаме́нтът **му**	*his flat* ⎫		
апартаме́нтът **й**	*her flat* ⎬	апартаме́нтът **им**	*their flat*

Insight

Note that **ѝ**, the little word for *her*, is *always* written with a grave accent so as to distinguish it from the word **и** meaning *and*. The word stresses, by way of contrast, are indicated in this book by an acute accent.

Exercises

1 Have another look at the dialogue, then rearrange the following words to form sentences:

a едно́, и́мам, дете́
b ли, омъ́жена, сте?
c преводачка, е, г-жа́ Ко́линс
d профе́сията Ви, е, госпо́жо Ко́линс, каква́?
e ли, за пъ́рви път, в Бълга́рия, е, г-жа́ Ко́линс?
f г-жа́ Ко́линс, са, и, откъде́, г-н Ко́линс?
g добре́, страна́та ви, позна́вам

2 Match these questions and answers (often the gender will be a useful clue):

i От Ма́нчестър ли е г-жа́ Ко́линс?	**a** От Ирла́ндия (*Ireland*) съм.
ii Преводач ли е г-н Ко́линс?	**b** Не. От Шотла́ндия (*Scotland*) съм.
iii Откъде́ си?	**c** Ле́кар съм.
iv От Ирла́ндия ли сте?	**d** Да, тя е от Ма́нчестър.
v Какъ́в сте?	**e** Той е от Ва́рна.
vi Какви́ са Марк и Виоле́та Де́йвис?	**f** Не, той не е́ преводач.
vii И́мате ли деца́?	**g** Той е америка́нец, а тя е бъ́лгарка.
viii Откъде́ е Никола́й?	**h** Да, и́мам две деца́.

3 Complete the dialogues (a) to (d). Use **какъ́в** or **каква́** to form the appropriate question and choose the correct gender form from the list of occupations and nationalities:

Model: Учи́телка ли сте?
        Не, не съм учи́телка.

Каква́ сте?
Студе́нтка съм. (*I'm a student.*)

Ирла́ндец ли сте?
Не, не съм ирла́ндец.
Какъ́в сте?
Шотла́ндец съм.

преводач	ле́кар	америка́нец	шотла́ндка
студе́нт	учи́телка	ирла́ндка	ирла́ндец
секрета́рка	шофьо́р	англича́нка	шотла́ндец

a Ле́карка ли сте?
Не, не _____
_____ сте?
_____ съм.

b Бъ́лгарка ли сте?
Не, не _____
_____ сте?
_____ съм.

c Сервитьо́р ли сте?
Не, не _____
_____ сте?
_____ съм.

d Англича́нин ли сте?
Не, не _____
_____ сте?
_____ съм.

4 The following people have provided some personal information when registering for an internet blog. Write out full sentences, then go to the answers in the Key and read them out loud. This exercise will help you to learn some words for the professions and also to practise using the words for marital status:

Model: Г-н Ко́линс е учи́тел. Той е от Ма́нчестър. Той е же́нен (or не е же́нен).

a Марк Де́йвис – журнали́ст – Са́нта Ба́рбара – же́нен
b Миле́на – фотогра́фка (*photographer*) – Со́фия – неомъ́жена
c А́ндрю – студе́нт – Гла́згоу – неже́нен
d г-жа́ Ко́линс – преводачка – Ма́нчестър – омъ́жена
e На́дя – секрета́рка – Пло́вдив – неомъ́жена
f Ма́йкъл Джо́нсън – бизнесме́н – Че́лмсфорд – же́нен
g г-н Анто́нов – дире́ктор (*director*) – Бурга́с – же́нен
h Никола́й – програми́ст (*programmer*) – Ва́рна – неже́нен

Now give your own name, say what you do for a job and where you come from and indicate your marital status.

5 Complete with the appropriate masculine or feminine definite forms (**-ът** or **-та**):

a Журналист . . . е от Са́нта Ба́рбара.
b Фотогра́фка . . . е от Со́фия.
c Студе́нт . . . е от Гла́згоу.
d Преводачка . . . е от Ма́нчестър.
e Секрета́рка . . . е от Пло́вдив.
f Бизнесме́н . . . е от Че́лмсфорд.
g Дире́ктор . . . е от Бурга́с.
h Програми́ст . . . е от Ва́рна.

6 To practise the use of the alternative (**-ят**) form of the masculine definite article, read and then answer the questions:

a Джеймс Ми́лър е ле́кар. Той е шотла́ндец.
  Какъ́в е ле́карят?
b Джордж Ко́линс е учи́тел. Той е англича́нин.
  Какъ́в е учи́телят?
c Ча́ят е ху́бав. Той е от А́нглия.
  Какъ́в е ча́ят? Откъде́ е той?

QUICK VOCAB

запозна́йте се . . .!	*meet . . . !*
но	*but*
то́пъл, то́пла	*warm, hot*
ви́за	*visa*
резерва́ция	*reservation*
биле́т	*ticket*
гра́ница	*border*
река́	*river*
сто́лица	*capital*
град	*town, city*
(на) за́пад	*(in/to) the west*
(на) и́зток	*(in/to) the east*
(на) се́вер	*(in/to) the north*
(на) юг	*(in/to) the south*
Ду́нав	*the Danube*

Гъ́рция	Greece
Македо́ния	Macedonia
Румъ́ния	Romania
Съ́рбия	Serbia
Тýрция	Turkey
че́рен, че́рна	black
Че́рно мо́ре	the Black Sea

◀) CD 1, TR 20

7 Mr Antonov introduces his wife to Michael Johnson and says: Запозна́йте се – жена́ ми! *Meet my wife!* (lit. *Get to know one another – my wife*). What would you say when introducing the following people to a new Bulgarian acquaintance? (Beware of the vanishing definite article with the words for certain relatives!):

a your husband **d** your brother
b your son **e** your sister
c your daughter

8 Answer the questions that follow by using this model:

Как се ка́зва мъжъ́т Ви/ти? Мъжъ́т ми се ка́зва Ива́н.
Как се ка́зва ма́йка Ви/ти? Ма́йка ми се ка́зва Еле́на.

a Как се ка́зва синъ́т Ви/ти? (А́ндрю)
b Как се ка́зва дете́то Ви/ти? (Ви́ктор)
c Как се ка́зва ма́йка Ви/ти? (Ири́на)
d Как се ка́зва жена́ Ви/ти? (Мари́я)
e Как се ка́зва дъщеря́ Ви/ти? (Си́лвия)
f Как се ка́зва баща́ ти? (Пол)

9 Mrs Collins has taught her husband some expressions to use in restaurants. He is in Bulgaria for the first time and likes his coffee, soup and tea hot. Read the model and then practise with him. Don't forget that **кафе́, сýпа, чай** should be referred to as **то, тя** and **той** respectively!

Model: **Сервитьо́р** Кафе́то Ви, господи́не!
г-н Ко́линс Но то е студе́но! (*But it's cold!*)

40

a	Сервитьóр	Сýпата Ви, господúне!
	г-н Кóлинс	_____
b	Сервитьóр	Чáят Ви, господúне!
	г-н Кóлинс	_____

Neither does Mrs Collins like her beer, wine, water or gin warm. Complete and read out the following:

c	Сервитьóр	Бúрата Ви, госпóжо!
	г-жá Кóлинс	_____
d	Сервитьóр	Вúното Ви, госпóжо!
	г-жá Кóлинс	_____
e	Сервитьóр	Водáта Ви, госпóжо!
	г-жá Кóлинс	_____
f	Сервитьóр	Джúнът Ви, госпóжо!
	г-жá Кóлинс	_____

◄)) **CD 1, TR 21**

10 If asked to show your passport, your reply would be: Заповя́дайте, товá е паспóртът ми. How would you reply if asked to show your visa, your reservation or your ticket?

11 Look at the map of Bulgaria that follows. Then complete and write out the sentences.

    a Товá е _____ на Бългáрия.
    b На úзток грáницата е _____.
    c На сéвер грáницата е рекá. Рекáта се кáзва _____.
    d На юг са _____ и _____.
    e Стóлицата на Бългáрия е град _____.

Insight

Frequently на corresponds to the English preposition *on*, but it is also commonly used to join two nouns as an equivalent of *'s* or *of* as in стóлицата **на** Бългáрия *the capital of Bulgaria* or Товá е секретáрката **на** Боя́н Антóнов *This is Boyan Antonov's secretary/the secretary of . . .*

In addition, do try to learn **на** as part of a phrase, as in на рáбота *at work,* на úзток *in the east.*

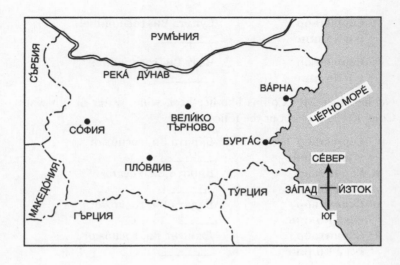

Another small step forward

🔊 **CD 1, TR 22–23**

Dialogue 2 В асансьóра *In the lift*

Nikolai and Milena meet in the lift on their way to see Nadya, the secretary. They work for the same advertising agency, but they don't yet know one another.

Николáй	Здравéйте!
Милéна	Дóбър ден! Познáваме ли се?
Николáй	Не. Да се запознáем! Кáзвам се Николáй Димитрóв. А Вúе как се кáзвате?
Милéна	Аз се кáзвам Милéна Марúнова.
Николáй	Прия́тно ми е! (*They go into the office.*) Éто и Нáдя, секретáрката. Здравéй, Нáдя!
Нáдя	Здравéйте! Мóля, заповя́дайте! Вúе познáвате ли се?
Николáй	И да, и не. Милéна, Вúе каквá сте?
Милéна	Фотогрáфка съм.
Нáдя	Милéна е фотогрáфката на фúрмата. Тя мнóго рабóти с компю́тър.
Николáй	Разбúрам. Товá е мнóго интерéсна профéсия.

Миле́на	А Ви́е какъ́в сте?
Никола́й	Аз съм програми́ст.
На́дя	Никола́й е програми́стът на фи́рмата.
Миле́на	Съ́що интере́сна профе́сия.
На́дя	И́мате ли вре́ме за едно́ кафе́?
Миле́на	Да, разби́ра се.
Никола́й	Аз съ́що. За кафе́ ви́наги и́мам вре́ме!

да се запозна́ем!	let's get acquainted!
прия́тно ми е!	pleased to meet you!
е́то	here is
фи́рма	firm
фотогра́фка	photographer (woman)
рабо́ти	(she) works
компю́тър	computer
разби́рам	I understand
разби́ра се	of course
интере́сен, интере́сна	interesting
програми́ст	(computer) programmer
съ́що	too, also
ви́наги	always

Test yourself

1 To see how well you have understood Dialogue 2, identify the true statements and correct any false ones:

a Никола́й и Миле́на не се́ позна́ват.

b Миле́на е секрета́рката на фи́рмата.

c Миле́на и́ма интере́сна профе́сия.

d Никола́й е програми́ст.

e Никола́й и Миле́на ня́мат вре́ме за кафе́.

2 Use another way of saying whose secretary or interpreter Nadya, Elena and Vassil are:

a На́дя е секрета́рка на Боя́н → На́дя е секрета́рката ____.

b Еле́на е секрета́рка на г-жа́ Анто́нова → Еле́на е секрета́рката ____.

c Васи́л е прево́дач на г-н и г-жа́ Ми́лър → Васи́л
е прево́дачът ____.

Now say that Vassil is your interpreter and your secretary is Elena.

3 How would you say:

    a Me too.
    b Of course.
    c What is your nationality? (for a woman? and for a man?)
    d Pleased to meet you.

Now can you:
- ask where someone comes from?
- ask what someone does for a job?
- say where you come from and what you do for a living?
- give your marital status?
- refer to your relatives?
- reply when people introduce themselves?
- ask *what kind of?*
- make a noun definite by adding the equivalent of *the*?

4

Кóлко?
В кóлко часá?
How much? How many?
At what time?

In this unit you will learn:

- To ask about quantity
- To ask and tell the time
- To use some more numbers

Dialogue 1

◀) **CD 1, TR 24–25**

The morning after Mr Johnson's arrival at the hotel, Nevena, the ever-obliging receptionist, stops him in the foyer.

Невéна	Дóбър ден, г-н Джóнсън! Ѝмате писмá днес.
г-н Джóнсън	Писмá? Кóлко писмá?
Невéна	Три – заповя́дайте! Ѝскате ли бъ́лгарски вéстници?
г-н Джóнсън	Съжаля́вам, но не разбѝрам добрé бъ́лгарски.
Невéна	Нѝе ѝмаме вéстници и списáния и на англѝйски езѝк. Заповя́дайте!
г-н Джóнсън	Товá е чудéсно! Благодаря́! Лек ден!
Невéна	Извинéте, г-н Джóнсън, ѝмате ли óще мáлко врéме?
г-н Джóнсън	(hesitatingly) Ѝмам срéща в цéнтъра . . .
Невéна	В кóлко часá е срéщата Ви?

г-н Джо́нсън	То́чно в двана́йсет.
Неве́на	Зна́чи и́мате о́коло пет мину́ти.
г-н Джо́нсън	Въпро́си ли и́мате?
Неве́на	Са́мо еди́н въпро́с. За ко́лко вре́ме сте в Бълга́рия?
г-н Джо́нсън	За две се́дмици.
Неве́на	Това́ пра́ви четирина́йсет но́щи в хоте́ла, нали́?
г-н Джо́нсън	То́чно така́.
Неве́на	Благодаря́.
г-н Джо́нсън	Това́ ли е вси́чко!
Неве́на	Да, да. Ня́мате вре́ме. Ве́че е двана́йсет без два́йсет и пет.
г-н Джо́нсън	Добре́. Дови́ждане!

И́мате писма́ днес.	*You have some letters today.*
Ко́лко писма́?	*How many letters?*
И́скате ли бъ́лгарски ве́стници?	*Do you want any Bulgarian newspapers?*
не разби́рам добре́ бъ́лгарски.	*I don't understand Bulgarian very well.*
Ни́е и́маме ве́стници и списа́ния и на англи́йски ези́к.	*We have newspapers and magazines in English, too.*
Това́ е чуде́сно!	*That's wonderful/marvellous!*
Извине́те.	*Excuse me.*
о́ще ма́лко	*a little more*
И́мам сре́ща в це́нтъра	*I have an appointment in the centre.*
В ко́лко часа́ е сре́щата Ви?	*At what time is your appointment?*
То́чно в двана́йсет	*At twelve precisely.*
Зна́чи и́мате о́коло пет мину́ти.	*So it means you have about five minutes.*
Въпро́си ли и́мате?	*Do you have any questions?*
Са́мо еди́н въпро́с.	*Just one question.*
За ко́лко вре́ме сте в Бълга́рия?	*How long are you in Bulgaria for?*
За две се́дмици.	*For two weeks.*
Това́ пра́ви четирина́йсет но́щи в хоте́ла, нали́?	*That makes fourteen nights in the hotel, doesn't it?*

Тóчно такá.	*Exactly so.*
Вéче е дванáйсет без	*It's already twenty-five to*
двáйсет и пет.	*twelve.*

1 Questions

a Кóлко писмá и́ма за г-н Джóнсън?

b Добрé ли разби́ра бъ́лгарски г-н Джóнсън?

c В кóлко часá и́ма срéща той? (Don't forget to repeat **в** in the answer.)

d Къдé е срéщата на г-н Джóнсън?

e Кóлко врéме и́ма г-н Джóнсън?

f За кóлко врéме е той в Бългáрия? (Repeat **за** in the answer.)

2 True or false?

Write out correct versions of the false statements:

a За г-н Джóнсън и́ма три писмá.

b Г-н Джóнсън не и́ска бъ́лгарски вéстници.

c В хотéла ня́ма англи́йски вéстници и списáния.

d Невéна и́ма мнóго въпрóси.

e Г-н Джóнсън е в Бългáрия за еднá сéдмица.

f Часъ́т е единáйсет без двáйсет и пет.

....

Doing things the Bulgarian way

Morning, noon and night

The Bulgarians have no real equivalent for *a.m.* and *p.m.* To avoid misunderstanding, especially when referring to opening times of shops or to bus or train times, they use the 24-hour clock. Alternatively, in situations not involving travel, immediately after giving the time, they insert the word **сутринтá** *in the morning*, **следóбед** *in the afternoon*, **вечертá** *in the evening* and **през нощтá** *at night*. So, if your plane arrives at 9.30 p.m. you will say: **самолéтът присти́га в двáйсет и еди́н часá и три́йсет мину́ти**, but if you are merely getting together with a friend in the evening, you will arrange to meet **в дéвет и половинá вечертá**.

Interestingly, where, in English, we would say *at one* (or *two*) *in the morning*, the Bulgarians say **в еди́н** (or **два**) **часа́ през нощта́**. For us, the night would seem to end at midnight, while for the Bulgarians, it goes on at least until two in the morning!

One further important thing to note is that the Bulgarian word **о́бед** or **обя́д** means *lunch* or *lunchtime* as well as *noon* or *midday*. Punctuality is not a national trait, neither is noon such a precise time for Bulgarians. It is, rather, the general period between midday and two. So, if someone invites you for lunch (**на о́бед**) at midday (**по о́бед**), make sure you also agree on a precise time or you could be in for a long wait for your meal!

How do you say it?

- Asking *How many?* and *How much?*

Ко́лко писма́ и́мате?	*How many letters do you have?*
Ко́лко вре́ме и́мате?	*How much time do you have?*

- Asking *At what time?* and *For how long?*

В ко́лко часа́?	*At what time?*
За ко́лко вре́ме сте в Бълга́рия?	*How long are you in Bulgaria for?*

- Asking, and saying, what the time is

Ко́лко е часъ́т?	*What is the time?*
Часъ́т е то́чно двана́йсет.	*It is exactly twelve o'clock.*

- Begging someone's pardon

Извине́те! or **Извиня́вайте!**	*Excuse me!/I beg your pardon.*

- Seeking agreement or confirmation using **нали́**?

Ви́е сте в Со́фия за четирина́йсет дни, нали́?	*You are in Sofia for fourteen days, aren't you?*

48

Г-н Джо́нсън е в Со́фия за 14 дни, нали́?	Mr Johnson is in Sofia for 14 days, isn't he?

- Agreeing and approving

То́чно така́!	That's right!/Exactly so!/ Precisely!
Така́ е.	That is so.
Това́ е чуде́сно!	That's wonderful!

- Indicating the time of day

сутринта́	in the morning
следо́бед	in the afternoon
вечерта́	in the evening
през нощта́	at night

Grammar

1 Ко́лко? *How many? How much?*

Ко́лко is the question word for quantity:

Ко́лко писма́ и́ма за г-н Джо́нсън?	How many letters are there for Mr Johnson?
Ко́лко вре́ме и́ма той?	How much time has he got?
За ко́лко дни е г-н Джо́нсън в Бълга́рия?	How many days is Mr Johnson in Bulgaria for?

When **ко́лко** refers to quantity, it is used to express both *how many?* (with naming words for concrete or countable things) and *how much?* (with abstract or uncountable things).

You also use **ко́лко** when asking questions about the time, such as *what's the time?* or *at what time?*

Ко́лко е часъ́т?	What's the time?
В ко́лко часа́ е самоле́тът за Ло́ндон?	What time is the plane for London?
До ко́лко часа́ рабо́ти о́фисът?	Until what time is the office open? (lit. *is working*)

2 Мно́го for quantity and quality

As a quantity word **мно́го** stands for *many*, *much* and *a lot of*. Its counterpart is **ма́лко**, which is an equivalent of *few*, *a few*, *a little*, *not many*, *not much*.

И́мам мно́го/ма́лко писма́ днес.	*I have a lot of/few letters today.*

Мно́го is also used to express the intensity of a quality as an equivalent of the English *very* or *very much*:

Г-жа́ Ко́линс разби́ра бъ́лгарски **мно́го добре́**.	*Mrs Collins understands Bulgarian very well.*
Хоте́лът е **мно́го ху́бав**.	*The hotel is very beautiful/ nice.*
Благодаря́ **мно́го**.	*Thank you very much.*
Извиня́вайте **мно́го**!	*I am very sorry!*

3 Plural of nouns

The most common (but not the only) plural ending is **-и**. It occurs with both masculine and feminine nouns.

Masculine nouns

The plural ending **-и** is attached to masculine words in a number of ways:

a by simply adding **-и** to the singular:

автобу́с	автобу́с**и**	*buses*
рестора́нт	рестора́нт**и**	*restaurants*
биле́т	биле́т**и**	*tickets*
ле́кар	ле́кар**и**	*doctors*
тури́ст	тури́ст**и**	*tourists*
о́фис	о́фис**и**	*offices*

Note that all these masculine nouns, as well as the following ones, have more than one syllable! Most masculine nouns of only one syllable form their plurals differently. You will learn them in Unit 7.

b by adding **-и** and also changing the final consonant of the singular. One of the most frequent changes is **-к** to **-ц**:

ве́стник	ве́стни**ци**	*newspapers*
ези́**к**	ези́**ци**	*languages, tongues*
климати́**к**	климати́**ци**	*air conditioners*
часо́вни**к**	часо́вни**ци**	*watches, clocks*

c by adding **-и** and also dropping the vowel that comes before the final consonant of the singular. Certain combinations of vowel and consonant, such as **-ец** or **-ър**, favour this method, but there is no simple rule:

америка́**нец**	америка́**нци**	*Americans*	⎫
чужден**е́ц**	чужден**ци́**	*foreigners*	⎬ **-ец** (**е** is dropped)
шотла́нд**ец**	шотла́нд**ци**	*Scots*	⎭
компю́т**ър**	компю́т**ри**	*computers*	⎫
ли́т**ър**	ли́т**ри**	*litres*	⎬ **-ър** (**ъ** is dropped)
ме́т**ър**	ме́т**ри**	*metres*	⎭
д**е**н	д**ни**	*days*	(**е** is dropped)

d by substituting **-и** for the singular ending in **-й**:

музе́**й**	музе́**и**	*museums*
трамва́**й**	трамва́**и**	*trams*
троле́**й**	троле́**и**	*trolleybuses*

Feminine nouns

The plural of feminine nouns is always **-и**, which replaces the singular ending **-а** or **-я**:

англича́н**ка**	англича́н**ки**	*English women*
ка́р**та**	ка́р**ти**	*cards*
се́дми**ца**	се́дми**ци**	*weeks*
дъщер**я́**	дъщер**и́**	*daughters*
резерва́ци**я**	резерва́ци**и**	*reservations*
ста́**я**	ста́**и**	*rooms*

Insight

The few feminine nouns that end in a consonant form their plural by adding **-и** to the singular. You have already come across **ве́чер**, **нощ** and **су́трин**:

една́ ве́чер	мно́го ве́чери	*many evenings*
една́ нощ	мно́го но́щи	*many nights*
една́ су́трин	мно́го су́трини	*many mornings*

Neuter nouns

The most common plural endings for neuter nouns are **-а** and **-я**.
The choice is determined by the endings in the singular.

a nouns in **-о** replace the final **-о** by **-а**:

| писмо́ | писма́ | *letters* |
| семе́йство | семе́йства | *families* |

Note that the stress sometimes moves to the final syllable:

| ви́но | вина́ | *wines* |

b nouns in **-ие** replace the final **-е** by **-я**:

| списа́ние | списа́ния | *magazines* |
| съобще́ние | съобще́ния | *messages* |

(More neuter plurals in Unit 8!)

4 Разби́рам *I understand* and и́скам *I want* (a-pattern verbs)

As with **и́мам** and **присти́гам**, the endings of these verbs contain
the vowel **-а-**. We can refer to them as **a**-pattern verbs. They are also
known as verbs of Conjugation 3. This is the most regular and the
most common pattern, and also the easiest to learn:

аз	разби́р**ам**	*I understand*	ни́е разби́ра**ме**	*we understand*
ти	разби́р**аш**	*you understand*	ви́е разби́р**ате**	*you understand*
той ⎫				
тя ⎬	разби́р**а**	*he, she, it*	те разби́р**ат**	*they understand*
то ⎭		*understands*		

52

5 Пра́вя *I make, I do* and рабо́тя *I work* (и-pattern verbs)

аз	пра́вя/ рабо́тя	*I make/do, work*	ни́е пра́вим/ рабо́тим	*we make/do, work*
ти	пра́виш/ рабо́тиш	*you make/do, work*	ви́е пра́вите/ рабо́тите	*you make/do, work*
той тя то	пра́ви/ рабо́ти	*he, she, it makes/ does, works*	те пра́вят/ рабо́тят	*they make/do, work*

As you can see, **пра́вя** and **рабо́тя** have -**и**- in all their endings except the forms for *I* and *they*. Verbs like **пра́вя** and **рабо́тя** belong to the **и**-pattern and are known as verbs of Conjugation 2.

Пра́вя can mean both *I make* and *I do*. Here, too, Bulgarian conveniently has one word with a number of different meanings in English. Compare:

Две и две пра́ви че́тири.   *Two and two makes four.*
Какво́ пра́виш?   *What are you doing?*

....

Insight

Among friends, **какво́ пра́виш?** – (you'll hear **кво пра́иш?**) – is commonly used to ask *How are you?* **Какво́ рабо́тиш?** or **какво́ рабо́тите?** is another way to ask *What's your job?* (see the 'How do you say it?' section in Unit 3).

....

6 -a and -я: the short definite article

In Unit 3, you were introduced to the Bulgarian equivalent of the English definite article *the*. You learnt to add the endings -**ът** or -**ят** to masculine nouns. These forms, known as the full forms, are, however, only used when the noun is the subject in the sentence, determining the ending of the verb, as in the sentence: хоте́лът е мно́го ху́бав *the hotel is very nice*.

Masculine nouns are also used with a short form of the definite article. This happens when the noun is not the subject in the sentence. The most obvious position is after prepositions. For example, if you

want to say you are *in* the hotel, **хотéлът** becomes **хотéла**: Аз съм
в хотéла.

The short forms of the definite article (with masculine nouns only,
remember) are **-a** or **-я**. This makes them look *and* sound like
feminines, while the long forms only sound like feminines – so listen
carefully and keep your wits about you! Compare:

	Цéнтърът на Сóфия е красúв.	*The centre of Sofia is beautiful.*
and	Úмам срéща в цéнтъра.	*I have a meeting in the centre.*
	Музéят е на úлица Ивáн Вáзов.	*The museum is on Ivan Vazov Street.*
and	Úма мнóго турúсти в музéя.	*There are a lot of tourists in the museum.*

Insight

You will now understand why we wrote **Паспóрта, мóля** in
the first dialogue of Unit 1 and **В ресторáнта** as the heading
of the second dialogue – **паспóрт** and **ресторáнт** are both
used here with the short form of the definite article. And you
will now appreciate the difference, when written, between
Кóлко е часъ́т? and **В** кóлко часá? (although часá and часъ́т
are both pronounced часъ́!).

Street sign in Sofia

> **улица**
> **ИВАН ВАЗОВ 21ᴬ→37**

◀) CD 1, TR 26

7 Numerals 11 to 100

11	единáйсет	14	четиринáйсет	17	седемнáйсет
12	дванáйсет	15	петнáйсет	18	осемнáйсет
13	тринáйсет	16	шестнáйсет	19	деветнáйсет

The numbers from 11 to 19 are formed by the addition of **-нáйсет** (the
equivalent of the English *-teen*) to the numbers from 1 to 9. For 11,

you add **-на́йсет** to the masculine **еди́н** and for 12, you add **-на́йсет** to **два** not to **две**.

20	два́йсет (два́десет)	25	два́йсет и пет
21	два́йсет и едно́/еди́н/една́	26	два́йсет и шест
22	два́йсет и две/два	27	два́йсет и се́дем
23	два́йсет и три	28	два́йсет и о́сем
24	два́йсет и че́тири	29	два́йсет и де́вет

From 20 upwards the numerals are formed on the principle of *twenty and one*, *twenty and two*, etc. with the word for *and* **и** being inserted between **два́йсет**, **три́йсет**, **чети́рисет**, etc. and **едно́**, **две**, **три**, etc. There are alternative more formal spellings and pronunciations – given in brackets – for some numbers.

Insight

Be careful to distinguish between **двана́йсет** (12) and **два́йсет** (20) – all the teens are longer!

30	три́йсет (три́десет)	70	седемдесе́т
40	чети́рисет (чети́ридесет)	80	осемдесе́т
50	петдесе́т	90	деветдесе́т
60	шейсе́т (шестдесе́т)	100	сто

Remember that **едно́** has different forms for the three genders. Also that **две** has an alternative form **два**, as in **два часа́** *two o'clock*. (More about this in Unit 8.)

8 Final -т in pronunciation

Although in written Bulgarian a distinction is still made between the short and long forms of the definite article (section 6 in this unit), when speaking it is normal to ignore the final **т** of the full form and to pronounce the endings as if they were the short form. So, for both **трамва́ят** and **трамва́я** you will hear **трамва́йъ**, for both **учи́телят** and **учи́теля** you will hear **учи́телйъ** and for both **хоте́лът** and **хоте́ла** – **хоте́лъ**.

The loss of final **-т** in pronunciation is also conspicuous in the numbers – most people say едина́йсе, двана́йсе, два́йсе, три́йсе.

Only in formal speech, in news bulletins on the radio or television, for example, or when people feel they need to be 'ultra-correct' in their speech, will you hear the long form articulated in full with the final **-т** pronounced. As you listen to the different speakers on the recording, see if you can detect any difference. (For further pronunciation changes in everyday speech, look again at the Appendix.)

9 Telling the time

> **Ко́лко е часъ́т?** What is the time?
> **Часъ́т е...** The time is ...

When telling the time in Bulgarian, you begin with the hours and move on to the minutes. For times up to the half hour, you give the hour first and add the minutes using the word **и**. As in English, the words for *hours* and *minutes* can be omitted:

Ко́лко е часъ́т?

Едина́йсет часа́ и де́сет мину́ти.   *(The time is)*
or   *ten past*
(Часъ́т е) едина́йсет и де́сет.   *eleven.*

Ко́лко е часъ́т?

Де́вет часа́ и два́йсет и пет   *(The time is) twenty-five*
мину́ти.   *past nine.*
or
(Часъ́т е) де́вет и два́йсет и пет.

For times after the half hour you give the number of the next hour first and take away the minutes from the next hour using the word **без** (*without* or *less*):

Ко́лко е часъ́т?

(Часъ́т е) се́дем **без** де́сет.   *(The time is*
                                                     ten to seven.)

Ко́лко е часъ́т?

(Часъ́т е) три без пет.   *(The time is five to three.)*

Bulgarian has alternative forms for half past and the quarters:

      Óсем **и полови́на**   *Half past eight*
or о́сем **и трийсет**   or *eight thirty.*

      Пет **без че́твърт**   *A quarter to five*
or пет **без петна́йсет**   or *four forty-five.*

      Шест **и че́твърт**   *A quarter past six*
or шест **и петна́йсет**   or *six fifteen.*

10 Нали́? *Isn't it so?*

In conversational Bulgarian, you will often hear the word **нали́** tagged on the end of statements making them into questions seeking confirmation. In English, there is no proper one-word equivalent for **нали́** and you have to repeat the verb to achieve the same effect. Bulgarians learning English have great difficulty with our different forms, but as you will see from the following examples, **нали́** is very easy for us to use:

Хоте́лът е мно́го ху́бав, **нали́**?   *The hotel is very nice, **isn't it?***

Ви́е не сте́ бъ́лгарка, **нали́**?   *You are not Bulgarian, are you?*

Úмате са́мо еди́н въпро́с, **нали́**?   *You do only have one question, **don't you?***

Той не и́ска бъ́лгарски ве́стници, **нали́**?   *He doesn't want Bulgarian newspapers, **does he?***

Exercises

РАЗПИСАНИЕ (Timetable)		
За (to)	Заминава (departs)	Пристига (arrives)
Мальовица	6.35	9.15
Банкя	10.10	10.45
Самоков	11.20	13.30
Боровец	13.50	17.25

1 Make full sentences using the information on the above bus departures and arrivals board. Best use the 24-hour clock!

Model: Автобусът за ＿＿＿ заминава в ＿＿＿ часа и ＿＿＿ минути и пристига в ＿＿＿ часа и ＿＿＿ минути.

Now use the short version of the times omitting **часа** and **минути**.

2 Looking at the timetable again, answer the following questions (the actual time is given in brackets):

Model: (Часът е десет без пет.) След колко минути заминава автобусът за Банкя? *In how many minutes does the bus leave for Bankya?*

• Автобусът за Банкя заминава след петнайсет минути.

   a (Часът е единайсет и петнайсет.) След колко минути заминава автобусът за Самоков?

   b (Часът е един и половина.) След колко минути заминава автобусът за Боровец?

   c (Часът е шест и двайсет и пет.) След колко минути заминава автобусът за Мальовица?

3 Answer these questions reading out the times on the clocks:

   a В колко часа заминава автобусът за Пловдив?

   b Кога пристига самолетът от Лондон?

58

c Когá и́ма самолéт за Вáрна?

d Когá заминáваш за Сóфия?

e В кóлко часá е срéщата на г-н Джóнсън?

4 Answer the following questions, presuming that:

a you are staying in Bulgaria for 12/15/20 days
b you are staying in the hotel for 3/13 nights
c you are staying in Varna for one/two weeks

i За кóлко дни сте в Бългáрия?
ii За кóлко нóщи сте в хотéла?
iii За кóлко сéдмици сте във Вáрна? (When **в** is used before words beginning with the letters **в** or **ф** it is extended to **във**.)

5 Read the notices that follow:

ЦЕНТРÁЛНА ПÓЩА Рабóтно врéме (*opening hours*) от (*from*) 7 до (*to*) 20.30 часá

АПТÉКА (*pharmacy*) Рабóтно врéме от 9 до 21 часá

РЕСТОРÁНТ Рабóтно врéме от 18 до 23 часá

ПОДÁРЪЦИ (*gifts*) сýтрин от 8 до 12 часá следóбед от 16 до 20 часá

СЛАДКÁРНИЦА (*patisserie, café*) сýтрин от 10 до 13 часá следóбед от 14 до 19 часá

A more natural way to read the notices would be to use **рабо́ти** and a 12-hour clock, for example:

> Магази́нът за пода́ръци рабо́ти от о́сем часа́ сутринта́ до двана́йсет часа́ на о́бед и от че́тири часа́ следо́бед до о́сем часа́ вечерта́.

Now complete the sentences as if answering the question **До ко́лко часа́ рабо́ти . . . ?** using the 12-hour clock:

a По́щата _____ от 7 часа́ сутринта́ до 8.30 часа́ _____.

b Апте́ката рабо́ти от 9 _____ _____ до 9 _____ _____.

c Рестора́нтът рабо́ти _____ 6 _____ 11 часа́ _____.

d _____ рабо́ти _____ 10 часа́ _____ до еди́н часа́ на о́бед и от 2 часа́ _____ до 7 часа́ _____.

◀) CD 1, TR 27

6 To practise using **ко́лко**, ask questions to which the following could be answers. Concentrate on the numbers involved and don't forget to repeat the prepositions:

a В хоте́ла и́ма две америка́нки.

b Г-н Джо́нсън е в Бълга́рия за две се́дмици.

c Брат ми присти́га след че́тири дни.

d Г-н и г-жа́ Ко́линс са в Со́фия от три дни.

e Автобу́сът замина́ва в де́сет часа́.

f Днес и́маш три съобще́ния и две ка́ртички (*postcards*).

g Г-н Джо́нсън и́ма две деца́.

7 Do you take milk and sugar? Read, checking the Quick vocab, and answer the questions:

Секрета́рката На́дя пи́е кафе́ с Никола́й и Миле́на. На́дя пи́е кафе́то с ма́лко за́хар. Никола́й и́ска кафе́ с мно́го за́хар, а Миле́на и́ска кафе́ без за́хар. Те оби́чат кафе́то с ма́лко мля́ко.

a Какво́ пра́ви На́дя?

b С ко́лко за́хар пи́е кафе́то На́дя?

c С ко́лко за́хар пи́е кафе́то Никола́й?

d Какво́ кафе́ и́ска Миле́на?

e Как оби́чат те кафе́то – с мно́го или́ с ма́лко мля́ко?

f Как оби́чате кафе́то Ви́е?

ка́ртички	postcards
за́хар (f)	sugar
мля́ко	milk
пи́е	(s/he) is drinking
оби́чат	(they) like/love
със за́хар	with sugar
без за́хар	without sugar
с мно́го/ма́лко за́хар	with a lot of/little sugar
с мно́го ма́лко за́хар	with very little sugar
легло́	bed
продава́чка	shop assistant (f)
чужденка́	foreigner (f)
теа́тър	theatre
парк	park

Insight

Със за́хар: when **с** is used before a word beginning with **с** or **з** it is extended to **със** – remember what happened to **в** before **в** and **ф**?

8 Continuing the milk and sugar theme, this exercise will help you practise different ways of saying the same thing. The short dialogues on the left present situations identical to those on the right. Complete the right-hand column using the model. Don't forget to use the short definite form with **чай**:

Тури́стка	Ча́ят е със за́хар, нали́?	В ча́я и́ма за́хар, нали́?
Сервитьо́рка	Да, с ма́лко за́хар.	Да, и́ма ма́лко за́хар.
Тури́стка	Кафе́то е със за́хар, нали́?	a _____
Сервитьо́рка	Да, с ма́лко за́хар.	_____
Тури́стка	Кафе́то е с мля́ко, нали́?	b _____
Сервитьо́рка	Да, с ма́лко мля́ко.	_____
Тури́стка	Ча́ят е с мля́ко, нали́?	c _____
Сервитьо́рка	Да, с ма́лко мля́ко.	_____

9 You can also use **нали** in negative questions. Try it here, adapting the statements with **без**. Notice that the answer can be with **не** or **да**:

Туристка	Чáят е без млякó, налú?	В чáя нямá млякó, налú?
Сервитьóрка	Да, без млякó е.	Не, нямá/ Да, нямá.
Туристка	Кафéто е без млякó, налú?	a _____
Сервитьóрка	Да, без млякó е.	_____
Туристка	Кафéто е без зáхар, налú?	b _____
Сервитьóрка	Да, без зáхар е.	_____
Туристка	Чáят е без зáхар, налú?	c _____
Сервитьóрка	Да, без зáхар е.	_____

10 Use the words in brackets in the plural:

a Г-н и г-жá Кóлинс úскат стáя с две _____ (леглó).

b Г-н и г-жá Кóлинс са _____ (чужденéц).

c _____ ли са г-н и г-жá Кóлинс? (америкáнец).

d Мáйкъл Джóнсън не úска бъ́лгарски _____ (вéстник).

e Николáй úма мнóго _____ (въпрóс).

f Мáйкъл Джóнсън разбúра мнóго _____ (езúк).

g В ЦУМ úма мнóго _____ (продавáчка).

h На булевáрд Вúтоша úма спúрка на _____ нóмер 1, 7 и 9 (трамвáй).

i В сладкáрницата úма мнóго _____ (чужденкá).

11 Finally, to practise using the full and short definite article, answer the following questions, using the words in brackets with the preposition **до**:

a Къдé е óфисът? (ресторáнт) **d** Къдé е теáтърът? (магазúн)

b Къдé е ресторáнтът? (óфис) **e** Къдé е музéят? (парк)

c Къдé е магазúнът? (теáтър) **f** Къдé е пáркът? (музéй)

Another small step forward

🔊 CD 1, TR 28–29

Dialogue 2 В óфиса *In the office*

Mr Antonov has some good news for Nikolai.

г-н Антонов	Николай, заповядай в офиса.
Николай	Благодаря.
г-н Антонов	Имам хубава новина. Заминаваш за Англия.
Николай	Но аз не разбирам английски!
г-н Антонов	О, програмист без английски не може.
Николай	Така е, зная ...
г-н Антонов	Нищо. Във фирмата има един англичанин, който разбира малко български.
Николай	Много интересно! В кой град е фирмата?
г-н Антонов	В Челмсфорд.
Николай	Не зная къде е Челмсфорд.
г-н Антонов	Челмсфорд е малък град близо до Лондон.
Николай	Нов проект ли имаме с фирмата?
г-н Антонов	Да, работим с английски специалисти.
Николай	Чудесно! Кога заминавам?
г-н Антонов	След три седмици.
Николай	За колко дни?
г-н Антонов	За двайсет дни. Хубава новина, нали?
Николай	Разбира се. Благодаря много!

QUICK VOCAB

заповядай в офиса!	*come into the office*
новина	*(piece of) news*
заминавам, -ваш	*to leave/depart*
английски	*English (language)*
програмист без английски не може	*a programmer can't do without English*
нищо	*no matter, never mind*
зная, -аеш	*to know*
кой град	*which town*
малък, малка	*small, little*
нов проект	*a new project*
специалист	*specialist*

Insight

The colloquial form of **зная** is **знам**. The verb remains an **e**-pattern in all other persons.

Test yourself

1 To see how well you have understood Dialogue 2, identify the true statements and correct any false ones:

a Николай заминава за Шотландия.
b Той разбира английски добре.
c Един англичанин от фирмата разбира всичко на български.
d Фирмата е в Честърфийлд.
e Фирмата е в малък град близо до Лондон.
f Николай не знае къде е Челмсфорд.
g Проектът с фирмата не е нов.
h Той заминава след десет дни.

2 How would you say:

a Wonderful, isn't it?
b Very interesting.
c What's the time?
d I don't understand Bulgarian very well.
e Excuse me.
f What are you doing?

3 Turn these plural words into the singular, dividing into masculine and feminine:

часовници	музеи	трамваи
офиси	чужденци	нощи
компютри	американки	шотландци
седмици	туристи	вечери
стаи	езици	

Now can you:

- give the time and ask what the time is?
- say *How much?* and *How many?*
- count from 20 to 100? (backwards too?)
- indicate the times of the day?
- express agreement and approval?

5

Говóрите ли англи́йски?
Do you speak English?

In this unit you will learn:

- How to ask people if they speak your language
- How to ask people what languages they speak
- How to say what languages you know

Dialogue 1

🔊 **CD 1, TR 30–31**

Although you do not need a third person to introduce you to someone in Bulgaria, Nevena's natural Bulgarian curiosity enables the English hotel guests to get to know one another.

Невéна	Г-н Джóнсън, знáете ли, че в хотéла и́ма и дрýги англичáни?
г-н Джóнсън	Ни́що чýдно. Англичáни и́ма в мнóго страни́ по светá.
Невéна	Но не мнóго англичáни говóрят бъ́лгарски! Ви́е говóрите бъ́лгарски добрé, но г-жá Кóлинс говóри пó-добрé.
г-н Джóнсън	Кой говóри пó-добрé?
Невéна	Г-жá Кóлинс.
г-н Джóнсън	Но коя́ е г-жá Кóлинс? Не зня́я коя́ е тя.
Невéна	Говóря за англичáнката, коя́то живéе в стáя нóмер дéсет.
г-н Джóнсън	А Ви́е говóрите ли англи́йски, Невéна?
Невéна	За съжалéние, не. Но говóря ня́колко дрýги ези́ка.

г-н Джо́нсън	Какви́ези́ци зна́ете?
Неве́на	Фре́нски, ру́ски и испа́нски. Фре́нски е ези́кът, който зна́я на́й-добре́.
г-н Джо́нсън	Мно́го бъ́лгари гово́рят чу́жди ези́ци.
Неве́на	Това́ е вя́рно. А, е́то г-н и г-жа́ Ко́линс! (*Calls out to them.*) Г-н Ко́линс, г-жа́ Ко́линс, извине́те за мину́та!
г-жа́ Ко́линс	Разби́ра се, госпо́жице. Здраве́йте!
Неве́на	Мо́ля, запозна́йте се. Това́ е господи́н Джо́нсън, англи́йски бизнесме́н, който живе́е в Че́лмсфорд.
г-жа́ Ко́линс	Мно́го ми е прия́тно!
г-н Ко́линс	(*Echoing Mrs Collins in Bulgarian.*) Прия́тно ми е!
Неве́на	(*Aside.*) Ко́лко интере́сно! Англича́ни, който гово́рят бъ́лгарски!

QUICK VOCAB

дру́ги англича́ни	*other English people*
Ни́що чу́дно.	*(That's) hardly surprising.*
по света́	*in the world*
Но не мно́го англича́ни гово́рят бъ́лгарски.	*But not many English people speak Bulgarian.*
Ви́е гово́рите бъ́лгарски добре́, но г-жа́ Ко́линс гово́ри по́-добре́.	*You speak Bulgarian well, but Mrs Collins speaks better.*
Кой гово́ри по́-добре́?	*Who speaks better?*
Но коя́ е г-жа́ Ко́линс?	*But who is Mrs Collins?*
Не зна́я.	*I don't know.*
Гово́ря за англича́нката, коя́то живе́е в ста́я но́мер де́сет.	*I'm speaking about the English woman who is staying in room number ten.*
А Ви́е гово́рите ли англи́йски?	*And do you speak English?*
за съжале́ние	*unfortunately*
Но гово́ря ня́колко дру́ги ези́ка.	*But I speak several other languages.*
Какви́ ези́ци зна́ете?	*What languages do you know?*
фре́нски	*French*
ру́ски	*Russian*
испа́нски	*Spanish*
Фре́нски е ези́кът, който зна́я на́й-добре́.	*French is the language I know best.*

	QUICK VOCAB
Мно́го бъ́лгари гово́рят чу́жди ези́ци.	A lot of Bulgarians speak foreign languages.
Това́ е вя́рно.	That's true.
извине́те за мину́та	excuse me, just a minute
англи́йски бизнесме́н, кой́то живе́е в Че́лмсфорд	an English businessman who lives in Chelmsford
Ко́лко интере́сно!	How interesting!
Англича́ни, кой́то гово́рят бъ́лгарски!	English people who speak Bulgarian!

1 Questions

a Къде́ и́ма англича́ни?
b Какъ́в чужд ези́к гово́ри г-жа́ Ко́линс мно́го добре́?
c Коя́ е г-жа́ Ко́линс?
d Ко́лко ези́ка гово́ри Неве́на?
e Какви́ ези́ци зна́е Неве́на?
f Къде́ живе́е г-н Джо́нсън?

2 True or false?

Write out correct versions of the false statements:

a Мно́го англича́ни гово́рят бъ́лгарски.
b Г-жа́ Ко́линс е америка́нката, коя́то живе́е в ста́я но́мер де́сет.
c Г-жа́ Ко́линс гово́ри бъ́лгарски мно́го добре́.
d Неве́на не зна́е англи́йски.
e Тя гово́ри ру́ски най-добре́.
f Ма́лко бъ́лгари гово́рят чу́жди ези́ци.

Doing things the Bulgarian way

Does anyone speak English?

You should already be able to cope using your Bulgarian in a number of different situations. However, you will be reassured to know that English is now quite widely spoken in Bulgaria, especially by the younger generation in the larger towns. You will usually find English speakers on the reception desks of big hotels, in money-changing bureaux, in tourist and airline offices and also in the more prestigious places for eating out. When speaking English, they will most probably shake their head for **не** and nod for **да** (see the vital word of warning in the 'Alphabet and pronunciation' section at the beginning of this book). With shop assistants, taxi drivers and policemen, however, although you might still venture a timid **говорите ли английски?**, you would probably do best to resort to your Bulgarian straightaway.

Big or small? When to use capital letters

Bulgarian uses far fewer capital letters than English. The names of nationalities and the national languages all begin with small letters. You will therefore find, for example, **американец, американка** (**американски**); **англичанин, англичанка** (**английски**); **испанец, испанка** (**испански** – *Spanish*); **италианец, италианка** (**италиански** – *Italian*); **немец, немкиня** (**немски** – *German*), and **французин, французойка** (**френски** – *French*).

Names of places begin with capital letters, but when the place name consists of more than one word, the second often begins with a small letter: **Златни пясъци** (*Golden Sands*), **Слънчев бряг** (*Sunny Beach*) and **Черно море** (*the Black Sea*).

Adjectives formed from the names of places also begin with small letters: Лондон: **лондонски**, София: **софийски**, Варна: **варненски.**

Phone matters

In Bulgarian, as in English, there is no single pattern for writing or reading out the individual digits in phone numbers. Some speakers group the digits in pairs, others in threes, depending on the amount of digits in the number. However, the need for ever-increasing strings of numbers, coupled with the widespread use of mobile phones (**мобилен телефон** or **джиесем** from the English **GSM**), means that the simplest way to give your phone number is by reading out the individual digits, one by one.

Curiously, the Bulgarian for a *text message* is **есемес** from the original English *Short Message Service (SMS)*.

When you answer the phone, it's best to follow the Bulgarian practice and, without giving your name, say «**Áло?**» or «**Да, мóля?**» or just «**Да?**» and wait for the person making the call to open the conversation.

When making a call yourself, be prepared to respond to an answerphone (**телефóнен секретáр** or just **секретáр** for short). The standard message on landlines goes something like this: '**Тук е телефóнният секретáр на** . . . [the name of the person]. **Мóля, оставéте съобщéние след сигнáла.**' ('*This is the answerphone of . . . Please leave your message after the beep.*') With mobiles you may also need to leave a **глáсова пóща** *voicemail* (*message*).

ФОТО
СТУДИО ИНДЕР
БЛ.111 ВХ.Б ЕТ.2
ТЕЛ. 847 89 47

Abbreviations used in this sign are: БЛ. = блок (*block*), ВХ. = вход (*entrance*), ЕТ. = етаж (*floor*) and ТЕЛ. = телефон (*telephone*).

How do you say it?

🔊 CD 1, TR 32

• Asking whether a person speaks a foreign language

Говóрите ли англи́йски?	*Do you speak English?*
Знáете ли фрéнски?	*Do you speak (know) French?*

| Какъ́в (чужд) ези́к говори́те/зна́ете? | *What (foreign) language do you speak/know?* |
| Какви́ (чу́жди) ези́ци говори́те? | *What (foreign) languages do you speak?* |

- Answering whether, and how well, you speak a language

Говоря́ добре́ фре́нски.	*I speak French well.*
Разби́рам испа́нски, но не говоря́ добре́.	*I understand Spanish but I don't speak (it) well.*
Зна́я ма́лко ру́ски.	*I know a little Russian.*
Не разби́рам бъ́лгарски.	*I don't understand Bulgarian.*
Говоря́ фре́нски най-добре́.	*I speak French best.*

- Responding to what you hear

| Това́ е вя́рно. | *That's true.* |
| Ни́що чу́дно. | *(That's) hardly surprising.* |

- Expressing interest, agreement or regret

Ко́лко интере́сно!	*How interesting!*
разби́ра се	*of course/naturally*
за съжале́ние	*unfortunately/sadly*

Grammar

1 Some more plurals

Nationalities and masculine nouns ending in -(н)ин

This is one of the endings that form names of nationalities or inhabitants of a place. The plural of such names is once again **-и**, but it is not added to the singular. Instead, the **-н** of the singular is dropped:

англича́нин	*Englishman*	англича́ни	*Englishmen*
бъ́лгарин	*Bulgarian*	бъ́лгари	*Bulgarians*
гра́жданин	*citizen*	гра́ждани	*citizens*
лондонча́нин	*Londoner*	лондонча́ни	*Londoners*

Plural of adjectives and other defining words

In the plural, no matter what the gender of the noun they describe, all adjectives in Bulgarian end in **-и**. Compare:

чужд езѝк	*a foreign language*	чу̀жди езѝци	*foreign languages*
чу̀жда страна̀	*a foreign country*	чу̀жди странѝ	*foreign countries*
чу̀ждо списа̀ние	*a foreign magazine*	чу̀жди списа̀ния	*foreign magazines*

Similarly, you will find the **-и** ending in **какви̂** (*what*), the plural form of **какъ̀в, каква̀, какво̀**:

Какъ̀в езѝк гово̀рите?	*What language do you speak?*
Какви̂ езѝци гово̀рите?	*What languages do you speak?*

Insight

Adjectives that end in **-ски** in the masculine singular remain the same in the plural:

англѝйски вѐстник	*an English newspaper*
америка̀нски бизнесмѐн	*an American businessman*
бъ̀лгарски куро̀рт	*a Bulgarian resort*
ру̀ски гра̀жданин	*a Russian citizen*
англѝйски вѐстници	*English newspapers*
америка̀нски бизнесмѐни	*American businessmen*
бъ̀лгарски куро̀рти	*Bulgarian resorts/spas*
ру̀ски гра̀ждани	*Russian citizens*

2 Друг/дру̀ги *Another/other*

друг, дру̀га, дру̀го	*another*
дру̀ги	*other*
нѐщо дру̀го	*something else*

3 Special masculine plural after numbers

In the dialogue, you came across two plurals of **езѝк** *language*, one ending in **-и** and the other in **-а**:

Какви̂ **езѝци** зна̀ете?	*What languages do you know?*
Зна̀я ня̀колко **езѝка**.	*I know several languages.*

The first is the regular plural (remember the change of **-к** to **-ц**!). The second is the plural form used after any number or after the word

ня́колко *several.* This plural form only occurs in masculine nouns for things and always ends in **-a** or **-я**. If the noun refers to people, you use the regular plural: **ня́колко учи́тели** *several teachers.* Here are some examples:

Неве́на зна́е **три ези́ка**.	*Nevena knows three languages.*
Де́сет биле́та, мо́ля.	*Ten tickets, please.*
В Га́брово и́ма **ня́колко музе́я**.	*In Gabrovo, there are several museums.*

You must also use this special numerical masculine plural in questions after **ко́лко** *how many*:

Ко́лко ези́ка зна́е Неве́на?	*How many languages does Nevena know?*
Ко́лко биле́та и́скате, мо́ля?	*How many tickets do you want, please?*
Ко́лко музе́я и́ма в Га́брово?	*How many museums are there in Gabrovo?*

4 Гово́ря *I speak*

This is an **и**-pattern, Conjugation 2 verb (like **пра́вя** and **рабо́тя** in grammar section 5 in Unit 4):

аз	гово́ря	*I speak*	ни́е	гово́рим	*we speak*
ти	гово́риш	*you speak*	ви́е	гово́рите	*you speak*
той тя то	гово́ри	*he/she/it speaks*	те	гово́рят	*they speak*

5 Зна́я *I know*, игра́я *I play*, живе́я *I live* (e-pattern verbs)

These verbs contain the vowel **-е-** in most of their present tense endings. They are examples of Conjugation 1, **e**-pattern verbs. Notice that once again the final vowel is the same in the *I* form and in the *they* form:

аз	зна́я/игра́я/живе́я	ни́е	зна́ем/игра́ем/живе́ем
ти	зна́еш/игра́еш/живе́еш	ви́е	зна́ете/игра́ете/живе́ете
той тя то	зна́е/игра́е/живе́е	те	зна́ят/игра́ят/живе́ят

Insight

The **-я, -ят** endings of the *I* and *they* forms are pronounced **-йъ, -йът**. Similarly, the **-a** and **-ат** endings are pronounced **-ъ** and **-ът** as in **чета́** *I read* **чета́т** *they read*. Listen carefully to the recording and you will hear this!

6 The present tense: patterns and meanings

To summarize, Bulgarian verbs have three patterns or conjugations:

Conjugation 1 verbs follow the **e**-pattern
Conjugation 2 verbs follow the **и**-pattern
Conjugation 3 verbs follow the **a**-pattern

The present tense in Bulgarian corresponds in meaning to two distinct tense forms in English. **Неве́на гово́ри фре́нски** might mean, depending on the context, either *Nevena speaks French* or *Nevena is speaking French*. Similarly, **аз у́ча бъ́лгарски** might mean either *I learn Bulgarian* or *I am learning Bulgarian*.

Insight

From now on in the vocabulary lists, you will find verbs given with the endings of both the *I* and the *you* forms (1st and 2nd sing). This will help you to identify the correct conjugation pattern. The endings of the *you* form will always be preceded by the letter to which the endings for the other forms need to be added:

Conjugation 1 живе́я, -е́еш; пи́я, -и́еш (*I drink*)
Conjugation 2 гово́ря, -риш; ми́сля, -лиш (*I think*);
 у́ча, -чиш (*I learn*)*

> **Conjugation 3** да́вам, -ваш (*I give*); запо́чвам, -ваш
> разби́рам, -раш
>
> *After ж, ч and ш the -я in all the *I* and *they* forms appears as -a.

7 Кой? *Who?*

The question word for *who* in Bulgarian is **кой**. It stands in place of a noun and you use it to ask for the subject of a sentence no matter whether the subject is masculine, feminine, neuter or even plural:

Ма́йкъл Джо́нсън живе́е в Че́лмсфорд.

Кой живе́е в Че́лмсфорд?	*Who lives in Chelmsford?*

Г-жа́ Ко́линс гово́ри бъ́лгарски по́-добре́.

Кой гово́ри бъ́лгарски по́-добре́?	*Who speaks Bulgarian better?*

Мно́го бъ́лгари гово́рят чу́жди ези́ци.

Кой гово́ри чу́жди ези́ци?	*Who speaks foreign languages?*

8 Кой? коя́? кое́? and кои́? *Which?*

Кой also means *which* when used before a noun and then it has a different form for each of the three genders and for the plural:

Masculine

Кой? В **кой град** е фи́рмата?	*Which town is the firm in?*
Кой ези́к гово́рите най-добре́?	*Which language do you speak best?*

Feminine

Коя́? В **коя́ ста́я** сте?	*Which room are you in?*

Neuter

Кое́? **Кое́ списа́ние** и́скате?	*Which magazine do you want?*

Plural

Кои́? **Кои́ ези́ци** зна́ете?	*Which languages do you know?*

74

When a feminine, neuter or plural noun (or pronoun) is mentioned in the question itself, the correct alternative form of **кой** has to be used, no matter whether it means *who* or *which*:

Коя́ е г-жа́ Ко́линс?	*Which one is Mrs Collins?*
Кое́ е това́ дете́?	*Who is that child?*
Кои́ са те?	*Who are they? or Which are they?*

9 Госпожа́та, коя́то ... *The woman who ...*

In expressions like these, the words *who* and *which* relate to the last person or thing mentioned. They are called relative pronouns. In Bulgarian, you have to concentrate not on the distinction between persons and things, but rather on whether the preceding noun is masculine, feminine, neuter or plural. In the singular, you have to use **ко́йто** (кой+то) for masculine, **коя́то** (коя+то) for feminine and **кое́то** (кое+то) for neuter nouns. The plural form is **кои́то** (кои+то). All the forms must be preceded by a comma:

Masculine
Това́ е **господи́нът, ко́йто**
  гово́ри бъ́лгарски.

This is the man who speaks Bulgarian.

Feminine
Госпожа́та, коя́то присти́га
  днес, у́чи бъ́лгарски.

The woman who arrives/is arriving today is learning Bulgarian.

Neuter
Дете́то, кое́то гово́ри,
  е синъ́т на г-н Анто́нов.

The child who is speaking is Mr Antonov's son.

Plural
Г-н и г-жа́ Ко́линс са
  англича́ни, кои́то живе́ят
  в Ма́нчестър.

Mr and Mrs Collins are English people living/ who live/in Manchester.

Insight

Note that while, in English, you can sometimes omit the words *who* and *which*, in Bulgarian, the relative pronoun can *never* be omitted.

10 Аз зная, че ... *I know that ...*

Че is the Bulgarian equivalent of *that*. It is used as the connecting word (conjunction) after certain verbs and, unlike *that*, can never be omitted. It must always be preceded by a comma:

Аз зная, **че** София е столицата на България.	*I know (that) Sofia is the capital of Bulgaria.*
Знаете ли, **че** много българи говорят английски?	*Do you know (that) many Bulgarians speak English?*

11 Doing *well, better* or *best of all* – comparison

In Bulgarian, when you want to compare the way in which something is done, you change the adverb, in this case **добре** (*well*), by adding **по-** and **най-** on the front. You add **по-** when comparing the way in which two things are done and **най-** when you want to compare more than two. The **по-** and **най-** are pronounced with an emphasis and in the book, we will add a stress mark to remind you of this. Here are some examples:

Г-н Джонсън говори български **добре**, но г-жа Колинс говори **по-добре**.	*Mr Johnson speaks Bulgarian well, but Mrs Collins speaks better.*
Невена говори няколко езика, но знае френски **най-добре**.	*Nevena speaks several languages, but knows French best of all.*

In the same way, the adverbs **близо** *near* and **бързо** *quickly, fast* become:

по-близо *nearer*	**най-близо** *nearest* (of all)
по-бързо *more quickly*	**най-бързо** *quickest* (of all)

In Bulgarian, you use **от** in comparisons much as you use *than* in English:

Г-жа Колинс говори български **по-добре от** г-н Джонсън.	*Mrs Collins speaks Bulgarian better than Mr Johnson.*
Г-жа Колинс говори **по-бързо от** г-н Джонсън.	*Mrs Collins speaks more quickly than Mr Johnson.*

Exercises

1 Turn the following sentences into questions requiring the answer 'yes' or 'no' by making the words in bold type the focus of your questions. Remember to put the verb immediately after the question word **ли**:

Model: Г-жа́ Ко́линс е **англича́нка. Англича́нка ли** е г-жа́ Ко́линс? Да.

a В хоте́ла и́ма **мно́го англича́ни**.
b **Мно́го бъ́лгари** гово́рят англи́йски.
c Г-н Анто́нов и Никола́й са **бъ́лгари**.
d Във фи́рмата рабо́тят **бъ́лгари и англича́ни**.
e Г-н и г-жа́ Ко́линс са **англича́ни**.

банкома́т	*cashpoint, ATM*
цига́ра	*cigarette*
къ́мпинг	*campsite*
моте́л	*motel*
бензиноста́нция	*petrol/gas station*
га́ра	*railway station*
су́пермаркет	*supermarket*
серви́рам, -раш	*to serve*

QUICK VOCAB

2 The following questions may be useful when you want to ask for something else, or something different, using the Bulgarian equivalent of *another* or *other*. Use **друг, дру́га, дру́го** or **дру́ги** as appropriate:

a И́мате ли _____ въпро́си?
b Какво́ _____ ви́но и́мате?
c Къде́ и́ма _____ ба́нка?
d Какви́ _____ ези́ци гово́рите?
e И́ма ли _____ банкома́т до хоте́ла?
f Какви́ _____ цига́ри и́мате?
g Кога́ и́ма _____ автобу́с за Малько́вица?
h И́мате ли _____ дете́?
i Зна́ете ли къде́ и́ма _____ апте́ка?
j И́мате ли _____ свобо́дни места́?

БАНКОМАТ

3 A tourist, map in hand, stops a passer-by and asks which of two places on the map is closer:

i Тук на ка́ртата и́ма два хоте́ла. Кой (хоте́л) е по́-бли́зо?

How would you ask about:

a рестора́нт   **d** къ́мпинг
b град   **e** моте́л
c куро́рт

When asking the same question about places that are feminine, remember, you have to use **коя́**:

ii На ка́ртата и́ма две туристи́чески аге́нции. Коя́ (аге́нция) е по́-бли́зо?

How would you ask the same question about:

a апте́ка   **b** бензиноста́нция   **c** спи́рка

4 Use **кой** or **коя́** as appropriate:

a _____ град е на́й-бли́зо до куро́рта Зла́тни пя́съци?
b _____ трамва́й е на́й-бли́зо до у́лица Ра́ковски?
c _____ спи́рка е на́й-бли́зо до га́рата?
d _____ магази́н е на́й-бли́зо до хоте́л «Ше́ратон»?

e _____ туристическа агенция е най-близо до спирката?

f _____ супермаркет е най-близо до пощата?

5 Ask questions with **колко**, remembering to put the subject at the end of the question, as in the model: Г-н и г-жа Колинс искат два чая. Колко чая искат г-н и г-жа Колинс?

a Невена говори три чужди езика.

b Те искат десет билета.

c Сервитьорът сервира три джина.

d Майкъл Джонсън знае няколко чужди езика.

6 In this exercise, you need to change a word from the normal masculine plural form to the special numerical plural. (The two forms are often used very near to one another.)

Турист   Извинете, има ли магазини до гарата?

Гражданин   Да, до гарата има няколко магазина.

Compose questions and answers based on the model using:

a хотел   **c** музей

b ресторант   **d** офис

7 Choose the correct combinations to make sentences:

(a)	мъжа,	което живее в стая номер десет.
Познавам	жената,	който пристига от Лондон.
	англичани,	която говори хубаво български.
	семейството,	които живеят в България.

(b)	българина,	която е омъжена за англичанин?
Познаваш ли	англичани,	който не пият уиски?
	шотландци,	който заминава за Англия?
	българката,	които са женени за българки?

8 This exercise draws your attention to the fact that what looks like the same masculine form may have two distinct meanings. For instance, **хотела** can be either *the hotel*, in the non-subject form, or, when used after a numeral, *hotels*.

Compare: Това е хотелът.

with: Ето хотела.   *Here's the hotel.*

           Ето два хотела.   *Here are two hotels.*

Using the examples as a model, practise pointing to one or two of the following:

a трамва́й **c** автобу́с **e** компю́тър
b троле́й **d** къ́мпинг **f** банкома́т

You will see from the example that after **е́то** you need to add the short definite article, not the full form, to the noun.

◀) **CD 1, TR 33**

9 Michael Johnson writes down his home address and shows it to Nevena saying: **Е́то адре́са ми**.
What would you say while showing or pointing to the following?

a your ticket **d** your son
b your passport **e** your luggage (**бага́ж**)
c your husband

10 This exercise will help you practise giving telephone numbers the Bulgarian way (see 'Phone matters', earlier in this unit). First, give the numbers as single digits, then group the double digits together: 0888 32 18 91; 0898 15 67 42; 789 02 66; 947 54 26.

Another small step forward

◀) **CD 1, TR 34-35**

Dialogue 2 У́ча англи́йски *I'm studying English*

Milena goes into the office and sees Nikolai who seems busy at the computer.

Миле́на	Здраве́й, Никола́й. Какво́ пра́виш?
Никола́й	У́ча англи́йски по и́нтернет. Ти зна́еш ли англи́йски?
Миле́на	Да, но не мно́го добре́. Ми́сля, че е мно́го тру́ден ези́к.
Никола́й	И аз така́ ми́сля. И́мам ну́жда от учи́тел.
	Позна́ваш ли учи́тели по англи́йски?
Миле́на	О да, позна́вам ня́колко учи́тели, кои́то живе́ят бли́зо.
Никола́й	Чуде́сно. И́мам ну́жда и от уче́бници по англи́йски.
Миле́на	Аз и́мам два уче́бника и ня́колко компа́ктдиска.
	И́мам съ́що фи́лми без пре́вод на ди́види.

80

Никола́й	Мно́го добре́, но и́мам мно́го ма́лко вре́ме.
Миле́на	Не се́ опла́квай! Ве́че сме в Евро́па, нали́? Сега́ деца́ на че́тири-пе́т годи́ни у́чат чужд ези́к.
Никола́й	Ми́сля, че ве́че съм стар за чу́жди ези́ци.
Миле́на	На ко́лко годи́ни си?
Никола́й	На два́йсет и шест.
Миле́на	Е да, вя́рно, мно́го си стар . . .

тру́ден, тру́дна	difficult
така́	so, likewise
и́мам ну́жда от	I need
уче́бник, -ици	textbook
компа́ктдиск	CD
пре́вод	translation
филм	film
ди́види́	DVD
Не се́ опла́квай	Don't complain.
Евро́па	Europe
стар	old
на ко́лко годи́ни си?	how old are you?

Test yourself

1 To see how well you have understood Dialogue 2, identify the true statements and correct any false ones:

a Никола́й у́чи фре́нски.

b Никола́й и́ма ну́жда от учи́тел.

c Миле́на не позна́ва учи́тели по англи́йски.

d Миле́на и́ма три уче́бника по англи́йски.

e Никола́й ня́ма ну́жда от уче́бници.

f Никола́й ми́сли, че е ве́че стар за чу́жди ези́ци.

g Никола́й е на три́йсет и шест годи́ни.

2 You need to match four photos to four CVs. Ask which is/are:

a На́дя   **b** Васи́л   **c** Джон и Кен

3 How would you say:

    a Do you understand English?
    b Do you know French?
    c I speak a little Bulgarian.

Now can you:
- ask someone if they speak English?
- say that you speak/understand a little Bulgarian?
- tell someone where you live?
- use the Bulgarian question words for *who* and *which*?
- say whether something is done *well, better* or *best*?
- use the special plural form of nouns after numbers?
- use adjectives in the plural?

6

Искате ли да . . . ?

Would you like to . . . ?

In this unit you will learn:

- How to say *would you like to ... ?* and *may I ... ?*
- How to respond to *would you like to ... ?* and *may I ... ?*
- How to say *you must* or *have to* do something

Dialogue 1

🔊 **CD 1, TR 36–37**

Michael Johnson is keeping his appointment with Boyan Antonov at the advertising agency.

г-н Джо́нсън	(*Knocking on the office door and going in.*) Мо́же ли? До́бър ден! Ка́звам се Ма́йкъл Джо́нсън.
На́дя	О, г-н Джо́нсън, добре́ дошли́! Мо́ля, заповя́дайте.
г-н Джо́нсън	Благодаря́. Тук ли е г-н Анто́нов? Аз и́мам сре́ща с не́го.
На́дя	Да, разби́ра се. Г-н Анто́нов Ви ча́ка.
г-н Джо́нсън	(*At the door into the director's office.*) Мо́же ли?
г-н Анто́нов	Заповя́дайте, г-н Джо́нсън. Седне́те! Ра́двам се да се запозна́я с Вас.
г-н Джо́нсън	Аз съ́що.
г-н Анто́нов	Как се чу́вствате в Со́фия? Надя́вам се, че сте дово́лен от хоте́ла.
г-н Джо́нсън	Да, вси́чко е наре́д.
г-н Анто́нов	И́скате ли да обя́дваме за́едно?

г-н Джо́нсън	Разби́ра се, ня́мам ни́що проти́в. Мо́же ли пъ́рво да оти́дем в ба́нката? Тря́бва да обменя́ пари́.
г-н Анто́нов	Ня́ма пробле́ми. Ба́нката не é дале́че, а рестора́нтът е до не́я.
г-н Джо́нсън	Извиня́вайте, г-н Анто́нов, мо́же ли да гово́рите по́-ба́вно?
г-н Анто́нов	Мо́же, разби́ра се. Ра́двам се, че ня́маме ну́жда от прево́дач. Ми́сля, че Ви́е гово́рите бъ́лгарски мно́го добре́.
г-н Джо́нсън	Но аз и́скам да разби́рам бъ́лгарски о́ще по́-добре́! И́скам да гово́ря по́-добре́ от г-жа́ Ко́линс.

QUICK VOCAB

Мо́же ли?	*May I (come in)?*
О, г-н Джо́нсън, добре́ дошли́!	*Oh, Mr Johnson, welcome!*
Мо́ля, заповя́дайте.	*Please, do come in.*
Г-н Анто́нов Ви ча́ка.	*Mr Antonov is expecting you.*
Седне́те!	*Do sit down!*
Ра́двам се да се запозна́я с Вас.	*Pleased to/meet you/make your acquaintance.*
Аз съ́що.	*So am I/Me too.*
Как се чу́вствате в Со́фия?	*How do you feel to be in Sofia?*
Надя́вам се, че сте дово́лен от хоте́ла.	*I hope you are happy with the hotel.*
Да, вси́чко е наре́д.	*Yes, everything is fine.*
И́скате ли да обя́дваме за́едно?	*Would you like to have lunch together?*
Разби́ра се, ня́мам ни́що проти́в.	*Certainly, why not?*
Мо́же ли пъ́рво да оти́дем в ба́нката?	*Could we (possibly) go to the bank first?*
Тря́бва да обменя́ пари́.	*I have to change some money.*
Ня́ма пробле́ми.	*No problem.*
Ба́нката не é дале́че, а рестора́нтът е до не́я.	*The bank is not far and the restaurant is next to it.*
мо́же ли да гово́рите по́-ба́вно?	*could you (please) speak more slowly?*

Мо́же, разби́ра се.	*I can, of course.*
Ра́двам се, че ня́маме	*I am glad we do not*
ну́жда от прево́да́ч.	*need an interpreter.*
Но аз и́скам да разби́рам	*But I want to understand*
бъ́лгарски о́ще по́-добре́!	*Bulgarian even better.*

1 Questions

a Кой и́ма сре́ща с г-н Анто́нов?
b Кой ча́ка г-н Джо́нсън?
c И́ма ли г-н Джо́нсън пробле́ми в Со́фия?
d Къде́ и́ска да оти́де пъ́рво г-н Джо́нсън?
e Кой тря́бва да обмени́ пари́?
f Как тря́бва да гово́ри г-н Анто́нов?

2 True or false?

a Г-н Джо́нсън не е́ дово́лен от хоте́ла.
b Г-н Анто́нов и́ска да обя́два за́едно с г-н Джо́нсън.
c Ба́нката и ресторáнтът са дале́че от о́фиса.
d Г-н Джо́нсън тря́бва да гово́ри по́-ба́вно.
e Г-н Анто́нов и г-н Джо́нсън и́мат ну́жда от прево́да́ч.
f Г-н Джо́нсън и́ска да разби́ра бъ́лгарски по́-добре́.

....

Doing things the Bulgarian way

Responding to words of welcome

Мо́ля, you will remember, is the set response to **благодаря́**. The Bulgarians also have set formal responses to the traditional words of welcome **Добре́ дошъ́л!, Добре́ дошла́!** and **Добре́ дошли́!** These responses are **Добре́ зава́рил!, Добре́ зава́рила!** and **Добре́ зава́рили!** (lit. *Well met!*). Once again, notice, you use differing forms for the masculine, feminine and plural. Both the words of welcome and the responses, which are often immediately preceded or followed by **благодаря́**, are used particularly when someone has arrived safely after a long journey. If you cannot manage the full responses, nowadays **благодаря́** will also suffice.

Knocking and entering

In the dialogue at the beginning of this unit, you will have noticed Mr Johnson knocked at the door to Nadya's office and immediately went in. In the English-speaking world, this would have been considered rude. Being in Bulgaria, however, he was right not to wait, for it is normal, especially in offices, to knock and enter immediately. When knocking and entering you would do well simultaneously to give out a **Мо́же ли?** in the hope that, if you are a stranger, someone will eventually respond, inviting you to state your business with a **Да, мо́ля?** or a **каже́те!** *Can I help you?* (lit. *Say!*).

Changing money

ОБМЕННО БЮРО		
ВСИЧКИ СВЕТОВНИ ВАЛУТИ И МОНЕТИ		
ALL WORLD CURRENCIES AND COINS		
ВАЛУТА	БАНКНОТИ	
	КУПУВА	ПРОДАВА
EUR	1,94	1,95
USD	1,23	1,25
GBP	2,25	2,30
CHF	1,22	1,23
CYP	3,34	3,38
JPY	1,19	1,22
CAD	1,21	1,23
AUD	1,16	1,19

Sooner or later (probably sooner rather than later), you will need to change some money. This is not difficult in Bulgaria, especially not in the bigger towns and the main tourist resorts. You will find all manner of agencies, from the larger hotels and banks to numerous small 'change' bureaux, all keen to take your **валу́та** (*currency*) banknotes in exchange for the local Bulgarian *lev*. The 'change' bureaux are indicated by notices such as **ОБМЕ́ННО БЮРО́, ОБМЯ́НА НА ВАЛУ́ТА** or simply **CHANGE**. Travellers' cheques can only be exchanged in banks. All the banks and agencies should present you with a certificate of exchange, which you should check carefully before you leave against the sum paid out to you.

Before changing any money, make sure you know the exchange rates. These can differ considerably from dealer to dealer, but are clearly displayed. The boards list, from left to right, the currency to be exchanged, then the rate at which the bureau buys and sells for levs. Commission is not usually charged, but, like everything else, it's worth checking!

How do you say it?

🔊 **CD 1, TR 38**

- Saying *Welcome!*

To a man:	**Добре́ дошъ́л!**
To a woman:	**Добре́ дошла́!**
To more than one person (and polite):	**Добре́ дошли́!**

- Attracting attention

  Мо́же ли?　　　　　　*May I? Excuse me, but . . .*

- Requesting politely

Мо́же ли да гово́ря с Вас?	*May I have a word with you?*
Мо́же ли да оти́дем в ба́нката?	*Could we (possibly) go to the bank?*
Мо́же ли да гово́рите по́-ба́вно?	*Could you (please) speak more slowly?*

- Asking *May I . . . ?/Can I . . . ?* and responding to the same request

Мо́же ли да обменя́ пари́ тук?	*Can I change (some) money here?*
Да, мо́же.	*Yes, you can.*
Не, не мо́же.	*No, you can't.*

- Saying *I'm pleased to/that . . .* , *I'm glad . . .*

| Ра́двам се да се запозна́я с Вас. | *Pleased to meet you.* |
| Ра́двам се, че сте тук. | *I'm pleased/glad (that) you are here.* |

- Expressing satisfaction with the state of affairs

| Вси́чко е наре́д. | *Everything is fine.* |
| Ня́ма пробле́м(и). | *No problem(s).* |

- Agreeing with a proposal

| Ня́мам ни́що проти́в. | *Why not?/I don't mind if I do.* |

- Saying *I need/don't need*

| И́мам ну́жда от учи́тел. | *I need a teacher.* |
| Ня́мам ну́жда от преводи́ч. | *I don't need an interpreter.* |

Grammar

1 И́скам да *I want to/would like to*

Verbs like **и́скам** *I want* and **тря́бва** *I must* need another verb to complete their meaning. When two (or more) verbs are combined in Bulgarian the second verb is introduced by **да**. (Do not confuse it with **да** meaning *yes*!) The **да** form of the Bulgarian verb corresponds to the English infinitive with or without *to*. An essential difference from English, however, is that the **да** form has personal endings just like a main verb.

The personal endings of the main verb and the **да** form may agree or be different, depending on the meaning:

(*a*) When the two verbs share the same subject, both agree with that subject. The following examples go through all the persons:

И́скам да гово́ря бъ́лгарски по́-добре́.	*I want to speak Bulgarian better.*
И́скаш ли да у́чиш англи́йски?	*Do you want to study English?*
Миле́на и́ска да оти́де в А́нглия.	*Milena wants to go to England.*

Ние **искаме** да **обменим** пари.	We want/would like to change some money.
Искате ли да **отидете** в ба́нката?	Do you want to go to the bank?
Миле́на и Никола́й **искат** да **пия́т** кафе́.	Milena and Nikolai want to drink coffee.

(**b**) When the two verbs have different subjects, each agrees with its own subject (although the subject word may be omitted!). In the dialogue, Mr Antonov asks:

И́скате ли да обя́дваме за́едно?

This literally means *Do **you** want that **we** have lunch together?* Now compare the two – with the same subject and with different subjects:

И́ск**ам** да обя́дв**ам** с тях.	*I want to have lunch with them.*
Те и́ск**ат** да обя́дв**ам** с тях.	*They want me to have lunch with them.*
Той и́ск**а** да обя́дв**а** с тях.	*He wants/would like to have lunch with them.*
Той и́ск**а** да обя́дв**аш** с тях.	*He wants you to have lunch with them.*

So, to make sure you clearly express who wants to do what with whom you have to choose the endings of the **да** form very carefully. One letter can make all the difference between who gets a meal and who doesn't!

2 Тря́бва да... Must or have to...

You use **тря́бва да** + verb for both *must* and *have to.* As with **мо́же ли да...?** below, **тря́бва да...** itself stays the same for all persons. The verb that follows changes to fit the subject, which is not always expressed. Again, therefore, you have to be very careful to listen for the ending of the verb to work out the correct meaning:

| (аз) | тря́бва да оти́д**а** в Пло́вдив. | *I have to go to Plovdiv.* |
| (ти) | тря́бва да оти́д**еш** в по́щата. | *You must go to the post office.* |

Миле́на тря́бва да се запозна́е с г-н Джо́нсън.	*Milena must get to know Mr Johnson.*	
(ни́е)	тря́бва да оти́дем в ба́нката.	*We have to go to the bank.*
(ви́е, Ви́е)	тря́бва да обмени́те пари́.	*You must change some money.*
(те)	тря́бва да оти́дат в о́фиса.	*They have to go to the office.*

Insight

Note that some verbs can be used in the present tense only when preceded by **да**. You will learn more about these verbs in Unit 12, but from now on in vocab lists, they will all be preceded by (**да**).

---

3 Мо́же ли . . . ? *May I . . . ? Could you . . . ?*

Мо́же ли . . . ? is a commonly used phrase that never changes its form. It is used to attract attention, to ask whether something is possible or permitted or to make a polite request. **Мо́же** is, in fact, the *it* form of the verb meaning *can* or *be able*.

Мо́же ли on its own

Мо́же ли is used on its own to attract attention or to ask *Is it all right?* (for me to do this, that or the other) or *Could you?* (do this, that or the other for me). For instance, you say **Мо́же ли?** on its own:

(*a*) at the door when you want permission to go in
(*b*) when people are in your way and you want to get past
(*c*) when you need to interrupt someone

In a restaurant, you use **мо́же ли** on its own just to attract the waiter's attention or you may add another word to make your meaning clear:

Мо́же ли меню́то?   *Could you bring (pass etc.) the menu?*

Similarly, at table, if you want someone to pass something, the milk, for example, you would say:

Мо́же ли мля́кото?   *Could you pass (bring etc.) the milk?*

Мо́же ли да . . . ? *May I . . . ?*

This is used to ask if something is possible or permitted. **Мо́же ли да** + main verb is used to formulate full questions. When the main verb involves the speaker (*I* or *we*), **Мо́же ли да . . . ?** can be used to ask for permission, in which case the answer will be **Мо́же**, or **Да, мо́же** and, if you are unlucky, **Не мо́же**, or **Не, не мо́же**:

Мо́же ли да гово́ря с г-н Анто́нов?	*Can I speak to Mr Antonov?*
Не, сега́ не мо́же.	*No, it isn't possible now.*
Мо́же ли да оти́дем в ба́нката?	*Could we (possibly) go to the bank?*
Мо́же, разби́ра се.	*We could, of course.*
Мо́же ли да се́днем до вас?	*Can we sit next to you?*
Разби́ра се, заповя́дайте!	*Certainly, go ahead!*

Мо́же ли да гово́рите по́-ба́вно? *Could you please speak more slowly?*

When the main verb is addressed to someone else, in the 2nd person singular or plural, **Мо́же ли да . . . ?** is used to make a polite request:

Мо́же ли да гово́риш по́-ба́вно?	*Would you please speak more slowly?*
Мо́же ли да се оба́дите по́-късно?	*Could you please ring/ call later?*

4 И́мам сре́ща с не́го *I've a meeting with him*

As in English, personal pronouns have different forms when they are not used as subjects, for instance after prepositions. Compare: *I have a meeting with him* (**аз и́мам сре́ща с не́го**), and *he has a meeting with me* (**той и́ма сре́ща с ме́не**). Both subject and non-subject (full) forms are given in the table side by side for comparison:

И́скате ли да обя́двате с ме́не?	*Would you like to have lunch with me?*
Г-н Джо́нсън и́ма сре́ща с не́го.	*Mr Johnson has a meeting with him.*
Това́ е ба́нката, а ресторантъ́т е до не́я.	*That is the bank and the restaurant is next to it.*
И́ма три писма́ за Вас.	*There are three letters for you.*
На́дя пи́е кафе́ с тях.	*Nadya is drinking coffee with them.*

Subject forms		Non-subject (full) forms	
Singular	аз	с мéне	*with me*
	ти	от тéбе	*from you*
	той	с нéго	*with him*
	тя	от нéя	*from her*
	то	до нéго	*next to it*
Plural	нíе	до нас	*near us*
	вíе (Вíе)	с вас (Вас)	*with you*
	те	от тях	*from them*

NB You'll find more on non-subject forms in Units 7 and 11.

5 Getting to know one another

Verbs that are accompanied by the 'satellite' word **се** are known as reflexive verbs. One of the uses of a reflexive verb is to express the meaning *each other* or *one another*.

Sometimes the same verb can be used with and without **се** with different meanings. Compare the non-reflexive *without* **се**:

Невéна íска да запознáе г-н Джóнсън със семéйство Кóлинс.	*Nevena wants to introduce Mr Johnson to the Collins family.*
Г-н Джóнсън разбíра бъ́лгарски.	*Mr Johnson understands Bulgarian.*

Now the same verbs used *with* **се**:

Николáй и Милéна íскат да се запознáят.	*Nikolai and Milena want to meet (one another).*
Г-н Антóнов и г-н Джóнсън се разбíрат без преводáч.	*Mr Antonov and Mr Johnson understand one another without an interpreter.*

A number of reflexive verbs, usually denoting feelings or emotions, never appear without **се**: **надя́вам се** *I hope*, **рáдвам се** *I am glad*. (There's more about reflexives in Unit 20.)

6 Where to place 'се'

Strict rules govern the position of **се**. Most importantly, it can never be the very first word in a sentence. Like a satellite it remains close to its verb, but:

(a) it comes before the verb if there are other words in first position such as pronouns, adverbs, question words or even little words like **да** in a **да** form or the negative **не**

(b) it follows the verb if the verb is the first word in the sentence:

Before the verb	After the verb
Той се надя́ва, че г-н Джо́нсън е дово́лен.	Надя́вам се, че сте дово́лен.
He hopes Mr Johnson is pleased.	*I hope you are pleased.*
Как се чу́вствате?	Чу́вствам се добре́.
How do you feel?	*I feel well.*
Не се́ чу́вствам добре́.	
I don't feel well.	

(The Appendix has a table to help you with word order.)

Exercises

1 Form short dialogues following the model:

* И́мате ли резерва́ция?
    – Не. Тря́бва ли да и́мам резерва́ция?
* Да, тря́бва.

Use **паро́ла** (*password*), **кре́дитна ка́рта** (*credit card*), **пи́нкод** (*PIN number*) instead of **резерва́ция**.

2 Using the model: И́скате ли да оти́дем на рестора́нт? ask someone to go:

a to the opera
b to a concert
c to a café
d to a disco
e to the theatre
f on an excursion
g skiing
h to the beach

Logo of the National Palace of Culture in Sofia, Национа́лен Дворе́ц на Култу́рата (НДК, pronounced «еН-Де-Ка́»)

дискоте́ка	disco
екску́рзия	excursion
на ски́	skiing
плаж	beach
сол (f)	salt
бар	bar
ма́са	table
пи́там, -таш	to ask
мо́же да напра́ви	(she) can make

3 You fear you have misheard an important telephone message. On the basis of the following questions and answers, see if you can write out the original message in just one sentence:

Кой тря́бва да оти́де в А́нглия? – Никола́й.

В кой град тря́бва да оти́де Никола́й? – в Че́лмсфорд.

Кога́ тря́бва да оти́де Никола́й в Че́лмсфорд? – След три се́дмици.

4 Which of the **мо́же ли?** questions might you use in the following situations. In some of them, a variety of questions may be appropriate:

i	at the information desk	**a**	Мо́же ли?
ii	looking for a place in a restaurant	**b**	Мо́же ли да гово́ря с Миле́на?
iii	in a crowded bus	**c**	Мо́же ли това́?
iv	at table	**d**	Мо́же ли да се́дна до Вас?
v	pointing at something in a shop	**e**	Мо́же ли да обменя́ пари́ тук?
vi	asking for Milena on the phone	**f**	Мо́же ли солта́?
vii	at the bank		
viii	entering a room	**g**	Мо́же ли една́ ка́рта на Со́фия?
ix	attracting the attention of a waiter	**h**	Мо́же ли еди́н въпро́с?

5 By using pronouns instead of the names and the nouns in the next two exercises, you will be able to practise using the non-subject forms:

a Познаваш ли Невена? Имам писмо от _____.

b Познаваш ли Марк? Имам среща с _____.

c Познаваш ли г-н и г-жа Колинс? Има билети за _____.

6 You are giving directions using a well-known place as reference point. Complete with the appropriate personal pronoun:

a Знаете къде е барът, нали? Кафето е до _____.

b Знаете къде е кафето, нали? Дискотеката е до _____.

c Знаете къде е дискотеката, нали? Бюро «Информация» е до _____.

d Знаете къде е бюро «Информация», нали? Пощата е до _____.

e Знаете къде е пощата, нали? Музеят е до _____.

f Знаете къде е музеят, нали? Магазинът е до _____.

7 Introduce yourself and, using **трябва да има** (*there should be*), ask for the things in the following list:

Model: Казвам се _____. Трябва да има стая за мене.

билети/писма/покана/вестници/маса

8 Read the following text and make it into a conversation between Nikolai, Mr Antonov and Nadya. It will help you practise using verbs in the *I* form:

Николай иска да говори с г-н Антонов. Г-н Антонов съжалява, но сега няма време за него. Той има среща с г-н Джонсън. Надя пита има ли г-н Антонов нужда от нея. Г-н Антонов мисли, че те нямат нужда от преводач. Той пита Надя може ли да направи кафе за тях. Надя няма нищо против.

◀) CD 1, TR 39

9 This exercise will help you ask for things you might need. Prefacing your answer by **Имам нужда от**, use the words in the following list to reply to the question: **От какво имате нужда?**

a ютия

b чадър

c количка

e носач

d такси

f пари

10 Now for a few useful reflexives. Complete the following sentences without forgetting to alter the position of **ce**. Here is a model to guide you:

Ра́двам се да се запозна́я с Вас! – И аз **се ра́двам.**

a Надя́вам се да оти́да във Ва́рна. – И аз _____
b Ра́двам се, че замина́ваш за А́нглия. – И аз _____
c Чу́вствам се добре́. – И аз _____

_____

Another small step forward

◀ CD 1, TR 40–41

Dialogue 2 Зае́та ли си? *Are you busy?*

(*The telephone rings.*)

Nadya asks a client to ring back later and the office staff then arrange to meet up after work.

На́дя	Да, мо́ля?
Клие́нт	А́ло, мо́же ли да говоря́ с дире́ктора г-н Анто́нов?
На́дя	Съжаля́вам, г-н Анто́нов е зае́т в моме́нта. Мо́же ли да се оба́дите пак?
Клие́нт	Кога́ да се оба́дя?
На́дя	По́-къ́сно следо́бед, мо́ля.
Клие́нт	Благодаря́. Дочу́ване.
****	

96

Николай	Дире́кторът с г-н Джо́нсън ли е?
На́дя	Да, ти тря́бва да се запозна́еш с не́го.
Николай	По́-късно. Сега́ г-н Джо́нсън и г-н Анто́нов са зае́ти.
На́дя	Вя́рно, те гово́рят за прое́кта в моме́нта.
Николай	Миле́на, ти зае́та ли си днес след ра́бота? И́скаш ли да оти́дем на те́нис?
Миле́на	Добра́ иде́я. Мо́же ли и брат ми да игра́е с нас?
На́дя	Су́пер! Да оти́дем зае́дно на те́нис! Брат ти мо́же да игра́е с ме́не, а Никола́й – с те́бе.
Миле́на	Добре́, но пъ́рво тря́бва да гово́ря с брат ми.

QUICK VOCAB

клие́нт	*client, customer*
а́ло	*hello* (on the phone)
зае́т	*busy; occupied*
в моме́нта	*at the moment*
(да) се оба́дя, -диш	*to call, to ring*
пак	*again*
по́-късно	*later*
дочу́ване	*goodbye* (on the phone)
иде́я	*idea*

Test yourself

1 To see how well you have understood Dialogue 2, answer the following questions:

   a Кой и́ска да гово́ри с дире́ктора?
   b Свобо́ден ли е г-н Анто́нов?
   c Кога́ тря́бва да се оба́ди клие́нтът?
   d Къде́ и́ска да оти́де Никола́й след ра́бота?
   e И́ска ли На́дя да оти́де с Никола́й и Миле́на?

2 Complete the sentences:

   a _____ ли да обме́ня пари́ тук?
   b Г-н Анто́нов е _____ в моме́нта.
   c Миле́на, свобо́дна ли си днес _____ ра́бота?
   d И́скаш ли да _____ на те́нис?
   e Пъ́рво _____ да се оба́дя на брат ми.

3 Provide questions to which the following could be responses:

a _____

Съжаля́вам, сега́ не мо́жете да гово́рите с г-н Джо́нсън.

b _____

Чу́вствам се добре́.

c _____

Мо́же, разби́ра се. Заповя́дайте, седне́те!

Now can you:

- ask if someone would like to do something and say what you would like to do?
- make polite requests?
- say that you must or have to do something?
- say that you are pleased?
- attract somebody's attention?
- distinguish between the meanings of some non-reflexive verbs and their reflexive counterparts with ce?
- use the right forms of pronouns after prepositions?

7

Ко́лко стру́ва . . . ?
How much is . . . ?

In this unit you will learn:

- How to point out and ask for things
- How to ask *how much does it cost?*
- How to shop at Bulgarian open-air fruit markets

Dialogue 1

◀） CD 1, TR 42–43

After consulting Nevena for advice, Mr and Mrs Collins go to the market to buy fresh fruit and vegetables.

г-жа́ Ко́линс	Неве́на, покаже́те ни, мо́ля, откъде́ да ку́пим плодове́ и зеленчу́ци.
Неве́на	За съжале́ние магази́нът за плодове́ и зеленчу́ци не е́ бли́зо. На́й-добре́ е да оти́дете на паза́ра. Плодове́те и зеленчу́ците там не са́ е́втини, но са на́й-пре́сни.
г-жа́ Ко́линс	Бли́зо ли е паза́рът?
Неве́на	Да, да, не е́ дале́че.

At the market, Mrs Collins is so carried away she speaks to her husband in Bulgarian and Mr Collins shows he is learning fast!

г-жа́ Ко́линс	Виж, Джордж, та́зи жена́ прода́ва ху́бави зеленчу́ци. Да ку́пим дома́ти от не́я.
г-н Ко́линс	Зеленчу́ци? Дома́ти? А-ха́ . . .

Продавачка	Заповядайте, моля! Вземете си!
г-н Колинс	Какви са тези зеленчуци?
Продавачка	Това са тиквички, господине. Да Ви дам ли?
г-н Колинс	Не, благодаря. Жена ми не обича тиквички.
Продавачка	Много мило! В България не са много мъжете, които пазаруват.
г-н Колинс	Моля? Не разбирам.
г-жа Колинс	Пазар – пазарувам. Жената иска да каже, че мъжете в България не обичат да пазаруват.
г-н Колинс	О, аз нямам нищо против да пазарувам! Дайте ми, моля, един килограм домати. Жена ми обича домати.
г-жа Колинс	Колко струват доматите?
Продавачка	Три лева.
г-жа Колинс	А пъпешите?
Продавачка	Два и петдесет за килограм.
г-жа Колинс	Дайте ми този пъпеш, ако обичате.
Продавачка	Готово – пъпешът е два килограма и половина. Искате ли още един плик за пъпеша?
г-жа Колинс	Да благодаря. Джордж, какви други плодове искаш?
Продавачка	Имаме хубави ябълки, праскови и грозде.
г-жа Колинс	Дайте ни един килограм от тези ябълки и половин килограм бяло грозде.
Продавачка	Всичко дванайсет лева и осемдесет стотинки.
г-жа Колинс	Джордж, плати, ако обичаш. (*Popping a grape into her mouth.*) Ммм, гроздето е много сладко. Джордж, купи още половин кило.
г-н Колинс	Добре, добре. Още има мъже, които пазаруват с удоволствие. Много мило!

QUICK VOCAB

Покажете ни, моля откъде да купим плодове и зеленчуци.	*Please show us where to buy fruit and vegetables from.*
Най-добре е да отидете на пазара.	*You'd do best to go to the market.*
магазинът за плодове и зеленчуцин	*greengrocer's (shop)*
евтин	*cheap*
най-пресни	*freshest*

100

Виж, Джордж, тáзи женá продáва хýбави зеленчýци.	Look, George, this woman is selling nice vegetables.
Да кýпим домáти от нéя.	Let's buy (some) tomatoes from her.
Вземéте си!	Help yourselves!
тéзи	these
тúквички	courgettes/zucchinis
Да Ви дам ли?	Shall I give you some?
Женá ми не обúча тúквички.	My wife doesn't like courgettes.
мнóго мúло!	very sweet/kind!
Не сá мнóго мъжéте, който пазарýват!	There aren't many men who do the shopping.
Женáта úска да кáже, че мъжéте в Бългáрия не обúчат да пазарýват.	What the woman means is that men in Bulgaria don't like shopping.
О, аз нямам нúщо протúв да пазарýвам.	Oh, I don't mind shopping.
Дáйте ми, мóля, едúн килогрáм домáти.	Please give me one kilogram of tomatoes.
Кóлко стрýват домáтите?	How much are the tomatoes?
три лéва	three levs
А пъпешите?	And the melons?
два и петдесéт за килогрáм	two fifty a kilogram
Дайте ми тóзи пъпеш, акó обúчате.	Give me this melon if you please.
Готóво!	There you go (lit. ready)!
Пъпешът е два килогрáма и половúна.	The melon is 2 1/2 kilograms.
óще едúн плик	another plastic bag
каквú дрýги плодовé úскаш?	what other fruit would you like?
Úмаме хýбави ябълки, прáскови и грóзде.	We have apples, peaches and grapes.
едúн килогрáм от тéзи ябълки половúн килогрáм бяло грóзде	a/one kilogram of these apples half a kilogram of white grapes
платú, акó обúчаш	pay, (if you) please

Гро́здето е мно́го сла́дко.
Купи́ о́ще полови́н кило́.
О́ще и́ма мъже́, кои́то
   пазару́ват с удово́лствие.

The grapes are very sweet.
Buy me another half kilo.
There still are men who gladly
   do the shopping.

1 Questions

a Къде́ е на́й-добре́ да оти́дат г-н и г-жа́ Ко́линс?
b Какви́ са плодове́те и зеленчу́ците на паза́ра?
c Какво́ не оби́ча г-жа́ Ко́линс?
d Ко́лко килогра́ма дома́ти и́ска г-н Ко́линс?
e Какви́ дру́ги плодове́ прода́ва жена́та?
f Ко́лко стру́ва вси́чко?

2 True or false?

a Г-н и г-жа́ Ко́линс и́скат Неве́на да им пока́же магази́н за чай и кафе́.
b Г-н Ко́линс и́ска да ку́пи ти́квички.
c Г-н Ко́линс е еди́н от те́зи мъже́, кои́то оби́чат да пазару́ват.
d Г-жа́ Ко́линс и́ска да взе́ме еди́н пъпеш.
e Г-жа́ Ко́линс и́ска едно́ кило́ пра́скови.
f Гро́здето е мно́го сла́дко и г-жа́ Ко́линс и́ска да ку́пи о́ще.

Doing things the Bulgarian way

More about money

Since the early 1880s, shortly after the liberation of Bulgaria from the Ottoman Empire, the basic Bulgarian currency unit has been the **лев** (*lev*, lit. *lion*, after the rampant lion that is the official emblem of free Bulgaria). The sub-unit (one hundred to every lev) is the **стоти́нка** (*stotinka*, from **сто** meaning *hundred*).

In English, the plural of 'lev' should rightly be 'levs'. The temptation, however, is to say 'leva' or 'levas', influenced by the masculine counting form **два ле́ва, три ле́ва** etc., which is far more frequently heard than the straight singular **лев**. Similarly, the plural of 'stotinka' in English should be 'stotinkas', but you will most likely be tempted to say 'stotinki', influenced by the Bulgarian feminine plural **стотинки**.

The Bulgarian for 'one dollar' – whether US or Canadian – is **един долар**, so you say **сто долара** (only one **л** remember!) The pound sterling has a feminine and masculine form: **една английска лира** or **един британски паунд**, so 'one hundred pounds' would be either **сто английски лири** or **сто британски паунда**. The euro is neuter and has no plural: **едно евро, сто евро** etc.

The Bulgarian national coat of arms:
UNION MAKES STRENGTH

In everyday conversation, you will often hear **левче** or **едно левче** used instead of **един лев**. This is the affectionate, diminutive form. There are coins for 1, 2, 5, 10, 20 and 50 stotinkas, and also for one lev(che). Notes come in denominations of 2, 5, 10, 20, 50 and 100 levs.

Buying fruit

The best place to buy fruit is at one of the many open-air markets. Here you will find a variety of local and imported fruit and vegetables being offered for sale by individual stallholders, all eager that you should leave your money with them. Sometimes the stallholder will even offer you something to taste. It is common practice for you to select your own fruit, but some stallholders may object to your handling it, so be prepared with an apology: **Извинете!** (*I'm sorry!/Excuse me!*).

Fruit and vegetables are sold by the kilogram and even cucumbers and melons are usually sold by weight. When buying quantities less than a kilogram, the weight is usually calculated in grams or fractions of a kilogram. So if you want half a kilogram of tomatoes, you say **Половин килограм домати, моля**. And if you want 300 grams of feta cheese, you say **триста грама сирене, моля**.

Bulgaria is a Mediterranean-type country and a 'bridge to the East', but you will not be expected to haggle over the prices of fruit and vegetables. Although not always marked up, the prices you will be given when you ask **Колко струва?** (or **Колко струват?**) will be firm. As with waiters, the arithmetic of stallholders can be unreliable and overcharging is not unknown. So do tot up the various items yourself, preferably in Bulgarian and out loud!

In Bulgaria, courgettes (or zucchinis if you prefer) are more like small marrows. They are light in colour and larger than the ones we are used to.

How do you say it?

🔊 CD 1, TR 44

- Asking someone to give you/show you something

Дáйте ми, мóля, дéсет билéта за метрóто!	*Please give me ten tickets for the metro.*
Покажéте ми, мóля, товá списáние!	*Please show me this magazine.*

- Asking how much something costs

Кóлко стрýва пъпешът?	*How much is the melon?*
Кóлко стрýват ябълките?	*How much do the apples cost?*

- Making suggestions

Да отúдем на пазáра!	*Let's go to the market.*
Да кýпим домáти от тáзи женá!	*Let's buy some tomatoes from this woman.*

- Giving advice

Нáй-добрé е да отúдете на пазáра!	*You'd do best to go to the market.*

- Expressing your likes and dislikes

Обúчам грóзде.	*I like grapes.*
Обúчам да пазарýвам.	*I like shopping.*

104

Не оби́чам пра́скови.	*I don't like peaches.*
Не оби́чам да у́ча.	*I don't like studying.*

Grammar

1 More masculine plurals

Masculine nouns of one syllable have a plural ending all of their own. If they end in a consonant, they add **-ове** to the singular. If they end in **-й**, they add **-еве**. Some nouns keep the stress on the first syllable, while, in others, the stress jumps either to the middle or to the final syllable:

клуб	–	клу́б**ове**	*clubs*			
ключ	–	клю́ч**ове**	*keys*	плод	–	плод**ове́** *fruit*
плик	–	пли́к**ове**	*envelopes*	брой	–	бро́**еве** *numbers;*
сок	–	со́к**ове**	*juices*			*copies*
нож	–	нож**о́ве**	*knives*			
град	–	град**ове́**	*towns*			

Note that це́нтър (*centre*), although more than one syllable, has the plural це́нтрове.

Insight

Only very few masculine nouns of one syllable form their plurals differently. Two common examples are:

брат – бра́тя	*brothers*	мъж – мъже́	*men/husbands*

2 Using *the* with plural nouns: adding -те and -та

The Bulgarian equivalent of *the* is added to the end of the word, as we saw earlier:

Singular		with *the*	
пъпеш	*a melon*	пъпеш**ът**	*the melon*
Plural		with *the*	
пъпеши	*melons*	пъпеши**те**	*the melons*

There are two alternative plural forms of *the*: **-те** and **-та**. Which you need depends entirely on the final letters of the plural form. Gender plays no part whatsoever. Once again, however, you will notice an element of rhyme or vowel harmony.

(*a*) **-те** is added to plurals in **-и** or **-е**:

зеленчу́к: зеленчу́**ци**	–	зеленчу́ци**те**	*the vegetables*
плод: плодов**é**	–	плодов**éте**	*the fruit*
пра́скова: пра́скови	–	пра́скови**те**	*the peaches*
я́бълка: я́бълки	–	я́бълки**те**	*the apples*

(*b*) **-та** is added to plurals in **-а** and **-я**:

ви́но: вин**á**	–	вин**áта**	*the wines* (note the stress change!)
се́ло: сел**á**	–	сел**áта**	*the villages* (stress change here too!)
дете́: дец**á**	–	дец**áта**	*the children*
писмо́: писм**á**	–	писм**áта**	*the letters*
брат: бра́т**я**	–	бра́т**ята**	*the brothers*

(There are more neuter plurals in Unit 8.)

3 Telling people what to do

Да́йте ми, мо́ля!	*Please give me.*
Вземе́те си, мо́ля!	*Please help yourself.* (lit. *take to yourself*)
Покаже́те ми, мо́ля!	*Please show me.*

These are all commands or requests in the polite plural. You have already come across a number of similar forms (all ending in **-те**) **заповя́дайте!, здраве́йте!** and **каже́те!** These forms are known as imperatives. There is a singular imperative, for situations when you would need to use the singular **ти** form, and a plural imperative, for situations when you would use **Ви́е** or **ви́е**.

The endings of the imperative are either **-й** (**-йте**) or **-и́** (**-éте**).

(*a*) In **а**-pattern verbs and verbs with an *I* form ending in two vowels you replace the present tense endings of the *I* form with **-й** or **-йте**:

106

Present tense	Imperative singular	Imperative plural	
парки́рам (*I park*)	не парки́рай!	не парки́рай**те**!	*don't park!*
ра́двам се	ра́двай се!	ра́двай**те** се!	*be happy!*
игра́я	игра́й!	игра́й**те**!	*play!*
пи́я	пи́й!	пи́й**те**!	*drink!*

(*b*) In most **e**- and **и**-pattern verbs the ending of the *I* form of the present tense is replaced by **-и** in the singular and **-éте** in the plural:

Present tense	Imperative singular	Imperative plural	
(да) пока́жа	покаж**и́**!	покаж**éте**!	*show!*
(да) сéдна	седн**и́**!	седн**éте**!	*sit down!*
(да) ку́пя	куп**и́**!	куп**éте**!	*buy!*
(да) платя́	плат**и́**!	плат**éте**!	*pay!*

Insight

In these verbs, the stress is on the final syllable in the singular and on the penultimate syllable in the plural.

Some common irregular imperatives:

Present	Singular	Plural	
(да) ви́дя	виж!	ви́жте!	*look!*
(да) дам	дай!	да́йте!	*give!*
(да) ям	яж!	я́жте!	*eat!*
(да) до́йда	ела́!	ела́те!	*come!*

4 (Да) дам *I give*

This verb follows the **e**-pattern, but the *I* form is irregular. In the present tense, **дам** only occurs after **да**. The examples that follow are therefore accompanied by **тря́бва**:

аз	тря́бва да дам	I must give	ни́е тря́бва да даде́м	we must give
ти	тря́бва да даде́ш	you must give	ви́е тря́бва да даде́те	you must give
той тя то	тря́бва да даде́	he, she, it must give	те тря́бва да дада́т	they must give

5 Да́йте ми! покаже́те ми! *Give me, show me*

When using verbs like *give* and *show,* you usually need to mention both what you give or show (the direct object) and the person to whom the thing is given or shown (the indirect object):

Да́йте **ми**, мо́ля, еди́н килогра́м гро́зде!	*Please give **me** a kilogram of grapes.*
Покаже́те **ми**, мо́ля, та́зи ка́ртичка!	*Please show **me** this postcard.*
Купи́ **ми** я́бълки, мо́ля.	*Buy me (some) apples, please.*

In English, you often need two words (a preposition such as *to* or *for* and a naming word or a pronoun such as *me*) to express the indirect object: *Give it **to me*** or *Buy some **for me***. Bulgarian, however, usually manages without a preposition. Happily, the forms of the most common indirect object pronouns (the so-called 'short forms') are the same as those used to express possession (see Unit 3). Here is a list of those short indirect object pronouns with the subject forms in brackets:

(аз)	**ми**	*to me*	(ни́е)	**ни**	*to us*
(ти)	**ти**	*to you*	(ви́е)	**ви**	*to you*
(той)	**му**	*to him*			
(тя)	**й**	*to her*	(те)	**им**	*to them*
(то)	**му**	*to it*			

6 Where to put the indirect object pronoun

Like the reflexive pronoun **се**, the short indirect object pronoun usually comes immediately before the verb:

И́скам да **ти** пока́жа Со́фия.	*I want to show **you** Sofia.*
Мо́же ли да **ни** пока́жете паза́ра?	*Could you show **us** the market?*

108

Insight

Watch the stress of (**да**) **пока́жете**. This is the *you* form, *not* the imperative **покажéте**!

If the verb is the first word in the sentence, the pronoun comes immediately after the verb:

Покажéте **ни** меню́то, мóля.   *Please show us the menu.*
Да́йте **ми** меню́то, мóля.   *Please give me the menu.*

7 Да Let's! and shall we?

Да can be used with the *we* form to express the English *let's!* or *shall we?*:

Да отѝдем на паза́ра!   *Let's go to the market!*
Да кỳпим пъ̀пеша!   *Let's buy the melon!*
Да платѝм!   *Let's pay!*

If we add **ли** and turn these examples into questions, the affirmative answer will involve two different usages of **да**:

Да отѝдем ли на паза́ра?   *Shall we go to the market?*
Да, да отѝдем!   *Yes, let's!*
Да кỳпим ли пъ̀пеш?   *Shall we buy a melon?*
Да, да кỳпим!   *Yes, let's!*

8 Тóзи, та́зи, товá and тéзи: this, these

In situations in which, in English, you use *this* or *these* – when pointing to or referring to something or someone nearby – in Bulgarian, you have to select one of four slightly different forms:

Masculine	**тóзи** голя́м магазѝн	*this large shop*
Feminine	**та́зи** ста́ра жена́	*this old woman*
Neuter	**товá** хỳбаво детé	*this beautiful child*
Plural	**тéзи** мла́ди мъжé	*these young men*

In spoken Bulgarian, you will often hear their simplified forms: **тóя** or **тоз** for **тóзи**, **та́я** or **таз** for **та́зи** and **тéя** or **тез** for **тéзи**.

9 Éвтин, пó-éвтин *Cheap, cheaper*

To say that something is cheaper, bigger or more beautiful, for example (i.e. to make the comparative form of the adjective), all you do is place **пó-** on the front, as you did with the adverbs in Unit 5. The adjectives, however, have to be changed according to gender, depending on what noun they go with. So you say:

Тóзи пъ̀пеш е éвтин/
   пó-éвтин.
This melon is cheap/cheaper.

Тáзи кáртичка е хýбава/
   пó-хýбава.
This card is beautiful/ more beautiful.

Товá вѝно е слáдко/
   пó-слáдко.
This wine is sweet/sweeter.

Тéзи крáставици са éвтини/
   пó-éвтини.
These cucumbers are cheap/cheaper.

As with the adverbs, the **пó-** is emphasized and we will again add a stress mark to remind you of this.

If you want to compare one thing (or person) with another, you use **от** in place of the English *than*, just as you did with the adverbs:

Я́бълките са пó-éвтини
   от прáсковите.
The apples are cheaper than the peaches.

Невéна е пó-хýбава **от** Нáдя.
Nevena is more beautiful than Nadya.

When there is a preposition before the noun, you have to use **откóлкото** instead of **от**:

В Бългáрия зеленчýците са
   пó-евтѝни **откóлкото**
   в Áнглия.
In Bulgaria, the vegetables are cheaper than in England.

На пазáра плодовéте са
   пó-прéсни **откóлкото**
   в магазѝните.
At the market, the fruit is fresher than in the shops.

Exercises

1 Select from the regular and numerical plural forms in the box (all masculines!) to complete these sentences:

110

a Ѝмате ли _____ .

b Невѐна ѝска да кýпи два _____ .

| пли́ка, пли́кове |

c Два _____ , мо́ля.

d Оби́чаш ли _____ ?

| бана́на, бана́ни |

e Да ви дам ли два _____ ?

f Г-жа́ Ко́линс обича _____ .

| пъ́пеша, пъ́пеши |

g Мо́ля, да́йте ни _____ !

h Ѐто тук ѝма ня́колко _____ .

| но́жа, ножо́ве |

i Г-н Джо́нсън ѝска да оти́де
в ня́колко бъ́лгарски _____ .

j Рýсе и Тъ́рново са
_____ в Бълга́рия.

| гра́да, градове́ |

2 Public notices are often instructions, sometimes given in the singular, sometimes in the plural. You would do well to note – and observe! – the following common instructions:

Бутни́! *Push.* **Дръпни́!** *Pull.* **Не пи́пай!** *Don't touch!*
Плате́те на ка́сата! *Pay at the cash desk.*
Пазе́те чистота́! *No litter* (lit. *Observe cleanliness*).
Не газе́те трева́та! *Keep off the grass!* (lit. *Don't trample down the grass*)

Which of the notices would you expect to find:

a in a shop or bank?   **c** on doors into a shop?

b in a park?   **d** near live electricity cables?

бана́н	*banana*
павилио́н	*kiosk*
плик	*envelope*
ма́рка	*stamp*
крем	*cream*
ча́ша	*cup, glass*
лека́рство	*medicine*
кра́ставица	*cucumber*
пътýвам, -вате	*to travel*
ка́рам, -раш ски	*to go skiing*

QUICK VOCAB

3 Ask the appropriate questions using the following phrases and choosing between **павилио́н, по́ща, апте́ка** and **ба́нка**:

Model: Мо́же ли да ми ка́жете къде́ и́ма павилио́н? Тря́бва да ку́пя биле́ти.

a Тря́бва да ку́пя пли́кове и ма́рки.
b Тря́бва да обменя́ пари́.
c Тря́бва да ку́пя аспири́н.
d Тря́бва да ку́пя ве́стници.

4 Imagine you are in a pharmacy/drugstore. Ask for the items in the following list using Мо́же ли да ми пока́жете and **a** то́зи, **b** та́зи, **c** това́ or **d** те́зи:

ка́рта	списа́ние	списа́ния	ча́ши
чадъ́р	ножо́ве	кре́мове	лека́рство
крем	ча́ша		

5 You've now moved to the open-air market. Ask for the items that follow using the model: Ко́лко стру́ват дома́тите? Да́йте ми едно́ кило́ дома́ти:

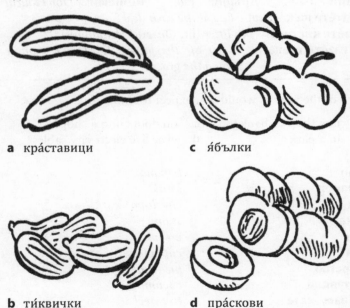

a кра́ставици
c я́бълки

b ти́квички
d пра́скови

6 Give affirmative answers to these questions following the model:
Да ку́пим ли крем? Да, да ку́пим!

  a Да оти́дем ли на Ви́тоша?
  b Да оти́дем ли на те́нис?
  c Да плати́м ли сега́?
  d Да се оба́дим ли на Никола́й?

7 To practise saying what you do and do not like doing and also
to make sure you have not forgotten how to use the construction
with **да**, answer the following questions:

  a Оби́чате ли да пъту́вате?
     Да, мно́го оби́чам _____.
  b Оби́чаш ли да игра́еш на компю́тър?
     Не, не оби́чам _____.
  c Оби́чате ли да пазару́вате? Не, не оби́чам _____.
  d Оби́чате ли да ка́рате ски?
     Да, мно́го оби́чам _____.
  e Оби́чаш ли да чете́ш?
     Да, мно́го оби́чам _____.

8 First, read aloud these polite (plural) forms of a number of common
instructions. Then use their familiar, singular forms, as if you were
talking to a child or a good friend:

  a Купе́те мля́ко, мо́ля!
  b Ела́те, мо́ля!
  c Седне́те, мо́ля!
  d Ви́жте, мо́ля!
  e Каже́те, мо́ля!
  f Да́йте, мо́ля!

9 Practise some comparisons by making complete sentences out of
the following words. With the exception of (**d**), you have to use
the definite forms throughout:

Model: Пъпеш/бана́н/голя́м
     Пъпешъ́т е по́-голя́м от бана́на.

  a Я́бълки/пра́скови/е́втини
  b Дома́ти/ти́квички/пре́сни
  c Пъпеш/гро́зде/сла́дък

d Надя/Невéна/заéта

e Крáставици/тúквички/голéми

Another small step forward

🔊 CD 1, TR 45–46

Dialogue 2 Подáръци *Presents*

Nevena is on her way to a birthday party. She stops off in a flower shop and finds everything she needs.

Невéна	Едúн букéт рóзи, мóля.
Продавáчка	Éто букéтите. Кой да Ви дам?
Невéна	Тóзи, голéмият, е мнóго красúв. Кóлко стрýва?
Продавáчка	Осемнáйсет лéва.
Невéна	Хм, покажéте ми пó-éвтини букéти, мóля.
Продавáчка	Éто, вúжте, лалéтата са пó-éвтини. Тóзи букéт е сáмо шест лéва.
Невéна	Сýпер. Úскам да кýпя и нéщо за подáрък.
Продавáчка	Úмаме красúви вáзи. Да Ви покáжа ли?
Невéна	Да, тáзи мáлка вáза е мнóго симпатúчна. И еднá кáртичка, мóля.
Продавáчка	От кой?
Невéна	Нéщо от Сóфия.
Продавáчка	Éто, вúжте – с Нарóдния теáтър, с Парламéнта, с Университéта…
Невéна	Тáзи с Нарóдния теáтър, мóля.
Продавáчка	Да Ви дам ли плик за подáръка?
Невéна	Каквú плúкове úмате?
Продавáчка	Мáлки плúкчета от осемдесéт стотúнки и пó-голéми плúкове от лев и петдесéт.
Невéна	Дáйте ми два плúка от лев и петдесéт. Кóлко трябва да Ви дам всúчко?
Продавáчка	Товá прáви осемнáйсет и петдесéт.

букéт	*bunch, bouquet*
рóза	*rose*
краси́в	*beautiful*
лалé	*tulip*
вáза	*vase*
симпати́чен, -чна	*nice*
Нарóдният теáтър	*the National Theatre*
Парламéнт	*Parliament*
(да) покáжа, -жеш	*to show*
плик	*(gift)bag*
пли́кче	*small (plastic) bag*

Test yourself

1 To see how well you have understood Dialogue 2, answer the questions that follow:

   a Кóлко стру́ва голéмият букéт рóзи?
   b Кои́ цветя́ са пó-éвтини?
   c Каквó óще и́ска да ку́пи Невéна?
   d Какви́ пли́кове и́ма в магази́на?
   e Кóлко тря́бва да плати́ Невéна?

2 Complete the sentences:

   a Кóлко _____ тóзи букéт?
   b Покажéте _____ пó-éвтини букéти.
   c Лалéтата са _____ -éвтини.
   d _____ Ви дам ли плик?
   e _____ ми два пли́ка.

3 Try rearranging the words that follow to make proper sentences:

   a ли, да дам, Ви, солтá?
   b покáжете, стáята, мóже ли, да, ни?
   c ни, дáйте, мóля, ключá!
   d товá, покажéте, списáние, ми, мóля!
   e да, мóже ли, пъпеш, ми, дадéте, тóзи?

Now can you:

- inquire how much something costs?
- point out and ask for things?
- indicate the quantity of something you wish to purchase?
- make suggestions using the Bulgarian equivalent of *let's*?
- form and use comparative adjectives?
- use indirect object pronouns in phrases like *show me* and *tell me*?

1904

The Ivan Vazov National
Theatre

8

Какво́ предла́гате?
What is your suggestion?

In this unit you will learn:

- How to order a meal in a restaurant
- How to say what Bulgarian dishes you prefer
- How to suggest dishes to someone else

Dialogue 1

◀) CD 1, TR 47–48

Mr Antonov and Mr Johnson are about to order a meal.

г-н Анто́нов	Какво́ да поръ́чаме?
г-н Джо́нсън	Мо́же ли да ви́дя меню́то?
г-н Анто́нов	Заповя́дайте! (*Opening the menu and pointing.*) Е́то, това́ са су́пите и сала́тите. Това́ са бъ́лгарските специалите́ти.
г-н Джо́нсън	Какво́ ми предла́гате да взе́ма?
г-н Анто́нов	Шо́пската сала́та е типи́чно бъ́лгарска. Тя е с дома́ти, кра́ставици и си́рене.
г-н Джо́нсън	Добре́, една́ шо́пска сала́та за ме́не.
г-н Анто́нов	И́скате ли тарато́р?
г-н Джо́нсън	Какво́ е тарато́р?
г-н Анто́нов	Това́ е су́па от ки́село мля́ко и кра́ставици. Серви́ра се студе́на. Мно́го е вку́сна.
г-н Джо́нсън	Не, благодаря́. Предпочи́там то́пла су́па. (*Reading and pointing.*) Е́то та́зи – пи́лешка су́па.

г-н Антонов	Тогава Ви предлагам да вземете този български специалитет – пълнени чушки.
г-н Джонсън	Добре, да вземем пълнени чушки.
г-н Антонов	(*To the waitress.*) Може ли . . . ?
Сервитьорка	Заповядайте, моля.
г-н Антонов	Две шопски салати, една пилешка супа, един таратор и два пъти пълнени чушки.
Сервитьорка	Колко хляб?
г-н Антонов	Четири бели хлебчета, моля.
Сервитьорка	Нещо за пиене?
г-н Антонов	А, да. Да вземем ли бутилка вино, г-н Джонсън?
г-н Джонсън	Не, благодаря. Аз обичам българските вина, но на обед не пия алкохол. Имате ли натурални плодови сокове?
Сервитьорка	Не, за съжаление. Само газирани напитки.
г-н Джонсън	За мене една газирана вода, ако обичате.
Сервитьорка	А за Вас, господине? Бялото вино е много хубаво.
г-н Антонов	Добре, тогава за мене чаша бяло вино, моля.
Сервитьорка	Нещо друго?
г-н Антонов	Не, благодаря.

QUICK VOCAB

Какво да поръчаме?	*What shall we order?*
Може ли да видя менюто?	*Can I see the menu?*
Ето, това са супите и салатите.	*Look, here are the soups and the salads.*
Това са българските специалитети.	*These are the Bulgarian specialities.*
Какво ми предлагате да взема?	*What do you suggest I take?*
Шопската салата е типично българска.	*The 'shopska' salad is typically Bulgarian.*
сирене	*feta cheese*
таратор	*tarator* (Bulgarian cold summer soup)
Това е супа от кисело мляко и краставици.	*It is a soup made of yoghurt and cucumbers.*
Сервира се студена.	*It is served cold.*
Много е вкусна.	*It is delicious.*
Предпочитам топла супа.	*I prefer a hot soup.*

Éто тáзи – пúлешка сýпа.	*This one here – chicken soup.*
Тогáва Ви предлáгам да взéмете тóзи бългáрски специалитéт.	*Then I suggest you take this Bulgarian speciality.*
пълнени чýшки	*stuffed peppers*
два пъти	*twice*
Кóлко хляб?	*How much bread?*
чéтири бéли хлéбчета	*four white bread rolls*
Нéщо за пúене?	*Anything to drink?*
Да взéмем ли бутúлка вúно?	*Shall we take a bottle of wine?*
На óбед не пúя алкохóл.	*I don't drink alcohol at lunchtime.*
Úмате ли натурáлни плóдови сóкове?	*Have you any natural fruit juices?*
газúрани напúтки	*fizzy drinks*
акó обúчате	*if you please*
Бялото вúно е мнóго хýбаво.	*The white wine is very good.*
Тогáва за мéне чáша бяло вúно.	*A glass of white wine for me, then.*
Нéщо дрýго?	*Anything else?*

1 Questions

a Каквó úска да вúди г-н Джóнсън?
b Каквó предлáга г-н Антóнов на г-н Джóнсън?
c Каквó е таратóр?
d Каквó предпочúта г-н Джóнсън?
e Каквó úска г-н Джóнсън за пúене?
f Кой úска да поръча чáша вúно?

2 True or false?

a Шóпската салáта е с кúсело мляко и крáставици.
b Таратóрът се сервúра студéн.
c Пълнените чýшки са бългáрски специалитéт.
d Г-н Антóнов и г-н Джóнсън не úскат хляб.
e Г-н Джóнсън úска нéщо за пúене, но не алкохóл.
f На óбед г-н Антóнов пúе сáмо лимонáда.

Doing things the Bulgarian way

Food and eating out

Bulgarians enjoy eating out. They go as much for the company as for the food, which is often served warm rather than hot. They eat lots of bread – not just with their soup course – and spend a long time over their meals, especially in the evenings. The more popular, smaller restaurants often get very busy, noisy and full of cigarette smoke, so go early. And if the weather is good, try and find a table outside. For the more popular establishments, it's best to make a reservation (**резервация**). If you want to try and escape from the cigarette smoke, ask for a **маса за непушачи** (*a table for non-smokers*). If you like the smoke, ask for a **маса за пушачи**. Service can be slow, so allow plenty of time for your meal and enjoy the company and the atmosphere!

If you go out in a group, you may be asked on entering **Колко души сте?** *How many (people) are you?* and **Имате ли резервация?** *Do you have a reservation?*

All restaurants serve alcohol – at any time of the day or night. Most have tables set aside for non-smokers, but the smokers do not always observe the instructions. Specifically vegetarian restaurants are few and far between, but you can usually make up a very decent vegetarian meal from the standard dishes on offer. When ordering your meal, remember that the courses, often beginning with fresh salads as a starter, are served in strict sequence. Subsequent courses will not be brought until everyone at your table has finished their starter. So if you want a starter as your main course or a salad with your main course, you need to tell the waitress.

Restaurants in tourist areas usually have menus in more than one language. In hotels with restaurants (**хотел-ресторант**), the restaurants are generally open to non-residents, unless they have been pre-booked for a closed function. They offer a wide choice of dishes, many of them 'international'. Some of these restaurants are quite formal, with waiters in black ties.

In the larger towns, there are plenty of eating places to choose from and a wide variety of traditional restaurants. Most of the well-known western food chains are represented. There are innumerable Italian restaurants, both large and small, serving traditional pizza and pasta dishes. If you are wanting a Chinese restaurant, look for **китáйски ресторáнт**.

For a quick bite, there are lots of informal snack bars, very functional, self-service establishments, often with limited seating. Pop in for a sandwich, maybe toasted, a Bulgarian **бáничка** (*pasty*), a cup of coffee or a **кóла** – usually Coca-Cola or Pepsi. Many of these establishments have foreign names, usually English. There are also many small eating places offering dishes such as grilled chicken to take away (**пúле на грил за вкъщи**). Some sell Middle Eastern food and have appropriate Middle Eastern names.

Grilled meat dishes are served in most establishments and are (rightly) very popular. Look for the word **скáра** (*grill*) in the menu. If you want something traditional, tasty and inexpensive, go for freshly grilled meatballs (**кюфтéта**) – the really hot ones are called **нервóзни** – or delicious, spicy grilled sausages (**кебáпчета**). Order any number – of either or both – and eat with plenty of bread and **лютеница**, a piquant red sauce made of tomatoes, red peppers and finely chopped onions. Wash down with beer or red wine. Delicious!

There are many small street bars – look for **бар** or **кафé** – with tables out on the pavement in the summer. Here you can find soft drinks, a variety of alcoholic drinks, coffee, hot chocolate, tea etc. Although traditionally in Bulgaria, you only drank tea (without milk) when you were unwell, you can find all kinds of tea, including tea made from a variety of different herbs. Remember, though, that if you do want a traditional 'cuppa', **чёрен чай** (*black tea*), you will probably be presented with a cup or, more likely, a glass of hot water, some sugar and a teabag. You will be expected to brew up yourself at the table. And if you want milk, you will have to ask for it!

How do you say it?

- Asking *What do you suggest or offer?* and suggesting or offering something yourself

Какво́ ми предла́гаш?	*What do you suggest (for me)?*
Предла́гам да поръ́чаш та́зи су́па.	*I suggest you order this soup.*
Предла́гаме това́ ви́но.	*We suggest this wine.*

- Asking for someone's preference and expressing your own

Ви́е какво́ предпочи́тате?	*What do you prefer?*
Предпочи́там то́пла су́па.	*I prefer hot soup.*

- Saying *once, twice,* etc.

еди́н път	*once* (lit. *one time*)
два пъ́ти	*twice*
три пъ́ти	*three times*
че́тири пъ́ти, etc.	*four times*

- Asking for something to eat or drink

Не́що за я́дене, мо́ля!	*Something to eat, please.*
Не́що за пи́ене, мо́ля!	*Something to drink, please.*

◀) CD 1, TR 49

- Saying *please* in a more formal way

ако́ оби́чате	*if you please*

- Saying a *glass of* . . . , *a cup of* . . . , *a bottle of* . . .

чáша винó	a glass of wine
чáша кафé	a cup of coffee
бутѝлка винó	a bottle of wine

Grammar

1 *The* with adjectives

When an adjective is added to a noun used with the definite article, the definite article moves from the noun to the adjective:

Feminine	салáта**та**	becomes	шóпска**та** салáта
	the salad		*the 'shopska' salad*
Neuter	винó**то**	becomes	червéно**то** винó
	the wine		*the red wine*
Plural	сýпи**те**	becomes	тóпли**те** сýпи
	the soups		*the hot soups*

As you can see, the definite article added to adjectives is the same as the definite article added to nouns of the same gender. Only with masculine nouns is there any change. (You will learn more about this in Unit 9.)

Insight

If you use more than one adjective, you only put the definite article on the end of the first adjective:

| специалитéти**те** | becomes | хýбави**те** бъ́лгарски специалитéти |
| *the specialities* | | *the lovely Bulgarian specialities* |

2 More neuter plurals

Many neuter nouns ending in -(**ч**)**е** form their plural by adding **-та**:

еднó хлéбче	чéтири хлéбчета	*four bread rolls*
еднó кафé	три кафéта	*three coffees*
еднó парчé	две парчéта	*two pieces*
еднó плѝкче	мнóго плѝкчета	*many small (plastic) bags*

Some words adopted from other languages, words like **интервю́, меню́, такси́** and **уи́ски**, which are considered neuter nouns, also take this plural ending:

мно́го интервю́та	*many interviews*
ня́колко меню́та	*several menus*
мно́го такси́та	*many taxis*
ня́колко уи́скита	*several whiskies*

Insight

Be careful not to confuse these plurals with singular feminine nouns used with the definite article – they both end in **-та**!

When neuter plurals like **меню́та** and **парче́та** are used with the definite article, they end in a double **-тата**, and the resulting 'rhyme' creates the distinctive Bulgarian 'machine-gun' effect:

хле́бче**тата**	*the bread rolls*	меню́**тата**	*the menus*
кафе́**тата**	*the coffees*	такси́**тата**	*the taxis*
парче́**тата**	*the pieces*	уи́ски**тата**	*the whiskies*

3 Два and две: two times two

You have already briefly come across these two forms of the numeral for two in Unit 4. **Два**, as in **два часа́**, remember, goes with masculine nouns denoting things and animals (but not persons). **Две** goes with neuter and feminine nouns:

Masculine		Feminine	Neuter
два тарато́ра	but	две сала́ти	две парче́та
два со́ка		две ма́рки	две писма́
два пли́ка		две ча́ши	две такси́та
два килогра́ма		две ста́и	две места́

4 Два́ма *two* and три́ма *three* (*people*)

You have to use special forms of certain numerals with masculine nouns for people. These forms exist for the numerals from *two* to

124

six, but you will probably only come across **двáма** *two* and **трúма** *three*. These numerals are used with the normal plural of the noun only, not with the special counting form:

двáма англичáни и трúма   *two Englishmen and three*
  американци   *Americans*
двáма студéнти и трúма   *two students and three*
  учúтели   *teachers*

двáма дýши   *two people* (lit. *two souls*)

5 Бя́ло and бéли, я and e: fickle vowels

Depending on stress and the vowels that occur in the following syllable, you will find that the vowels **я** and **e** may alternate. Happily, the rules governing these alternations are well defined. The changes are confusing, though, and you would do well to learn the rules, perhaps putting a slip of paper between these pages, so you can find them easily:

я is used either	(*a*)	if it is stressed and the vowel in the following syllable is **a, o, y** or **ъ**
or	(*b*)	if it is stressed and occurs in the final syllable.
e is used either	(*a*)	if it is stressed and the vowels **e** or **и** occur in the following syllable
or	(*b*)	if it is unstressed.

So you will find:

бял, бя́ла, бя́ло *white*   but   **бéли**
мя́сто *place*   but   **местá** (note the stress change!)
свят *world*   but   по **светá** *around the world*

Insight

You will also hear mixed, 'incorrect' forms like **бя́ли**. Sometimes there are two correct forms of the same word – some speakers say **óбед** and others say **обя́д**.

6 Плод, плóдов сок *Fruit, fruit juice*

By adding **-ов** (**-ова, -ово, -ови**) to a noun you can often form an adjective with the meaning *made of* . . . If the noun is feminine or neuter, you first have to remove the final vowel:

плод:	плóд**ов** сок	*fruit juice*
	плóд**ова** тóрта	*fruit gateau*
	плóд**ово** мля́ко	*fruit-flavoured milk*
	плóд**ови** тóрти	*fruit gateaux* or *pieces of fruit gateau*
грóзде:	грóзд**ова** раки́я	*grape brandy*
сли́ва:	сли́в**ова** раки́я	*plum brandy*
портокáл:	портокáл**ов** сок	*orange juice*
я́бълка:	я́бълк**ов** сок	*apple juice*

Exercises

1 The Bulgarian verbs for *order* (**да**) **поръ́чам** and *prefer* **предпочи́там** sound very much alike. Practise them using the following words in place of the words in bold:

Model: Сервитьóрката предлáга **бя́ло ви́но**, но аз предпочи́там **червéно**. Да поръ́чаме **червéно ви́но!**

a пи́лзенска (*Pilsner*) би́ра, бъ́лгарска би́ра
b грóздова раки́я, сли́вова раки́я
c пи́лешка сýпа, зеленчýкова (*vegetable*) сýпа

2 Here are the ingredients for tarator soup:

> **ки́село мля́ко**
> **еднá крáставица**
> **чéсън** (*garlic*)
> **сол**
> **óлио** (*vegetable oil*)
> **óрехи** (*walnuts*)

Now answer the question: Каквó и́ма в таратóра?

126

3 Read the following list of drinks and cakes out loud:

> нéс(кафе) = *instant* (*coffee*)
> кафé еспрéсо = *espresso*
> чéрен чай
> мéнтов чай
> бúлков чай
> плóдова тóрта
> шоколáдова (*chocolate*) тóрта
> óрехова тóрта
> портокáлов сок
> грóздов сок
> я́бълков сок
> сок от я́годи (*strawberries*)

Now, using **úма**, say what is on offer in the way of:

a coffee   **c** cakes
b tea   **d** fruit juices

Words you might need to know are: **бúлка** *herb*, **мéнта** *peppermint* and **óрех** *walnut*.

4 So as to fix in your mind the correct use of the different Bulgarian words for *two*, use **два, две** or **двáма** as appropriate. Here you can again see the special plural form of masculine nouns used after numbers – but not after **двáма** and **трúма**:

a Дáйте ми _____ парчéта пúца (*pizza*) и _____ óрехови тóрти.

b Да порѣчаме _____ грóздови сóка и _____ салáти.

c Там úма _____ свобóдни местá.

d _____ децá игрáят тéнис. (Remember the singular of децá is детé.)

e Да кýпим _____ плúка и _____ мáрки.

f Дáйте ни _____ лимóнови сладолéда (*lemon ice creams*), мóля.

g В стáята úма _____ бѣлгарски студéнти.

h Úскаш ли да порѣчаме _____ таратóра?

i В хотéла úма _____ англичáнки.

j Ни́е сме са́мо _____ ду́ши. *(There are only two of us.)*
k И́маме ну́жда от _____ ча́ши.
l До га́рата и́ма _____ магази́на.

5 Choose a soup and another item from the following list and order:

> **Меню́**
> зеленчу́кова су́па
> вегетариа́нска (*vegetarian*) су́па
> омле́т (*omelette*) със си́рене
> пи́ца с кашкава́л (*yellow cheese*)
> омле́т с шу́нка (*ham*)
> кюфте́та (*meatballs*)

a just for yourself
b another combination for yourself and a companion
c a third combination for your family of four

6 Using the model Предла́гам да поръ́чаме черве́**ното** ви́но, suggest to your dining companion in a Bulgarian restaurant that you should order:

a бя́ло ви́но   **d** шокола́дова то́рта
b сли́вова раки́я   **e** бъ́лгарски специалите́ти
c вегетариа́нска су́па **f** пи́лзенска би́ра

◀)) CD 1, TR 50

7 You go into a snack bar with a group of friends. Complete the dialogue, acting as the customer:

Продава́чка	За вас, мо́ля? *(What would it be for you?)*
Клие́нт	(Ask what sandwiches they have.)
Продава́чка	И́маме са́ндвичи с шу́нка и с кашкава́л.
Клие́нт	(Ask for two sandwiches with ham and one with cheese.)
Продава́чка	Дру́го? *(Anything else?)*
Клие́нт	(Ask for one orange juice, two cokes and three coffees.)

8 Now you want two sausages, two bread rolls and two meatballs. Ask how much they are in two ways, with and without the numeral:

  i a Колко струват две _____ ?   (кебапчета, кебапчетата)
    b Колко струват _____ ?

  ii a Колко струват две _____ ? (хлебчета, хлебчетата)
    b Колко струват _____ ?

  iii a Колко струват две _____ ? (кюфтета, кюфтетата)
    b Колко струват _____ ?

9 Your dining partner praises the food – all except the chicken soup and the Bulgarian yoghurt. You agree. Using the words in brackets, follow the model to give your reaction in more precise terms:

Your partner	Салатата е много вкусна!
You	Да, шопската салата е много вкусна!

This will help you remember that the definite article moves from the noun to the defining word!

  a Супата е много вкусна!   (вегетерианска)
  b Чушките са много вкусни!   (пълнени)
  c Гроздето е много вкусно!   (бяло)
  d Супата не е много вкусна!   (пилешка)
  e Ябълките са много вкусни!   (червени)
  f Тортата е много вкусна!   (плодова)
  g Хлебчетата са много вкусни! (бели)
  h Млякото не е много вкусно! (българско, кисело)

Another small step forward

🔊 **CD 1, TR 51–52**

Dialogue 2 В кафето *At the café*

Nadya and Milena meet in front of the office early one morning.

Надя	Здравей, Милена. Още е рано за работа. Да отидем в кафето.
Милена	Не е ли затворено?

На́дя	Ко́лко е часъ́т?
Миле́на	О́сем и полови́на.
На́дя	Тря́бва да е отво́рено ве́че.

(*Inside.*)

Сервитьо́р	Добро́ у́тро. Каже́те, мо́ля!
На́дя	Какво́ и́ма за заку́ска?
Сервитьо́р	Са́ндвичи, ки́фли, ба́нички.
Миле́на	Не́що сла́дко?
Сервитьо́р	И́ма кроаса́ни, кекс, и́ма съ́що пло́дова то́рта.
На́дя	За ме́не еди́н са́ндвич и парче́ то́рта.
Миле́на	За ме́не съ́щото.
Сервитьо́р	Зна́чи два са́ндвича и две парче́та то́рта. Дру́го?
На́дя	И две кафе́та.
Сервитьо́р	Нес или́ еспре́со?
Миле́на	Еспре́со, мо́ля. Какви́ напи́тки и́ма?
Сервитьо́р	Натура́лни со́кове, ко́ла, гази́рана вода́.
Миле́на	Добре́, два я́бълкови со́ка, ако́ оби́чате.

(*The waiter comes back with the order.*)

На́дя	Мо́же ли да плати́м ведна́га?
Сервитьо́р	Разби́ра се. Е́то, това́ е сме́тката.

ра́но	*early*
сла́дък, сла́дка	*sweet*
затво́рен	*closed*
отво́рен	*open*
заку́ска	*breakfast, snack*
ки́фла	*bun*
ба́ничка	*(cheese) roll, pasty*
не́що сла́дко	*something sweet*
кроаса́н	*croissant*
кекс	*(sponge) cake*
са́мо	*only*
(да) платя́, -ти́ш	*to pay*
ведна́га	*immediately*
сме́тка	*bill*

Test yourself

1 To see how well you have understood Dialogue 2, answer the following questions:

   a Колко е часът?
   b Рано ли е за работа?
   c Затворено ли е кафето?
   d Какво има за закуска?
   e Какво искат Надя и Милена за ядене?
   f Какво искат те за пиене?

2 Complete the sentences:

   a Какво има за _____ ?
   b За _____ един сандвич.
   c Два ябълкови _____ , ако обичате.
   d Ето, това е _____ .

3 In a restaurant, which of the Bulgarian words for *order*, *offer* and *prefer* would you use to complete these sentences?

   a Каква супа _____ -ате?
   b Г-н Антонов иска да _____ -а бутилка вино.
   c Кое вино _____ -ате, червеното или бялото?
   d Г-н Антонов _____ -а пълнените чушки.
   e Да _____ -ме този български специалитет!
   f Г-н Джонсън _____ -а плодов сок, а не вино.
   g Искате ли да _____ -ате шопска салата?

Now can you:

- order different dishes for a restaurant meal?
- distinguish between the Bulgarian for *I prefer* and *I suggest*?
- use *two* with people and nouns of different genders?
- turn nouns into adjectives meaning *made of*?
- use the definite article with combinations of adjective(s) plus noun?

С какво́ мо́га да Ви помо́гна?

How can I help you?

In this unit you will learn:

- How to ask for and offer help
- How to express possession
- How to describe things and people

Dialogue 1

◀) CD 1, TR 53–54

Violeta and Mark Davies are preparing to leave their hotel.

Виоле́та	А́ло, аз съм Виоле́та Де́йвис. Неве́на ли е?
Неве́на	Каже́те, госпо́жо Де́йвис, с какво́ мо́га да Ви помо́гна?
Виоле́та	Мо́ля, поръ́чайте едно́ такси́ за лети́щето.
Неве́на	За ко́лко часа́?
Виоле́та	За де́сет и петна́йсет. Мо́ля съ́що пи́колото да ни помо́гне с бага́жа.
Неве́на	Разби́ра се, госпо́жо Де́йвис.
Виоле́та	Благодаря́. Дочу́ване!

(Violeta is now in the hotel lobby.)

Пи́коло	Бага́жът ви е ве́че във фоайе́то, но такси́то о́ще го ня́ма.
Виоле́та	Благодаря́ ти, момче́.
Пи́коло	Ня́ма защо́.
Виоле́та	Хм, това́ не е́ са́мо на́шият бага́ж. Тук и́ма ку́фари и ча́нти на дру́ги го́сти на хоте́ла.
Пи́коло	И те ча́кат такси́.

Виоле́та	Е́то, това́ на́шето такси́ ли е?
Пи́коло	Не, ми́сля, че дру́гото такси́ е за вас.
Виоле́та	Мъжъ́т ми о́ще го ня́ма. Мо́жете ли пак да ми помо́гнете с бага́жа?
Шофьо́р	Да́йте, аз мо́га да Ви помо́гна. Покаже́те ми кой бага́ж е Ваш.
Виоле́та	Благодаря́ мно́го. Че́рният ку́фар и си́нята ра́ница са на́ши. Но къде́ е ча́нтата на мъжа́ ми?
Шофьо́р	Не мо́жете ли да я наме́рите? Как изгле́жда тя?
Виоле́та	Голя́ма че́рна ча́нта.
Пи́коло	Ви́жте зад о́нзи син ку́фар.
Виоле́та	Ня́ма я . . .
Пи́коло	Мно́го неприя́тно. Пи́тайте Неве́на.
Виоле́та	А, е́то го Марк. Той но́си своя́та ча́нта!
Пи́коло	Зна́чи ня́ма пробле́м.
Виоле́та	Да, вси́чко е наре́д. Марк, дай не́що на момче́то.
Пи́коло	Благодаря́. Прия́тен път.

С какво́ мо́га да Ви помо́гна?	*How can I help you?*
лети́ще	*airport*
Мо́ля съ́що пи́колото да ни помо́гне с бага́жа.	*Let the bellboy also help us with the luggage, please.*
фоайе́	*foyer/lobby*
такси́то о́ще го ня́ма	*the taxi is still not here*
момче́	*boy, lad*
Ня́ма защо́.	*You're welcome./Don't mention it.*
на́шият бага́ж	*our luggage*
го́сти на хоте́ла	*residents at the hotel*
Мо́жете ли пак да ми помо́гнете с бага́жа?	*Could you help me with the luggage again?*
аз мо́га да Ви помо́гна	*I can help you*
Покаже́те ми кой бага́ж е Ваш.	*Show me which luggage is yours.*
Че́рният ку́фар и си́нята ра́ница са на́ши.	*The black suitcase and the blue rucksack are ours.*
ча́нта	*bag*
Не мо́жете ли да я наме́рите?	*Can't you find it?*

QUICK VOCAB

Как изглѐжда тя?	*What does it look like?*
Виѐжте зад ѐнзи син кѐфар.	*Look behind that blue suitcase.*
Мнѐго неприѐтно.	*Very unpleasant.*
Пѐтайте Невѐна.	*Ask Nevena.*
Той нѐси свѐята чѐнта.	*He's carrying his (own) bag.*
всѐчко е нарѐд	*everything's fine*

1 Questions

a Каквѐ ѐска да порѐча Виолѐта?
b С каквѐ ще помѐгне пѐколото?
c Каквѐ кѐфари и чѐнти ѐма във фоайѐто?
d Каквѐ не мѐже да намѐри Виолѐта?
e Каквѐ нѐси Марк?
f Как изглѐжда чѐнтата на Марк?

2 True or false?

a Виолѐта ѐска да порѐча таксѐ за единѐйсет и половѐна.
b Мѐжѐт на Виолѐта ѐще го нѐма във фоайѐто.
c Шофьѐрѐт предлѐга да помѐгне с багѐжа.
d Сѐният кѐфар и чѐрната рѐница са на Марк и Виолѐта.
e Чѐнтата на Марк не ѐ зад сѐния кѐфар.

Doing things the Bulgarian way

Getting about in town

For travel within the larger towns, you will find well-developed networks of trams, buses, trolleybuses and minibuses. Movement is slow in the centre and – especially in the rush hours – not always a pleasant experience. And beware of pickpockets! Services are, however, frequent and still relatively cheap. The only underground in Bulgaria is a single line in Sofia running from the Obelya district in the northwest into the centre of town and out to the huge housing estates to the southeast. Further extensions crossing this line are under construction to the north and south.

In Sofia, there are no conductors on buses, trams or trolleybuses. Best buy your tickets in a block (**талѐни**) of 10 in advance – it's cheaper! Do this at one of the many small street kiosks with their minuscule, low-down windows through which, if you are lucky, you will just be able to see the assistant's hands and the tickets. The kiosks display signs **ГРА́ДСКИ ТРА́НСПО́РТ – БИЛЕ́ТИ И КА́РТИ** and the tickets are all one price for bus, tram and trolleybus. Make sure you use the validating key ticket – number 10 in the block – last and always have it with you.

You get on by any door. Once on, and in rush hours, you may have to push a bit, make sure you punch a ticket as soon as possible in one of the small machines fixed to the side of the vehicle. The driver will not want to see your ticket. Ticket inspectors will, though. Dressed in plain clothes, armed with passes and usually in groups, they make collective raids to deter ticket dodgers. To be caught without a punched ticket inevitably leads to altercation and most probably a fine. Most locals have season tickets.

If you want to move about more quickly, take a taxi or a minibus. There are plenty of both, but different taxi firms have differing tariffs, so check the charges. Taxis all have meters registering distance and time. Seatbelts are fitted and should be worn, but the driver may suggest you ignore them or merely lay them across your lap. The minibuses (**маршру́тни такси́та**, or, more colloquially, **маршру́тки**) ply predetermined routes, but pick up and set down on request anywhere along the route. No tickets, but pay the driver – there is a single fixed fare for any distance. So, far cheaper than taxis, but more expensive than the normal tram ticket. Good for longer distances, bad for short.

How do you say it?

- Asking for and offering help

Мо́жете ли да ми помо́гнете?	*Can you help me?*
С какво́ мо́га да Ви помо́гна?	*How can I help you?*
Мо́га ли да Ви помо́гна с не́що?	*Can I help you with anything?*

- Saying that *something* or *somebody* is missing

(Къде́ е ча́нтата?)	
Ня́ма я./Ча́нтата я ня́ма.	*It's missing./ The bag is missing.*
(Къде́ е г-н Анто́нов?)	
Ня́ма го./Г-н Анто́нов го ня́ма.	*He's not in./ Mr Antonov is not in.*
(Там ли е г-жа́ Ко́линс?)	
Ня́ма я./Г-жа́ Ко́линс я ня́ма.	*She's not in./ Mrs Collins is not in.*

- Saying *one (of the . . .)*

Masculine
Еди́ният ку́фар го ня́ма.   *One (of the) case(s) is missing.*

Feminine
Една́та ча́нта е голя́ма.   *One (of the) bag(s) is large.*

Neuter
Едно́то момче́ е тук.   *One (of the) boy(s) is here.*

- Responding to unpleasant news

Мно́го неприя́тно!   *Very unpleasant.*

- Responding to being thanked

Ня́ма защо́.	*You're welcome.*
(Ня́ма) ни́що.	*(It's) nothing./Don't*
	mention it.

Grammar

1 Мо́га да *I can, I am able to*

The Bulgarian verb expressing ability or a particular skill to do things is **мо́га** *I can/I am able to/I am in a position to*. **Мо́га** belongs to the e-pattern. The *he/she/it* form **мо́же** with its distinct usage will be familiar to you from Unit 6. In addition to the change of personal endings, there is a change of **г** to **ж** in all forms containing **e** in the ending:

(аз)	мо́га	(ни́е)	мо́жем
(ти)	мо́жеш	(ви́е)	мо́жете
(той)		(те)	мо́гат
(тя) ⎬	мо́же		
(то)			

Мо́га requires a **да** form of the following main verb:

(Аз) мо́га да ка́рам ски.	*I know how to ski.*
(Ти) мо́жеш да гово́риш англи́йски.	*You can speak English.*
Те не мо́гат да наме́рят бага́жа.	*They cannot find the luggage.*

2 -ият and -ия: *the* with masculine adjectives

(a) To make a masculine adjective definite, you add **-ият** to the simple masculine form (or **-ия** if the phrase is not the subject in the sentence):

| ху́бав мъж | *a handsome man* | ху́бавия(т) мъж | *the handsome man* |
| млад мъж | *a young man* | мла́дия(т) мъж | *the young man* |

(b) If the adjective ends in **-ски**, you only need to add **-ят** or **-я**:

английски – английския(т) ре́чник
бъ́лгарски – бъ́лгарския(т) ре́чник

(c) If the adjective loses **ъ** or **e** from its ending in the feminine, neuter and plural, then it does so in the definite form as well (see Appendix):

добъ́р (добра́, добро́, добри́)
добри́я(т) бъ́лгарин *the kind Bulgarian*

че́рен (че́рна, че́рно, че́рни)
че́рния(т) чадъ́р *the black umbrella*

(d) If there is **я** in the basic form, it will naturally be affected by the rules governing the change of **я** to **e** before **и** (see Unit 8):

бял – бе́лия(т)
голя́м – голе́мия(т)

(e) If you use more than one adjective, you only add **-ият** or **-ия** to the first adjective:

| хуба́в**ият** млад мъж | *the handsome young man* |
| голе́м**ият** че́рен ку́фар | *the large black case* |

3 *My, your, his, her*, etc.

When you say **мъжъ́т ми** *my husband*, **ку́фарът Ви** *your suitcase* or **бага́жът им** *their luggage*, you are using a noun in the definite form followed by a short possessive pronoun (see Unit 3). It is also possible to express the same meaning, but with a different emphasis, by a full possessive adjective, which comes before the noun and bears the definite article. Like all adjectives, the full possessive adjectives have different endings depending on whether they are used with masculine, feminine, neuter or plural words. Here are examples used with the Bulgarian for *my, your, our* and *their*:

ку́фарът ми/ти	becomes	**мо́ят/тво́ят** ку́фар	*my/your case*
ча́нтата ми/ти	becomes	**мо́ята/тво́ята** ча́нта	*my/your bag*
дете́то ми/ти	becomes	**мо́ето/тво́ето** дете́	*my/your child*
деца́та ми/ти	becomes	**мо́ите/тво́ите** деца́	*my/your children*

багáжът ни/им	becomes	**нáшият/тéхният** багáж	*our/their luggage*
стáята ни/им	becomes	**нáшата/тя́хната** стая	*our/their room*
таксúто ни/им	becomes	**нáшето/тя́хното** таксú	*our/their taxi*
рáниците ни/им	becomes	**нáшите/тéхните** рáници	*our/their rucksacks*

(See end of Appendix for a full list of possessive adjectival forms. Look at the list when you do the exercises.)

4 Багáжът ми or мóят багáж?

Normally, you can use the short possessive pronoun, as explained in Unit 3. However, for purposes of contrast, when the ownership is being emphasized, as in the sentence *this bag is mine, not yours*, for example, you must use the *full* possessive adjective with the definite article:

Мóите кýфари са голéми.	*My cases are big.*
Твóите са мáлки.	*Yours are small.*
Твóят син е в Áнглия.	*Your son is in England.*
Мóят син е в Бългáрия.	*My son is in Bulgaria.*
Товá не é **мóят** багáж.	*This is not my luggage.* (i.e. it belongs to someone else)
Товá **твóята** чáнта ли е?	*Is this your bag?* (i.e. not someone else's?)

5 Чáнтата е мóя *The bag is mine*

The possessive adjective can sometimes be used without the definite article to render the English independent possessives like *mine, yours, his, hers,* etc. Usually this happens when there is no word following the possessive word as in:

Твóя ли е тáзи чáнта?	*Is this bag yours?*
Да, чáнтата е мóя.	*Yes, the bag is mine.*
Твой ли е тóзи багáж?	*Is this luggage yours?*
Не, не é мой.	*No, it isn't mine.*
Твóе ли е товá детé?	*Is this child yours?*

Да, мо́е е.	*Yes, it is mine.*
Тво́и ли са те́зи ку́фари?	*Are these suitcases yours?*
Да, мо́и са.	*Yes, they are mine.*

Insight

Here is a summary of the different ways in which you can express possession. Remember that the full possessive forms are used for stronger emphasis or contrast:

Та́зи ча́нта е на Марк.	*This bag is Mark's.*
Та́зи ча́нта е не́гова.	*This bag is his.*
Това́ е ча́нтата на Марк.	*This is Mark's bag.*
Това́ е не́говата ча́нта.	*This is his bag.*
Това́ е ча́нтата му.	*This is his bag.*

6 Свой, своя́, сво́е and сво́и *Mark's own or someone else's?*

In English, when you say *Mark is carrying his bag* or *they can't find their suitcases*, it is not clear whether Mark is carrying his own or somebody else's bag and whether they can't find their own or someone else's suitcases. In Bulgarian, to emphasize *own* and avoid this ambiguity, you use the special words listed in the heading, most frequently in their definite forms, as shown in the following box.

Here are the different definite forms:

Subject pronoun	Masculine	Feminine	Neuter	Plural
той/то/тя/те	своя́(т)	своя́та	сво́ето	сво́ите

These are adjectives, so no matter whether you want to say *his*, *her* or *their own*, the masculine, feminine, neuter and plural forms go with the gender and number of the word that follows.

Compare:
Марк но́си **своя́та ча́нта**.   *Mark is carrying his (own) bag.*
with
Шофьо́рът но́си **не́говата ча́нта**. *The driver is carrying his (i.e. Mark's) bag.*

140

and
Виоле́та ча́ка **своя́ мъж**.

Violeta is waiting for her (own) husband.

with
Неве́на ча́ка **не́йния мъж**.

Nevena is waiting for her (i.e. Violeta's) husband.

also
Го́стите не мо́гат да наме́рят **свои́те ку́фари**.

The residents can't find their (own) suitcases.

with
Момче́тата не мо́гат да наме́рят **те́хните ку́фари**.

The boys can't find their (i.e. the residents') suitcases.

7 Ня́ма го *He isn't here*

With **ня́ма**, you don't use **той, тя, то, те** but rather **го, я, го** and **ги** for the person(s) absent or the thing(s) missing. These are short object pronouns, the Bulgarian non-subject equivalents for *him, her, it, them*. (You will learn more about them in Unit 11.)

Къде́ е бага́жът? Ня́ма **го**.	*Where is the luggage? It's missing.*
Къде́ е ча́нтата? Ня́ма **я**.	*Where is the bag? It's missing.*
Къде́ са ку́фарите? Ня́ма **ги**.	*Where are the cases? They're missing.*

Oddly enough, you have to use the short object pronoun even if you also name the person or thing, so you get a repetition:

Ча́нтата я ня́ма.	*The bag is missing.*
Момче́то го ня́ма.	*The boy is not here.*
Ку́фарите ги ня́ма.	*The suitcases are missing.*
Бага́жът им го ня́ма.	*Their luggage is missing.*

8 Помогне́те ми! *Help me!/Give me a hand!*

The Bulgarian verb (**да**) **помо́гна** is used more like the English phrase *to give help to* rather than just *to help*. So you need to use the indirect object pronouns as explained in Unit 7:

Мо́жете ли да **ми** помо́гнете?	*Can you help me?* (as if you were saying *Can you give help to me?*)

Exercises

1 Answer the following questions as appropriate to your own skills and abilities:

a Мо́жете ли да игра́ете те́нис?

b Мо́жеш ли да ка́раш ски?

c Мо́жете ли да плу́вате?

d Мо́жете ли да ка́рате кола́?

e Мо́жеш ли да игра́еш на ка́рти?

2 Read the following short dialogue:

You	Извине́те, мо́жете ли да ми пока́жете къде́ е спи́рката на трамва́й но́мер четирина́йсет?
Passer-by	Съжаля́вам, не мо́га. Аз съ́що съм тури́ст.

Now use the same pattern to ask to be shown the way to:

142

a the chemist's
b the underground/subway
c the Sheraton Hotel
d the stop for trolleybus No. 2
e the Central Railway Station

3 Match the questions with the answers on the right:

i Кой пъпеш искате,
голе́мия или ма́лкия?

a Не, ста́рият.

ii Кой е Ва́шият ку́фар?

b Англи́йския.

iii Мла́дият мъж ли
е англича́нин?

c Че́рния.

iv Кой ве́стник искате?

d Си́ният.

v Кой чадъ́р да Ви дам?

e Ма́лкия.

4 Repeat the dialogue that follows substituting the word in bold with different words from the Quick vocab. Make sure you change the defining words (all underlined) according to gender:

Your friend	Тво́ята ча́нта ли е това́?
You	Не, <u>та́зи</u> ча́нта не е́ <u>мо́я</u>. <u>Мо́ята</u> ча́нта е <u>по́-голя́ма</u>.

ку́фар	*suitcase*
портмоне́	*purse, wallet*
чадъ́р	*umbrella*
па́пка	*folder*
моби́лен телефо́н	*mobile phone*
моли́в	*pencil*
беле́жник	*diary*
химика́лка	*ballpoint pen*

5 Disaster has struck: you have lost your purse, your luggage, your umbrella, your diary, your folder and your money. Making up separate sentences for each item, tell a policeman that they are missing. You may find the words in Exercise 4 useful.

Insight

Don't forget that the word for *money* пари́ is always plural!

6 Read the following story about a tourist who has lost his way in Sofia. First, answer the questions to test your understanding, then turn the story into a dialogue between a tourist and a policeman:

Турист пита един полицай (*policeman*) може ли да му помогне. Туристът не може да намери своя хотел. Полицаят пита как се казва неговият хотел. Туристът отговаря (*answers*), че не знае името на хотела. Той знае само, че хотелът е близо до спирката на тролей номер едно и тролей номер пет. Полицаят пита знае ли господинът на коя улица е хотелът. Туристът отговаря, че не знае улицата, но знае, че хотелът е близо до Университета. Полицаят казва, че има два хотела близо до Университета. Единият се казва «София Радисън», другият се казва хотел «България». Туристът сега вече знае името на хотела. Неговият хотел се казва «София Радисън». Той благодари на полицая.

a Какво не може да намери туристът?

b Знае ли туристът името на хотела?

c Къде е хотелът?

d Колко хотела има до Университета?

e Как се казва неговият хотел?

7 This exercise is based on the **Getting about in town** section. Are the following statements true or false?

a В големите градове на България има метро.

b Шофьорът продава билети.

c Вие трябва да купите билети за трамвай от павилиона.

d Талоните са по-евтини.

e Вие можете да поръчате маршрутка по телефона.

◀) CD 1, TR 55

8 Complete the answers in the following dialogue using **го, я** or **ги** as appropriate:

На телефона: **a** Извинете, там ли е Невена?

Няма ____.

b Извинете, там ли е г-н Джонсън?

Няма ____.

c Извинете, там ли е директорът?

Няма ____.

144

d Извинéте, там ли са Николáй и Милéна?
   Няма _____.

e Извинéте, там ли е секретáрката?
   Няма _____.

f Извинéте, там ли е пúколото?
   Няма _____.

Another small step forward

◆) CD 1, TR 56–57

Dialogue 2 Да се запознáем! *Let's get acquainted!*

Milena goes into a café and sees that there are two free seats at the table where Mr and Mrs Collins are having coffee.

Милéна	Извинéте, мóже ли да сéдна до вас?
г-жá Кóлинс	Разбúра се, заповя́дайте! Местáта са свобóдни.
Милéна	(*To the waitress.*) Еднó кафé и едúн сладолéд, мóля. (*To Mr and Mrs Collins.*) Днес е мнóго тóпло, налú?
г-жá Кóлинс	Да, наúстина. Врéмето е хýбаво за турúсти.
Милéна	На почúвка ли сте в Бългáрия?
г-жá Кóлинс	Да, úскаме да отúдем с мъжá ми на Злáтни пя́съци, но пъ́рво úмаме мáлко рáбота в Сóфия.
Милéна	Вúе говóрите мнóго добрé бългáрски.
г-жá Кóлинс	Благодаря́, аз тря́бва да говóря добрé бългáрски, защóто бългáрският езúк е мóята профéсия.
Милéна	Разбúрам. Сúгурно сте преводáчка.
г-жá Кóлинс	Тóчно такá.
Милéна	Да се запознáем! Кáзвам се Милéна Марúнова.
г-жá Кóлинс	Прия́тно ми е, Виктóрия Кóлинс.
г-н Кóлинс	Аз съм Джордж Кóлинс.
Милéна	Вúе сúгурно сте англичáни.
г-жá Кóлинс	Да, англичáни сме.
Милéна	Едúн мой колéга заминáва скóро за Áнглия. И аз úскам да отúда ня́кой ден.
г-жá Кóлинс	Пожелáвам Ви скóро да мóжете да отúдете.
Милéна	Надя́вам се. Мóга ли да ви помóгна с нéщо, докáто сте в Сóфия?
г-жá Кóлинс	Мúсля, че мóжете. Тря́бва да отúдем в Централна пóща, а не знáем къдé е.

найстина	*indeed*
време	*weather*
на почивка	*on holiday*
отговарям, -ряш	*to answer*
защото	*because*
сигурно сте преводачка	*you must be an interpreter*
един мой колега (m)	*a colleague of mine*
пожелавам ви да ...	*I wish you (to do something)*
докато	*while*

QUICK VOCAB

Test yourself

1 To see how well you have understood Dialogue 2, identify the true statements and correct any false ones:

  a До г-н и г-жа Колинс няма свободни места.
  b Времето е много топло.
  c Г-н и г-жа Колинс са на почивка в България.
  d Г-н и г-жа Колинс нямат работа в София.
  e Г-жа Колинс говори добре български, защото е преводачка.
  f Милена заминава скоро за Англия.
  g Г-н и г-жа Колинс знаят къде е Централна поща.

2 Complete the sentences:

  a Извинете, _____ да седна до вас?
  b Да, _____ се, заповядайте!
  c _____ език е моята професия.
  d _____ ли да ви помогна?
  e Мисля, че _____.
  f Пожелавам _____ да отидете в Англия.

3 Look again at Dialogue 1 and then rearrange the words that follow to make sentences:

  a Ви, мога, да, помогна, какво, с?
  b от, имат, гостите, Америка, такси, нужда, от
  c не, чантата, Виолета, на своя мъж, да намери, може
  d багаж, не, това, моят, е
  e синя, на, малката, е, чанта, Марк

Now can you:

- ask for and offer help?
- describe things and people?
- manage the different ways of expressing possession?
- say that you are or are not able to do something?
- say that something or someone is not (t)here?

10

Какво́ ще бъ́де вре́мето?
What will the weather be?

In this unit you will learn:

- How to discuss the weather
- How to offer your opinion
- How to talk about future events

Dialogue 1

🔊 **CD 1, TR 58–59**

Nikolai and Nadya make plans for two outings and keep an eye on the weather.

Никола́й	*(Nikolai rushes into the office.)* На́дя, здраве́й! Мо́жеш ли да ми помо́гнеш? Тря́бва да организи́рам екску́рзия до Ви́тоша за г-н Анто́нов и за на́шия гост от А́нглия.
На́дя	По́-споко́йно, Никола́й! Говори́ по́-ба́вно. Защо́ бъ́рзаш то́лкова?
Никола́й	Защо́то тря́бва да поръ́чам такси́ и да запа́зя ма́са в рестора́нта за у́тре.
На́дя	Ня́ма пробле́ми. Най-ва́жно е вре́мето да бъ́де ху́баво.
Никола́й	Вя́рно. И́маш ли ве́стник с прогно́за за вре́мето?
На́дя	Не, но мо́жем да чу́ем прогно́зата по ра́диото.
(Some time later they are listening to the radio.)	
Ра́дио	У́тре вре́мето ще бъ́де слъ́нчево, но ветрови́то. По висо́ките планини́ ще е о́блачно. Възмо́жно е да вали́. Температу́рите ще бъ́дат между́ осемна́йсет и два́йсет и два гра́дуса.

148

(Later...)	
Николай	Жа́лко, вре́мето на Ви́тоша ня́ма да е мно́го ху́баво. Си́гурно ще вали́ дъжд. И си́гурно г-н Джо́нсън не но́си марато́нки.
На́дя	Ни́що, не е фата́лно. Предла́гам да оти́дете на юг – в Ме́лник. Там вре́мето си́гурно ще е ху́баво. На Ви́тоша мо́же да оти́дете в съ́бота.
Николай	Добра́ иде́я, но какво́ ще е вре́мето в съ́бота?
На́дя	Спо́ред прогно́зата в кра́я на се́дмицата ня́ма да вали́ и ще бъ́де по́-то́пло.
Николай	Ше́фът ще се съгласи́ ли с но́вия план?
На́дя	Ще се съгласи́. Аз ще гово́ря с не́го. В Ме́лник е изключи́телно краси́во.
Николай	Да, зна́я. На́дя, предла́гам и ти да до́йдеш. Съгла́сна ли си?
На́дя	Съгла́сна съм. Ще до́йда с удово́лствие!

QUICK VOCAB

да организи́рам екску́рзия до Ви́тоша	*to organize an outing to Mount Vitosha*
По́-споко́йно!	*Take it easy!*
Защо́ бъ́рзаш то́лкова?	*What's the hurry?*
да поръ́чам такси́ и да запа́зя ма́са	*to order a taxi and reserve a table*
у́тре	*tomorrow*
На́й-ва́жно е вре́мето да бъ́де ху́баво.	*The main thing is for the weather to be fine.*
прогно́за за вре́мето	*weather forecast*
Мо́жем да чу́ем прогно́зата по ра́диото.	*We can hear the forecast on the radio.*
Вре́мето ще бъ́де слъ́нчево.	*The weather will be sunny.*
ветрови́то	*windy*
По висо́ките планини́ ще е о́блачно.	*Over the high mountains it will be cloudy.*
Възмо́жно е да вали́.	*It is likely to rain.*
Температу́рите ще бъ́дат между́ осемна́йсет и два́йсет и два гра́дуса.	*The temperatures will be between 18° and 22° Centigrade*
Жа́лко.	*What a pity.*
Вре́мето на Ви́тоша ня́ма да е мно́го ху́баво.	*The weather on Mount Vitosha isn't going to be very good.*

Си́гурно ще вали́ дъжд.	It will most probably rain.
Си́гурно г-н Джо́нсън не но́си марато́нки.	Mr Johnson surely doesn't have trainers with him.
не е́ фата́лно	it isn't fatal
Предла́гам да оти́дете на юг.	I suggest you go south.
Там вре́мето си́гурно ще е ху́баво.	The weather is sure to be good there.
в съ́бота	on Saturday
Какво́ ще е вре́мето?	What is the weather going to be like?
Споре́д прогно́зата в кра́я на се́дмицата ня́ма да вали́.	According to the forecast at the end of the week it isn't going to rain.
Ше́фът ще се съгласи́ ли с но́вия план?	Will the boss agree to the new plan?
Аз ще гово́ря с не́го.	I'll speak to him.
изключи́телно краси́во	exceptionally beautiful
Предла́гам и ти да до́йдеш.	I suggest you come too.
Съгла́сна ли си?	Do you agree?
Съгла́сна съм!	I agree!
Ще до́йда с удово́лствие!	I'd love to come! (lit. I'll come with pleasure!)

1 Questions

a Защо́ бъ́рза Никола́й?

b Как мо́гат Никола́й и На́дя да разбера́т (*find out*) прогно́зата?

c Какво́ ще бъ́де вре́мето у́тре по висо́ките планини́?

d Какво́ предла́га На́дя?

e Каква́ е прогно́зата за кра́я на се́дмицата?

f Кой ще гово́ри с ше́фа?

2 True or false?

a Никола́й тря́бва да организи́ра екску́рзия до Ви́тоша за г-н Джо́нсън и г-н Анто́нов.

b Той тря́бва да ку́пи биле́ти за автобу́с за у́тре.

c Във ве́стника и́ма прогно́за за вре́мето, но На́дя ня́ма ве́стник.

d У́тре вре́мето на Ви́тоша ще бъ́де ху́баво.

150

e Г-н Джо́нсън си́гурно но́си марато́нки.

f Ше́фът ня́ма да се съгласи́ да оти́де в Ме́лник.

....

Doing things the Bulgarian way

Relying on the weather

Bulgaria has a continental climate – hot summers and cold winters. The extremes of temperatures are, however, tempered by the Black Sea in the east and the Aegean to the south. At the Black Sea resorts, even in the summer there is usually a slight breeze and the temperatures are bearable. In the winter, you will find the coldest weather to the north of the Balkan Mountains, which stretch from the west to the east of the country. In the Thracian Plain to the south of the Balkan range, and in the valleys leading down towards Greece, the winters are milder.

In the spring and autumn, the weather is less reliable. Particularly in March and April, and sometimes into May, you can expect a good deal of rain, so do take an umbrella. In the higher mountains, of course, rain at these times usually means snow and snow in Bulgaria means skiing. In the Rila and Pirin Mountains to the south of Sofia and also on Mount Vitosha, which rises majestically to nearly 2300 metres, just half an hour's drive from the centre of the capital city, you can often ski into May.

Getting out of town

There are mountains everywhere in Bulgaria. Having access to the mountains is, of course, wonderful, but do go prepared for rapid changes of weather, especially in the spring and autumn. It can be sunny and warm in the valleys and snowing hard higher up.

The distances in Bulgaria are not great and it is well worth hiring a car to get out of town. (Book well in advance!) There are some very good roads – as well as many very bad ones. Do remember, though, that Bulgarian driving patterns are rather like the climate, a mixture of continental and Mediterranean. Remember too that Bulgarian traffic police make on-the-spot fines (**глоба**) and are particularly hot on speeding and unauthorized overtaking.

The rail network is small and trains are slow, so, unless you hire a car, you may prefer to try the large selection of cross-country minibuses and long-distance coaches. It's safer to buy your tickets in advance and do take your passport with you. In fact, it's best to take your passport wherever you go – just in case!

How do you say it?

- Asking *what will the weather be like?*

  Каквó ще е/бъ́де врéмето?   *What will the weather be?*

🔊 **CD 1, TR 60**

- Describing the weather

Тóпло е.
It's warm.

Студéно е.
It's cold.

Слъ́нчево е.
It's sunny.

Óблачно е.
It's cloudy.

Ветровúто е.
It's windy.

Валú дъжд.
It's raining.

Валú сняг.
It's snowing.

- Evaluating a situation

Ху́баво е/Не é ху́баво.	It's fine/not good.
Интере́сно е/Не é интере́сно.	It's interesting/not interesting.
Ва́жно е/Не é ва́жно.	It's important/not important.
Не é фата́лно.	It's not fatal.
Възмо́жно е.	It's possible/likely.

- Suggesting what to do

| Предла́гам да оти́дем на Ви́тоша. | I suggest we go to Mount Vitosha. |
| Предла́гам да оти́дете в Ме́лник. | I suggest you go to Melnik. |

- Agreeing or disagreeing

For a man

| Съгла́сен съм. | I agree. |
| Не съм съгла́сен. | I disagree. |

For a woman

| Съгла́сна съм. | I agree. |
| Не съм съгла́сна. | I disagree. |

- Expressing regret

| Жа́лко! | What a pity! |

Grammar

1 Слъ́нчево е *It's sunny*

When describing the weather in Bulgarian, you do not need an equivalent of the English *it*:

| Слъ́нчево е. | It is sunny. |
| Я́сно е. | It is clear. |

As you see, you use the neuter form of the corresponding adjective and put the verb **e** after the 'weather' word. You follow the same pattern for sentences describing the situation in more general terms:

| Тъ́мно е. | It is dark. | Къ́сно е. | It is late. |
| Ра́но е. | It is early. | Жа́лко е. | It is a pity. |

You can also begin with the actual word for *weather*:

Врéмето е мнóго лóшо днес.   *The weather is very bad today.*
Врéмето днес е ясно.   *The weather is clear today.*

Very often weather sentences begin with a reference to where and when it is warm, cold, dark, etc. In such cases, the verb **e** comes before the neuter adjective:

В Мéлник винаги е тóпло.   *In Melnik, it is always warm.*
През зимата е студéно.   *In winter it is cold.*
В стáята е тъмно.   *It is dark in the room.*

2 Вали (дъжд) *It's raining*

For descriptions of the weather involving precipitation Bulgarian uses the *it* form of an old verb meaning *fall*: вали. Depending on the context, вали can mean *it is raining* or *it is snowing*. To be more specific you add the word for *rain* or *snow*:

Вали дъжд.   *It is raining.*
Вали сняг.   *It is snowing.*

3 Чудéсно е, че . . . *It is wonderful that . . .*

Some evaluating expressions such as *'wonderful'* or *'important'* are linked to further statements. If the linking word in English is *that*, in Bulgarian, you use **че**:

Чудéсно е, **че** сте тук!   *It's wonderful (that) you are here.*

Жáлко е, **че** нямаме врéме.   *It's a pity (that) we have no time.*

Insight

Don't forget that in Bulgarian, you can *never* leave out **че**.

If what follows in English is an infinitive (*to* + verb), the verb in Bulgarian must be preceded by **да**:

Вáжно е **да пристигнем** наврéме.   *It's important (for us) to get there on time.*
Приятно е **да пътуваш** с колá.   *It's pleasant to travel by car.*

154

Note that the verb **е** always comes second no matter what other word is used in first position:

Не é вя́рно, че . . .   *It is not true that . . .*
Мно́го е прия́тно да . . .   *It is very pleasant to . . .*

4 (Аз) Ще до́йда *I will come* (future tense)

It is very easy to refer to future events in Bulgarian. You merely insert **ще** in front of the verbal forms for the present tense. With (**да**) **до́йда**, therefore, you say:

(аз)	**ще** до́йда	*I'll come*	(ни́е)	**ще** до́йдем	*we'll come*
(ти)	**ще** до́йдеш	*you'll come*	(ви́е)	**ще** до́йдете	*you'll come*
(той)					
(тя)	**ще** до́йде	*he/she/it*	(те)	**ще** до́йдат	*they'll come*
(то)		*will come*			

To say *I will not, you will not,* etc. instead of **ще** you insert **ня́ма** followed by **да**:

(аз)	**ня́ма да** до́йда	*I won't come*
(ти)	**ня́ма да** до́йдеш	*you won't come*
(той)	**ня́ма да** до́йде	*he won't come*
(ни́е)	**ня́ма да** до́йдем	*we won't come*
(ви́е)	**ня́ма да** до́йдете	*you won't come*
(те)	**ня́ма да** до́йдат	*they won't come*

5 Аз ще съм and аз ще бъ́да *I will be*

You have two verb forms to choose from to express *I will be* or *I am going to be,* etc. The form with **бъ́да**, etc. tends to be more formal:

(аз)	ще съм/ ще бъ́да	*I will be*	(ни́е)	ще сме/ ще бъ́дем	*we will be*
(ти)	ще си/ ще бъ́деш	*you will be*	(ви́е)	ще сте/ ще бъ́дете	*you will be*
(той)					
(тя)	ще е/ ще бъ́де	*he/he/it will be*	(те)	ще са/ ще бъ́дат	*they will be*
(то)					

| Аз ще съм/бъда в Пло́вдив у́тре. | I will be in Plovdiv tomorrow. |
| Той ще е/бъ́де на екску́рзия в съ́бота. | He will be going on an excursion on Saturday. |

To say *I will not*, etc. you simply replace **ще** with **ня́ма да**:

Ня́ма да съм/бъ́да в Со́фия.	Ня́ма да сме/бъ́дем свобо́дни.
Ня́ма да си/бъ́деш свобо́ден.	Ня́ма да сте/бъ́дете въ́в фи́рмата.
Ня́ма да е/бъ́де на те́нис.	Ня́ма да са/бъ́дат в Пло́вдив.

6 In what manner?

A great number of words that tell us *how* or *in what manner* something is done (adverbs) can be formed from adjectives. In English, you often add *-ly* to adjectives to form adverbs. In Bulgarian, many adverbs look exactly like the neuter form of an adjective because they end in **-о**:

Adverbs

| Той гово́ри мно́го бъ́рзо. | He speaks very quickly. |
| Тря́бва да гово́риш по́-споко́йно. | You must speak more calmly. |

Adjectives

| Такси́то е мно́го бъ́рзо. | The taxi is very quick. |
| Оби́чам споко́йно мо́ре. | I like a calm sea. |

Adverbs are also used to make adjectives more specific as in:

| Вре́мето ще бъ́де **мно́го** ху́баво. | The weather will be very nice. |
| Ме́лник е **изключи́телно** краси́во градче́. | Melnik is an exceptionally beautiful little town. |

7 Най- for *biggest* and *best* – superlative

To say that something or someone is *the biggest* or *the best* or *the most beautiful*, (i.e. to make the superlative form of the adjective), you place **най-** on the front of the adjective and, usually, the definite article on the end:

| **Най**-голе́мият пъ́пеш е тук. | The biggest melon is here. |

Тази англичанка
   е **най**-хубава**та**.
Това е **най**-сладко**то** вино.
Най-евтини**те** краставици
   са на пазара.

This English woman is the
*   most beautiful one.*
This is the sweetest wine.
The cheapest cucumbers are
*   at the market.*

But, as in English, you can sometimes use the superlative without the definite article:

Времето е **най**-топло
   в Мелник.

The weather is hottest
*   in Melnik.*

Exercises

1 To practise talking about the weather, first read the following short dialogue:

– Днес е слънчево, но ветровито. Утре ще бъде ли също слънчево и ветровито?
• Не, утре няма да бъде слънчево и ветровито.

Now complete these dialogues following the same pattern:

a Днес е облачно и мрачно. _____?
   Не, _____.
b Днес е мъгливо. _____?
   Не, _____.
c Днес е топло и слънчево. _____?
   Не, _____.
d Днес е студено и влажно. _____?
   Не, _____.
e Днес е дъждовно. _____?
   Не, _____.

мрачно	*dull*
мъгливо	*foggy*
влажно	*damp*
дъждовно	*rainy*
горещо	*hot*
късно	*late*

QUICK VOCAB

забáвно	*amusing*
удóбно	*convenient, comfortable.*
бѐрзо	*quickly*
трýдно	*not easily, with difficulty*
тѝхо	*quietly*

2 Agree or disagree with the following comments, using the model:

– Интерéсно е.

• Наѝстина, мнóго е интерéсно. (*Indeed, it is very interesting.*)

• Не съм съглáсен/съглáсна. Изобщо не é интерéсно. (*I don't agree. It isn't interesting at all.*)

a Горéщо е.
b Кѐсно е.
c Забáвно е.
d Удóбно е.
e Възмóжно е.

3 Use **бѐрзо**, **трýдно** or **пó-тѝхо** to complete these sentences:

a Г-н Антóнов ще се съгласѝ _____.
b _____ ще намéрим гáрата.
c Шшш! Говорѝ _____!
d _____ ще намéрим багáжа.

◄» **CD 1, TR 61**

4 You turn on the radio and hear the following weather forecast:

Ѝтре в цялата странá ще бѐде ясно и горéщо. По Черноморието ще ѝма слаб до умéрен ѝзточен вятър. Температýрата на въздуха: междý двáйсет и óсем и трѝйсет и два грáдуса, а на мóрската водá – óколо двáйсет и три грáдуса.

Now, using full sentences, try to answer the following questions:

a Óблачно ли ще бѐде ýтре?
b Ще ѝма ли сѝлен вятър по Черномóрието?
c Кóлко горéщо ще бѐде?
d Каквá ще бѐде температýрата на морéто?

цял	*whole*
Черномо́рието	*the Black Sea coast*
слаб	*light*
уме́рен	*moderate*
и́зточен, -лна	*east*
въ́здух	*air*
мо́рската вода́	*the sea water*
ля́то	*summer*
обу́вки	*shoes*
кита́йски	*Chinese* (adj)
си́лен, -лна	*strong*
все пак	*all the same*
я́ке	*jacket*

5 Choose a good reason for the statements that follow from the list on the right:

i Г-н Джо́нсън ня́ма да оти́де на екску́рзия, _____

ii Ня́ма да оти́да на Ви́тоша, _____

iii Тря́бва да поръ́чаме такси́, _____

iv В Бълга́рия и́ма мно́го тури́сти, _____

v Кита́йският ресторáнт е затво́рен, _____

a защо́то е къ́сно и ня́ма трамва́и.

b защо́то е мно́го ра́но.

c защо́то ля́тото е дъ́лго и то́пло.

d защо́то ня́ма удо́бни обу́вки.

e защо́то ще вали́ дъжд.

6 Imagine you are Nikolai and complete this conversation:

Миле́на	Ще до́йдеш ли днес с нас на те́нис, Никола́й?
Никола́й	(*I won't come because I haven't got time.*)
Миле́на	Жа́лко. Кога́ ще и́маш вре́ме?
Никола́й	(*Tomorrow.*)
Миле́на	Къде́ предла́гаш да оти́дем у́тре?
Никола́й	(*I suggest we go on an outing. Do you agree?*)
Миле́на	Какво́ ще бъ́де вре́мето?
Никола́й	(*The weather will be sunny and warm.*)
Миле́на	Добре́, съгла́сна съм. Но все пак ще взе́ма я́ке.
Никола́й	(*Good. I'll take my jacket too.*)

Another small step forward

🔊 CD 1, TR 62–63

Dialogue 2 Елá с нас! *Come with us!*

Milena succumbs to gentle GSM* persuasion and agrees to go to Melnik.

(*Bulgarian mobile phone, джиесéм remember?)

Николáй	Здравéй, Милéна.
Милéна	Ти ли си, Николáй? Защó не си на екскýрзия?
Николáй	Врéмето е лóшо.
Милéна	Не изглéжда лóшо. Слънчево е.
Николáй	Да, но има силен вятър и на Витоша е студéно.
Милéна	Вярно, там винаги е пó-студéно.
Николáй	Да, защóто е висóко. Затовá искаме ýтре да отидем в Мéлник.
Милéна	В Мéлник е чудéсно. Сигурно ще бъде тóпло, защóто е на юг.
Николáй	Но все пак ще взéмем якета. Искаш ли да дóйдеш и ти, Милéна?
Милéна	Възмóжно ли е?
Николáй	Разбира се, че е възмóжно. Елá с нас! Нáдя също ще дóйде. Ще бъде пó-интерéсно с две хýбави момичета.
Милéна	Добрé, съглáсна съм. Когá заминáвате?
Николáй	В сéдем и половина.
Милéна	Сериóзно? Но товá е ужáсно рáно!
Николáй	Не, не, шегýвам се, защóто знáя, че не обичаш да стáваш рáно. Срéщата ни е в дéвет и половина пред хотéла на г-н Джóнсън.
Милéна	Добрé, ще дóйда.

Insight

Although **момиче** means *girl*, the word itself is neuter! So, too, is **момчé** *boy*.

висóко	*high*
изглéждам, -даш	*to look, seem*

160

затова́	*that is why*
сериóзно?	*are you serious?*
ужáсно	*terribly*
шегу́вам, -ваш се	*to joke*
стáвам, -ваш	*to get up*
пред	*in front of*

Test yourself

1 To see how well you have understood Dialogue 2, identify the true statements and correct any false ones:

a Николáй не é на екску́рзия, защóто врéмето на Ви́тоша е лóшо.

b На Ви́тоша ви́наги е пó-тóпло.

c Мéлник е на и́зток.

d Милéна е съглáсна да оти́де в Мéлник.

e Милéна оби́ча да стáва рáно.

f Срéщата на Николáй с г-н Джóнсън е пред хотéла му.

2 Complete the sentences:

a Врéмето не изглéжда _____ .

b В Мéлник си́гурно ще _____ тóпло.

c Нáдя съ́що _____ дóйде.

d Ще _____ пó-интерéсно с две ху́бави моми́чета.

3 How would you say:

a What a pity!
b It's wonderful.
c It's late.
d It's possible.
e It's convenient.

Now can you:

• talk about the weather?
• refer to future events?
• evaluate a situation?
• express agreement and disagreement?

11

План за следващата седмица
A plan for the coming week

In this unit you will learn:

- How to refer to the days of the week
- Some time expressions
- How to give the date
- Some more numbers

Dialogue 1

🔊 **CD 2, TR 1–2**

Mr Johnson firms up plans for his second week in Bulgaria.

г-н Антóнов	(*Looking at his diary.*) Мáйкъл, днес е четвъртък, четиринáйсети май. Вéче е четвъртият ден от Вáшия престóй. Остáват óще дéсет дни. Трябва да напрáвим план за слéдващата сéдмица.
г-н Джóнсън	В понедéлник úскам да отúда в Бóровец, за да разглéдам хотéлите. Женá ми и синът ми úскат да дóйдат през зúмата на ски в Бългáрия.
г-н Антóнов	Úскате ли някой да Ви придружú?
г-н Джóнсън	Не, благодаря. Ще наéма колá и ще отúда сам.
г-н Антóнов	Добрé, кáкто предпочúтате. Във втóрник преди óбед сме покáнени на излóжба на плакáти. След товá е запланýван óбед с дизáйнера, който организúра излóжбата. Слéдобед трябва да отговóрим на фúрмата, от коята ще кýпим компютри. Úмам

	една молба́ към Вас – да ни даде́те съве́т за на́й-изго́дните цени́.
г-н Джо́нсън	Разби́ра се. Ще оти́дем ли в Пло́вдив сле́дващата се́дмица?
г-н Анто́нов	Да. Пло́вдивският панаи́р запо́чва на два́йсети май, в сря́да. Ще оти́дем на пъ́рвия ден, за да и́маме вре́ме да разгле́даме вси́чко.
г-н Джо́нсън	Кога́ ще бъ́дат пре́говорите?
г-н Анто́нов	На вто́рия и тре́тия ден. Тря́бва да поръ́чаме ня́кои материа́ли и маши́ни за фи́рмата. Ва́шата по́мощ е добре́ дошла́.
г-н Джо́нсън	Разби́ра се, аз съм тук, за да помо́гна на фи́рмата Ви.
г-н Анто́нов	За съжале́ние, на два́йсет и вто́ри май тря́бва да се въ́рна в Со́фия. На то́зи ден тря́бва да посре́щна делега́цията, коя́то присти́га от Япо́ния. Никола́й ще бъ́де с Вас до кра́я на се́дмицата.
г-н Джо́нсън	Тога́ва, ще обясня́ на Никола́й кой материа́ли са на́й-подходя́щи и кои́ са на́й-моде́рните маши́ни.
г-н Анто́нов	Отли́чно, това́ ще е изключи́телно поле́зно за нас. На́дя, обади́ се на Никола́й. Пи́тай го свобо́ден ли е. Кажи́ му за програ́мата на г-н Джо́нсън. Обясни́ му защо́ и́маме ну́жда от не́го сле́дващия пе́тък.
г-н Джо́нсън	Извине́те, Боя́не, кога́ ще се въ́рнем от Пло́вдив?
г-н Анто́нов	А, да! С Никола́й ще се въ́рнете в съ́бота, а в неде́ля сте у нас на го́сти.
г-н Джо́нсън	Благодаря́. Вто́рата ми се́дмица в Бълга́рия изгле́жда до́ста интере́сна!

Днес е четвъ́ртък, четирина́йсети май.	*Today is Thursday May 14.*
четвъ́ртият ден от Ва́шия престо́й	*the fourth day of your stay*
Оста́ват о́ще де́сет дни.	*There are still ten days left.*
Тря́бва да напра́вим план за сле́дващата се́дмица.	*We must do a plan for the coming week.*
в понеде́лник ...	*on Monday ...*
за да разгле́дам хоте́лите	*(in order) to take a look at the hotels*
И́скате ли ня́кой да Ви придружи́?	*Would you like someone to accompany you?*
Ще нае́ма кола́.	*I'll hire a car.*

ка́кто	*as*
Във вто́рник преди́ о́бед сме пока́нени на изло́жба на плака́ти.	*On Tuesday, before lunch, we are invited to a poster exhibition.*
След това́ е заплану́ван о́бед с диза́йнера, ко́йто организи́ра . . .	*After that a lunch has been planned with the designer who is organizing . . .*
И́мам една́ молба́ към Вас.	*I have a favour to ask of you.*
съве́т за на́й-изго́дните цени́	*advice concerning the most favourable prices*
Пло́вдивският панаи́р запо́чва на два́йсети май.	*The Plovdiv Trade Fair begins on May 20.*
в сря́да	*on Wednesday*
на пъ́рвия ден	*on the first day*
да разгле́даме вси́чко	*to look round everything*
Кога́ ще бъ́дат пре́говорите?	*When will the talks be?*
на вто́рия и тре́тия ден	*on the second and third day*
ня́кои материа́ли и маши́ни	*certain materials and machines*
Ва́шата по́мощ е добре́ дошла́.	*Your help is welcome.*
за да	*(in order) to*
На два́йсет и вто́ри май тря́бва да се въ́рна в Со́фия.	*On May 22 I must return to Sofia.*
На то́зи ден тря́бва да посре́щна делега́цията, коя́то присти́га от Япо́ния.	*That day I must meet the delegation arriving from Japan.*
до кра́я на се́дмицата	*until the end of the week*
Ще обясня́ на Никола́й кой материа́ли са на́й-подходя́щи.	*I'll explain to Nikolai which materials are the most suitable.*
кой са на́й-моде́рните маши́ни	*which are the most up-to-date machines*
отли́чно	*excellent*
поле́зно	*useful*
Пи́тай го свобо́ден ли е.	*Ask him whether he is free.*
Кажи́ му за програ́мата на г-н Джо́нсън.	*Tell him about Mr Johnson's programme/schedule.*
Обясни́ му защо́ и́маме ну́жда от не́го сле́дващия пе́тък.	*Explain to him why we need him next Friday.*

164

| В неде́ля сте у нас на го́сти. | *On Sunday you are guests at our place.* |
| до́ста | *quite, very* |

1 Questions

a За кого́ тря́бва да напра́вят план г-н Анто́нов и г-н Джо́нсън?
b Защо́ г-н Джо́нсън и́ска да оти́де в Бо́ровец?
c Кога́ са пока́нени на изло́жба г-н Джо́нсън и г-н Анто́нов?
d Защо́ ще оти́дат на панаи́ра на пъ́рвия ден?
e Кога́ тря́бва да се въ́рне в Со́фия г-н Анто́нов?

2 True or false?

a Г-н Джо́нсън и́ска ня́кой да го придружи́ до Бо́ровец.
b Панаи́рът в Пло́вдив запо́чва на два́йсети май.
c Пре́говорите ще бъ́дат на пъ́рвия и вто́рия ден.
d Г-н Анто́нов ще посре́щне делега́ция, коя́то присти́га от Фра́нция.
e Ма́йкъл Джо́нсън и Никола́й ще се въ́рнат от Пло́вдив в съ́бота.

....

Doing things the Bulgarian way

Of high days and holidays

Although Bulgaria is on the south-eastern fringe of Europe and, for nearly five centuries, was within the Ottoman Empire, the people share with us most of the traditional feast days in the Christian calendar. They belong, however, to the Eastern Orthodox branch of Christianity and occasionally there are differences of emphasis. They place less importance on Christmas (**Ко́леда**) and more on Easter (**Вели́кден**), for example, and sometimes the dates of Easter in Bulgaria and in western Europe and America do not coincide.

The Bulgarian Orthodox service on the Saturday night before Easter Sunday is a very beautiful occasion with candles, rich vestments and wonderful singing.

The Bulgarians also have a number of special days in their calendar that are to do with nationality, their cultural identity and the political experiences of their recent past rather than with religion. March 3 (**трети март**), for example, is Bulgaria's day of national liberation and is a public holiday. Bulgarians then celebrate the end of the Russo-Turkish War of 1877–8 and their liberation from the Ottoman Empire.

May 24 (**двайсет и четвърти май**) is a very old holiday. It has a cultural significance for all the Slav peoples and has survived numerous changes of regime. It is dedicated to the 9th-century Saints Cyril and Methodius, the so-called 'Apostles of the Slavs' whom the Bulgarians regard very much as their own and who played a major role in bringing enlightenment to other Slav peoples. This holiday, which is probably Bulgaria's most popular 'high day', celebrates the achievements of Bulgarian education and culture through the ages and has traditionally seen street parades, singing, dancing and other public festivities.

How do you say it?

⏺ CD 2, TR 3

- Giving the date

  Днес е шести юни.   *Today is June 6.*

- Saying *on* with a date

  на петнайсети май   *on May 15*

- Saying *on* with days of the week

в понеделник	*on Monday*
във вторник	*on Tuesday*
в сряда	*on Wednesday*
в четвъртък	*on Thursday*
в петък	*on Friday*
в събота	*on Saturday*
в неделя	*on Sunday*

- Asking for advice/a favour

Мо́ля, да́йте ми съве́т. *Please give me some advice.*
Какъ́в съве́т ще ми даде́те? *What advice would you give me?*
И́мам една́ молба́ към Вас. *I have a favour to ask of you.*

- Stating your purpose

Ще оти́дем ра́но, за да *We'll go early so as to have*
и́маме вре́ме. *time.*
Обади́ се на Никола́й, за да *Get in touch with/*
го пи́таш кога́ ще до́йде. *Ring Nikolai (in order) to ask*
him when he'll be coming.

- Inviting someone home

Ела́(те) у нас на го́сти. *Come to our place.*

Grammar

1 Пъ́рви, вто́ри, тре́ти *First, second, third*

The numerals indicating order (ordinals) are used as adjectives:

Masculine		Feminine	Neuter
пъ́рви	*first*	пъ́рва	пъ́рво
вто́ри	*second*	вто́ра	вто́ро
тре́ти	*third*	тре́та	тре́то
четвъ́рти	*fourth*	четвъ́рта	четвъ́рто

From *fifth* on, you obtain the masculine forms by adding **-и** to the number. For feminine and neuter words you replace **-и** with **-а** or **-о** as above. Note the occasional shift of stress:

(пет)	пе́ти	*fifth*		едина́йсети	*eleventh*
(шест)	ше́сти	*sixth*		двана́йсети	*twelfth*
(се́дем)	се́дми	*seventh*	(with loss of **е**	трина́йсети	*thirteenth*
(о́сем)	о́сми	*eighth*	before **м**)	четирина́йсети	*fourteenth*
(де́вет)	деве́ти	*ninth*		петна́йсети	*fifteenth*
(де́сет)	десе́ти	*tenth*		шестна́йсети	*sixteenth*

For numbers consisting of more than one word you add **-и (-а, -о)**
only to the last part of the number:

два́йсет и пъ́рв**и**	*twenty-first*
два́йсет и втóр**и**	*twenty-second*
два́йсет и трéт**и**	*twenty-third*

Like all other adjectives, the ordinal numerals also have definite
forms:

вто́ра**та** сéдмица	*the second week*
четвъ́ртия**т** ден	*the fourth day*

(You will find a full list of all the numerals early on in the Appendix.)

◀) **CD 2, TR 4**

2 Пъ́рви януа́ри *January 1*

To give the date in Bulgarian you say **днес е** *today is* followed by the
day and the masculine ordinal numeral (an adjective, remember!) in
the indefinite form:

(днес е) вто́рник, тре́ти февруа́ри	*(today is) Tuesday 3 February*

Here are some dates together with the names of all the months.
Certain of the dates are particularly important in the Bulgarian
calendar. The significance of some of them was explained earlier:

пъ́рви	**януа́ри**	*1 January*	(1.I.)
о́сми	**февруа́ри**	*8 February*	(8.II.)
тре́ти	**март**	*3 March*	(3.III.)
два́йсет и деве́ти	**апри́л**	*29 April*	(29.IV.)
два́йсет и четвъ́рти	**май**	*24 May*	(24.V.)
вто́ри	**ю́ни**	*2 June*	(2.VI.)
се́дми	**ю́ли**	*7 July*	(7.VII.)
четирина́йсети	**а́вгуст**	*14 August*	(14.VIII.)

шести	**септември**	6 September	(6.IX.)
трийсети	**октомври**	30 October	(30.X.)
десети	**ноември**	10 November	(10.XI.)
двайсет и пети	**декември**	25 December	(25.XII.)

The names of the months and the days of the week are spelt with a small letter. When you write the number of the month in figures, you normally use Roman numerals, as shown in the brackets.

◀) **CD 2, TR 5**

3 101 and above

101	сто и едно	600	шестстотин
110	сто и десет	700	седемстотин
123	сто двайсет и три	800	осемстотин
200	двеста	900	деветстотин
300	триста	1 000	хиляда
400	четиристотин	2 000	две хиляди
500	петстотин	1 000 000	един милион

Insight

The words for *(one) thousand* and *(one) million* are nouns and have the respective plural forms: **две хиляди** (f pl), **два милиона** (special m pl after numbers). Note the change of stress in **хиляда** and **две хиляди**!

4 През две хиляди и единайсета година *In 2011*

To say *in* with the year in Bulgarian, you use the preposition **през**. The year is given in thousands (**хиляда** *thousand* or **две хиляди** *two thousand*), followed by the hundreds and the tens. Only the last element of the number is an ordinal, the feminine form agreeing with **година**:

Роден съм **през хиляда деветстотин осемдесет и втора година**.	*I was born in 1982.* (In Bulgarian you have to say *I am born.*)

Note that **и** comes before the final numeral (see Unit 4).

5 *When*: prepositions in time expressions

Here are some of the most common prepositions used with time expressions. Try to learn the expressions as whole phrases:

в сря́да	*on Wednesday*
до десе́ти ное́мври	*before/until November 10*
за две се́дмици	*for two weeks*
	(looking to the future)
от една́ се́дмица	*for a week*
	(looking to the past)

Insight

With expressions such as от една́ се́дмица when they answer the question *How long have you been here for?* Bulgarian uses the present tense:

От ко́лко вре́ме сте в България?	*How long have you been in Bulgaria (for)?*
В Бълга́рия съм от една́ се́дмица.	*I've been in Bulgaria for a week.*

на о́сми март	*on March 8*
от сря́да **до** пе́тък	*from Wednesday till Friday*
преди́ о́бед	*before lunch*
преди́ три дни	*three days ago*
през деня́	*during the day*
през есента́	*in autumn*
през нощта́	*at night*
през пролетта́	*in spring*
през (ме́сец) януа́ри	*in January*
след една́ се́дмица	*a week later/in a week*

6 Го and я *Him/it* and *her*

When they are not subjects, things and persons are most frequently substituted by the short object pronouns. Unlike English, these little words usually precede the verb. They are normally unstressed:

Кой ще напра́ви план?	*Who is going to do a plan?*
Секрета́рката ще **го** напра́ви.	*The secretary will do it.*

170

| Кой нóси чáнтата? | *Who is carrying the bag?* |
| Мъжъ́т на Виолéта **я** нóси. | *Violeta's husband is carrying it.* |

However, after **не** the short object pronouns are stressed and, if the verb comes first in the sentence, they follow it.

Не **мé** чáкай!	*Don't wait for me!*
Пи́тай **го** свобóден ли е.	*Ask him whether he's free.*
Придружéте **ме** до бáнката, мóля.	*Accompany me to the bank, please.*

Here are all the short object pronouns (corresponding subject forms in brackets). For a list of the full forms, see Unit 6 (non-subject forms after prepositions):

(аз)	**ме**	*me*	(ни́е)	**ни**	*us*
(ти)	**те**	*you*	(ви́е)	**ви/Ви**	*you*
(той)	**го**	*him/it*			
(тя)	**я**	*her/it*	(те)	**ги**	*them*
(то)	**го**	*it*			

(You'll find the short indirect object pronouns in Unit 7 and parallel lists in the Appendix.)

7 Ще обясня́ на Николáй *I'll explain to Nikolai*

In Unit 7, you learned what pronouns to use with verbs that require an indirect object – the person to whom or for whom something is done. If, however, you want to use the person's name or a noun, you need to introduce it by the preposition **на** (which in most cases corresponds to the English *to*). Here are examples with some of the most common verbs that require an indirect object in Bulgarian: (да) дам, (да) помóгна, (да) обясня́ and (да) кáжа:

Той ще дадé съвéт **на момчéто**.	*He will give the boy some advice.*
Невéна ще помóгне **на Марк и Виолéта**.	*Nevena will help (give help to) Mark and Violeta.*
Мáйкъл Джóнсън ще обясни́ свóите плáнове **на Николáй**.	*Michael Johnson will explain his plans to Nikolai.*
Николáй ще кáже **на Милéна** за нóвия план.	*Nikolai will tell Milena about the new plan.*

8 Ще му обясня́ *I'll explain to him*

Compare the examples in the last section with their alternatives where the short indirect object pronouns replace **на** + noun and move to the left of the verb:

Той ще **му даде́** съве́т.	*He'll give him some advice.*
Неве́на ше **им помо́гне.**	*Nevena will help them.*
Ма́йкъл Джо́нсън ще **му обясни́** сво́ите пла́нове.	*Michael Johnson will explain his plans to him.*
Никола́й ще **й ка́же** за но́вия план.	*Nikolai will tell her about the new plan.*

When **на** is used with the full non-subject pronoun as an alternative to the short pronoun to the left of the verb, this highlights a contrast. Compare:

	Ще се оба́дя **на не́я** (не на не́го!).	*I'll ring her (not him).*
with	Ще **й** се оба́дя.	
	Ще помо́гна **и на те́бе** (не са́мо на тях!).	*I'll help you too (not just them).*
with	Ще **ти** помо́гна.	

9 Ни́е сме пока́нени *We are invited*

Some verbal forms can be used with the verb *to be* as in *we are* or *we have been invited*. In such sentences, you are not interested in who does the inviting but who is or has been invited. That is why they are called passive sentences. Such -ed forms of the verb are known as passive participles and are used as adjectives. In Bulgarian, you form the passive participle of most verbs by replacing the personal endings of the past form with **-ен**:

(да) пока́н**я** *to invite* becomes пока́н**ен** *invited*:
аз съм пока́нен   *I am invited*

This is the masculine form to which you can then add the feminine, neuter or plural endings: **тя е пока́нена, то е пока́нено, ни́е сме пока́нени.**

A-pattern verbs add **-ан**, so заплану́вам *to plan* becomes **заплану́ван** (**-а, -о, -и**) *planned*:

Конфере́нцията **е**	*The conference is planned*
заплану́вана за се́дми	*for September 7.*
септе́мври.	

A small number of verbs add **-ян** or **-т**. You will find some of them among the participles listed in the Appendix.

Exercises

◄》 CD 2, TR 6

1 Read this notice found just inside the entrance to a department store:

ПА́РТЕР (*ground floor*):	пода́ръци и козме́тика (*cosmetics*)
I ЕТА́Ж (*floor*):	вси́чко за дете́то
II ЕТА́Ж:	обу́вки
III ЕТА́Ж:	телеви́зори (*televisions*),
	компю́три. моби́лни телефо́ни
IV ЕТА́Ж:	кили́ми (*carpets*)
V ЕТА́Ж:	рестора́нт, тоале́тна

Now answer Какво́ и́ма:

a на па́ртера?

b на пъ́рвия ета́ж?

c на вто́рия ета́ж?

d на тре́тия ета́ж?

e на четвъ́ртия ета́ж?

f на пе́тия ета́ж?

2 Still looking at the notice, say on which floor they sell the indicated items. На кой ета́ж прода́ват:

a марато́нки?

b парфю́ми? (*perfumes*)

c компю́три

d шампоа́ни? (*shampoos*)

3 Try using some object pronouns by filling the spaces with the Bulgarian for *him, her*, etc.

Обади́ се:

a на Марк и _____ покани́ у нас на го́сти.

b на Неве́на и _____ покани́ у нас на го́сти.

c на Никола́й и _____ покани́ у нас на го́сти.

d на г-н и г-жа́ Анто́нови и _____ покани́ у нас на го́сти.

4 You are looking at your diary and making plans for the days ahead. Following the model, complete the sentences with the appropriate days of the week or time expressions:

Днес е понеде́лник. След три дни ще бъ́де четвъ́ртък. Ще ку́пя биле́т (for за) четвъ́ртък.

a Днес е четвъ́ртък. След два дни ще бъ́де _____. Ще запа́зя ма́са (for) _____.

b Днес е неде́ля. След пет дни ще бъ́де _____. Ще оти́да на изло́жбата (on) _____.

c Днес е вто́рник. У́тре ще бъ́де _____. Ще ку́пя биле́т (for tomorrow) _____.

5 Look carefully at this page from a brochure, then answer the questions below in Bulgarian. (For the rounded, long-hand letters look back at the 'Bulgarian alphabet' in the 'Alphabet and pronunciation' section.)

БЕЛГРАД
ЕДИН ПРИЯТЕН УИКЕНД

ДАТИ НА ЗАМИНАВАНЕ	ЦЕНА
април – 26	193 лв.
май – 31	193 лв.
август – 2	193 лв.
септември – 6	193 лв.
октомври – 11	193 лв.

1 ДЕН – Отпътуване в 6,00 ч. по маршрут София - Белград. Пристигане в Белград в ранния следобед. Настаняване. Кратка почивка. Панорамна обиколка на Белград с екскурзовод на български език. Свободно време. По предварителна заявка – вечеря в бохемския квартал «Скадарлия». Нощувка.

2 ДЕН – Закуска. Целодневна екскурзия до Нови Сад с екскурзовод на български език. Разглеждане на Старата Патриаршия и Катедралата; посещение на манастира Ново Хопово; разглеждане на средновековната крепост Петроварадин. Свободно време. Връщане в Белград. По желание – разходка с корабче по р. Дунав и р.Сава. Нощувка.

3 ДЕН – Закуска.
Отпътуване за България.
Пристигане в София в
късния следобед.

ЦЕНАТА ВКЛЮЧВА
- транспорт с луксозен
  автобус (климатик,
  видеосистема, мини бар -
  безплатни топли напитки);
- 2 нощувки със закуски в
  хотел в центъра на
  Белград;
- панорамна обиколка на
  Белград с екскурзовод на
  български език;
- целодневна екскурзия до
  Нови Сад с екскурзовод на
  български език;
- застраховка.

ЦЕНАТА НЕ ВКЛЮЧВА
- вечеря в бохемския
  квартал «Скадарлия»;
- разходка с корабче по
  р.Дунав и р. Сава;
- входни такси и билети за
  музеи.

ОТСТЪПКИ
- ученици и студенти: 8
  лв.;
- деца до 12 г., настанени
  в стаята на двамата си
  родители: 18 лв.;
- пенсионери: 8 лв.

a How does the agency describe the trip to Belgrade?
b What is the means of transport?
c Where will the participants be staying?
d Reckoning on two nights away, what will the return dates be
   for the different departures?
e What trips does the price include?
f What language will the guide use?
g Does the price include entrance tickets to museums?

Туристическа агенция •
ГЕОГРАФСКИ СВЯТ лиценз №222

6 Read the following page from Nadya's diary for the week ahead.
This exercise will help you practise talking about future events:

Понеде́лник	Да помо́гна на Никола́й с докуме́нтите (*the documents*).
Вто́рник	Да ка́жа на ше́фа за да́тата (*the date*) на изло́жбата.
Сря́да	Да отгово́ря на писмо́то на диза́йнера.
Четвъ́ртък	Да изпра́тя пока́ни (*send invitations*) на вси́чки, който рабо́тят във фи́рмата.
Пе́тък	Да се оба́дя на коле́гата в Пло́вдив.
Съ́бота	Да ку́пя пода́рък на сина́ на Анто́нови.
Неде́ля	Да пока́жа на Миле́на но́вите плака́ти.

Answer Какво́ ще пра́ви На́дя?

a в понеде́лник?
b във вто́рник?
c в сря́да?
d в четвъ́ртък?
e в пе́тък?
f в съ́бота?
g в неде́ля?

Now, instead of using the days of the week, use dates starting from Monday, May 18, to ask Nadya **Какво́ ще пра́виш на . . . ?**

Another small step forward

◀》 CD 2, TR 7–8

Dialogue 2 На добъ́р пъ́т! *Have a good journey!*

Jim, a young American staying at the same hotel as the Collinses, changes his air ticket – with a little help from his friends.

Невéна	Добрó ýтро, г-жá Кóлинс! Заминáвате ли вéче?
г-жá Кóлинс	Да, отúваме във Вáрна. Предú да замúнем úмам еднá молбá. Акó нáкой ни тáрси, мóля, дáйте тóзи телефóн. Ще бáдем в хотéл «Одéса» до четвáрти юни.
Невéна	Разбúра се, ще го напрáвя. На добáр пáт и приáтно изкáрване! (*She sees Jim, obviously anxious to speak to Mrs Collins.*) Вúжте, тóзи америкáнец úска да Ви кáже нéщо.
г-жá Кóлинс	(*After having exchanged a few words with Jim.*) Невéна, товá е Джим. Той úска да вáрне свóя билéт на áвиокомпáнията. Нáма да мóже да пáтува на двáйсет и втóри юли. Úска да отúде в Копрúвщица, за да вúди фолклóрния фестивáл.
Невéна	Добрé. Ще се опúтам да помóгна и на нéго. Úмам приáтелка в тáзи áвиокомпáния. Едúн момéнт, ще úскам съвéт от нéя. (*After speaking on the phone.*) Такá, всúчки éвтини билéти от двáйсет и втóри юли до дванáйсети áвгуст са продáдени. Úма билéти за тринáйсети áвгуст, срáда.
г-жá Кóлинс	Мóля, запазéте едúн билéт за тринáйсети áвгуст.
Невéна	(*Finishes conversation and rings off.*) Кажéте на Джим, че мóже да отúде в агéнцията в понедéлник и да вáрне билéта на приáтелката ми. Тя говóри англúйски.
г-жá Кóлинс	Благодарá Ви за помощтá!
Джим	Благодарá, Невéна!
Невéна	Нáма защó. Аз съм тук, за да помáгам на гóстите на хотéла.

Insight

The verb **помáгам** is a 'twin' of **да помóгна** *to help* (Unit 9). You will learn more about verbal twinning in Unit 12.

(да) замúна, -неш	*to leave*
На добáр пáт!	*Have a good/safe journey!*
Приáтно изкáрване!	*Have a good time/pleasant stay!*
áвиокомпáния	*airline*
фолклóрен фестивáл	*folk festival*
тáрся, -сиш	*to look/ask for*

QUICK VOCAB

(да) опи́там, -таш	to try
прода́вам, -ваш	to sell
прода́ден	sold
по́мощ (f)	help

Test yourself

1 To see how well you have understood Dialogue 2, identify the true statements and correct any false ones:

  a Ако́ ня́кой тъ́рси г-н и г-жа́ Ко́линс, Неве́на ще му даде́ те́хния телефо́н.

  b Г-н и г-жа́ Ко́линс ще бъ́дат във Ва́рна до четвъ́рти юли.

  c Джим и́ска да въ́рне сво́я биле́т.

  d Джим мо́же да пъту́ва на два́йсет и вто́ри юли.

  e Вси́чки е́втини биле́ти от два́йсет и вто́ри юли до двана́йсети а́вгуст са прода́дени.

  f Джим тря́бва да оти́де в аге́нцията във вто́рник.

2 Answer the questions.

  a На кого́ ще помо́гне Неве́на?

  b Защо́ Джим ня́ма да мо́же да пъту́ва на два́йсет и вто́ри юли?

  c Какъ́в ден от се́дмицата е трина́йсети а́вгуст?

  d Кога́ Джим ще въ́рне биле́та?

3 Complete the sentences:

  a И́мам една́ _____.

  b Ще бъ́дем в хоте́л Оде́са до _____ (04.06.).

  c Джим _____ да мо́же да пъту́ва на два́йсет и вто́ри юли.

  d И́ма биле́ти за _____ (13.08).

  e Вси́чки е́втини биле́ти са _____.

  f На добъ́р пъ́т и прия́тно _____!

Now can you:

• say *on* with days of the week?
• remember the names of all the months?

178

- form ordinal numbers and give the date?
- use prepositions in time expressions?
- count in hundreds from one hundred to a thousand?
- recognize passive participles used as adjectives?

12

Почáкай, не порѣчвай óще!
Wait, don't order yet!

In this unit you will learn:

- How to use negative imperatives to tell people not to do things
- How to choose between two verbs describing the same situation
- How to talk about being on time
- How to select a table in a café or restaurant using spatial prepositions

---

Dialogue 1

🔊 **CD 2, TR 9–10**

Nadya and Milena are looking for a table in a café.

Милéна	Нáдя, елá! Тук и́ма свобóдна мáса.
Нáдя	Не оби́чам да ся́дам до вратáта.
Милéна	Хáйде да сéднем до прозóреца тогáва.
Нáдя	Добрé, каквó ще порѣчаме?
Милéна	Не порѣчвай óще. Николáй тря́бва да дóйде след мáлко. Да го почáкаме.
Нáдя	Ня́мам ни́що проти́в, но той ви́наги закъсня́ва.
Милéна	Такá ли? Надя́вам се, че днес ня́ма да закъснéе. Нóся му два англи́йски учéбника.
Нáдя	Той ня́ма да дóйде за учéбниците, а за да те ви́ди.
Милéна	Каквó и́скаш да кáжеш?

На́дя	Не ви́ждаш ли, че те харе́сва?
Миле́на	О, не зна́я, мо́же би . . . Все едно́, не оби́чам да ча́кам.
На́дя	Не сé опла́квай! (*Milena takes out her mobile.*) Какво́ пра́виш?
Миле́на	Ще се оба́дя на Никола́й и ще го попи́там защо́ не и́два.
На́дя	Неде́й да се оба́ждаш! Поча́кай о́ще ма́лко. Си́гурна съм, че ще до́йде. А, е́то го, и́два.
Никола́й	Здраве́йте, моми́чета. Извине́те за закъсне́нието. Отда́вна ли ме ча́кате?
На́дя	Не, са́мо от две мину́ти.
Миле́на	(*Significantly.*) Ка́кто ка́зва На́дя, ти ви́наги си то́чен . . .
Никола́й	Ха-ха! На́дя и́ма чу́вство за ху́мор.
На́дя	Ха́йде, ня́ма ли да се́днеш?
Никола́й	Ще се́дна, разби́ра се. Оби́чам да ся́дам до ху́бави моми́чета!

Не оби́чам да ся́дам до врата́та.	*I don't like sitting by the door.*
Ха́йде да се́днем до прозо́реца тога́ва.	*Come on, let's sit by the window then.*
Не поръ́чвай о́ще.	*Don't order yet.*
Никола́й тря́бва да до́йде след ма́лко.	*Nikolai should be coming soon.*
Да го поча́каме.	*Let's wait for him.*
той ви́наги закъсня́ва	*he's always late*
днес ня́ма да закъсне́е	*today he won't be late*
Но́ся му два англи́йски уче́бника.	*I'm bringing him two English textbooks.*
Той ня́ма да до́йде за уче́бниците.	*He won't be coming for the textbooks.*
за да те ви́ди	*(in order) to see you*
Не ви́ждаш ли, че те харе́сва?	*Can't you see he likes you?*
мо́же би	*maybe*
все едно́	*all the same*
Ще се оба́дя на Никола́й.	*I'm going to phone Nikolai.*
ще го попи́там защо́ не и́два	*I'll ask him why he isn't coming*
Неде́й да се оба́ждаш.	*Don't ring.*
Поча́кай о́ще ма́лко.	*Wait a bit longer.*

Си́гурна съм, че ще до́йде.	*I'm sure he'll come.*
Извине́те за закъсне́нието.	*Sorry I'm late.*
Отда́вна ли ме ча́кате?	*Have you been waiting long for me?*
Ка́кто ка́зва На́дя, ти ви́наги си то́чен ...	*As Nadya says, you are always punctual ...*
Ха-ха!	*Ha-ha!*
чу́вство за ху́мор	*sense of humour*
ня́ма ли да се́днеш?	*won't you sit down?*
Ще се́дна.	*I will sit down.*

ГАРАЖ
НЕ ПАРКИРАЙ

1 Questions

a Какво́ не оби́ча На́дя?

b Защо́ Миле́на ка́зва на На́дя да не поръ́чва о́ще?

c Защо́ споре́д На́дя ще до́йде Никола́й?

d Защо́ Миле́на и́ска да се оба́ди на Никола́й?

e И́ма ли Миле́на моби́лен телефо́н (джи́есе́м)?

f Къде́ оби́ча да ся́да Никола́й?

2 True or false?

a Никола́й тря́бва да до́йде след полови́н час.

b На́дя ка́зва, че Никола́й ви́наги е то́чен.

c Никола́й харе́сва Миле́на.

d Миле́на ня́ма ни́що проти́в да ча́ка.

e На́дя е си́гурна, че Никола́й ще до́йде.

182

How do you say it?

◀) CD 2, TR 11

- Saying *Don't* (do something)

Не сé оплáквай!/Не сé оплáквайте!	*Don't complain.*
Недéй да поръ́чваш!	
Недéйте да поръ́чвате! }	*Don't order.*

- Saying *Come on!* and *Come on, let's . . .!*

Хáйде!	*Come on!*
Хáйде да сéднем!	*Come on, let's sit down!*

- Asking someone to wait

Почáкай/почáкайте мáлко!	*Wait a minute.*

- Excusing yourself for being late

Извинéте за закъснéнието.	*Forgive me for being late.*
Извиня́вайте за	*I am sorry for the delay.*
закъснéнието.	

- Asking someone to be more explicit

Каквó и́скаш да кáжеш?	*What do you mean?*

- Saying *Maybe*

Мóже би ще дóйда.	*Maybe/Perhaps I'll come.*

- Saying *by* and *behind*

до вратáта	*by the door*
зад вратáта	*behind the door*

Grammar

1 Verb twinning

If you look carefully at the dialogue, you will notice that it contains a number of verbs that differ slightly in Bulgarian, but which are translated in a similar way in English. Here, with a couple added, is a list of these 'twinned' verbs in alphabetical order with the significant differences highlighted:

A	B	
ви́ждам	(да) ви́дя	*to see*
закъсня́вам	(да) закъсне́я	*to be late*
и́двам	(да) до́йда	*to come*
извиня́вам се	(да) се извиня́	*to apologize*
ка́звам	(да) ка́жа	*to say*
оба́ждам се	(да) се оба́дя	*to ring, call*
пома́гам	(да) помо́гна	*to help*
поръ́чвам	(да) поръ́чам	*to order*
пра́вя	(да) напра́вя	*to do, make*
прода́вам	(да) прода́м	*to sell*
ся́дам	(да) се́дна	*to sit*
харе́свам	(да) харе́сам	*to like*
ча́кам	(да) поча́кам	*to wait*

In Bulgarian, an action can be seen from two different points of view, or *aspects*: either as incomplete and still going on (column A) or as momentary and complete (column B). We refer to verbs in column A as imperfective and those in column B as perfective verbs. In fact, you can think of most Bulgarian verbs as having a 'twin' with which it forms an 'aspectual pair'.

Insight

In the English–Bulgarian vocabulary we have, where appropriate, given both verbs.

When you come across a new verb you should try and learn it together with its twin.

Formally, the verbs in a pair may differ in one of four main ways:

(a) Imperfective verbs (A) often have the suffix **-ва-**, as in закъсня́**ва**м, ка́з**ва**м and поръ́ч**ва**м.
(b) Perfective verbs (B) often have the suffix **-на-**, as in се́д**на**, запо́ч**на** and ста́**на** (*to get up*).

(c) Perfective verbs frequently have extra letters (a prefix) added on the front as in **напра́вя**, **по**пи́там and **по**ча́кам.

(d) There may be some other internal alternation of letters, often a change of vowel or consonant, as in разби́рам – (да) разбера́, затва́рям – (да) затво́ря (*to close*), оти́вам – (да) оти́да (*to go*), оба́ждам се – (да) се оба́дя (*to ring, call*) and разгле́ждам – (да) разгле́дам (*to take a look at, inspect*).

Some verbs such as **обя́двам, организи́рам, парки́рам** and **пъту́вам** have the same form for both imperfective and perfective. They are identical twins!

Occasionally, two very different verbs form an imperfective/perfective pair, **и́двам** and **(да) до́йда,** for example. In Dialogue 1, remember, you came across Е́то го, **и́два** and Никола́й тря́бва да **до́йде** след ма́лко.

2 Imperfective and perfective: which to use when

Which of a pair with the present tense?

In the present tense, you always use an imperfective verb because the action is still going on:

Какво́ пра́виш?	*What are you doing?*
Какво́ ка́зва той?	*What is he saying?*
Ви́ждаш ли табе́лката?	*Can you see the notice?*

You also use an imperfective verb when making generalizations:

Г-н Джо́нсън оби́ча ху́баво ви́но.	*Mr Johnson loves good wine.*
Никола́й ви́наги закъсня́ва.	*Nikolai is always late.*

You normally cannot use perfective verbs to describe actions in the present tense. The only exception is when you envisage a completed action that is not really taking place yet – it is still potential. This happens:

(a) when you say that you *want to, have to* or *can* do something using verbs like **и́скам (да), тря́бва (да), мо́же (да)**:

И́скам **да поръ́чам** сала́та.	*I want to order a salad.*
Тря́бва **да оти́да** в ба́нката.	*I have to go to the bank.*
Мо́же ли **да се́дна** до Вас?	*May I sit next to you?*

(b) after words such as **когато** (*when*) and **ако** (*if*) indicating that an action will only take place if certain conditions are fulfilled, as in **когато дойде** (*when he comes*) and **ако дойде** (*if he comes*).

(c) after **за да** (*in order to*) or just **да** on its own, when there is a sense of purpose or a need to 'get something done'. Here again there is an emphasis on the completion of an action:

Той идва, **за да те види.**	*He is coming (in order) to see you.*
Ще се обадя **да го попитам.**	*I'll ring to ask him.*

Which of a pair with the future tense?

You will usually need to use the perfective twin when talking about future events:

Ще седна до прозореца.	*I'll take a seat by the window.*
Утре **няма да закъснея.**	*Tomorrow I won't be late.*
Ще направя както ми казвате.	*I'll do what you tell me.*
Ще Ви донеса менюто.	*I'll bring you the menu.*

In all these examples, you are concerned with one specific occasion and concentrating on getting something done.

Sometimes, however, when you are not concerned with one specific occasion or not concentrating on getting something done, you use the imperfective twin:

(a) Винаги **ще ставам** рано.	*I'll always get up early.*
(b) **Ще чакам** до 11 часа.	*I'll wait until 11 o'clock.*

Here you are referring either (*a*) to something you are going to do regularly in the future, or (*b*) to something that is going to go on for some time.

3 With да and without

The verbs that have been listed with (**да**) are all perfective verbs. They were listed in this way so as to indicate that perfective verbs cannot be used without a 'prop' such as **да** (or **когато** or **ако**) in the present tense.

You should note, however, that **да** is not used exclusively with perfective verbs. In generalizations, when there is no concentration on the need to complete an action or achieve a result, it can also be used with imperfectives. Thus you can say **обичам да помагам** *I like to help* and **не обичам да сядам до прозореца** *I don't like sitting by the window*. In both of these cases, you are making generalizations.

4 Do and don't

If you look back at Unit 7 where – among other things – you learnt how to give instructions, you will see that almost all the verbs were used in their perfective forms: **вземете си!, дайте ми!, плати!** etc. In fact, you almost always use the perfective twin in positive instructions, when you are telling someone to do something specific on a particular occasion:

Седнете до прозореца!	*Sit by the window.*
Затвори вратата!	*Close the door.*
Направи кафе!	*Make some coffee.*
Обади се!	*(Do) ring/call!*

You use the imperfective twin, however, in negative instructions, when you want to stop someone from doing something, no matter whether it is on a specific occasion or as a general rule:

Не сядайте до прозореца!	*Don't sit by the window.*
Не затваряйте вратата!	*Don't close the door.*
Не прави кафе!	*Don't make any coffee.*
Не се обаждай!	*Don't ring/call!*

Almost the only time you use the imperfective twin in positive instructions is when you issue a general prohibition valid not just on one particular occasion. You will find the following notice on doors, for example:

Затваряйте вратата!   *Close the door.* (i.e. always)

You will also find that Bulgarians use the imperfective **Извинявайте много!** in preference to the perfective **Извинете!** for *Excuse me!* when they want to be especially polite or insistent.

5 Недей(те) да *Don't*!

Instead of using **не** with the special command (imperative) forms of the verb, you can tell someone not to do something by using **недей да** or **недейте да**:

Недей да спираш тук!	*Don't stop here.*
Недейте да спирате тук!	
Недей да закъсняваш!	*Don't be late.*
Недейте да закъснявате!	

You can see that this is followed by the normal present tense endings of the *you* form of the verb, in the singular or plural as the occasion demands. The verb must be in the imperfective, remember, because it is a negative command. You will also have noticed that, in Bulgarian, imperative forms are usually followed by an exclamation mark, thereby emphasizing the urgency of the situation.

(Don't forget that there is a list of imperatives in the Appendix and that positive command forms are explained in Unit 7.)

6 Обичам and харесвам *To love* and *to like*

Both **обичам** and **харесвам** may be translated as *I like*:

Обичам класическа музика.	*I like/love classical music.*
Харесвам тази музика.	*I like/love this music.*
Обичам сладолед.	*I like/love ice cream.*
	(i.e. all ice cream)
Харесвам този сладолед.	*I like/love this ice cream.*

As you can see from these examples, however, **харесвам** is normally used with individual, specified things, while **обичам** is used for more general statements. But when you use **обичам** with people it always means *I love*:

Обичам това момиче.	*I love that girl.*
Обичам те!	*I love you!*

When **харесвам** is used with people it simply means *I like*, nothing more exciting, alas!

Not true! It can mean "to fancy someone"! But it's context dependent.

188

Do remember, though, that when you want to say you like doing something, you have to use **обичам да**, as in **обичам** (or more likely **не обичам**) **да чакам** I like/don't like waiting.

Exercises

1 In the short dialogue that follows you will find the 'twin' verbs for to leave: **оставям** (**а-/я**-pattern and imperfective) and (**да**) **оставя** (**и**-pattern and perfective). First, work out which is which and note how they are used:

В хотела	
Николай	Ако искаш, остави лаптопа (laptop) в стаята.
Милена	Няма да го оставя.
Николай	Защо?
Милена	Виж, има табелка: Не оставяйте ценности в стаята! (Don't leave valuables in the room.)
Николай	Вярно. Не е добра идея. Недей да го оставяш. Остави само чадъра.

Now complete the following sentences with the appropriate verb for to leave:

a _____ тази тежка чанта вкъщи (at home)!

b Сигурно ще вали. Няма да _____ чадъра вкъщи.

c Недей да _____ вратата отворена.

d Не _____ ценности в стаята на хотела.

e (To the taxi driver.) _____ ме пред хотела, моля.

2 Here are some common Bulgarian notices with their English equivalents:

a

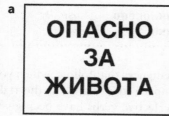

ОПАСНО ЗА ЖИВОТА

DANGER OF DEATH!

b

НЕ Е ВХОД

NO ENTRY

**ПАЗЕТЕ
ЧИСТОТА!**

NO LITTER!

**СНИМАНЕТО
ЗАБРАНЕНО**

NO PHOTOGRAPHY!

**СЛУЖЕБЕН
ПАРКИНГ**

OFFICIAL PARKING

**ПУШЕНЕТО
ЗАБРАНЕНО**

NO SMOKING!

Now see if you can match the notices with these negative imperatives, which have been translated literally:

i	Не влизайте!	*Don't go in.*
ii	Не пипай!	*Don't touch.*
iii	Не паркирай!	*Don't park.*
iv	Не пушете!	*Don't smoke.*
v	Не хвърляйте отпадъци!	*Don't throw litter.*
vi	Не правете снимки!	*Don't take pictures.*

Insight

The following time words usually go with imperfective verbs:

вѝнаги	*always*	обикновѐно	*usually*
чѐсто	*often*	ря́дко	*rarely*

---

3 Look for these time words in the sentences that follow, which you should complete, choosing the imperfective verb and the right personal ending. (For once, the perfective verbs have been given without **да**!):

a Г-н Кóлинс чéсто (помáгам/помóгна) на свóята женá.

b Нúе вúнаги (стáвам/стáна) (*to get up*) рáно.

c Обикновéно Нáдя (úдвам/дóйда) на рáбота в óсем и половúна.

d Мáйкъл Джóнсън рáдко (порýчвам/порáчам) вúно за обáд.

4 Here, Nevena is talking to another receptionist and enviously watching a very smart lady enter the restaurant. Nevena is describing what she sees using imperfective verbs. Try to complete her story choosing the correct form of the perfective verb after **úскам да . . .**, **хáйде да . . .**, **за да . . .**, **ще** and **мóга да**. (Use the English–Bulgarian vocabulary to track down the twins.)

Невéна Виж, úдва еднá мнóго красúва женá. Úскам да (*I, see*) úма ли срéща. Ще (*you, come*) ли с мéне? Éто, úдва едúн хýбав мъж. Те влúзат в ресторáнта. Хáйде да (*we, go in*) и нúе. Те сáдат на мáсата до прозóреца и избúрат нéщо за пúене. Úскам да (*we, sit*) на тáзи мáса и нúе да (*we, choose*) нéщо. Мóжеш ли да ги (*you, see*)? Аз ги вúждам – порýчват джин. Хáйде да (*we, order*) и ниé два джúна. Сегá мъжýт се обáжда по джúесéма. А тя каквó прáви? Виж, и тя úска да (*she, make a call*), но джúесéмът ѝ не рабóти. Ще (*she, take a picture*) снúмка на ресторáнта. Úскам да (*I, go*) пó-блúзо, за да (*I, hear*) на какýв езúк говóрят. Почáкай ме мáлко . . . Красúвата женá е америкáнка! Óще ýтре ще (*I begin*) да ýча англúйски!

5 Read this passage, following Nadya's thoughts when she fails to make a meeting with Milena:

Милéна **ще дóйде**, **ще вúди**, че не съм там и **ще влéзе** в сладкáрницата. **Ще вúди** свобóдна мáса и **ще сéдне**. **Ще избéре** (*choose*) нéщо за закýска и веднáга **ще порýча**. Сервитьóрката **ще донесé** кафé и сáндвич сáмо за нéя. **Нáма да ме почáка** дори (*even*) пет минýти! **Ще платú**, **ще стáне** (*get up*) и ще отúде в ЦУМ – без мéне!

Now imagine you are observing Milena and, beginning with **Éто**, recount what you see, turning all the verbs into the present. You will need to replace each perfective verb with its imperfective twin.

6 Оби́чам or **харе́свам?** Choose one of the verbs to complete the sentences:

a Неве́на _____ да гово́ри с чужденци́.

b Никола́й _____ Миле́на.

c Г-н Ко́линс _____ да игра́е голф.

d На́дя _____ та́зи изло́жба.

e Г-жа́ Ко́линс _____ кафе́ без за́хар.

f Ви́е си́гурно ще _____ то́зи град. (Use the perfective: (**да**) **харе́сам**)

g Те _____ бъ́лгарските специалите́ти.

h Не _____ да ча́кам.

i Ма́йкъл Джо́нсън _____ бъ́лгарско ви́но.

j Миле́на ще _____ то́зи нов при́нтер. (Again you need (**да**) **харе́сам**)

k Никола́й не _____ то́зи уче́бник.

Another small step forward

🔊 CD 2, TR 12–13

Dialogue 2 Внима́ние! *Danger! Watch Out!*

Michael Johnson has a hard time on his own in out-of-season Borovets.

Полица́й	Мо́ля, не парки́райте тук. Опа́сно е. Ви́жте табе́лката.
г-н Джо́нсън	Ви́ждам я, но не я́ разби́рам. Аз съм чужде́нец. Какво́ зна́чи «Внима́ние! Па́дащи предме́ти»?
Полица́й	Това́ зна́чи, че хоте́лът е в ремо́нт и поня́кога па́дат те́жки предме́ти. Мо́же не́що да па́дне върху́ кола́та Ви.
г-н Джо́нсън	Така́ ли? Къде́ мо́же да парки́рам? Тъ́рся рестора́нт, но не ви́ждам па́ркинг нао́коло.
Полица́й	Па́ркингът е зад хоте́ла. Ще ви́дите табе́лката. В кой рестора́нт оти́вате?
г-н Джо́нсън	Не зна́я. Каже́те ми кой рестора́нт е на́й-добъ́р.
Полица́й	Предла́гам Ви да оти́дете в ма́лкия рестора́нт до ли́фта. Сега́ ня́ма мно́го тури́сти и ми́сля, че ня́ма да ча́кате дъ́лго.
г-н Джо́нсън	Благодаря́ за съве́та. Ще напра́вя ка́кто ми ка́звате.

(*Later, in the small restaurant by the ski lift, Mr Johnson is about to take a seat at a corner table.*)

Сервитьóрка	Извинявайте мнóго, господúне, но не сядайте на тáзи мáса, акó обúчате. Мáсата в ъ́гъла е запáзена.
г-н Джóнсън	Съжалявам, грéшката е мóя. Сегá вúждам табéлката. Изглéжда днес прáвя всúчко не кáкто трябва.
Сервитьóрка	Заповядайте, седнéте до прозóреца. Товá е мáса за непушáчи. Имá чудéсен úзглед към планинáта. Сегá ще Ви донесá менюто. Ще дóйда за пор*ъ*чката след катó изберéте.
г-н Джóнсън	Мóля, недéйте да бъ́рзате. Аз избúрам мнóго бáвно, защóто не разбúрам всúчко.
Сервитьóрка	Тогáва úдвам веднáга. Ще Ви помóгна да изберéте.
г-н Джóнсън	Благодаря мнóго. Запóчвам да харéсвам Бóровец.

опáсно	*dangerous*
внимáние!	*danger!, watch out!, attention!*
пáдащи предмéти	*falling objects*
понякога	*sometimes*
пáдам, -даш	*to fall*
тéжък, тéжка	*heavy*
(да) пáдна, -неш	*to fall*
такá ли?	*really? is that so?*
пáркинг	*car park, parking lot*
наóколо	*nearby*
зад	*behind*
лифт	*ski/chairlift*
ъ́гъл	*corner*
запáзен	*reserved*
непушáч	*non-smoker*
úзглед	*view*
(да) донесá, -сéш	*to bring*
пор'ьчка	*order*
избúрам, -раш	*to choose*
(да) изберá, -рéш	*to choose*
влúзам, -заш	*to enter*
вход	*entrance*
живóт	*life*

забране́но	*forbidden, not allowed*
отпа́дък, -ъци	*litter, rubbish*
пу́ша, -шиш	*to smoke*
пу́шене	*smoking*
служе́бен, -бна	*official, for staff only*
хвъ́рлям, -ляш	*to throw*
чистота́	*cleanliness*

Test yourself

1 To see how well you have understood Dialogue 2, answer the following questions:

a Защо́ г-н Джо́нсън не тря́бва да парки́ра до табе́лката?
b Къде́ е па́ркингът?
c Защо́ полица́ят предла́га ма́лкия рестора́нт?
d Защо́ г-н Джо́нсън не мо́же да се́дне на ма́сата в ъ́гъла?
e Как г-н Джо́нсън ка́зва на сервитьо́рката да не бъ́рза?
f Защо́ сервитьо́рката ще помо́гне на г-н Джо́нсън да избере́ не́що за я́дене?

2 Complete the sentences:

a Мо́ля, не _____ тук.
b Не _____ на та́зи ма́са, ако́ оби́чате.
c Ма́сата в ъ́гъла е _____.
d Мо́ля, _____ да бъ́рзате.

3 Put the following phrases in two columns according to the type of verb in bold face – perfective or imperfective:

ни́е **оби́чаме** ди́ско, ха́йде **да се́днем**, не **поръ́чвай**, **надя́вам се**, ще **харе́саш** то́зи град, неде́й **да и́дваш** ра́но, отда́вна ли **ча́кате**?, той тря́бва **да до́йде**, ще **напра́вя** кафе́, и́скам **да помо́гна**, мо́же ли **да ви́дя**?, какво́ ще **ка́жеш**?, ху́баво е да **пома́гаме** на прия́тели.

194

Now can you:

- tell someone not to do something?
- choose from a pair of verbs describing the same event?
- remember the time words which usually go with imperfective verbs?
- correctly use the Bulgarian words for *I love* and *I like*?
- use the Bulgarian for *by* and *behind*?
- recognize some common Bulgarian notices?

13

Как да стигнем до хотел «Одеса»?

How can we get to the Odessa Hotel?

In this unit you will learn:

- How to ask the way
- How to give and understand directions
- How to talk about events in the past

Dialogue 1

◀ CD 2, TR 14–15

Mr and Mrs Collins have just arrived in Varna. Mr Collins stops the car so Mrs Collins can ask a policeman the way.

г-жа́ Ко́линс	Извине́те, мо́жете ли да ни ка́жете как да сти́гнем до хоте́л «Оде́са»?
Полица́й	Хоте́л «Оде́са» е бли́зо до це́нтъра. Ка́райте напра́во и ще сти́гнете до еди́н площа́д. На не́го и́ма църква. Ще зави́ете наля́во и ще ка́рате до пъ́рвия светофа́р. На светофа́ра зави́йте надя́сно. Ще пресече́те еди́н булева́рд и ще сти́гнете до вхо́да на еди́н парк. Това́ е Мо́рската гради́на. Хоте́л «Оде́са» е вдя́сно, срещу́ Мо́рската гради́на.
г-жа́ Ко́линс	Благодаря́ мно́го.
Полица́й	Ня́ма защо́. Ако́ загу́бите пъ́тя, попи́тайте пак.

196

(Mr and Mrs Collins do lose their way and it is rather late when they eventually arrive at the hotel.)

г-жá Кóлинс	Дóбър вéчер. Ѝмаме запáзена стáя в тóзи хотéл.
Администрáторка	Дóбър вéчер. Ѝмето, мóля?
г-жá Кóлинс	Джордж и Виктóрия Кóлинс.
Администрáторка	Да, ѝма стáя за вас. Добрé дошлѝ! Не вѝ очáквахме тóлкова късно. Имахте ли проблéми по пътя?
г-жá Кóлинс	Не, пътýването бéше приятно. Проблéмите започнаха, когáто пристѝгнахме във Вáрна, защóто нямахме кáрта на градá.
Администрáторка	Когá пристѝгнахте?
г-жá Кóлинс	Пристѝгнахме предѝ óколо два чáса, към сéдем часá. Бéше óще свéтло.
Администрáторка	Не попѝтахте ли за пътя?
г-жá Кóлинс	Да, попѝтахме едѝн полицáй. Кáрахме напрáво, но не стѝгнахме до площáда с църквата. Ѝлицата бéше в ремóнт и ѝмаше отклонéние. На слéдващата ýлица завѝхме налявo и загýбихме пътя.
Администрáторка	Защó не попѝтахте пак?
г-жá Кóлинс	В товá врéме започна да валѝ и нямаше хóра по ýлиците. Нямаше когó да попѝтаме.
Администрáторка	Как намéрихте пътя?
г-жá Кóлинс	Едѝн шофьóр на таксѝ ни помóгна.
Администрáторка	Сѝгурно сте уморéни и глáдни. Ресторáнтът е óще отвóрен.
г-жá Кóлинс	О, да. Умѝраме за чáша чай.
Администрáторка	Заповядайте, ресторáнтът е на пáртера вляво.
г-жá Кóлинс	Благодаря мнóго. Кудé мóжем да остáвим багáжа?
Администрáторка	Пѝколото ще напрáви товá. Стáята ви е на четвъртия етáж, коридóрът вдясно. Приятна почѝвка! Лéка нощ!

The city crest of Varna

администра́торка	*receptionist*
как да сти́гнем до	*how we can get to*
ка́райте напра́во	*drive straight ahead*
ще сти́гнете до еди́н площа́д	*you'll get to a square*
цъ́рква	*church*
ще зави́ете наля́во	*you (will) turn left*
светофа́р	*traffic lights*
надя́сно	*to the right*
ще пресече́те	*you (will) cross*
Мо́рската гради́на	*the Marine Park*
вдя́сно	*on the right*
ако́ загу́бите пъ́тя . . .	*if you lose the way . . .*
И́махте ли пробле́ми по пъ́тя?	*Did you have any problems on the way?*
пъту́ването бе́ше прия́тно	*the journey was pleasant*
Пробле́мите запо́чнаха, кога́то присти́гнахме във Ва́рна.	*The problems started when we arrived in Varna.*
ня́махме	*we didn't have*
преди́ о́коло два ча́са	*about two hours ago*
към се́дем часа́	*at about 7 o'clock*
бе́ше о́ще све́тло	*it was still light*
Не попи́тахте ли за пъ́тя?	*Didn't you ask the way?*
попи́тахме еди́н полица́й	*we asked a policeman*
ка́рахме напра́во	*we drove straight ahead*
не сти́гнахме до площа́да с цъ́рквата	*we didn't get to the square with the church*
у́лицата бе́ше в ремо́нт	*the road was under repair*
и́маше отклоне́ние	*there was a diversion*
зави́хме наля́во	*we turned left*
загу́бихме пъ́тя	*we lost the way*
запо́чна да вали́	*it started raining*
ня́маше хо́ра по у́лиците	*there weren't any people out in the streets*
Как наме́рихте пъ́тя?	*How did you find the way?*
Еди́н шофьо́р на такси́ ни помо́гна.	*A taxi driver helped us.*
Си́гурно сте умо́рени и гла́дни.	*You must be tired and hungry.*

198

Умираме за чаша чай.	*We are dying for a cup of tea.*
вляво	*on the left*
Лека нощ!	*Good night!*

1 Questions

Imagine you are Mrs Collins: see if you can answer the questions she and her husband are asked on arrival at the hotel:

a Към колко часа пристигнахте?
b Как беше пътуването ви?
c Защо имахте проблеми?
d Кога започнаха проблемите ви?
e Тъмно ли беше, когато пристигнахте?
f Защо не стигнахте до площада с църквата?

2 True or false?

a Г-н и г-жа Колинс ще завият наляво и ще стигнат до една църква.
b Хотел «Одеса» е вляво, зад Морската градина.
c Г-н и г-жа Колинс пристигнаха във Варна към шест и половина.
d Един шофьор на такси им помогна.
e Ресторантът е в коридора вдясно.

How do you say it?

• Asking the way

Как да стигна до гарата?	*How do I get to the station?*
В коя посока е пощата?	*In which direction is the post office?*
Можете ли да ми покажете пътя за . . . ?	*Can you show me the way to . . . ?*

◀) CD 2, TR 16

• Giving directions

Карайте направо./Вървете направо.	*Drive straight on./Go straight on.*

Завийте наляво.	*Turn to the left.*
Завийте надясно.	*Turn to the right.*
Върнете се обратно.	*Go back.*
В обратната посока	*In the opposite direction.*

- Saying *on the left/on the right*

Третата врата вляво.	*The third door on the left.*
Коридорът вдясно.	*The corridor on the right.*
Фоайето е вдясно/	*The foyer is on the right/*
вляво от асансьора.	*on the left of the lift.*

- Giving approximate times

Пристигнахме преди около половин час.	*We arrived about half an hour ago.*
Стигнахме Варна за около шест часа.	*We reached Varna in about six hours.*
Пощата е на около пет минути.	*The post office is about five minutes away.*
Започна да вали към три часа.	*It started to rain towards three o'clock.*
Николай ще дойде към единайсет часа.	*Nikolai will come towards eleven o'clock.*

- Saying *I am tired* and *Good night*

Уморен съм/уморена съм.	*I am tired.*
Уморени сме.	*We are tired.*
Лека нощ!	*Good night!*

Grammar

1 Past tense

Verbs describing past events also have special endings. In the following sentences, which take you from the *I* form to the *they* form, these endings (-х, -, -, -хме, -хте, -ха) and the preceding vowel have been highlighted. You will see that in the *you* (familiar) and *he/she/it* forms there is no special ending added to the vowel:

Купих нова програма за компютъра.	*I bought a new computer program.*

Ти пи**та** ли къде́ е площа́дът?		*Did you ask where the square is?*				

Ти пи**та** ли къде́ е площа́дът?   *Did you ask where the square is?*

Тя помо́г**на** на г-жа́ Ко́линс.   *She helped Mrs Collins.*

Присти́г**нахме** във Ва́рна   *We arrived in Varna about*
към се́дем часа́.   *7 o'clock.*

Сти́г**нахте** ли до площа́да?   *Did you get to the square?*

Деца́та игра́**ха** до къ́сно.   *The children played until late.*

The endings are the same for all three verb patterns, but they are added to a variety of vowels and this makes forming the past tense in Bulgarian a little tricky. You will, however, be able to take things gradually, learning in this and the following units which vowels go with which groups of verbs. To make things easier we will move from the regular to the less regular forms.

(a) Verbs that add past endings to -**a**-

With all **a**-pattern verbs (Conjugation 3) like пи́т**ам**, ка́р**ам** *to drive*, (**да**) разгле́д**ам** *to look at* you replace the -**м** of the *I* form with the special past endings. So пи́та-**м**, which is the imperfective twin of (**да**) попи́т**ам**, becomes:

(аз)	пи́т**ах**	*I asked*	(ни́е)	пи́т**ахме**	*we asked*
(ти)	пи́т**а**	*you asked*	(ви́е)	пи́т**ахте**	*you asked*
(той)			(те)	пи́т**аха**	*they asked*
(тя) }	пи́т**а**	*he/she/it asked*			
(то)					

Insight

You will notice that there is no difference between the past той пи́т**а** and the present той пи́т**а**. You therefore have to rely on the context to tell you whether it means *he asked*, *he asks* or *he is asking*.

You form the past tense of some **e**-pattern verbs in the same way: (**да**) сти́гна, (**да**) присти́гна, (**да**) запо́чна, (**да**) помо́гна, for example. You can recognize this group by the presence of -**на** in the dictionary form:

Сти́г**нах** до хоте́ла.   *I reached the hotel.*

Вче́ра Никола́й запо́ч**на** да   *Yesterday Nikolai began to*
у́чи англи́йски.   *study English.*

Помо́гнахме на америка́неца.   *We helped the American.*
Присти́гнаха къ́сно във Ва́рна.   *They arrived late in Varna.*

(b) Verbs adding past endings to **-и-**

Most **и**-pattern verbs (Conjugation 2) have the vowel **-и-** before the past endings: (**да**) **загу́бя** *to lose*, (**да**) **ку́пя**, (**да**) **наме́ря**, (**да**) **напра́вя** as well as **пра́вя**, **рабо́тя**, **тъ́рся**, etc.:

(аз)	ку́пих	*I bought*	(ни́е)	ку́пихме	*we bought*
(ти)	ку́пи	*you bought*	(ви́е)	ку́пихте	*you bought*
(той)			(те)	ку́пиха	*they bought*
(тя)	ку́пи	*he/she/it*			
(то)		*bought*			

Тъ́рсих г-н Анто́нов,   *I looked for Mr Antonov*
 но не го **наме́рих**.   *but didn't find him.*
На́дя **напра́ви** кафе́   *Nadya made coffee for*
 за вси́чки.   *everyone.*
Какво́ **загу́бихте**?   *What did you lose?*

(c) For the past tense forms of **е**-pattern verbs in **-и́я** and **-а́я** like (**да**) **зави́я** *to turn*, **пи́я** *to drink*, **игра́я** *to play* you simply replace the **-я** of the first person *I* form by the appropriate past endings. The resulting forms look just like the ones we saw in (*a*) and (*b*):

Та́зи су́трин **пих** мля́ко.   *This morning I drank some milk.*
Кола́та **зави́** надя́сно.   *The car turned to the right.*
Деца́та **игра́ха** до къ́сно.   *The children played until late.*

2 И́мах *I had* and ня́мах *I didn't have*

When describing past situations – states rather than actions – both **и́мам** and **ня́мам** have different past endings in the *you* (familiar) and *he/she/it* forms:

(аз)	и́мах/ня́мах	*I had/didn't have*	(ни́е)	и́махме/ня́махме	*we had/didn't have*
(ти)	и́маше/ ня́маше	*you had/ didn't have*	(ви́е)	и́махте/ня́махте	*you had/ didn't have*
(той)		*he*	(те)	и́маха/ня́маха	*they had/didn't have*
(тя)	и́маше/ня́маше	*she*			
(то)		*it* *had/didn't have*			

202

(You will find out more about these past forms in Unit 17.)

3 Аз бях *I was*

(аз)	**бях**	*I was*	(ние)	**бяхме**	*we were*
(ти)	**беше**	*you were*	(вие)	**бяхте**	*you were*
(той)			(те)	**бяха**	*they were*
(тя) }	**беше**	*he/she/it was*			
(то)					

4 When and how to use the past forms

The verb endings for the past are used when you want to describe an action that was fully completed in the past. You can use them either with the perfective or with the imperfective twin, but they tend to be used more with the perfective. There are other ways of describing past actions and you will learn about them in later units.

When describing past actions using two and more verbs linked by **да**, you should remember that only the first (main) verb needs the past endings. The verb(s) after **да** remain in the present tense:

Започна **да вали**.	*It started to rain.*
Един полицай ни помогна **да намерим** пътя.	*A policeman helped us find the way.*
В Лондон имах възможност **да видя** катедралата «Свети* Павел».	*In London, I had a chance to see St Paul's Cathedral.*

*Света (f)

5 Кой or кого *Who or whom*

Кого *whom* is a form of **кой** *who* and is used in the non-subject position:

Subject position			Non-subject position	
Кой попита?	*Who asked?*	but	**Кого** попитахте?	*Whom did you ask?*
Кой помогна?	*Who helped?*	but	**На кого** помогнахте?	*Whom did you help?*
			Нямаше кого да питаме.	*There was nobody (whom) we could ask.*

6 Еди́н/една́/едно́: An alternative for *a* or *a certain*

Very often **еди́н/една́/едно́** (see Unit 2) doesn't mean *one* in a counting sense. Instead it can be an equivalent of the English *a* or *a certain* as in:

Ще сти́гнете до **еди́н** площа́д. *You'll come to a square.*
Еди́н шофьо́р на такси́ *A taxi driver helped us.*
ни помо́гна.

You will also find the plural form **едни́** meaning *some* or *certain*:

Едни́ па́ркинги са по́-ма́лки, *Some/certain car parks are*
а дру́ги са по́-голе́ми. *smaller and others are larger.*

7 (Да) пресека́ у́лицата *To cross the street*: к changes to ч

Verbs with a **-к-** immediately before the ending of the *I* and the *they* forms change the **-к-** to **-ч-** in all the other persons:

(аз)	ще пресека́	*I will cross*	(ни́е)	ще пресече́м	*we will cross*
(ти)	ще пресече́ш	*you will cross*	(ви́е)	ще пресече́те	*you will cross*
(той)			(те)	ще пресека́т	*they will cross*
(тя)	ще пресече́	*he/she/it*			
(то)		*will cross*			

Exercises

1 Match the following questions and answers:

i На ко́лко мину́ти **a** Ела́те към се́дем часа́.
е га́рата? **b** За отклоне́нието
ii Напра́во ли е къмпинг зави́йте надя́сно на
«Оа́зис»? тре́тата у́лица.
iii Към ко́лко часа́ да **c** Тъ́рся секрета́рката
до́йдем? на фи́рмата.

iv Кого́ тъ́рсите?

v В та́зи посо́ка ли е цъ́рквата «Света́ Со́фия»?

vi Къде́ е отклоне́нието за магистра́лата (*motorway*)?

d Не, «Света́ Со́фия» е в обра́тната посо́ка.

e Га́рата е на о́коло де́сет мину́ти.

f Не, за къ́мпинг «Оа́зис» тря́бва да зави́ете наля́во.

2 To what questions might the following be answers? The important bits are highlighted!

a Запо́чна да вали́ **към 6 часа́**.

b Загу́бихме пъ́тя, **защо́то бе́ше тъ́мно**.

c Ба́нката е **вля́во от катедра́лата**.

d Пи́тахме **еди́н мъж** къде́ е магистра́лата.

e **Едно́ момче́** ни помо́гна да наме́рим пъ́тя.

f **На тре́тата у́лица** зави́хме надя́сно.

3 This exercise will help you use some key verbs in the past tense. Complete the answers following the model:

Model: И́скате ли да Ви **обясня́** къде́ живе́е г-н Анто́нов?
       Той ве́че ми **обясни́**.

a И́скате ли да **обя́дваме** за́едно?
   Аз ве́че _____

b Да **ку́пя** ли биле́ти за «Травиа́та»?
   На́дя ве́че _____

c Кога́ **ще зами́нат** г-н и г-жа́ Ко́линс?
   Те ве́че _____

d Да **напра́вя** ли кафе́?
   Неве́на ве́че _____

e Кога́ **ще запо́чне** конце́ртът?
   Той ве́че _____

f Да **попи́там** ли къде́ е магистра́лата?
   Ни́е ве́че _____

g Да **поръ́чам** ли такси́?
   Аз ве́че _____

h **Ще изпра́тиш** ли и́мейл в Че́лмсфорд?
   Никола́й ве́че _____

4 A friendly policeman tells you how to get to the museum by car:

Върнéте се по сѫщата ýлица. Ще стѝгнете до едѝн булевáрд. Завѝйте надя́сно и кáрайте напрáво. Катó стѝгнете до площáда, паркѝрайте на пáркинга и попѝтайте пак (*again*). Музéят не é далéче от площáда.

You successfully follow his instructions. Now tell your friend how you got there. You will need to put the verbs into the past and change them to the *I* form.

5 Look at the map that follows and tell a stranger how to get from the museum to the chemist's.

6 You, too, need to get to the chemist's. Having checked the instructions you gave in Exercise 5 (in the Key!), say how you and your companion drove there.

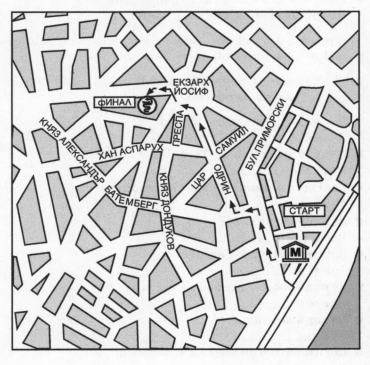

Another small step forward

🔊 CD 2, TR 17–18

Dialogue 2 В Пло́вдив *In Plovdiv*

Nadya is curious to hear about Mr Johnson's adventures in Bulgaria's second city.

На́дя	Дово́лен ли сте от престо́я в Пло́вдив?
Ма́йкъл Джо́нсън	Мно́го съм дово́лен. За ме́не бе́ше стра́шно интере́сно. Ня́мах предста́ва от бъ́лгарската исто́рия.
На́дя	И́махте ли вре́ме да разгле́дате ста́рия град?
Ма́йкъл Джо́нсън	Да, бях в на́й-интере́сните ста́ри къщи, разгле́дах Ри́мската стена́, ста́рия теа́тър и цъ́рквата «Свети́ Константи́н и Еле́на».
На́дя	Ху́баво ли бе́ше вре́мето?
Ма́йкъл Джо́нсън	Да, вре́мето бе́ше мно́го прия́тно. Не бе́ше мно́го горе́що.
На́дя	И́маше ли мно́го хо́ра?
Ма́йкъл Джо́нсън	О, да. На панаи́ра бе́ше пъ́лно с хо́ра от ця́ла Евро́па. (*Tongue in cheek.*) Да́же има́х възмо́жност да бъ́да прево́дач на една́ гру́па англича́ни.
На́дя	Защо́? Пробле́ми ли и́маха?
Ма́йкъл Джо́нсън	Не, ни́що серио́зно. Бях набли́зо, кога́то те присти́гнаха. Помо́гнах им да наме́рят своя́ прево́дач. Те го тъ́рсиха във фоайе́то вля́во от реце́пцията, а той бе́ше във фоайе́то вля́во от асансьо́ра.
На́дя	Напра́вихте ли сни́мки в ста́рия град?
Ма́йкъл Джо́нсън	Да, напра́вих сни́мки. За съжале́ние, загу́бих фо́тоапара́та си! Ще Ви пока́жа ка́ртичките, кои́то ку́пих. Е́то тук, вдя́сно от площа́да, е хоте́лът. А това́ е къ́щата на Ламарти́н, вля́во е Ри́мската стена́.
На́дя	Ра́двам се, че сте дово́лен. И ще бъ́дете о́ще по́-дово́лен, кога́то Ви ка́жа, че фо́тоапара́тът Ви не е́ загу́бен – у Никола́й е!

стра́шно интере́сно	*terribly interesting*
предста́ва	*idea*
исто́рия	*history*
Ри́мската стена́	*the Roman Wall*
да́же	*even*
възмо́жност (f)	*opportunity, chance*
гру́па	*group*
набли́зо	*nearby*
реце́пция	*reception*
фо́тоапара́т	*camera*
къща	*house*
Ламарти́н	*Lamartine* (French poet)
загу́бен	*lost*
у	*with*

Test yourself

1 To see how well you have understood Dialogue 2, identify the true statements and correct any false ones:

a Ма́йкъл Джо́нсън ня́маше предста́ва от бъ́лгарската исто́рия.

b Той ня́маше вре́ме да разгле́да ста́рия град.

c Той разгле́да цъ́рквата «Свети́ Константи́н и Еле́на».

d На панаи́ра ня́маше хо́ра.

e Ма́йкъл не напра́ви сни́мки.

f Той ку́пи ка́ртички от Пло́вдив.

2 Complete with the past endings of the verbs as in Dialogue 2:

a Има-_____ ли вре́ме да разгле́дате Пло́вдив?

b Ху́баво ли _____ вре́мето вче́ра?

c Бях набли́зо, кога́то присти́гн-_____ англича́ните.

d Аз има-_____ възмо́жност да бъ́да превода́ч.

e Напра́в-_____ ли сни́мки?

f За съжале́ние, загу́б-_____ фо́тоапара́та си.

g Това́ са ка́ртичките, които ку́п _____.

3 How would you say:

   a Go straight on.
   b Turn to the left/right.
   c I had no idea of Bulgarian history.
   d I looked round the old town.
   e There weren't many people on the street.

Now can you:
- ask someone the way?
- give and understand directions?
- give approximate times?
- talk about past events?
- say *there was/were* and *there wasn't/weren't*.

Plovdiv Trade Fair logo

14

Поздравя́вам те!
Congratulations!

In this unit you will learn:

- How to congratulate people on special occasions
- How to name items and places in the home

Dialogue 1

🔊 **CD 2, TR 19–20**

It is Sunday May 24, the day of Bulgarian letters and culture traditionally associated with Saints Cyril and Methodius. Nikolai meets Michael Johnson to take him to Mr Antonov's house.

Ма́йкъл	Никола́й, оти́ваме на го́сти, нали́? Какъ́в пода́рък се но́си на домаки́нята в Бълга́рия?
Никола́й	Обикнове́но се но́сят цветя́ или бонбо́ни.
Ма́йкъл	Ела́те да ку́пим цветя́ за г-жа́ Анто́нова. (*At the florist's.*) До́бър ден! Ви́ждам, че мно́го хо́ра купу́ват цветя́ днес.
Никола́й	Да, защо́то е пра́зник.
Ма́йкъл	Какъ́в пра́зник?
Никола́й	Днес се празну́ва деня́т на бъ́лгарската култу́ра.
Ма́йкъл	Тря́бва да ми разка́жеш по́вече. Те́зи ро́зи ми харе́сват. Ще ку́пя буке́т ро́зи.

(*At the Antonovs' Zlatka Antonova opens the door helped by Sashko, their 7-year-old son.*)

Зла́тка	Добре́ дошли́! Заповя́дайте. Какви́ краси́ви цветя́!
Са́шко	А за ме́не и́ма ли не́що?

Златка	Сашко!
Майкъл	Може би има нещо и за тебе, но първо ми кажи какво се казва, когато искаш да поздравиш някого.
Сашко	Можеш да ми кажеш «Честит рожден ден!»
Златка	Сашко, но днес не е твоят рожден ден!
Сашко	Да, но на рожден ден се получават подаръци.

(After some conferring with Nikolai, Michael gives Sashko a bar of chocolate and a set of coloured pencils.)

Майкъл	Честит празник! Заповядай – един шоколад и кутия моливи. Ти си ученик, нали? Поздравявам те по случай празника на Светите братя Кирил и Методий!
Сашко	Благодаря много. И аз те поздравявам, че ми донесе шоколад. И моливите ми харесват.
Златка	Сашко, много говориш. Иди и донеси вазата от спалнята. Внимавай да не я счупиш!
Боян	Златке, покани гостите в хола.
Майкъл	Колко красиво е наредена масата! Сашко, ти ли я нареди?
Златка	Да, той нареди вилиците, ножовете и салфетките. Той обича да помага.
Сашко	Мамо, донесох вазата. Може ли да донеса и виното за гостите?
Златка	Не, баща ти ще го донесе. Бояне, моля те донеси виното от кухнята.

(Boyan returns with the wine and pours it out.)

Боян	Готово! Да започваме! Наздраве! Честит празник!
Майкъл	Честит празник! Наздраве!
Златка	Заповядайте, докато е топла баницата. Надявам се, че ще ви хареса.

отиваме на гости	*we are going visiting*
Какъв подарък се носи на домакинята?	*What kind of present does one take to the lady of the house?*
Обикновено се носят цветя или бонбони.	*Usually one takes flowers or chocolates.*
много хора купуват цветя	*a lot of people are buying flowers*
празник	*a special day, festival, holiday*
Днес се празнува денят на ...	*Today we are celebrating the day of ...*

тря́бва да ми разка́жеш по́вече	you *must* tell me more
какво́ се ка́зва кога́то и́скаш да поздрави́ш ня́кого	what one says when you want to congratulate someone
Чести́т рожде́н ден!	Happy birthday!
На рожде́н ден се получа́ват пода́ръци.	On one's birthday one gets presents.
Чести́т пра́зник!	Congratulations!
кути́я моли́ви	a box of pencils
Поздравя́вам те по слу́чай пра́зника на Свети́те бра́тя Ки́рил и Ме́тодий!	I congratulate you on the occasion of the Festival of the Saints, brothers Cyril and Methodius!
че ми доне́се шокола́д	that you brought me a bar of chocolate
Иди́ и донеси́ ва́зата.	Go and bring the vase.
спа́лня	bedroom
Внима́вай да не я счу́пиш!	Watch you don't break it!
наре́ден	arranged
Покани́ го́стите в хо́ла.	Ask our guests into the living room.
Той нареди́ ви́лиците, ножо́вете и салфе́тките.	He arranged the forks, knives and serviettes.
Той оби́ча да пома́га.	He likes to help.
Доне́сох ва́зата.	I've brought the vase.
ку́хня	kitchen
Гото́во!	Ready!
Да запо́чваме!	Let's begin!
Наздра́ве!	Cheers!/Your good health!
докато́ е то́пла ба́ницата	while the banitsa (cheese) pasty is still warm
ще ви харе́са	you will like it

1 Questions

a Какво́ се но́си на домаки́нята, кога́то се хо́ди на го́сти в Бълга́рия?

b Какво́ се празну́ва днес?

c Защо́ Ма́йкъл Джо́нсън не мо́же да ка́же на Са́шко «Чести́т рожде́н ден»?

d За какво́ благодари́ Са́шко на Ма́йкъл Джо́нсън?

e Когá се получáват подáръци?
f Откъдé ще донесé вѝното Боя́н Антóнов?

2 True or false?

a Нѝкой (*nobody*) не купýва цветя́ днес.
b Мáйкъл купýва букéт рóзи, защóто рóзите му харéсват.
c На Сáшко му харéсват молѝвите.
d Злáтка ще покáни гóстите в кýхнята.
e Сáшко не обѝча да помáга.
f Злáтка се надя́ва, че бáницата ще им харéса.

How do you say it?

- Offering general congratulations on any festive occasion

Честѝто!/Честѝт прáзник!   *Congratulations!*

- Congratulating someone on an achievement

Поздравя́вам те/Ви с успéха!   *Congratulations on your success!*

Поздравлéния!   *Congratulations!*

- Offering good wishes on specific occasions

Поздравя́вам те/   *Many happy returns of*
  Ви с рождéния ден!   *the day!*
Честѝт рождéн ден!   *Happy birthday!*
Вéсела/Честѝта Кóледа!   *Merry/Happy Christmas!*
Честѝта Нóва Годѝна!   *Happy New Year!*
  (ЧНГ)

Insight

The abbreviation **ЧНГ** is used on New Year cards. Among friends you may hear a jocular **Чънъгъ́!** in place of **Честѝта Нóва Годѝна!**

За мнóго годѝни!   *Many happy returns!*
     (lit. *for many more years.*
     Also used on other festive
     occasions such as New Year.)

| Желáя ти/Ви здрáве и щáстие! | *I wish you health and happiness!* |

- Wishing someone *Good health* (on drinking!)

| Наздрáве! | *Cheers!* |

- Giving a warning

| Внимáвай(те)! | *Watch out!* |
| Внимáвай да не пáднеш! | *Mind you don't fall.* |

- Saying *on the occasion of* . . .

| По слýчай трéти март . . . | *On the occasion of the March 3 holiday . . .* |

Grammar

1 Каквó се прáви? *What do people do?*

There are two ways to generalize. You can either use the *you* singular form as in English, but leaving out **ти**:

| Когáто йскаш да поздравйш нýкого, кажú «Честúто!». | *When you want to congratulate someone, say 'Congratulations!'.* |

Or, with most verbs, you can put **се** in front of the *it* form making the verb reflexive:

Каквó **се прáви** на Кóледа в Бългáрия?	*What do people do (is done) for Christmas in Bulgaria?*
Каквó **се кáзва** на Кóледа?	*What do people say (is said) at Christmas?*
Каквó **се нóси** на домакúнята, когáто **се хóди** на гóсти?	*What does one take (is taken) to the lady of the house when one goes visiting?*
Как **се кáзва** «Happy birthday» на бъ́лгарски?	*How does one say 'Happy birthday' (is 'Happy birthday' said) in Bulgarian?*

214

Insight

Although there is no separate word for *one* in Bulgarian, this form with **ce** is, in fact, the Bulgarian equivalent. And remember too, that **какво** here is a singular word and is followed by a singular verb.

As you can see from the alternative translation given in brackets (*is . . . said*), and also from the little homily Езикът се учи, когато се говори *Language is learned when it is spoken*, there is more of an emphasis here on what is done and not so much on the person who does it. (Look back too to the True or false? section in Unit 8 and you will find the sentence: **Тараторът се сервира студен** *The tarator soup is served cold*.)

The **ce** may also be used with the *they* form of certain verbs, again when you want to emphasize what is done and not the person who does it:

Обикновено **се носят** цветя или бонбони.	*Usually people take flowers or chocolates (flowers or chocolates are taken).*
На рожден ден **се получават** подаръци.	*On one's birthday one receives presents (presents are received).*

(This is another way of expressing the passive which you came across in Unit 11 and about which you can discover more in the Appendix.)

You will find this generalizing form used widely in public notices and instructions:

Тук не се пуши!	*No smoking here.*
Тук се продават билети.	*Tickets sold here.*
Тук не се паркира.	*No parking here.*

Most of these constructions with **ce** have no subject: they are impersonal constructions.

тук
се продават
билети за
ГРАДСКИЯ
ТРАНСПОРТ

2 Another way of saying *I like*

In Unit 12, you learnt the verbs **обичам** and **харесвам/(да) харесам**. You can use **харесвам** and **(да) харесам** in a slightly different way, focusing not so much on your liking – or disliking – something, but rather on the effect something – or someone – has on you. So, instead of saying you like something, you are, in effect, saying it 'appeals' to you. You can therefore say:

Either Аз харесвам тези рози or Тези рози ми харесват (*I like these roses*).

Either Майкъл Джонсън хареса розите or Розите харесаха на Майкъл Джонсън (*Michael Johnson liked the roses*).

Either Той хареса розите or Розите му харесаха (*He liked the roses*).

In fact, the more usual form is the second one with the indirect object pronouns (cf. Unit 7) as in:

Надявам се, че баницата ще ви хареса.	*I hope you will like the banitsa.*
Баницата хареса на гостите.	*The guests liked the banitsa.*
Баницата им хареса.	*They liked the banitsa.*

Insight

You will notice that when you use a person's name or a noun (instead of a pronoun) you have to use **на**.

3 Present and past forms of *to bring/carry/take, to buy*, and *to see*

When you want to say that something is happening at the moment or happens often, you need to use the imperfective verb. So, in the following examples, you can see the imperfective verbs **нося**, **купувам** and **виждам** used in the present:

Милена **носи** два учебника на Николай.	*Milena is bringing two textbooks to Nikolai.*
Много хора **купуват** цветя днес.	*A lot of people are buying flowers today.*
Майкъл Джонсън не **вижда** табелката.	*Michael Johnson does not see the notice.*

216

To say the same things in the past, you need to choose the perfective equivalents of the verbs (**да**) **донеса́**, (**да**) **ку́пя** and (**да**) **ви́дя**:

Миле́на **доне́се** два уче́бника на Никола́й.	*Milena took two textbooks to Nikolai.*
Мно́го хо́ра **ку́пиха** цветя́ днес.	*A lot of people bought flowers today.*
Ма́йкъл Джо́нсън не **видя́** табе́лката.	*Michael Johnson did not see the notice.*

Insight

The plural of **чове́к** (*person*) is **хо́ра** *(people)*, a word 'borrowed' from the Greek, like the English *chorus*.

4 Some more about past endings

(a) Verbs adding past endings to **-я-**

These are **е**-pattern verbs in **-ея** (**пе́я** *to sing*, **живе́я** *to live*):

живя́х	I lived/used to live	живя́хме	we lived, used to live
живя́	you lived	живя́хте	you lived
живя́	he/she/ it lived	живя́ха	they lived

A small group of **и**-pattern verbs also belong here, especially ones with stress on the final syllable like **вървя́** *to walk* and **стоя́** *to stay/stand*. Although not with final stress, (**да**) **ви́дя** adds the past ending to **-я-**:

видя́х	I saw	видя́хме	we saw
видя́	you saw	видя́хте	you saw
видя́	he/she/it saw	видя́ха	they saw

(b) Past tense of (**да**) **до́йда** *to come*, (**да**) **донеса́** *to bring/carry/take*

Verbs of the **е**-pattern with **д, з, к, с** or **т** before their present endings have **-о-** in front of all their past endings, except in the 2nd and 3rd singular:

(аз)	до́йдо́х	доне́сох	(ни́е)	до́йдо́хме	доне́сохме
(ти)	до́йде́	доне́се	(ви́е)	до́йдо́хте	доне́сохте
(той)			(те)	до́йдо́ха	доне́соха
(тя)	до́йде́	доне́се			
(то)					

Note the different stress in the past. Other similar verbs you already know are: **(да) отѝда** *to go* and **(да) пресекá** *to cross*. Remember the change from **к** to **ч** (Unit 13)!

5 Хóдя and отѝвам *To go*

Usually, you use the same verb to say that something is happening at the moment or happens often. **Хóдя** and **отѝвам**, however, are special. You can only use **хóдя** when you go somewhere often, while **отѝвам** can only be used when you are going somewhere from here, now, this very moment:

Всéки ден хóдя на рáбота.	*Every day I go to work.*
Всѝко лѝто хóдя на морé.	*Every summer I go to the seaside.*
Всѝка недéля хóдя на цѝрква.	*Every Sunday I go to church.*

And the answer to: **Къдé отѝваш?** *Where are you going?* is:

Отѝвам на рáбота.	*I am going to work.* (Now!)
Отѝвам на морé.	*I am going to the seaside.* (Now!)
Отѝвам на цѝрква.	*I am going to church.* (Now!)

Only **отѝвам** has a perfective counterpart:

Трѝбва веднáга да **отѝда** на рáбота.	*I have to go to work immediately.*

6 Къдé and нѝкъде *Where* and *somewhere*

All question words can be made into indefinite words by adding **нѝ-**:

как	*how*	**нѝ**как	*somehow*
какѝв	*what sort of*	**нѝ**какѝв	*some sort of*
когá	*when*	**нѝ**кога	*sometime*
кóлко	*how many*	**нѝ**колко	*some, a few, several*
къдé	*where*	**нѝ**къде	*somewhere*

Нѝкой *somebody* or *someone* is formed in a similar way. It has the non-subject form **нѝкого**.

7 Златка and Златке: a special address form for names

You may just remember from way back in Unit 2, when addressing someone using their name or title, you often need to use special forms of address, as in:

господи́не! госпо́жо! госпо́жице!

Some names of people have similar special forms, usually involving the change or addition of a single letter:

Masculine names ending in consonants add **-e**:

(Боя́н) Боя́не! (Ива́н) Ива́не!

Most feminine names don't have a special form, but certain names ending in **-ка** change to **-ке**:

(Зла́тка) Зла́тке! (Ра́дка) Ра́дке!

Exercises

1 Using the model: Поздравя́вам Ви с рожде́ния ден. Чести́то!, congratulate a Bulgarian on:

a getting a new job   **d** some special achievement
b moving to a new flat   **e** a festive occasion
c getting married   **f** a good choice

You will find the new words in the Quick vocab – don't forget to make the nouns/adjectives definite!

апартаме́нт	*apartment, flat*
сва́тба	*wedding*
успе́х	*success, achievement*
пра́зник	*festive occasion, holiday*
и́збор	*choice*
пока́на	*invitation*
па́рти	*party*
кокте́йл	*cocktail party*
малоле́тен	*juvenile* (male)
отту́к	*from here*
ико́на	*icon*

QUICK VOCAB

| крипта | *crypt* |
| шампа́нско | *champagne* |

2 Read the sentences that follow and then alter them, using the model: Получихме пока́на за конце́рт/Пока́нени сме на конце́рт (*We have received an invitation for a concert/We've been invited to a concert*). Note the different use of **за** and **на**.

This exercise will help you practise using the right gender of the passive participles and the right form of **съм**:

a Миле́на получи пока́на за о́пера.
b Получих пока́на за сва́тба.
c Ма́йкъл Джо́нсън получи пока́на за изло́жба.
d Те получиха пока́на за па́рти.
e Получихте ли пока́на за коктейла?

3 Ask questions about the words in bold using the question words **къде́**, **какво́** and **кога́**:

a Валу́та се обме́ня **на ка́са 14**.
b Цига́ри и алкохо́л на малоле́тни не се́ прода́ват.
c Резерва́ции се пра́вят **всеки ден от 9 до 11 часа́**.
d С то́зи трамва́й се оти́ва **до поли́цията**.
e На та́зи ка́ртичка се ви́жда **хоте́л «Роди́на»**.
f Отту́к се ви́ждат **ЦУМ и хоте́л «Ше́ратон»**.

ТУК се продават фонокарти

Тук се продава
sim карта
Prima!

4 Now for some irregular verbs! First, read aloud this dialogue between two couples sightseeing in Sofia. Then change the dialogue to indicate that only you and a friend are talking. (The forms in bold will remind you which bits need altering.)

– Видя́**хте** ли катедра́лата «Свети́ Алекса́ндър Не́вски»?
● Да, видя́**хме** я.
– Харе́са ли **ви**?
● Мно́го **ни** харе́са.
– Разгле́да**хте** ли кри́птата?
● Да, разгле́да**хме** и не́я. Пред кри́птата се прода́ваха ико́ни. Ку́пи**хме** една́ ма́лка ико́на.
– Мо́же ли да я ви́**дим**?
● Разби́ра се. Ето я. Харе́сва ли **ви**?
– **Ни́е** не разби́ра**ме** от ико́ни, но та́зи **ни** харе́сва.

🔊 **CD 2, TR 21**

5 This exercise will help you practise saying *I like*. Give a full answer to the following short questions:

Model: Харе́сва ли ти шампа́нското? Да, шампа́нското мно́го ми харе́сва.

a Харе́сва ли Ви то́зи компа́ктдиск с бъ́лгарска му́зика?
b Харе́сва ли Ви тарато́рът?
c Харе́сва ли Ви ба́ницата?
d Харе́сват ли ти те́зи цветя́?
e Харе́сва ли Ви бъ́лгарското ви́но?
f Харе́сват ли ти пъ́лнените чу́шки?
g Харе́сват ли Ви бонбо́ните?
h Харе́сва ли Ви шо́пската сала́та?

6 First, read the following sentences out loud in which people are taking things somewhere. Then read the sentences again as if the various errands were completed yesterday:

Model: Аз но́ся те́жкия ку́фар. Вче́ра доне́сох те́жкия ку́фар.

a Ма́йкъл Джо́нсън и Никола́й но́сят ро́зи за Зла́тка Анто́нова.
b Миле́на но́си еди́н уче́бник за Никола́й.
c Ни́е но́сим брошу́ри от панаи́ра в Пло́вдив.

d Нóсите ли подáрък за свóите приятели?

e Мáйкъл Джóнсън нóси шоколáд за Сáшко.

f Г-н Антóнов и синъ́т му нóсят две бутúлки вúно от кýхнята.

Another small step forward

🔊 CD 2, TR 22–23

Dialogue 2 Приятелски съвéт *Friendly advice*

Michael Johnson consults an estate agent and then seeks advice from Boyan Antonov on a possible purchase.

Мáйкъл	Дóбър ден. Дойдóх при Вас за съвéт.
Брóкерка	Ще се рáдвам да Ви помóгна. Вúе англичáнин ли сте?
Мáйкъл	Да, úмам бúзнес контáкти с бългáрска фúрма. Чéсто пътýвам до Бългáрия. Искам да знáя как се купýва къ́ща тук.
Брóкерка	Предполáгам, че се интересýвате от къ́ща в провúнцията.
Мáйкъл	Да, да, извъ́н Сóфия.
Брóкерка	Сегá ще Ви покáжа ня́колко къ́щи на нáшия сайт. Катó изберéте къ́ща, добрé е да отúдете да я вúдите с Вáшия адвокáт.
Мáйкъл	Благодаря́. Ще дóйда пак при Вас.

(A few days later.)

Мáйкъл	Бóяне, хóдих да вúдя ня́колко къ́щи в провúнцията. Харéсах еднá романтúчна къ́ща блúзо до Бáнско.
Боя́н	Не тря́бва да се купýва без съвéт от специалúст. Мóже къ́щата да е мнóго стáра. Женá Ви видя́ ли я?
Мáйкъл	Тя я видя́ сáмо на снúмка. Éто, донéсох снúмката да Ви покáжа къ́щата.
Боя́н	Симпатúчна къ́ща, но úма ли градúна?
Мáйкъл	Да, градúната съ́що ми харéса.
Боя́н	Внимавáйте за шумá. Аз кýпих еднá къ́ща блúзо до дискотéка, къдéто се чýва мýзика ця́ла нощ …
Мáйкъл	Мнóго неприя́тно. И товá мя́сто не é мнóго тúхо, когáто úма прáзник илú свáтба.
Боя́н	Защó?

Майкъл	Къщата е до един манастир. Ходих там на празника на Свети Кирил и Методий. Имаше много хора и цветя.
Боян	Да, на този празник се носят цветя в църквите.
Майкъл	На нас ни харесва идеята да живеем до манастир. Така ще видим как се празнува в България.
Боян	Тогава, поздравления за добрия избор! Желая Ви щастливи дни и много празници в България!

брокерка	*(real) estate agent* (woman)
контакт	*contact*
често	*often*
предполагам, -гаш	*to suppose*
провинция	*the country (outside the capital)*
извън	*outside*
сайт	*(internet) site*
адвокат	*lawyer, attorney*
романтичен, -чна	*romantic*
манастир	*monastery*
щастлив	*happy*

QUICK VOCAB

Test yourself

1 To see how well you have understood Dialogue 2, answer the following questions:

   a Какво иска да знае г-н Джонсън?
   b Какъв е съветът на брокерката?
   c Къде е къщата, която г-н Джонсън харесва?
   d Кога се носят цветя в църквата?
   e Какво пожелава Боян Антонов на г-н Джонсън?

2 Complete the sentences:

   a Дойдох при Вас за _____.
   b Добре е _____ отидете да я видите.
   c Как се _____ къща в България?
   d Градината също _____ харесва.
   e На този празник се _____ цветя в църквите.

3 Opposite these perfective verb forms put their respective dictionary forms and those of their imperfective 'twins':

като изберете	купих
да я видите	ще ви покани
харесах	дойдох
донесох	

Now can you:

- talk about things in the home?
- congratulate people on special occasions?
- ask for advice on buying a flat or house in Bulgaria?
- generalize to say what is and what isn't done?
- use **ходя** and **отивам** correctly?
- form the past tense of **живея**, **(да) видя** and **(да) дойда**?

15

Бях на ле́кар
I went to see the doctor

In this unit you will learn:

- How to talk about feeling ill and getting better
- How to describe feelings

Dialogue 1

🔊 **CD 2, TR 24–25**

Nadya and Milena are coming to the end of their coffee break.

На́дя	И́скаш ли о́ще кекс?
Миле́на	Не, благодаря́.
На́дя	Не ти́ ли харе́са?
Миле́на	Мно́го ми харе́са, но не ми́ се яде́.
На́дя	Ти ви́наги внима́ваш какво́ яде́ш, гри́жиш се за килогра́мите си. Пак ли си на дие́та?
Миле́на	Не, не е́ това́. Не се́ чу́вствам добре́.
На́дя	Какво́ ти е?
Миле́на	Ло́шо ми е. От вче́ра ме боли́ стома́хът.
На́дя	Защо́ не оти́деш на ле́кар?
Миле́на	Бях на ле́кар та́зи су́трин. Страху́вах се, че и́мам апендиси́т. Сла́ва Бо́гу, не е́ апендиси́т. Ле́карят ка́за, че си́гурно е ня́какъв лек грип.
На́дя	Отиди́ си вкъ́щи, ако́ не си́ добре́.
Миле́на	Ня́ма ну́жда, ни́що дру́го не ме́ боли́. Ня́мам хре́ма или ка́шлица. Ка́кто ти ка́зах, и́мам бо́лки в стома́ха и непрекъ́снато ми се пи́е вода́.

Надя	За стома́х пий ме́нтов чай – мно́го пома́га. Сега́ ще ти напра́вя.
Миле́на	Неде́й, ня́ма ну́жда. Не ми́ се пи́е чай след кафе́то.
Надя	Студе́но ли ти е?
Миле́на	Не, не ми́ е студе́но, ня́мам температу́ра. Не се́ безпоко́й, ще ми ми́не.
Надя	Да, щом ня́маш температу́ра, ско́ро ще ти ми́не. Спо́мням си, ми́налата годи́на по това́ вре́ме и́мах стра́шен грип с висо́ка температу́ра и си́лна ка́шлица. Не можа́х да се опра́вя цял ме́сец. Тря́бваше да взи́мам антибио́тик.
Миле́на	Аз не оби́чам да взи́мам антибио́тици.
Надя	И аз не оби́чам, но чове́к тря́бва ви́наги да се грижи за здра́вето си.
Миле́на	Пра́ва си.

Не ти́ ли харе́са?	*Didn't you like it?*
Не ми́ се яде́.	*I don't feel like eating.*
Грижиш се за килогра́мите си.	*You're worrying about your weight.* (lit. *kilograms*)
на дие́та	*on a diet*
Не се́ чу́вствам добре́.	*I don't feel well.*
Какво́ ти е?	*What is the matter with you?*
Ло́шо ми е.	*I'm not well.*
От вче́ра ме боли́ стома́хът.	*I've had stomachache since yesterday.*
на ле́кар	*to the doctor's*
Страху́вах се, че и́мам апендиси́т.	*I was afraid I had appendicitis.*
Сла́ва Бо́гу!	*Thank heavens!*
ня́какъв лек грип	*a kind of mild flu*
Отиди́ си вкъ́щи, ако́ не си́ добре́.	*Go home if you are not (feeling) well.*
ни́що дру́го не ме́ боли́	*nothing else is hurting*
хре́ма	*cold* (in the head)
ка́шлица	*cough*
И́мам бо́лки в стома́ха.	*I have stomach pains.*
Непреку́снато ми се пи́е вода́.	*I feel like drinking water all the time.*
Не ми́ се пи́е чай.	*I don't feel like drinking tea.*

Студéно ли ти е?	*Are you cold?*
Не сé безпокóй.	*Don't worry.*
Ще ми мúне.	*It will pass./I'll be fine.*
щом нýмаш температýра	*since you don't have a temperature*
скóро	*soon*
спóмням си	*I remember*
мúналата годúна по товá врéме	*last year at this time*
Не можáх да се опрáвя цял мéсец.	*It took me a whole month to get over it.*
Трýбваше да взúмам антибиóтик.	*I had to take an antibiotic.*
Човéк трýбва вúнаги да се грúжи за здрáвето си.	*One always has to look after one's health.*

1 Questions

a Защó Милéна не úска пóвече (*more*) кекс?
b Каквó ѝ е?
c Каквó ѝ се пúе?
d Когá úмаше Нáдя грип с висóка температýра?
e За каквó трýбва да се грúжи човéк?

2 True or false?

a Милéна не úска кекс, защóто се грúжи за килогрáмите си.
b Кéксът не ѝ харéса.
c Милéна úма бóлки в стомáха от вчéра.
d Тя úма хрéма и кáшлица.
e Мúналата годúна Нáдя не можá да се опрáви от грип цял мéсец.

How do you say it?

◆) CD 2, TR 26

- Asking someone how they feel

  Как се чýвстваш?/чýвствате?   *How do you feel?*

- Asking someone what is the matter with them

Какво́ ти/Ви е?	*What is the matter with you?*
Какво́ те/Ви боли́?	*What is hurting?*

- Complaining of ill health

Не се́ чу́вствам добре́.	*I don't feel well.*
Чу́вствам се зле.	*I feel unwell.*
Ло́шо ми е.	*I'm not well.*
И́мам бо́лки в стома́ха.	*I have stomach pains.*

- Saying you'll get better

Ще ми ми́не.	*It'll pass.*
Ще се опра́вя.	*I'll get better.*

- Saying that you do or don't feel like doing something

Пи́е ми се вода́.	*I feel like a drink of water.*
Не ми́ се пи́е чай.	*I don't feel like tea.*
Яде́ ми се не́що сла́дко.	*I feel like something sweet.*
Не ми́ се рабо́ти.	*I don't feel like working.*

Grammar

1 Какво́ ти е? *What's the matter with you?*

To ask someone how they feel, physically or mentally, or what is the matter with them, you say **Какво́ ти е?** or **Какво́ Ви е?** You will notice that the indirect object pronouns (Unit 7) are used to refer to the person affected. Similarly, to tell someone how you feel, you describe your state (in the neuter!) e.g. студе́но *cold* and then refer to yourself using the indirect object pronoun **ми**:

Студе́но **ми** е.	*I am (feeling) cold.*

These expressions are related to the weather descriptions you came across in Unit 10. Here are some examples for all persons:

Ло́шо ми е.	*I'm not well./I'm sick/poorly.*
Горе́що ли ти/Ви е?	*Are you hot?*
Ло́шо ѝ е.	*She is sick/poorly/not well.*
Студе́но му е.	*He is (feeling) cold.*

Интере́сно ни е.	It is interesting for us./
	We find it interesting.
Ску́чно им е.	They are bored.

In the negative, **не** is placed first, the word coming immediately after **не** is stressed and the word expressing the feeling is placed after the verb:

Не ми́ е ло́шо.	I'm not unwell/sick/poorly.
Не ти́ ли е горе́що?	Aren't you hot?
Не му́ е студе́но.	He is not (feeling) cold.

You can also use the alternative ways to indicate the person affected (Unit 11):

на + name
| На На́дя ѝ е ло́шо. | Nadya is not feeling well. |

на + noun
| На секрета́рката ѝ е ло́шо. | The secretary is not feeling well. |

на + full pronoun
| На не́я ѝ е ло́шо. | She's not feeling well. |

You will have noticed that you still need to keep the indirect object pronoun. Here are some more examples:

На Никола́й/на не́го	Nikolai/He is cold.
му е студе́но.	
На го́стите/на тях	The guests/They are bored.
им е ску́чно.	

2 Боли́ ме *It hurts*

If you want to say that some particular part (or parts) of your body hurts (or hurt) you use **боли́** – or **боля́т** – with the short object pronoun **ме** (there's a full list in Unit 11):

Боли́ **ме** глава́та	My head hurts/
(*or* Глава́та **ме** боли́).	I have a headache.
Боля́т **ме** очи́те	My eyes hurt.
(*or* Очи́те **ме** боля́т).	

It is as though you were saying *My head hurts me* or *My eyes hurt me*. And the doctor might ask you **Какво́ Ви боли́?** (or **Какво́ те боли́?** if he knows you well) *What is hurting you?*

In the following examples, people, other than you, are in pain, and **ме** is replaced by the appropriate short object pronouns:

Боли́ ли те гъ́рлото?	*Does your throat hurt?*
Боли́ го ухо́то.	*His ear hurts/He has earache.*
Боли́ я кракъ́т.	*Her leg hurts.*
Боля́т ли те уши́те?	*Are your ears hurting?*
Боля́т го ръцéте.	*His hands/arms hurt.*
Боля́т я зъ́бите.	*Her teeth hurt.*
Боля́т ги кракáта.	*Their feet hurt.*

3 Ядé ми се *I'm hungry*

Another very useful way of saying how you feel is to use the *it* form of the verb with **се** (cf. Unit 14). You merely insert the indirect object pronoun between the verb and **се**:

Ядé **ми** се.	*I'm hungry.* (lit. *It eats to me.*)
Пи́е **ми** се.	*I'm thirsty.* (lit. *It drinks to me.*)
Спи **ми** се.	*I'm sleepy.* (lit. *It sleeps to me.*)

If you don't feel like doing something, put **не** first and the verb last:

Не **ми́** се ядé.	*I'm not hungry.*
Не **ми́** се пи́е.	*I'm not thirsty.*
Не **ми́** се спи.	*I'm not sleepy.*

This construction can be extended:

Яде́ **ми** се сладоле́д.	*I feel like an icecream.*
Пи́е **ми** се вода́.	*I feel like a drink of water.*

If you use a person's name you still have to use the pronoun:

На Са́шко не **му́** се спи.	*Sashko isn't sleepy.*
На Миле́на не **й** се яде́ сладоле́д.	*Milena doesn't feel like an icecream.*

You can use this pattern with almost any verb to express your wish to do (or not do) something:

Хо́ди **ми** се на мо́ре.	*I feel like going to the seaside.*
Не **ми́** се хо́ди на ра́бота.	*I don't feel like going to work.*
Не **ми́** се рабо́ти.	*I don't feel like working.*

4 Some awkward past tense forms

Past tense of *to say/tell* ка́звам/да ка́жа – ка́зах

In the present tense, you have to use the imperfective **ка́звам**, but in the past you change to the perfective (**да**) **ка́жа**:

Чу́ваш ли какво́ ти **ка́звам**?	*Do you hear what I'm telling you?*
Чу ли какво́ ти **ка́зах**?	*Did you hear what I told you?*

(**Да**) **ка́жа** belongs to a small group of **е**-pattern verbs that change their last consonant from the present to the past, in this case **ж** to **з**. (For other changes and other examples see the Appendix; and also **мо́га** with the change from **г** to **ж**.) Compare the forms of (**да**) **ка́жа**:

		Present		Past	
(тря́бва да)	ка́жа	*I must say*		ка́зах	*I said*
(тря́бва да)	ка́жеш	*you must say*		ка́за	*you said*
(тря́бва да)	ка́же	*he/she must say*		ка́за	*he/she said*
(тря́бва да)	ка́жем	*we must say*		ка́захме	*we said*
(тря́бва да)	ка́жете	*you must say*		ка́захте	*you said*
(тря́бва да)	ка́жат	*they must say*		ка́заха	*they said*

Past tense of *can* мо́га – можа́х

Не можа́хме да спим ця́ла нощ.	*We couldn't sleep all night.*

| Тя не можа́ да яде́ мно́го
от ке́кса. | *She wasn't able to eat much
of the cake.* |
| Не можа́х да се опра́вя
цял ме́сец. | *It took me a whole month
to get over it.* |

можа́х	*I was able*	можа́хме	*we were able*
можа́	*you were able*	можа́хте	*you were able*
можа́	*he/she was able*	можа́ха	*they were able*

Past tense of *must/had to* тря́бва – тря́бваше

Тря́бва has only one past form – **тря́бваше** – for all persons singular
and plural:

Тря́бваше да взи́мам антибио́тик.	*I had to take an antibiotic.*
Тря́бваше да ста́не ра́но.	*He/she had to get up early.*
Тря́бваше да ча́каме/ ча́кат дъ́лго.	*We/they had to wait a long time.*

Depending on the context, тря́бваше can also mean *should have* or
ought to have (but didn't), so тря́бваше да взи́мам антибио́тик could
mean *I ought to have* (or *should have*) *taken an antibiotic* (but didn't).

5 Possessive and reflexive pronoun си

(a) This is another difficult little word, not to be confused with the
си in **ти си**. It belongs to the group of short possessive pronouns
you first came across in Unit 3 and is a short form of **свой (своя́,
сво́е, свои́)** *his/her/their own* (cf. Unit 9). **Си** is very versatile
and can be used to replace any possessive adjective (**мой, твой,
не́гов** etc.) with any person, masculine or feminine, singular or
plural. Unlike the possessive adjective, however, it is placed after
the word to which it refers.

Note also that the definite article moves from the possessive adjective
to the noun:

| Ча́кам сво́я прия́тел =
Ча́кам прия́теля **си**. | *I am waiting for my friend.* |
| Ви́наги се гри́жиш за сво́е**то**
здра́ве = Ви́наги се
гри́жиш за здра́ве**то си**. | *You are always worrying
about your health* |

Тя се грижи за своите килограми = тя се грижи за килограмите си.	She is worrying about her weight (lit. kilograms).

(b) **Си** can also be used as an equivalent of *myself, yourself, himself, herself, itself, ourselves, yourselves* and *themselves*:

Ку́пих **си** моде́рна блу́за.	I bought **myself** a fashionable blouse.
Неве́на **си** ку́пи дъ́лга ро́кля.	Nevena bought **herself** a long dress.
Никола́й **си** ку́пи но́во ви́део.	Nikolai bought **himself** a new video.

(c) Some verbs you always have to use with **си**:

Почи́вам **си**.	I am taking a rest.
Спо́мням **си**.	I remember.

To other verbs **си** adds a personalized, intimate sense of doing something for oneself. There is a difference, for example, between **оти́вам** *I am going* and **оти́вам си** *I am going home*. In the Dialogue, when Nadya suggests Milena goes home, she says: отиди́ **си** вкъ́щи.

Insight

Like many other short grammatical words, **си** never appears as the first word in a sentence and is *always* stressed after **не**.

Exercises

1 Match the following questions and answers:

i Какво́ ти се пи́е?	a Яде́ ми се ки́село мля́ко.
ii Гъ́рло (*throat*) ли те боли́?	b Ло́шо ми е.
iii Какво́ те боли́?	c Пи́е ми се би́ра.
iv И́маш ли хре́ма?	d Студе́но ми е.
v Какво́ ти се яде́?	e Боли́ ме кракъ́т.
vi Какво́ ти е?	f Не, ня́мам хре́ма, но и́мам висо́ка температу́ра.
vii Как се чу́встваш?	g Не, боля́т ме уши́те.

2 You are interpreting for a Bulgarian doctor working with English-speaking tourists. Give a full negative answer to the doctor's questions using the model:

Боли́ ли го ухо́то? Не, не го́ боли́ ухо́то.

Watch the word order!

a   **i**   Боля́т ли го очи́те?   **iv**   Боли́ ли го коля́ното?
     ii   Боли́ ли я зъб?   **v**   Боли́ ли я ръка́та?
    iii   Боля́т ли ги крака́та?

Now give a full negative answer to the questions:

b   **i**   Хо́ди ли ти се на плаж?
     ii   Пи́е ли Ви се чай?
    iii   Гово́ри ли ти се бъ́лгарски?
    iv   У́чи ли ти се?
     v   Рабо́ти ли ти се на компю́тър?

3 Now your friend is unwell. Complete your role in the dialogue:

– Не се́ чу́вствам добре́.
• (*Ask your friend what is the matter with him.*)
– Боли́ ме кръстъ́т (*small of the back*).
• (*Ask him what the doctor said to him.*)
– Ле́карят ми ка́за да си почи́вам.
• (*Ask whether he's feeling sleepy.*)
– Не, не ми́ се спи.
• (*Ask him whether he is bored.*)
– Да, мно́го ми е ску́чно.
• (*Tell him not to worry and reassure him that he'll soon be OK again.*)
– Да, и аз се надя́вам, че ско́ро ще ми ми́не.

🔊 **CD 2, TR 27**

4 Now you've been to the doctor's and are answering your friend's questions. Using the model:

Какво́ ти ка́за ле́карят? Ле́карят ми ка́за, че и́мам але́ргия (*allergy*).

and, at the risk of giving your friend a heart attack, say that:

a you have flu
b you have appendicitis
c you have a high temperature

d you have a cold in the head
e you have hepatitis (хепати́т)

5 Using the past of **мо́га** fill in the answers. Follow the model:

Видя́хте ли фолкло́рния конце́рт? Не, не **можа́хме** да го **ви́дим**, защо́то закъсня́хме.

a Джон **оти́де** ли на го́сти?
_____, защо́то го боле́ше глава́та. (cf. Unit 17)

b **Доне́се** ли ча́нтата?
_____, защо́то ме боле́ше кръстъ́т.

c Те **разгле́даха** ли куро́рта?
_____, защо́то ги боля́ха крака́та.

d **Пра́тихте** (*send*) ли писмо́то?
_____, защо́то ня́махме ма́рки.

e **Я́де** ли от бъ́лгарските специалите́ти?
_____, защо́то и́мах бо́лки в стома́ха.

6 In this exercise, you can practise saying *came* and *went*. Read out the sentences, filling in the answers according to the model:

Защо́ не дойдо́хте с нас на екску́рзия?
Тря́бваше да посре́щнем прия́телите си. Оти́дохме да посре́щнем прия́телите си.

a Защо́ не дойде́ с нас на екску́рзия?
Тря́бваше да си ку́пя марато́нки. _____.

b Защо́ не дойдо́хте с нас на плаж?
Тря́бваше да си почи́нем (*have a rest*). _____.

c Защо́ не дойде́ с нас на вече́ря (*dinner, supper*)?
Тря́бваше да си ку́пя лека́рства. _____.

d Защо́ не дойде́ с нас на го́сти?
Тря́бваше да посре́щна дъщеря́ си. _____.

e Защо́ не дойде́ с ме́не на Ви́тоша?
Тря́бваше да оти́да на ле́кар. _____.

f Защо́ не дойдо́хте с ме́не на ски?
Тря́бваше да пра́тим писмо́ на роди́телите си. _____.

Another small step forward

◆ CD 2, TR 28–29

Dialogue 2 След плáжа *After the beach*

Mr and Mrs Collins are at the doctor's in Varna. As usual, Mrs Collins prefers to do the talking.

г-жá Кóлинс	Дóбър ден, дóктор Стоянов.
Лéкар	Дóбър ден. Кажéте. Зле ли се чýвствате?
г-жá Кóлинс	Не, не áз. Мъжът ми не сé чýвства добрé.
Лéкар	Каквó му е?
г-жá Кóлинс	Има силно главобóлие и все му е студéно.
г-н Кóлинс	Да, мнóго ми е студéно, а навън е тóлкова тóпло.
Лéкар	Имате ли температýра?
г-жá Кóлинс	Температýрата му не é мнóго висóка – 37.1 [тридесет и сéдем и еднó.]
Лéкар	Боли ли го гърло?
г-жá Кóлинс	Нито го боли гърло, нито има хрéма.
Лéкар	Виждам, че кóжата на ръцéте и кракáта му е дóста червéна.
г-жá Кóлинс	О, да. Той мнóго обича да стои на слънце. Вчéра цял ден бéше на плáжа.
Лéкар	На кóлко години сте г-н Кóлинс?
г-н Кóлинс	На шейсéт и две.
Лéкар	Имахте ли шáпка на главáта си, когáто бяхте на плáжа?
г-н Кóлинс	Не.
г-жá Кóлинс	Кáзах му, че слънцето е мнóго силно, но не можáх да го накáрам да слóжи шáпка.
Лéкар	Страхýвам се, че ще трябва да стоите на сянка няколко дни. От слънцето Ви е лóшо.
г-жá Кóлинс	Чýваш ли, Джордж? Трябваше да ми вярваш катó ти кáзвах, че слънцето тук е силно дори през май!

QUICK VOCAB

дóктор	*doctor* (only when addressing)
стоя, стоиш	*to stay*
зле	*unwell*
главобóлие	*headache*
все	*all the time*
навън	*outside*

нѝто ..., нѝто ...	*neither ..., nor ...*
кóжа	*skin*
шáпка	*hat*
главá	*head*
слѝнце	*sun*
(да) накáрам, -раш	*to make* (somebody do something)
(да) слóжа, -жиш	*to put on*
сѝнка	*shade*
вѝрвам, -ваш	*to believe*
катó	*when*

A pharmacy sign in Sofia

Test yourself

1 To see how well you have understood Dialogue 2, answer the following questions:

   a Кой не сé чýвства добрé?
   b Каквó му е на г-н Кóлинс?
   c Защó е червéна кóжата на г-н Кóлинс?
   d Каквó трѝбваше да слóжи на главáта си г-н Кóлинс?
   e Каквó трѝбва да напрáви той сегá?

2 Identify the true statements and correct any false ones:

   a Виктóрия се чýвства зле.
   b Температýрата на Джордж е мнóго висóка.
   c Болѝ го гѝрлото.
   d Все му е тóпло.
   e Джордж не обѝча да стоѝ на слѝнце.

3 Complete the sentences:

a Мъжъ́т ми не _____ _____ добре́.
b Мно́го _____ е студе́но.
c Ни́то го боли́ гъ́рло, _____ и́ма хре́ма.
d _____ се, че ще тря́бва да стои́те на ся́нка ня́колко дни.
e От слъ́нцето _____ е ло́шо.
f Цял ден не _____ да нака́рам Джордж да сложи́ ша́пка.

Now can you:

- ask someone how they feel?
- talk about feeling unwell?
- say which part of your body hurts?
- use the *it* form of the verb with ce to say how you or someone else feels?
- use *I said, I could(n't)* and *I had to*?

16

Акó бях на твóе мя́сто...
If I had been in your place...

In this unit you will learn:

- How to talk about things that might have happened but didn't (i.e. hypothetical situations)
- How to talk about giving presents and showing and sending things to people
- How to form the past tense of some awkward verbs

Dialogue 1

◀) CD 2, TR 30–31

Following Michael Johnson's return to London, there is a short discussion over a cup of coffee back in the Sofia office.

Боя́н Антóнов	Николáй, кажи́ как ми́на послéдният ден с Ма́йкъл Джóнсън.
Николáй	Вси́чко ми́на нормáлно. Сутринтá оти́дох да го взéма от хотéла. Плати́хме смéтката. Моми́чето на рецéпцията порѝча такси́ за два без петнáйсет. Г-н Джóнсън кáза, че е мнóго довóлен от хотéла. Осóбено от товá моми́че – ми́сля, че се кáзва Невéна. И́скаше да й подари́ нéщо за спóмен. Стрáшни са тéзи англичáни! Акó бях аз, щях да забрáвя дори́ да кáжа дови́ждане. Но г-н Джóнсън и́маше еди́н белéжник и й го подари́. Тя мнóго го харéса.

На́дя	Ако́ бях аз, и аз щях да го харе́сам!
Миле́на	А ако́ бях аз, ня́маше да го приема́!
Боя́н Анто́нов	Моми́чета, сти́га! Продължа́вай, Никола́й.
Никола́й	По́сле оти́дохме в магази́на за пода́ръци. Избра́хме една́ сре́бърна гри́вна за жена́ му.
Боя́н Анто́нов	Да́де ли му пода́ръка за жена́ му от мо́ята жена́?
Никола́й	Разби́ра се, да́дох му го.
Боя́н Анто́нов	Той пока́за ли ти програ́мата за твоя престо́й в Че́лмсфорд?
Никола́й	Не ми́ я пока́за. Ка́за, че ще ми я пра́ти с и́мейл.
Боя́н Анто́нов	Ще те посре́щне ли в Ло́ндон?
Никола́й	Да, ще до́йде на Хи́йтроу да ме посре́щне.
Боя́н Анто́нов	И ни́е щя́хме да го посре́щнем, но той не и́скаше. Иде́ята му бе́ше да хо́ди нався́къде сам, за да говори по́вече бъ́лгарски.
Никола́й	О, щях да забра́вя на́й-ва́жното – це́лия ден говори́хме на англи́йски. Той ка́за, че напре́двам, но аз о́ще и́мам чу́вството, че ни́що не знам.
На́дя	Сти́га, Никола́й! Ако́ бях на тво́е мя́сто, изо́бщо ня́маше да се безпокоя́.
Боя́н Анто́нов	Мо́ля ви, по́сле ще гово́рите. И́скам да разбера́ – ти изпра́ти ли Ма́йкъл до лети́щето?
Никола́й	Да, да, изпра́тих го. Сла́ва Бо́гу, не закъсня́хме за самоле́та!
Боя́н Анто́нов	Е, на́й-по́сле разбра́х това́, кое́то и́сках да зна́я . . .
На́дя	И́скате ли о́ще кафе́, господи́н Анто́нов?
Боя́н Анто́нов	Не, благодаря́. Не и́скам по́вече.

QUICK VOCAB

Кажи́ как ми́на после́дният ден.	*Tell me how the final day went.*
норма́лно	*OK, normally*
да го взе́ма	*to take him*
осо́бено	*especially*
да й подари́ не́що за спо́мен	*to give her something as a memento*
Стра́шни са те́зи англича́ни!	*Terrific/Awesome, these English!*
еди́н беле́жник	*a notebook*
Ако́ бях аз, щях да забра́вя дори́ да ка́жа дови́ждане.	*If it had been me, I'd have forgotten even to say goodbye.*

240

Акó бях аз, и аз щях да го харéсам!	If it had been me, I'd have liked it too!
А акó бях аз, нямаше да го приéма!	And if it had been me, I wouldn't have accepted it.
Стѝга!	Stop it!/Enough!
Продължáвай!	Go on!
Избрáхме еднá срéбърна грѝвна.	We chose a silver bracelet.
Дáде ли му подáръка?	Did you give him the present?
Той покáза ли ти прогрáмата?	Did he show you the programme?
Кáза, че ще ми я прáти.	He said he'd send it to me.
Ще те посрéщне ли . . .?	Will he be meeting you . . . ?
И нѝе щяхме да го посрéщнем.	And we too were intending to meet him.
навсякъде	everywhere
пóвече	more
Щях да забрáвя нáй-вáжното.	I nearly forgot the most important thing.
Той кáза, че напрéдвам.	He said I was making progress.
Акó бях на твóе място . . .	If I had been in your place . . .
нямаше да се безпокоя	I wouldn't have worried
нáй-пóсле разбрáх	at last I have found out
óще кафé	some more coffee
Не ѝскам пóвече.	I don't want any more.

1 Questions

Nikolai has been asked these questions. What should he answer?

a Каквó прáвихте послéдния ден с Мáйкъл Джóнсън в хотéла?

b Каквó подари Мáйкъл Джóнсън на Невéна?

c Какъв подáрък избрáхте за г-жá Джóнсън?

d Дáде ли на Мáйкъл Джóнсън подáръка от г-жá Антóнова?

e Как ще ти прáти той прогрáмата?

f На какъв езѝк говóрихте цéлия ден?

2 True or false?

a Невéна мнóго харéса белéжника, кóйто Мáйкъл Джóнсън й подарú.

b Нáдя на нéйно мя́сто сúщо щéше да го харéса.

c Мáйкъл Джóнсън избрá еднá срéбърна грúвна за дъщеря́ си.

d Той покáза на Николáй прогрáмата за нéговия престóй в Чéлмсфорд.

e Акó Нáдя бéше на нéгово мя́сто, тя щéше да се безпокóи.

f Боя́н Антóнов не можá да разберé товá, коéто úскаше да знáе.

How do you say it?

- Saying *If I were you*

  Акó бях на твóе мя́сто.   *If I had been in your place.*
  Акó бях аз.   *If it had been me.*

- Saying that you nearly forgot

  Щях да забрáвя.   *I nearly forgot.* (*That reminds me.*)

- Telling someone to stop doing something

  Стúга!   *Stop it!*
  Достáтъчно!   *Enough!*

- Saying *At last* and *Thank heavens!*

  Нáй-пóсле!   *At last!*
  Слáва Бóгу!   *Thank heavens!* (lit. *Glory to God!*)

- Asking for and declining more

  Úскам óще мáлко.   *I would like a little more.*
  Не úскам пóвече, благодаря́.   *I don't want any more, thank you.*

- Saying you would not have done something

  Ня́маше да отúда без тéбе.   *I would not have gone without you.*

242

Grammar

1 Past tense of (да) дам: да́дох

You will remember from Unit 7 that in all forms other than the *I* form of (**да**) **дам** there is a -**д**- before the present tense endings (**да**) **даде́ш**, (**да**) **даде́**, etc. As explained in Unit 14, the past endings are therefore added to -**о**-:

(аз)	да́до**х**	*I gave*	(ни́е)	да́до**хме**	*we gave*
(ти)	да́де	*you gave*	(ви́е)	да́до**хте**	*you gave*
(той)			(те)	да́до**ха**	*they gave*
(тя) да́де		*he/she/it gave*			
(то)					

Remember: (a) in the *you* singular and *he*, *she*, *it* forms an -**e** replaces the -**o**; (b) in the *he*, *she*, *it* form it is only the position of the stress that distinguishes between the present (**да**) **даде́** and the past **да́де**.

2 Past tense of (да) разбера́ and (да) избера́: разбра́х and избра́х

These verbs belong to a small group of **e**-pattern verbs that have -**ep**- in the present tense. So, too, does (**да**) **събера́** *to gather*. These verbs all drop the vowel -**e**- before -**p**- in the past tense:

(аз)	разбра́**х**	*I (have) understood*	(ни́е)	разбра́**хме**	*we (have) understood*
(ти)	разбра́	*you (have) understood*	(ви́е)	разбра́**хте**	*you (have) understood*
(той)			(те)	разбра́**ха**	*they (have) understood*
(тя) разбра́		*he/she/it (has) understood*			
(то)					

3 Past tense of и́скам: и́сках

И́скам has the same past endings as **и́мам** and **съм**:

(аз)	и́ска**х**	*I wanted*	(ни́е)	и́ска**хме**	*we wanted*
(ти)	и́ска**ше**	*you wanted*	(ви́е)	и́ска**хте**	*you wanted*

(той)			(те)	и́ска**ха**	*they wanted*
(тя)	и́ска**ше**	*he/she/it wanted*			
(то)					

Insight

So far you have come across two patterns of past forms: with and without -**ше** in the *you* singular and *he*, *she*, *it* forms. We have been concentrating on the one without -**ше**, which is used to describe a sequence of completed actions. Verbs like и́скам, и́мам and съм, however, stand for *states* rather than actions. That is why they are used in a past tense form with -**ше**, which is used for describing incomplete actions. (You will find more on how to use the past forms with -**ше** with other verbs too in Unit 17.)

4 Pronoun word order with giving, sending and showing verbs

With verbs of giving, like (**да**) **дам** and (**да**) **подаря́**, sending, (**да**) **пра́тя**, and showing (**да**) **пока́жа**, you usually need to mention both the thing that is given (or shown or sent) – the direct object – and the 'beneficiary' – the indirect object – of whatever has been given, shown or sent. (Look back to Unit 7!) When you use the short pronouns as direct and indirect objects, pay attention to the word order. Look at the following sentences taken from the dialogue:

Г-н Джо́нсън и́маше еди́н беле́жник и **й го** подари́. (i.e. на не́я, беле́жника)	*Mr Johnson had a notebook and gave it to her.*
Тя не **ми я** пока́за. (i.e. на ме́не, програ́мата)	*She did not show it to me.*
Той ще **ми я** пра́ти. (i.e. на ме́не, програ́мата)	*He will send it to me.*
Да́дох **му го**. (i.e. на г-н Джо́нсън, пода́ръка)	*I gave it to him.*

What you need to remember here is:

(a) most importantly, that the indirect object pronouns always come before the direct object ones

244

(b) when the verb is not the first word in the sentence, then both short pronouns come immediately before the verb

(c) when the verb does come first in the sentence, they both come immediately after the verb (cf. the last example).

5 Щях да *I was going to (but I didn't)*

To express things you wanted or intended to do, but didn't, you need to use the past forms of **ще**, which, in fact, comes from **ща**, an old verb meaning *to want*:

щях	*I intended*	**щяхме**	*we intended*
щеше	*you intended*	**щяхте**	*you intended*
щеше	*he/she intended*	**щяха**	*they intended*

Аз щях да дойда, но не можах.	*I was going to come, but I couldn't.*
Той щеше да дойде, но не можа.	*He was going to come, but couldn't.*

You also use this construction to refer to things that nearly happened (but didn't quite!):

Щях да закъснея, но взех такси.	*I would have been late, but I took a taxi.*
Той щеше да отиде без тебе.	*He was about to go without you.*

In either case, **щях** is followed by **да** and a verb in the present tense in the same person as the main verb.

6 Щях да забравя *I nearly forgot/That reminds me*

One of the most common occurrences of **щях** is in the phrase **щях да забравя** meaning *I nearly forgot* (but didn't quite!). Here are all the forms:

щях да забравя	*I nearly forgot*
щеше да забравиш	*you nearly forgot*
щеше да забрави	*he/she nearly forgot*
щяхме да забравим	*we nearly forgot*
щяхте да забравите	*you nearly forgot*
щяха да забравят	*they nearly forgot*

7 Нямаше да *I (you, he, she, it, we, etc.) would not have*

You will remember from Unit 10 that the negative form of **ще** is
нямa да, which stays the same for all persons. Its past form **нямаше**
да, which also stays the same for all persons, is used as the negative
of **щях:**

Аз нямаше да отúда без тéбе.	*I would not have gone without you.*
Нúе нямаше да отúдем без тéбе.	*We would not have gone without you.*

8 Акó . . . щях *I would have done it, if . . .*

Щях is often used with **акó** *if* to introduce conditions under which
something would have taken place, had the conditions been fulfilled
(which they weren't!) These are a type of so-called 'conditional'
sentences and you will find out more about them in Unit 20. There
are a number of examples in the dialogue:

Акó бях аз, щях да забрáвя да кáжа дорú довúждане.	*If it had been me, I'd have forgotten even to say goodbye.*
Акó бях аз, и аз щях да го харéсам.	*If it had been me, I'd have liked it too.*

Sometimes the *if* element, **акó**, may only be implied:

И нúе щяхме да го посрéщнем (implied: акó той úскаше), но той не úскаше.	*And we too were intending to meet him (implied: if he had wanted), but he didn't want us to.*

The negative form is again with **нямаше да:**

Акó бях аз, нямаше да го приéма.	*If it had been me, I wouldn't have accepted it.*
Акó бях на твóе място, нямаше да се безпокóя.	*If I had been in your place, I wouldn't have worried.*

9 Пóвече and óще *more*

Bulgarian has two different words for *more*: **пóвече** and **óще**. It is not always easy to choose the right one, but if you remember the following simple rules, it will help:

(a) **Пóвече** is to **мнóго** what *more* is to *much* or *many*. It is the irregular comparative of **мнóго**. It is used when you make comparisons and want to say that one person, for example, knows more words (or has more money!) than another:

Мáйкъл знáе **мнóго** бългáрски дýми.	*Michael knows a lot of Bulgarian words.*
Виктóрия знáе **пóвече** (бългáрски дýми).	*Victoria knows more (Bulgarian words).*
Той и́ма **мнóго** пари́; аз и́мам **пóвече**.	*He has a lot of money; I have more.*

(b) **Пóвече** is also used when you have had enough of something and don't want any more. It tends to be used with negatives and therefore has to do with not going beyond a limit that has already been reached:

И́скате ли óще би́ра? Не, не и́скам **пóвече**.	*Would you like some more beer? No, I don't want any more.*

(c) You use **óще** – and this is the difficult one! – when you are thinking of adding to what is (or **was**, if you are asking for **another** glass of beer!) already there:

И́скате ли óще би́ра? Да, и́скам **óще** мáлко.	*Would you like some more beer? Yes, I'd like a bit more.* (i.e. in addition)

10 Indirect (reported) speech

When you repeat something someone else has said, a question asked or an answer given, you are creating what is called 'indirect' or 'reported speech', forming 'indirect' questions and answers. This usually occurs after an introduction such as *she asked* or *she said*. In English, the tense of the verbs used in indirect speech is changed. (You will see this in the examples that follow, all of which are based on dialogues you have already studied.) In Bulgarian, in most instances, you can use the original verb tense of the question and answer. All you need to do is change the person of the speaker, from the *I* form to the *he* form, for example:

Ма́йкъл Джо́нсън
Мно́го съм дово́лен от хоте́ла. *I am very pleased with the hotel.*

Никола́й
Ма́йкъл Джо́нсън ка́за, че **е** *Michael Johnson said (that)*
мно́го дово́лен от хоте́ла. *he was very pleased with the hotel.*

Ма́йкъл Джо́нсън
Ще ти пра́тя програ́мата. *I'll send you the programme.*

Никола́й
Ма́йкъл Джо́нсън ка́за, че *Michael Johnson said (that)*
ще ми пра́ти програ́мата. *he would send me the programme.*

Боя́н Анто́нов (to Nadya)
Свобо́ден ли е Никола́й? *Is Nikolai free?*
На́дя (to Nikolai)
Ше́фът попи́та свобо́ден *The boss asked if you were*
ли **си**. *free.*

In questions like the last one, using **ли**, you can replace **ли** with **дали́** (*whether*). Note the change of word order:

На́дя
Ше́фът попи́та **дали́** *The boss asked whether you*
си свобо́ден. *were free.*

Exercises

1 This, and the following two exercises, will help you to practise talking about things that might have happened – but didn't. Read out loud the two sentences in which Mark and Violeta explain what they would have done if they hadn't had more pressing things to attend to:

Марк и Виоле́та И́скаме да оти́дем на екску́рзия.
Ако́ ня́махме дру́га ра́бота, ща́хме да оти́дем на екску́рзия.

Now read the following sentences out loud and following the model say what you would have done. Use **щя́хме да** or **щя́х да**:

a И́скахме да оти́дем на плаж. Ако́ ня́махме ва́жна сре́ща _____.

b И́сках да оти́да на Ви́тоша. Ако́ ня́мах дру́га ра́бота _____.

c И́скахме да оти́дем на те́нис. Ако́ ня́махме дру́га ра́бота _____.

d И́сках да оти́да на го́сти. Ако́ ня́мах ва́жна сре́ща _____.

e И́сках да оти́да на ски. Ако́ ня́мах дру́га ра́бота _____.

2 What would you buy from Bulgaria as a present? Using the words provided, write out sentences in answer to the question:

Ако́ и́скахте да ку́пите пода́рък от Бълга́рия, какъ́в пода́рък щя́хте да ку́пите?

кути́я бонбо́ни	**календа́р**
бути́лка (*bottle*) **ви́но**	**плака́т**
кути́я с луксо́зни (*deluxe*) **пли́кове**	**кни́га**

3 In the following sentences, you are being asked what you would have done, had you been in the position of the speaker. Read the model out loud, then answer the questions first using **да**, then using **не**:

Model: Ако́ бе́ше на мо́е мя́сто, ще́ше ли да оти́деш на лети́щето?

Да, ако́ бях на тво́е мя́сто, щях да оти́да на лети́щето.

Не, ако́ бях на тво́е мя́сто, ня́маше да оти́да на лети́щето.

a Ако́ бе́ше на мо́е мя́сто, ще́ше ли да прие́меш пока́ната?
b Ако́ бе́ше на мо́е мя́сто, ще́ше ли да ку́пиш цветя́?
c Ако́ бе́ше на мо́е мя́сто, ще́ше ли да изпра́тиш моми́чето?
d Ако́ бя́хте на мо́е мя́сто, щя́хте ли да донесе́те пода́рък?
e Ако́ бя́хте на на́ше мя́сто, щя́хте ли да посре́щнете америка́неца?

4 The next two exercises will help you to practise and then to choose correctly between **о́ще** and **по́вече**. The first exercise will also help you practise using the past tense of (**да**) **дам**. So, following the model, complete the sentences altering or replacing the words in bold as necessary:

Model: **Да́дох** две ка́ртички от Ри́лския манасти́р на Джим. Той **и́скаше** о́ще, но аз **ня́мах** по́вече.

a Неве́на _____ на Марк и Виоле́та. Те _____ .
b Ни́е _____ на тури́стите. Те _____ .
c Г-н и г-жа́ Ко́линс _____ на своя́ прия́тел. Той _____ .

5 Choose **о́ще** or **по́вече** in the sentences that follow, remembering that **о́ще** has the sense of *in addition* or *another* while **по́вече** tends to be used with negatives and in comparisons:

a И́скаш ли _____ кекс?
b _____ две би́ри, мо́ля.
c Ня́маме _____ вре́ме да ча́каме.
d Миле́на и́ма _____ англи́йски кни́ги от Никола́й.
e Г-жа́ Ко́линс полу́чи две писма́ от А́нглия и _____ едно́ писмо́ от Аме́рика.

250

f Благодаря́, не и́скам _____ ви́но.

g И́маме _____ пет мину́ти до замина́ването (*the departure*) на самоле́та.

6 This exercise will help you practise the awkward irregular past forms of (**да**) **дам**, (**да**) **избера́** and (**да**) **разбера́**. First, read the little story out loud:

Г-жа́ Анто́нова и́скаше да даде́ на Ма́йкъл Джо́нсън **ма́лък пода́рък**. Тя разбра́ от не́го, **че жена́ му мно́го оби́ча криста́лни** (*crystal*) **ва́зи**. Вче́ра сутринта́ тя оти́де **в магази́н за пода́ръци**. И́скаше да избере́ **на́й-краси́вата криста́лна ва́за**. Тя не ку́пи криста́лна ва́за, **защо́то криста́лните ва́зи бя́ха ужа́сно скъ́пи** (*expensive*). Г-жа́ Анто́нова избра́ **една́ краси́ва ико́на**. По́сле тя да́де пода́рька за г-жа́ Джо́нсън **на Никола́й**.

Now change the story into a dialogue between yourself and a friend. To do this, turn every sentence into a question. Your friend has the answers in the story. When asking questions, concentrate on the sections in bold type and use **какво́, къде́, защо́** or **на кого́**.

7 Using the questions and statements in the first of these sentence pairs, complete the second, making the necessary alterations for indirect speech. Try to think of two possible versions for the **ли** question in (**b**):

a Къде́ и́ма търго́вски це́нтър?
Г-н и г-жа́ Ко́линс пи́таха _____ .

b И́мате ли свобо́дно вре́ме?
Неве́на попи́та г-н Джо́нсън _____ .

c Кога́ Ма́йкъл Джо́нсън ще изпра́ти програ́мата?
Боя́н Анто́нов попи́та _____ .

d И́мам сре́ща в два часа́.
Миле́на ка́за, че _____ .

e Ще зами́нем за Ва́рна на два́йсет и о́сми май.
Джордж и Викто́рия ка́заха, че _____ .

f Благодаря́, не и́скам по́вече кафе́.
Ше́фът ка́за, че _____ .

Another small step forward

Dialogue 2 Чудéсна възмóжност *A wonderful opportunity*

Nikolai and Milena accept an offer to exhibit in England.

Николáй	Милéна, видя́ ли плакáта, кóйто ни подари́ Мáйкъл Джóнсън?
Милéна	Да, Нáдя ми го покáза.
Николáй	Мнóго е интерéсен, нали́? На англи́йски се кáзва «пóстер».
Милéна	И на бългáрски мóже да се кáже «пóстер».
Николáй	Мáйкъл кáза, че ще ни изпрáти óще реклáми.
Милéна	Мóже да ги дадé на тéбе да ги донесéш.
Николáй	Знáеш ли каквó? Той ми предлóжи да напрáвим изло́жба с нáши пóстери в Áнглия.
Милéна	Да, разбрáх от Нáдя. Ти каквó му отговóри?
Николáй	Кáзах, че ще поми́слим. Ти на мóе мя́сто щéше ли да се съгласи́ш веднáга?
Милéна	Разби́ра се, на твóе мя́сто веднáга щях да приéма. Товá е чудéсна възмóжност.
Николáй	Óще не é късно. Аз вéче избрáх нáй-хýбавите от нáшите плакáти. Акó и́скаш, донеси́ от твóите и аз ще му ги дам, като́ зами́на.
Милéна	Когá да ти ги донесá?
Николáй	Аз мóга да дóйда у вас да ги взéма. А, щях да забрáвя – ще ми дадéш ли и англи́йските списáния, кóйто и́маш?
Милéна	Акó знáех, че ги и́скаш, щях да ти ги донесá.
Николáй	Предпочи́там да те изпрáтя до вас. Мóже ли?
Милéна	Защó не? Акó ня́мах дрýга рáбота, щях да те покáня на гóсти.
Николáй	Ни́що. Ще ме покáниш, когáто и́маш пóвече свобóдно врéме.

QUICK VOCAB

(да) изпрáтя, -тиш	*to send*
реклáма	*advertisement*
(да) предлóжа, -жиш	*to offer*
пóстер	*poster*
(да) поми́сля, -лиш	*to think* (something) *over*
да те изпрáтя, -тиш до вас	*to see you home*

кристáлен, -лна	crystal
лукcóзен, -зна	deluxe
скъп	expensive, dear

Test yourself

1 To see how well you have understood Dialogue 2, answer the following questions:

a Каквó óще ще изпрáти Мáйкъл Джóнсън?
b На когó мóже да дадé реклáмите Мáйкъл Джóнсън?
c От когó разбрá Милéна за чудéсната възмóжност?
d Каквó щéше да напрáви Милéна, акó бéше на мя́стото на Николáй?
e Каквó щéше да напрáви Милéна акó знáеше, че той и́ска списáнията?
f Каквó предпочи́та Николáй?

2 Turn the verbs in bold type into the past tense:

a **Ще изберéм** подáрък за Мáйкъл.
b Милéна **ще дадé** плакáт на Николáй.
c Те **и́скат** да разберáт когá заминáва Джон.
d Викτóрия и Джордж **ще дадáт** свóя адрéс на Милéна.
e Аз **ще изберá** óще еднá кáртичка.
f Николáй **и́ска** да изпрáти Милéна.

3 How would you say:

a I gave it to him.
b Nadya showed me it.
c I'll see you home.
d I nearly forgot.
e Thank you, I don't want any more.

Now can you:

- talk about things you would have done, but didn't?
- position the pronouns correctly with verbs of giving, sending and showing?
- correctly form the irregular past tense forms of the verbs *to give*, *to understand* and *to choose*?
- ask for/decline more of something?

17

Какво правеше тя?
What was she doing?

In this unit you will learn:

- How to talk about things breaking down/not working
- How to ask for help if something is wrong in your hotel room
- How to ask for help if you have trouble with your car
- How to refer to past events

Dialogue 1

◄) CD 2, TR 34-35

Boyan Antonov's secretary, Nadya, is late for work and nobody at the office knows why.

Боян Антонов	Защо я няма още Надя? Преди винаги идваше навреме. Болна ли е?
Николай	Не, не é болна. Много съм учуден, че я няма, защото тази сутрин я видях от трамвая. Отиваше на работа с колата си.
Боян Антонов	Милена, ти знаеш ли защо я няма?
Милена	Нямам представа. Аз също я видях на улицата отдалече, но не беше с кола.
Боян Антонов	Какво правеше?
Милена	Говореше с един полицай пред болницата. Не можех да чуя какво говорят. Полицаят й показваше знака СПИРАНЕТО ЗАБРАНЕНО.

254

Николай	Ясно защо́ я ня́ма. Си́гурно и́ма неприя́тности с поли́цията.
Боя́н Анто́нов	Ко́лко пъ́ти ѝ ка́звах да не парки́ра пред бо́лницата! Сега́ ще тря́бва да плати́ гло́ба.

(A little later Nadya comes in.)

На́дя	Здраве́йте. Извиня́вайте за закъсне́нието, но и́мах неприя́тности с кола́та. Опи́твах мно́го пъ́ти да се оба́дя по телефо́на в о́фиса, но бе́ше заето́.
Миле́на	Да, аз гово́рех преди́ ма́лко. Кажи́ какво́ се слу́чи.
На́дя	Оти́вах на ра́бота с кола́та, но пред бо́лницата мото́рът спря́ и не мо́жеше да запа́ли. Ня́мах предста́ва какво́ му е. От ня́колко дни мото́рът не рабо́теше добре́, но аз продължа́вах да ка́рам кола́та. Не мо́жех да напра́вя ни́що дру́го осве́н да оста́вя кола́та там.
Миле́на	Аз те видя́х. Гово́реше с еди́н полица́й.
На́дя	О, ужа́сен бе́ше, нали́? Ка́зах му, че кола́та и́ма повре́да, а той все ми пока́зваше зна́ка.
Боя́н Анто́нов	Какво́ ста́на по́сле?
На́дя	За ща́стие, видя́х еди́н позна́т. Той стое́ше на ъ́гъла до бо́лницата. Купу́ваше си ве́стник. Той наме́ри повре́дата ведна́га.
Николай	Какво́ ѝ бе́ше на кола́та?
На́дя	*(Evasively.)* Ни́що осо́бено. Повре́дата не бе́ше в мото́ра.
Миле́на	Защо́ не ни ка́жеш каква́ по́-то́чно бе́ше повре́дата?
На́дя	Е, добре́. Ня́маше бензи́н . . . *(General mirth.)* За ща́стие, мо́ят позна́т и́маше бидо́нче с бензи́н в бага́жника.
Боя́н Анто́нов	Сле́дващия път ще бъ́де мото́рът. По́-добре́ иди́ ведна́га на серви́з!

СПИРАНЕТО ЗАБРАНЕНО

Преди́ ви́наги и́дваше наврéме.	Before, she always used to come on time.
Бо́лна ли е?	Is she ill?
Мно́го съм учу́ден.	I'm very surprised.
Оти́ваше на ра́бота.	She was going to work.
Ня́мам предста́ва.	I have no idea.
отдалéче	from afar
Какво́ пра́веше?	What was she doing?
Гово́реше с еди́н полица́й пред бо́лницата.	She was talking to a policeman in front of the hospital.
Не мо́жех да чу́я.	I wasn't able to hear.
Полица́ят й пока́зваше зна́ка СПИ́РАНЕТО ЗАБРАНЕ́НО.	The policeman was pointing out the NO STOPPING sign to her.
я́сно защо́	it's obvious why
И́ма неприя́тности с . . .	She is having trouble with . . .
Ко́лко пъ́ти й ка́звах . . .	The times I've told her . . .
гло́ба	a fine
опи́твах	I tried/kept trying
аз гово́рех	I was speaking
какво́ се слу́чи	what happened
мото́рът спря́	the engine stopped
не мо́жеше да запа́ли	(it) wouldn't start
от ня́колко дни	for the past few days
не рабо́теше добре́	(it wasn't) working properly
не мо́жех да напра́вя ни́що дру́го осве́н . . .	all I could do was . . .
ужа́сен бе́ше	he was awful
кола́та и́ма повре́да	the car has broken down
все ми пока́зваше зна́ка	he kept pointing to the sign
Какво́ ста́на по́сле?	What happened next?
за ща́стие	fortunately
позна́т	acquaintance
той стое́ше на ъ́гъла	he was standing on the corner
Купу́ваше си ве́стник.	He was buying (himself) (cf. Unit 15) a newspaper.
повре́дата	the fault
ни́що осо́бено	nothing special/nothing much

бензи́н	petrol/gas
бидо́нче	small can
бага́жник	boot/trunk
сле́дващия път	next time
иди́ ведна́га на серви́з!	go to a garage/service station immediately

1 Questions

Answer pretending to be the person to whom the question is addressed:

a Миле́на, бо́лна ли е На́дя?

b Никола́й, защо́ си учу́ден, че На́дя о́ще не е́ на ра́бота?

c Никола́й, какво́ пра́веше На́дя, кога́то я видя́?

d Г-н Анто́нов, къде́ не тря́бваше да паркира На́дя?

e На́дя, какво́ се слу́чи с кола́та?

f На́дя, ти какво́ ка́за на полица́я?

2 True or false?

a Полица́ят пока́зваше на На́дя къде́ е серви́зът.

b На́дя зна́еше добре́ какво́ му е на мото́ра.

c На́дя тря́бваше да оста́ви кола́та пред бо́лницата.

d На́дя видя́ еди́н позна́т, ко́йто си купу́ваше ве́стник.

e Не́йният позна́т не можа́ да наме́ри повре́дата.

f Кола́та и́маше серио́зна повре́да.

How do you say it?

- Saying that something is out of order

Ду́шът не рабо́ти.	The shower is not working.
Кола́та и́ма повре́да.	The car has broken down.
Повре́дата е в мото́ра.	The fault is in the engine.
Асансьо́рът е повре́ден.	The lift is out of order.
И́мам неприя́тности/ проблеми́ с кола́та.	I'm having trouble/problems with the car.

- Asking *What happened* or *What is the matter?*

Какво́ ста́на?	*What happened?*
Какво́ се слу́чи?	*What happened?*
Какво́ и́ма?	*What's the matter?*
Какво́ ста́ва?	*What's up? What's going on?*

- Answering *Nothing special*

Ни́що осо́бено.	*Nothing special.*

- Expressing ignorance or surprise

Ня́мам предста́ва.	*I've no idea.*
Мно́го съм учу́ден.	*I'm very surprised.*

- Saying *Fortunately*

за ща́стие	*fortunately/luckily*

(cf. **за съжале́ние** *unfortunately* Unit 5)

Grammar

1 The past imperfect

You will find examples of phrases describing not completed actions in the past but actions that are seen as going on at a given past moment at the end of this paragraph. Usually, these are background actions accompanying the description of a past event. In all such cases, you need to use a set of past forms known as the past imperfect:

Какво́ пра́веше тя? *What was she doing?*

Examples based on the dialogue:

На́дя оти́ваше на ра́бота.	*Nadya was going to work.*
Тя гово́реше с еди́н полица́й.	*She was talking to a policeman.*
Полица́ят ѝ пока́зваше зна́ка.	*The policeman was showing her the sign.*

Here the reference to another past event (which happened when this one was going on) is only implied, but it can also be mentioned either:

258

- in phrases like **в това́ вре́ме** *just then*, **по съ́щото вре́ме** *at the same time* and **през ця́лото вре́ме** *all that time*
- or in accompanying phrases introduced by **кога́то** *when*, that describe another action with the 'ordinary' past tense:

През ця́лото вре́ме Миле́на гово́реше (past imperfect) по телефо́на.	*All that time Milena was talking on the phone.*
В това́ вре́ме мо́ят позна́т си купу́ваше (past imperfect) ве́стник.	*Just then my acquaintance was buying (himself) a newspaper.*
На́дя оти́ваше (past imperfect) на ра́бота, кога́то я видя́х. ('ordinary' past')	*Nadya was going to work when I saw her.*

Аз продължа́вах да ка́рам кола́та *I went on driving the car*

The verb **продължа́вам** *to continue, to go on* is naturally used in the past imperfect because it describes the action as still going on. However, even without such a verb you can use the past imperfect forms to render English expressions such as *I went on* and *I kept (on)* (doing something):

На́дя опи́тваше да се оба́ди.	*Nadya kept (on) trying to get through (on the phone).*

Whenever you use time words like **все** *all the time* you also need the past imperfect:

Полица́ят **все** ми пока́зваше зна́ка.	*The policeman kept showing me the sign.*

Note, too, that a similar meaning of continuing for a period of time is present in the following examples:

От ня́колко дни мото́рът не рабо́теше добре́.	*(For) the past few days the engine wasn't working properly.*
Преди́ де́сет годи́ни г-н Анто́нов рабо́теше като́ журнали́ст.	*Ten years ago Mr Antonov was working as a journalist.*

Тя ви́наги и́дваше на вре́ме *She always used to come on time*

You also need to use past imperfect forms for actions that were habitual or were repeated in the past. Frequently, words like **мно́го пъ́ти** *many times*, **ко́лко пъ́ти** *how many times* and **че́сто** are used to reinforce this meaning:

Ко́лко пъ́ти ѝ ка́звах!	*The times I've told her!*
Ка́звах ѝ мно́го пъ́ти.	*I've told her many times.*

Very often you can conveniently use the past imperfect forms to convey the meaning of the phrase '*used to*' (do something):

Преди́ На́дя ви́наги **и́дваше** навре́ме.	*Before, Nadya always **used to come** on time.*
Тя че́сто **пъту́ваше** с трамва́й.	*She often **used to go** by tram.*
Че́сто я **ви́ждах** от трамва́я.	*I often **used to see** her from the tram.*

2 How to form the past imperfect

As you can see from the list that follows, the endings for the past imperfect are almost identical with those for the simple past tense, except for the *you* singular and *he*, *she*, *it* forms. The main difference lies in the vowel preceding the endings.

(a) Verbs adding past imperfect endings to **-a-**: all **a**-pattern verbs:

(аз)	оти́в**ах**	*I used to go/ was going*	(ни́е)	оти́в**ахме**	*we used to go/ were going*
(ти)	оти́в**аше**	*you used to go/ were going*	(ви́е)	оти́в**ахте**	*you used to go/ were going*
(той) (тя) } (то)	оти́в**аше**	*he/she/it used to go/was going*	(те)	оти́в**аха**	*they used to go/ were going*

(b) Verbs adding past imperfect endings to **-e-**: most verbs of **e**- and **и**-pattern except those in (**c**):

(аз)	гово́р**ех**	*I was speaking*	мо́ж**ех**	(ни́е)	гово́р**ехме** мо́ж**ехме**
(ти)	гово́р**еше**	*you were speaking*	мо́ж**еше**	(ви́е)	гово́р**ехте** мо́ж**ехте**

260

| (той)
(тя)
(то) | } говор**еше** | *he/she/it
was
speaking* | мо́ж**еше** | (те) | говор**еха** | мо́ж**еха** |

(c) Verbs adding past imperfect endings to a stressed **-я- (-á-** after
ж, ч, ш): these can be either verbs of **e-** or of **и-**pattern with the
stress on the final syllable. But do note the change of **-я-/-á-** to
-é- in the *you* (singular) and *he, she, it* forms, as shown below in
to stand **стоя́** and *to hold* **държа́:**

(аз)	стоя́х/ държа́х	*I was standing/ holding*	(ни́е)	стоя́хме/ държа́хме	*we were standing/ holding*
(ти)	стое́ше/ държе́ше	*you were standing/ holding*	(ви́е)	стоя́хте/ държа́хте	*you were standing / holding*
(той) (тя) (то)	стое́ше/ държе́ше	*he/she/it was standing/ holding*	(те)	стоя́ха/ държа́ха	*they were standing/ holding*

3 Compare 'ordinary' past with past imperfect

When you compare the two tenses you will see that the past imperfect
goes most naturally with imperfective verbs since they, too, describe
incomplete actions (Unit 12). That is why some verbs that make no
distinction in the past form between perfective/imperfective like **съм,**
и́мам (Unit 13) and **тря́бва** (Unit 15) normally appear in the past
imperfect only.

Compare the following examples based on the dialogue (left-hand
column), with similar sentences in the right-hand column using
the corresponding perfective 'twin':

Past imperfect tense
(used with imperfective verb)

Past tense
(used with perfective verb)

и́двам

Тя и́дваше навре́ме.
She used to come
  on time.

(да) до́йда

Вче́ра тя дойде́ навре́ме.
Yesterday she came
  on time.

отивам	**(да) отида**
На́дя оти́ваше на ра́бота.	На́дя оти́де на ра́бота в се́дем часа́.
Nadya was going to work.	*Nadya went to work at seven o'clock.*

пока́звам	**(да) пока́жа**
Полица́ят ми пока́зваше зна́ка.	Полица́ят ми пока́за зна́ка.
The policeman was showing me the sign.	*The policeman showed me the sign.*

купу́вам	**(да) ку́пя**
Мо́ят позна́т си купу́ваше ве́стник.	Мо́ят позна́т си ку́пи ве́стник.
My acquaintance was buying (himself) a newspaper.	*My acquaintance bought (himself) a newspaper.*

ка́звам	**(да) ка́жа**
Ка́звах ѝ мно́го пъ́ти.	Ка́зах ѝ вче́ра.
I've told her many times.	*I told her yesterday.*

опи́твам	**(да) опи́там**
На́дя опи́тваше да се оба́ди.	На́дя опи́та да се оба́ди.
Nadya kept trying to get through (on the phone).	*Nadya tried to get through (on the phone).*

4 Можа́х and мо́жех *I managed/I was able (to do something)*

Unlike the verbs used in the examples we have just looked at, **мо́га** *can, be able*, has no proper perfective counterpart. It does, however, still have both a past tense form **можа́х** – as you saw in Unit 15 – and a past imperfect form **мо́жех**. It is not easy to make a clear distinction between the usage of the two forms in English, but the following examples will show in practice the difference in meaning in Bulgarian:

Past tense

можа́х

Можа́х да обясня́.	*I managed to explain.*
Не можа́х да чу́я какво́ ка́за.	*I did not manage to hear what you/he/she said.*

Here there is a sense of having a go and then bringing the action to an end, either, as in the first example, because you managed to achieve what you wanted, or, as in the second, because you did not.

Past imperfect

мо́жех

| Ми́налата годи́на **не мо́жех** да гово́ря бъ́лгарски. | *Last year I couldn't/wasn't able to speak Bulgarian.* |
| **Мо́жех** да обясня́, но не обясни́х. | *I could have explained, but didn't.* |

Here it is more a case of having – or not having! – the ability or potential to do something over a period of time. It is a state rather than an action.

Insight

When *can* really means *being allowed* – or *not allowed*! – to do something, in the past you should always use the past imperfect form of **мо́га**. Compare these present and past usages:

Present

Там (не) мо́же да се парки́ра.

One can/cannot park there.
   (i.e. is/isn't allowed)

Мо́га да парки́рам там.
I can park there.
   (i.e. am allowed)

Past

Там (не) мо́жеше да се парки́ра.

One could/n't park there.
   (i.e. was/wasn't allowed)

Мо́жех да парки́рам там.
I could park there.
   (i.e. was allowed)

Exercises

1 In this story, you will learn about Nadya's misfortunes with the car in a slightly different way. Can you choose the missing words from the list?

От ня́колко дни кола́та на На́дя не _____ добре́. И́маше ня́какъв шум (*noise*) в _____. На́дя не оти́де на

_____ . Тя продължа́ваше да _____ кола́та, защо́то не оби́ча да хо́ди на ра́бота _____ трамва́й.

Вче́ра На́дя _____ неприя́тности. Кога́то оти́ваше на ра́бота, кола́та спря́ _____ бо́лницата. Тя ми́слеше, че кола́та и́ма повре́да, но не зна́еше каква́ е _____ . Тя _____ да оста́ви кола́та там. Пред бо́лницата _____ е забране́но. Еди́н полица́й и́скаше На́дя да плати́ _____ . На́дя и́скаше да му обясни́, че кола́та _____ повре́да, но той все ѝ пока́зваше зна́ка СПИ́РАНЕТО _____ . Еди́н _____ на На́дя ѝ помо́гна. Той разбра́ведна́га, че _____ не е́ повре́дена. Про́сто (*simply*) ня́маше _____ !

бензи́н	и́маше	серви́з	рабо́теше
гло́ба	ка́ра	повре́дата	с
ЗАБРАНЕ́НО	кола́та	позна́т	спи́рането
и́ма	мото́ра	пред	тря́бваше

2 Complete the short dialogues that follow, inserting **Какво́ пра́веше?** or **Какво́ пра́веха?** and the right personal pronoun. Read the sentences out loud and then try to repeat them without looking:

a Вче́ра видя́х Никола́й и Миле́на. _____?
Ни́що осо́бено.
Оти́ваха на о́пера.

b Вче́ра видя́х тво́я прия́тел. _____?
Ни́що осо́бено.
Ча́каше трамва́я.

c Вче́ра видя́х Неве́на. _____? Ни́що осо́бено.
Гово́реше с еди́н англича́нин.

d Вче́ра видя́хме Са́шко. _____? Ни́що осо́бено
Игра́еше фу́тбол.

e Вче́ра видя́х Викто́рия и Джордж Ко́линс. _____? Ни́що осо́бено.
Пи́еха кафе́.

f Видя́хме гру́па америка́нци. _____?
Ни́що осо́бено. Стоя́ха на пла́жа.

◄) CD 2, TR 37

3 Somebody has stolen your suitcase and a policeman is taking evidence from you. Answer his questions:

Полица́й	Кога́ ста́на това́?
Ви́е	(Say that it happened 15 minutes ago.)
Полица́й	Къде́ бя́хте Ви́е, кога́то това́ се слу́чи?
Ви́е	(Say you were in the hotel.)
Полица́й	Какво́ пра́вехте?
Ви́е	(Say you were waiting for a taxi.)
Полица́й	Има́ше ли мно́го хо́ра във фоайе́то на хоте́ла?
Ви́е	(Say there was only one man.)
Полица́й	Какво́ пра́веше той?
Ви́е	(Say that he was speaking on the phone.)
Полица́й	Къде́ бе́ше портие́рът (the doorman)?
Ви́е	(Say that he was standing in front of the hotel.)
Полица́й	Благодаря́. Ще оти́да да гово́ря с портие́ра.

4 Practise saying what you used to do for a job by changing the sentences to the *I* form:

a Преди́ те рабо́теха в еди́н магази́н.

b Преди́ две годи́ни На́дя рабо́теше в музе́я.

c Преди́ той рабо́теше като́ сервитьо́р. (Сервитьо́рка is *waitress*, remember!)

d Преди́ мно́го годи́ни Викто́рия и Джордж Ко́линс рабо́теха като́ учи́тели.

e Преди́ ни́е рабо́техме в ба́нката.

5 In this exercise, you can check how good you are at distinguishing between repeated and single actions in the past. Don't forget that repeated actions usually go with an imperfective verb and single actions with a perfective one. Choose from the pair given with each set of sentences:

a **и́дваше/дойде́?**

  i На́дя ви́наги _____ ра́но на ра́бота.

  ii Вче́ра На́дя _____ къ́сно на ра́бота.

b **ка́зваше/ка́за?**

  i Г-н Анто́нов че́сто _____ на На́дя да не парки́ра пред бо́лницата.

  ii Миле́на _____, че не зна́е къде́ е На́дя.

c **купу́вах/ку́пих?**

  i Вче́ра _____ пода́рък за бра́т ми.

  ii Преди́ аз че́сто _____ ве́стници.

Another small step forward

🔊 CD 2, TR 38–39

Dialogue 2 Прия́тна изнена́да *A pleasant surprise*

In the Odessa Hotel outside the Collins' room, there is a bouquet of birthday surprises for Victoria.

г-жа́ Ко́линс	(*Rather flustered.*) Мо́ля Ви, каже́те на реце́пцията, че не мо́га да спра ду́ша. Кра́нът е повре́ден. Осве́н това́, не зна́я къде́ е мъжъ́т ми. Тря́бва да го наме́ря.
Камерие́рка	Аз видя́х г-н Ко́линс преди́ ма́лко. Оти́ваше към Мо́рската гради́на.
г-жа́ Ко́линс	Така́ ли? Мно́го съм учу́дена. Той ни́къде не хо́ди без ме́не. Ще пи́там портие́ра дали́ зна́е къде́ е мъжъ́т ми.
Гост на хоте́ла	(*Overhearing and joining in.*) Аз съ́що видя́х г-н Ко́линс. Той гово́реше с една́ жена́ пред вхо́да на Мо́рската гради́на.
г-жа́ Ко́линс	Но той не позна́ва ни́кого тук. Чу́хте ли за какво́ гово́рят?
Гост на хоте́ла	Ни́що осо́бено . . . Г-н Ко́линс пи́таше за посо́ката, но не разбра́х къде́ и́скаше да оти́де.
г-жа́ Ко́линс	Но той не зна́е добре́ бъ́лгарски. Ко́лко пъ́ти му ка́звах да не изли́за сам! Той е то́лкова разсе́ян. Ще пресече́ у́лицата не ка́кто тря́бва и ще и́ма неприя́тности.
Портие́р	(*Seeing Mrs Collins in a state of agitation.*) Добро́ у́тро, г-жа́ Ко́линс. Неприя́тности ли и́мате?
г-жа́ Ко́линс	За съжале́ние, да. Пъ́рво кра́нът на ду́ша се разва́ли. От ня́колко дни ду́шът не рабо́теше добре́, а сега́ не мо́га да го спра. По́сле мъжъ́т ми изче́зна.
Портие́р	Не се́ безпоко́йте, аз съ́що видя́х г-н Ко́линс. Изгле́ждаше съвсе́м добре́. Купу́ваше не́що, но не можа́х да ви́дя какво́.

(*Mr Collins appears at the end of the corridor.*)

г-жа́ Ко́линс	Джордж, какво́ ста́на? Защо́ изли́заш сам, без ме́не? Страху́вах се, че ще загу́биш пъ́тя.

г-н Ко́линс	Е, ми́сля, че мо́га сам да ку́пя буке́т цветя́! (*Produces a bunch of flowers from behind his back.*) Чести́т рожде́н ден, ми́ла Ви́ки!
Вси́чки	Чести́т рожде́н ден, госпо́жо Ко́линс!
г-жа́ Ко́линс	Благодаря́. Каква́ прия́тна изнена́да!
Портие́р	Ни́е вси́чки зна́ехме къде́ е г-н Ко́линс.
Камерие́рка	О́леле, забра́вихме за кра́на! Тря́бва бъ́рзо да се оба́дя на ма́йстора.

изнена́да	*surprise*
кран	*tap*
освéн	*apart from, besides*
дали́	*whether*
излизам, -заш	*to go out*
разся́ен	*absent-minded*
кра́нът се развали́	*the tap is not working*
(да) изче́зна, -неш	*to disappear*
е!	*well, really!*
мил	*dear*
камерие́рка	*chambermaid*
о́леле!	*oh dear me!*
ма́йстор	*workman* (here: *plumber*)

Test yourself

1 To see how well you have understood Dialogue 2, answer the following questions:

  a Защо́ г-жа́ Ко́линс не мо́же да спре ду́ша?
  b Какво́ пра́веше г-н Ко́линс, кога́то го видя́ еди́н гост на хоте́ла?
  c Какви́ неприя́тности и́ма г-жа́ Ко́линс?
  d Какво́ пра́веше г-н Ко́линс, кога́то го видя́ портие́рът?
  e Какво́ зна́еха вси́чки?

2 Complete the sentences:

  a Кра́нът на ду́ша се _____.
  b Кола́та и́ма _____.
  c От ня́колко дни мото́рът не _____ добре́.

Unit 17 What was she doing? 267

3 How would you say:

a I have no idea.
b Nothing special.
c What's the matter?
d I'm having problems with the car.
e What were they doing?

Now can you:
- talk about things breaking down?
- ask what has happened?
- distinguish between past events viewed as completed and those viewed as having some duration in the past?
- correctly use two different past forms of the verb *I can/ am able?*

18

Вéче съм решúла
I've already made up my mind

In this unit you will learn:

- How to talk about results: things that did or did not happen in the past and have affected the present
- How to say you have forgotten something
- How to talk about your leisure
- How to express disbelief

Dialogue 1

◀ CD 2, TR 40–41

Nikolai has come to collect Milena for the opera but finds she is not yet dressed for going out.

Николáй	Милéна, óще не сú готóва. Не сú забрáвила, че тáзи вéчер сме на óпера, налú?
Милéна	Не, не съм, но óще не съм се облякла.
Николáй	Каквó прáви досегá?
Милéна	Еднá приятелка дойдé на гóсти. Бях я покáнила предú да кýпиш билéти за óпера.
Николáй	Óще ли не сú е отúшла?
Милéна	Отúде си предú петнáйсет минýти.
Николáй	Хáйде, ще закъснéем, акó не сé облечéш пó-бързо. Представлéнието запóчва в сéдем часá.
Милéна	Няма да закъснéем. Ще бъдем там в сéдем.
Николáй	Мнóго се съмнявам.

Миле́на	Ве́че съм реши́ла какво́ да облека́. Вече́рял ли си?
Никола́й	Не, не съм. Ми́сля да вече́ряме за́едно след представле́нието.

(Outside the opera house. They've made it for 7 o'clock but the place looks suspiciously empty. They go to the ticket office.)

Миле́на	Запо́чнало ли е представле́нието?
Касие́рка	О́ще не, госпо́жице. Представле́нието е от се́дем и полови́на.
Никола́й	Миле́на, съжаля́вам! Вина́та е мо́я. Ня́мам предста́ва как съм напра́вил така́ва гре́шка.
Миле́на	Ня́ма значе́ние, слу́чва се. Вре́мето е ху́баво. Ха́йде да се разхо́дим.
Никола́й	Съгла́сен съм. Така́ ще бъ́дем за́едно полови́н час по́вече. Мо́же да си ку́пим сладоле́д.
Миле́на	Разби́ра се. Ня́ма да ни бъ́де ску́чно.
Никола́й	О, не . . .! (After a pause, groaning and throwing up his arms.) Ами́ сега́?
Миле́на	Какво́ се е случи́ло?
Никола́й	Не съм взел пари́! Забра́вил съм ги в джо́ба на дъ́нките си.
Миле́на	Мно́го си сме́шен! Нали́ мо́жеш да плати́ш с кре́дитна ка́рта?
Никола́й	Ча́кай! . . . (with relief) О, тук е, не́я не съм забра́вил.
Миле́на	Ста́нал си мно́го разся́ен. Си́гурно си се умори́л от мно́го у́чене.
Никола́й	Да, ни́кога не съм бил то́лкова разся́ен. Но дали́ е са́мо от у́чене е друг въпро́с . . .

не си́ забра́вила	*you haven't forgotten*
О́ще не съм се обля́кла.	*I haven't dressed yet.*
досега́	*until now*
една́ прия́телка дойде́	*a friend came*
Бях я пока́нила.	*I had invited her.*
О́ще ли не си́ е оти́шла?	*Hasn't she gone yet?*
ако́ не се́ облече́ш	*if you don't get dressed*
представле́ние	*performance*
Мно́го се съмня́вам.	*I very much doubt it.*
Ве́че съм реши́ла.	*I've already made up my mind.*
Вече́рял ли си?	*Have you had supper?*

Не, не съм.	No, I haven't.
Започнало ли е представлението?	Has the performance started?
Вината е моя.	It's my fault.
как съм направил такава грешка	how I made such a mistake
Хайде да се разходим.	Let's go for a walk.
Няма да ни бъде скучно.	We won't be bored.
Ами сега?	And now what?!
Какво се е случило?	What's happened?/What's the matter?
Не съм взел пари!	I haven't taken any money!
Забравил съм ги в джоба на дънките си.	I (must) have left it in the pocket of my jeans.
смешен	funny
нея не съм забравил	that I haven't forgotten
Станал си много разсеян.	You have become very absent-minded.
Сигурно си се уморил от много учене ...	You must have got tired with all that studying ...
никога не съм бил толкова разсеян	I have never been so absent-minded
друг въпрос	a different matter

QUICK VOCAB

1 Questions

a Какво не е направила Милена?
b Отишла ли си е приятелката на Милена?
c Кога предлага Николай да вечерят?
d Защо не е започнало представлението?
e Какъв е станал Николай?
f От какво се е уморил Николай според Милена?

2 True or false?

a Милена беше поканила една приятелка преди Николай да купи билети.
b Ще закъснеят, защото Милена още не е решила какво да облече.

c Николáй вéче е вечéрял.

d Представлéнието óще не é запóчнало.

e Николáй нáма предстáва как е напрáвил такáва грéшка.

f Николáй мóже да плати с крéдитна кáрта.

g На Николáй ще му е скýчно с Милéна.

How do you say it?

- Acknowledging guilt

Винáта е мóя.	*It's my fault.*
Мóя е винáта.	*The fault is mine.*

- Asking someone if they have eaten

Вечéрял(а) ли си?	*Have you had supper?*
Вечéряли ли сте?	*Have you had supper?*

- Expressing disbelief

Съмнáвам се.	*I doubt it.*
Мнóго се съмнáвам.	*I very much doubt it.*
Не é вáрно.	*It's not true.*
Товá е друг въпрóс.	*That's a different matter.*

- Making little of something

Нáма значéние.	*It doesn't matter./Never mind.*

- Expressing panic and confusion

Ами сегá?	*Now what?!*
Óлеле!	*Oh dear me!*

- Saying *I've made up my mind*

Вéче съм реши́л(а).	*I've already made up my mind.*

Grammar

1 Вéче съм реши́л(а) *I've already made up my mind*

In Bulgarian, as in English, you need a special tense to talk about actions that happened in the past, but the results of which are still evident in the present. We can call this the **present perfect tense**. You usually use it when you are focusing on the effect a past action has on the here and now. You are not interested or not sure when it happened. Very often the meaning of result is reinforced by words like **вéче** *already* or **óще не** *not yet*.

Here are some examples based on the dialogue – all, notice, corresponding to an English form using *have* or *has*:

Не съм забрáвила.	*I haven't forgotten.*
Óще ли не си е отúшла?	*Hasn't she gone yet?*
Запóчнало ли е представлéнието?	*Has the performance started?*
Óще не é запóчнало.	*It hasn't started yet.*

2 How to form the present perfect tense

As in English, the **present perfect** is made up of two parts. However, instead of *have* or *has*, Bulgarian uses the present forms of **съм** together with a distinct form of the main verb, called the **past participle**. (In English, these are the words *forgotten*, *gone* and *started* in the translations of the sentences you have just read. The form often ends in *-ed* or *-en*.) The past participle in Bulgarian ends in **-л** in the masculine, but you can think of it as an adjective, for it changes its ending to **-ла** in the feminine, **-ло** in the neuter and **-ли** in the plural. You will find a list of past participles in the Appendix.

Here is a list of forms in all persons for **вечéрям**. Notice the word order!

вечéрял(а) съм/ не съм вечéрял(а)	*I have/have not had supper (i.e. dined!)*
вечéрял(а) си/ не си вечéрял(а)	*you have/ have not had supper*
вечéрял(а) е/ не é вечéрял(а)	*he/she has/ has not had supper*
вечéряли сме/ не смé вечéряли	*we have/ have not had supper*
вечéряли сте/ не стé вечéряли	*you have/ have not had supper*
вечéряли са/ не сá вечéряли	*they have/ have not had supper*

3 Word order again ...

Word order with the present perfect is awkward. Normally **съм** (or **си**, **е**, etc.) comes immediately before the past participle, as in the **не** (negative) forms just given and in the following examples:

Никола́й е напра́вил гре́шка.   *Nikolai has made a mistake.*
Миле́на не е́ забра́вила.   *Milena hasn't forgotten.*

You will remember, however, that **съм** (or **си**, **е**, etc.) can never come first in a sentence. When the past participle comes first, **съм** (or **си**, **е**, etc.) comes immediately after it, as in the positive forms we saw earlier.

Insight

Word order is particularly awkward when you have to use a verb with **се** like О́ще не съм се обля́кла *I haven't got dressed yet*. In the Appendix, you will find a table setting out the relative positions of **съм** and **се**.

4 How to form past participles

Regular past participles

To form regular past participles, you start from the past I form of the verb and replace the ending **-х** by **-л**, **-ла**, **-ло-**, **-ли**. Again, a look at the Appendix will help!

Past tense	Past participle
забра́вих	забра́вил, забра́вила, забра́вило, забра́вили (*forgotten*)
реши́х	реши́л, реши́ла, реши́ло, реши́ли (*decided*)
хо́дих	хо́дил, хо́дила, хо́дило, хо́дили (*gone, walked*)
вече́рях	вече́рял, вече́ряла, вече́ряло, вече́ряли (*dined*)
видя́х	видя́л, видя́ла, видя́ло, виде́ли* (*seen*)
запо́чнах	запо́чнал, запо́чнала, запо́чнало, запо́чнали (*begun*)

Irregular past participles

Now for some *irregular* past participles:
(a) With verbs ending in **-сох**, **-зох**, **-кох** (Unit 14), replace **-ох** by **-ъл** and drop the **-ъ-** in the feminine, neuter and plural:

облякох   облякъл, облякла, облякло, облекли* (*dressed*)
донесох   донесъл, донесла, донесло, донесли (*brought*)

(*See Unit 8 for the change from я to е.)

(b) (да) отида has отишъл (-шла, -шло, -шли) *gone* for its past participle, and (да) дойда has дошъл (-шла, -шло, -шли) *come, arrived*. You will recognize дошъл from the expression Добре дошъл! (Unit 6). Here too, notice, you drop the -ъ- in the feminine, neuter and plural:

Приятелката ми още не си е отишла.	*My friend has not yet gone.*
Николай още не е дошъл.	*Nikolai has not yet come.*

(c) The past participle of съм is бил, била, било, били:

Никога не съм бил по-щастлив.	*I've never been happier.*
Никога не съм била в Москва.	*I've never been to Moscow.*

5 *Ever* and *never* with the present perfect

The present perfect is frequently used in statements and questions including or implying the adverbs *ever* and *never*:

Ходили ли сте в Париж?	*Have you (ever) been to Paris?*
Не, никога не съм ходил в Париж./ Не, не съм.	*No, I've never been to Paris./ No, I haven't.*
Да, ходил съм.	*Yes, I have.*

Insight

In Bulgarian, the negative answer is, like the English, without the participle ходил. See Unit 11.5 for a special use of the Bulgarian present where English has present perfect *has/have been* – after от.

6 The past perfect

Бях я поканила (преди да купиш билети).	*I had invited her (before you bought tickets).*

You need this form – the past perfect tense – to refer to events that took place before other past events. It differs from the present perfect tense only in that you use the past forms of *to be* instead of the present. Here is a list of all forms of the verb *to go*:

аз **бях оти́шъл/-шла**	*I had gone*	ни́е **бя́хме оти́шли**	*we had gone*
ти **бе́ше оти́шъл/ -шла**	*you had gone*	ви́е **бя́хте оти́шли**	*you had gone*
той **бе́ше оти́шъл**	*he had gone*	те **бя́ха оти́шли**	*they had gone*
тя **бе́ше оти́шла**	*she had gone*		
то **бе́ше оти́шло**	*it had gone*		

7 (Да) Взе́ма *To take*

This verb loses the -м- in its past forms and also in its past participle:

Past tense

аз **взех**	*I took*	ни́е **взе́хме**	*we took*
ти **взе**	*you took*	ви́е **взе́хте**	*you took*
той		те **взе́ха**	*they took*
тя } **взе** *he/she/it took*			
то			

Past participle

взел, взе́ла, взе́ло, взе́ли (*taken*)

The verbs (**да**) **наема** *to rent, hire* (Unit 11) and (**да**) **приема** *to accept* and some other verbs related to (**да**) **взе́ма** (Unit 16) also lose the -м- in the same way:

Ма́йкъл Джо́нсън нае́ кола́ и оти́де в Бо́ровец.	*Michael Johnson rented a car and went to Borovets.*
Те прие́ха пока́ната.	*They accepted the invitation.*

8 (Да) се облека́ *To get dressed;* (да) се съблека́ *to get undressed*

A number of sound changes occur in these verbs and also in (**да**) **пресека́** *to cross* (the street). First, you replace -к- by -ч- before all endings containing -е-. Second, in the past, the shift of stress means that you have to change the first -е- to -я- (Unit 8):

Present

Тря́бва да {
се облека́ — *I must get dressed*
се облече́ш — *you must get dressed*
се облече́ — *he/she/it must get dressed*
се облече́м — *we must get dressed*
се облече́те — *you must get dressed*
се облека́т — *they must get dressed*

Past

Аз се обля́кох/обля́кох се — *I got dressed*
Ти се обле́че — *You got dressed*
Той/тя/то се обле́че — *He/she/it got dressed*
Ни́е се обля́кохме — *We got dressed*
Ви́е се обля́кохте — *You got dressed*
Те се обля́коха — *They got dressed*

What with the rules for positioning се, these sound changes may seriously undermine your desire to talk about getting dressed, or undressed, in Bulgarian. But it is still worth trying!

Exercises

1 Practise using the present perfect by rearranging the words so as to reproduce sentences from the dialogue:

   a е, представле́нието, ли, запо́чнало?
   b се, не, о́ще, съм, обля́кла
   c гре́шка, как, ня́мам, съм, предста́ва, напра́вил, така́ва!
   d слу́чило, какво́, е, се?
   e реши́ла, ве́че, какво́, съм, да облека́

◆) CD 2, TR 42

2 Read the sentences that follow in which a friend is inviting you to see what Nikolai has done:

   a Виж, Никола́й е доше́л!
   b Виж, Никола́й е доне́съл цветя́!
   c Виж, Никола́й е ку́пил бонбо́ни!
   d Виж, Никола́й е напра́вил кафе́!

Now you say it is not true (**Не е вярно**), it is Nadya who has done all these things. Don't forget to make the participle feminine!

3 The receptionist at the Odessa Hotel asks Mr and Mrs Collins whether they have been to Borovets: Ходили ли сте в Боровец?

Ask the following people the same question:

a a young girl
b the couple sharing your table
c an elderly gentleman
d a small boy

4 A friend, who has taken you out, suddenly says: Забравил съм да взема пари. Станал съм много разсеян! Now imagine:

a You are a woman and you have forgotten to take an umbrella.
b You are a man and you have forgotten to take a camera.
c You and your partner have forgotten to take any money.

What would you say? Don't forget the second half of the answer!

5 Read the following sentences and then, using the model: Нямаше мляко. Милена беше забравила да купи мляко, complete the other sentences in the same way:

a Нямаше бира. Г-н Антонов _____.
b Нямаше хляб. Г-жа Антонова _____.
c Нямаше домати. Г-н и г-жа Колинс _____.
d Нямаше газирана вода. Аз _____.

6 Continuing with our absent-minded, forgetful heroes, what would you say if you thought you'd taken, but now can't find:

(a) ФОТОАПАРАТ

(b) ШАПКА

278

(c) СНИ́МКИ

(e) КНИ́ГА

(d) БЕЛЕ́ЖНИК

(f) ВЕ́СТНИК

Base your answers on the model:

Взех чадъ́ра, но сега́ го ня́ма. Си́гурно съм го загу́бил/а.

Another small step forward

◀) CD 2, TR 43–44

Dialogue 2 Ску́чно ми е! *I am bored!*

Victoria Collins comes back from the beach. George, who still has not got over the mild sunstroke he suffered in Unit 15, has stayed back at the hotel. They increasingly speak Bulgarian to one another.

Викто́рия	Как се чу́встваш, Джордж?
Джордж	Го́ре-до́лу. Но глава́та о́ще ме боли́.
Викто́рия	О́ще не си́ се обля́къл. Какво́ си пра́вил ця́ла су́трин?
Джордж	Че́тох уче́бника по бъ́лгарски – *Complete Bulgarian*.
Викто́рия	Какво́ но́во научи́?
Джордж	В Бълга́рия и́ма ху́баво море́. В Бълга́рия и́ма ху́баво ви́но. И ве́че и́ма ху́бава би́ра.
Викто́рия	Мно́го добре́, мно́го си научи́л.

Джордж	Но ня́ма игри́ще за голф набпи́зо! Викто́рия, ти не мо́жеш да разбере́ш! Ску́чно ми е! I AM BORED!
Викто́рия	Съжаля́вам, Джордж. Вина́та е твоя́! Ако́ не бе́ше стоя́л на слъ́нце то́лкова, сега́ ще́ше да мо́жеш да хо́диш на плаж. И разби́ра се, че и́ма игри́ще за голф.
Джордж	Така́ ли? Защо́ не си́ ми ка́зала?
Викто́рия	Не си́ ме пи́тал.
Джордж	Къде́ и́ма игри́ще?
Викто́рия	И́ма едно́ бли́зо до Балчи́к. Това́ не е́ дале́че от Ва́рна. Ни́кога не сме́ хо́дили там.
Джордж	Ха́йде да оти́дем!
Викто́рия	Добре́, ще оти́дем. Но о́ще не сме́ обя́двали.
Джордж	А с какво́ ще игра́я? Не съм взел сти́ковете си.
Викто́рия	Предпола́гам, че там ще мо́жеш да взе́меш сти́кове под на́ем. Пи́тай францу́зина от съсе́дната ста́я. Той ве́че е бил там. Ще взе́меш и ша́пка за слъ́нцето!

го́ре-до́лу	*so-so* (lit. *up-down*)
чета́, -те́ш	*to read*
(да) науча, -чиш	*to learn*
игри́ще за голф	*golf course*
стик	*golf club* (instrument)
съсе́ден, -дна	*next (door), neighbouring*

Test yourself

1 To see how well you have understood Dialogue 2, answer the following questions:

  a Какво́ о́ще го боли́ Джордж?
  b Какво́ му е на не́го?
  c Какво́ не е́ ка́зала досега́ Викто́рия на Джордж?
  d Какво́ не е́ взел Джордж?
  e С какви́ сти́кове ще игра́е Джордж?
  f Кой ве́че е игра́л голф на игри́щето?

2 Complete the past participles with the correct endings:

  a Миле́на, не си́ забра́в ____ за о́перата, нали́?
  b Миле́на о́ще не се́ е обля́к ____ .

280

c Миле́на е пока́н ____ прия́телка на го́сти.

d Прия́телката о́ще не си́ е оти́ш ____ .

e Никола́й, вече́р ____ ли си?

f Запо́чн ____ ли е представле́нието?

g Никола́й е напра́в ____ гре́шка.

h Той е забра́в ____ пари́те в джо́ба.

i Никола́й е вз ____ кре́дитната ка́рта.

j Ни́е сме реш ____ къде́ да оти́дем.

3 How would you say:

a It's my fault.

b It doesn't matter.

c I've already made up my mind.

d I very much doubt it.

Now can you:
- talk about some leisure activities?
- express disbelief?
- talk about past events that affect the present?
- refer to events that took place before other events in the past?
- vary the gender of the past participle in -л?
- choose the right word order for the present and past perfect tenses?
- form the past tense of the irregular verb *to take*?

19

Ѝмате ли оплаквания?
Do you have any complaints?

In this unit you will learn:

- How to complain if things go wrong
- How to distinguish between reporting what you know first hand and what you know from other sources

Dialogue 1

◀) **CD 2, TR 45–46**

Nevena is listening to the complaints of a businessman who has not been lucky with his room.

Бизнесмен	Добро утро, госпожице! Искам да сменя стаята си. Не съм доволен от стаята, която сте ми дали.
Невена	Какви оплаквания имате?
Бизнесмен	Контактът за самобръсначка не работи. Прозорецът е счупен, вентилаторът в банята е развален. Снощи и кпиматикът се развали! Освен това, има много шум. Стаята е точно над дискотеката и музиката не спира цяла нощ!
Невена	Съжалявам да чуя това, господине. Ще опитам да Ви намеря по-добра стая. Моля, почакайте във фоайето.
Бизнесмен	Сега не мога да чакам, защото имам важна среща. Ще се върна в хотела към шест часа.
Невена	Добре, не се безпокойте. Аз ще говоря с управителя.

(Later, in the manager's office.)

Невéна	Господинът от стáя сто и дванáйсета йска да смени стáята си.
Упрáвител	От каквó се оплáква?
Невéна	Кáзва, че контáктът за самобръснáчка не рабóтел, прозóрецът бил счýпен. Вентилáторът и климатикът били развалéни.
Упрáвител	Е, не é тóлкова стрáшно. Кажи му, че всичко ще попрáвим.
Невéна	Нéго го нямa. Кáза, че имал вáжна срéща. Щял да се върне към шест часá.
Упрáвител	Мнóго добрé. Катó се върне, всичко в стáята му ще бъде нарéд.
Невéна	Страхýвам се, че пак нямa да бъде довóлен. Йска дрýга стáя, защóто имало мнóго шум от дискотéката.
Секретáрка	И дрýги гóсти се оплáкват от шум. Кáзват, че не мóжели да спят от шумá на трамвáите.
Упрáвител	Да, знáя. Тогáва ще го слóжим в стáя на дванáйсетия етáж. Там е пó-тихо.
Невéна	Добрá идéя. Да се надявaме, че асансьóрите рабóтят!

Йскам да сменя стáята си.	*I want to change my room.*
стáята, коátо сте ми дáли	*the room you have given me*
Каквй оплáквания ймате?	*What complaints do you have?*
контáктът за самобръснáчка	*shaver socket*
счýпен	*broken*
вентилáтор	*extractor fan*
е развалéн	*is broken/has gone wrong*
Снóщи и кмиматикът се развалй.	*Last night the air conditioner, too, went wrong.*
освéн товá	*apart from that*
шум	*noise*
Мýзиката не спира цялa нощ.	*The music doesn't stop all night.*
Съжалявам да чýя товá.	*I am sorry to hear that.*
ще опитам	*I'll try*
упрáвител	*manager, director*
От каквó се оплáква?	*What is he complaining about?*
контáктът за самобръснáчка не рабóтел	*(he says) the shaver socket doesn't work*
прозóрецът бил счýпен	*(he says) the window is broken*
вентилáторът и кпиматикът били развалéни	*(he says) the extractor fan and the air conditioner aren't working*

Не é тóлкова стрáшно.	That's not so terrible.
Всúчко ще попрáвим.	We'll put everything right.
úмал вáжна срéща	(he said) he had an important meeting
щял да се вѣрне	(he said) he'd be back
úмало мнóго шум	(he said) there was a lot of noise
И дрýги гóсти се оплáкват от шум.	Other hotel residents too complain of noise.
не мóжели да спят от шумá на трамвáите	(they say) they couldn't sleep because of the noise from the trams
Тогáва ще го слóжим в стáя на дванáйсетия етáж.	Then we'll put him in a room on the twelfth floor.

1 Questions

a Каквó úска бизнесмéнът?

b Каквú оплáквания úма той?

c Защó е шýмна стáята му?

d Защó бизнесмéнът не мóже да чáка?

e От какѣв шум се оплáкват и дрýги гóсти на хотéла?

f Къдé предлáга упрáвителят да слóжат бизнесмéна?

2 True or false?

a Бизнесмéнът кáза, че бил довóлен от стáята, коя́то са му дáли.

b Огледáлото (the mirror) билó счýпено.

c Бизнесмéнът кáза, че в стáята му úмало мнóго шум от дискотéката.

d Той щял да се вѣрне след мáлко.

e Дрýги гóсти сѣщо се оплáквали от шумá на трамвáите.

How do you say it?

- Asking to have something changed

Úскам да сменя́ стáята си.   I'd like to change my room.

- Saying something is damaged or broken

Дýшът е развалéн.   The shower has gone wrong.

Прозóрецът е счýпен.   The window is broken.

- Recognizing invitations for possible complaints

Ѝмате ли опла́квания?   *Do you have any complaints?/*
                                           Is there anything wrong?

Какви́ опла́квания и́мате?   *What complaints do you have?*

От какво́ се опла́квате?   *What is your complaint?*
                                           (The doctor may ask you
                                           this too!)

- Expressing dissatisfaction

Не съм дово́лен /дово́лна   *I'm not happy with the hotel.*
  от хоте́ла.

И́скам да се опла́ча.   *I want to make a complaint.*

🔊 **CD 2, TR 47**

- Apologizing

И́скам да се извиня́.   *I want to apologize.*

- Reassuring someone

Не се́ безпоко́й/-те!   *Don't worry.*

Grammar

1 Renarrated forms

(Ка́за, че) и́мало мно́го   *(He said) there was a lot of noise.*
шум.

You will have noticed in the dialogue that when Nevena repeats the businessman's complaints she puts them in a slightly different form:

Бизнесме́н	Конта́ктът . . . **не рабо́ти.**
Неве́на	Конта́ктът . . . **не рабо́тел.**
Бизнесме́н	Прозо́рецът **е счу́пен.**
Неве́на	Прозо́рецът **бил счу́пен.**
Бизнесме́н	Сега́ . . . **и́мам** ва́жна сре́ща.
Неве́на	Ка́за, че **и́мал** ва́жна сре́ща.

In Bulgarian, you have to observe a clear distinction between what you know from first-hand experience and what you know from other sources. The form which Nevena uses shows that she is conveying second-hand information and that she has not herself been a witness to any of the events or facts she is presenting. She is only passing the information on, retelling the events. That is why the verb forms she is using are called 'renarrated' forms.

Every so often in the book so far, we have actually found it quite difficult to avoid these renarrated forms, especially in the exercises. Go back briefly to the questions after the dialogue in Unit 13, for example. You were asked there to imagine you were Mrs Collins and, as it were, to answer from 'first-hand experience':

| Към кóлко часá пристúгнахте? | *What time did you arrive?* |
| Как бéше пътýването ви? | *How was your journey?* |

It was not possible for us to ask you to talk about the journey yourself, because you were not a participant. You only read about it in the dialogue! Let's now compare Mrs Collins' answers with what you would need to say if you were 'renarrating' what she answered:

Г-жá Кóлинс	**Пристúгнахме** към сéдем часá.
Вúе	Те (г-н и г-жá Кóлинс) **пристúгнали** към сéдем часá.
Г-жá Кóлинс	Пътýването **бéше** прия́тно.
Вúе	Пътýването **билó** прия́тно.

Insight

Fairy tales use the renarrated forms. So do history books, unless, of course, the writer was an eye-witness to the events described.

2 How to construct the renarrated forms

Getting to grips with all the Bulgarian renarrated forms would be a pretty formidable task, as each tense has its equivalent renarrated version. For practical purposes, however, you will only need to use one or two of them, usually in the *he*, *she*, *it* and *they* forms, so it is on these that we will concentrate, both here and in the Appendix. In the Appendix, incidentally, you will find a slightly fuller set of tables enabling you to recognize some additional forms.

To start with, the renarrated forms are all based on the past participles ending in **-л, -ла, -ло, -ли**. This makes them look like the present perfect tense, which you came across in Unit 18. The difference is that the renarrated form drops the **е** and **са**. Compare:

Present perfect tense

Той е пристѝгнал.	*He has arrived.*
Те са пристѝгнали.	*They have arrived.*

Renarrated

Той пристѝгнал.	(I hear/they said) *he has arrived.*
Те пристѝгнали.	(I hear) *they have arrived.*

3 Renarrating present and past events

Go back to the dialogue earlier in the unit. You will see that the secretary repeats a complaint made by other hotel residents: Не **мо́жели** да спят от шума́ на трамва́ите. The form **мо́жели** tells us that the original complaint was made in the present tense: Не **мо́жем** да спим от шума́ на трамва́ите.

If the hotel residents had complained in the past tense (Не **можа́хме** да спим от шума́), the secretary would have said: Не **можа́ли** да спя́т от шума́ на трамва́ите. To be technical for a moment, and if you've got this far, you'll surely manage to cope, the difference between **мо́жели** and **можа́ли** is in the *type* of past participle being used. **Мо́жел (-а, -о, -и)** comes from the past imperfect form **мо́жех** (Unit 17). As an imperfective form, it is suitable for reproducing the present or past imperfect tense. **Можа́л (-а, -о, -и)** comes from the past form for *completed* actions **можа́х** (Unit 15). It is therefore suitable for reproducing things said in the past tense. Luckily, for many verbs, the two participles are identical.

4 Щял да се въ́рне към шест *He will be back about six* (he said)

When you want to renarrate things said in the future tense, you merely replace **ще** with **щял** (**щя́ла, щя́ло** or **щя́ли/ще́ли**) **да** ... You may remember Nevena saying the businessman would be back about six:

Бизнесмен	Ще се върна към шест часа́.
Неве́на	Щял да се въ́рне към шест часа́.

5 The present perfect of (да) дам

Дал, да́ла, да́ло, да́ли are the past participle forms of the verb (да) дам *to give*. It is an irregular form, because it is not directly derived from the past tense form да́дох (Unit 16). Instead of just replacing -х by -л, the past participle loses the last three letters: -дох and then adds -л, -ла, -ло, -ли:

ста́ята, коя́то сте ми да́ли   *the room you've given me*

This happens with all verbs which end in -дох or -тох in the past, as with чета́ *to read* (past: че́тох) and (да) преведа́ *to translate* (past: преве́дох):

Аз съм чел та́зи кни́га.	*I have read this book.*
Г-жа́ Ко́линс е преве́ла ня́колко кни́ги.	*Mrs Collins has translated a number of books.*

6 Ста́ята, коя́то сте ми да́ли: where to put the short indirect object pronoun

In present perfect sentences such as ста́ята, коя́то сте ми да́ли, you put the short pronoun for the person who is given something between the appropriate form of съм and the past participle:

Аз **съм ти дал** една́ кни́га.	*I've given you a book.*
Ти **си ми дал** една́ кни́га.	*You've given me a book.*
Ни́е **сме му да́ли** една́ кни́га.	*We've given him a book.*
Ви́е **сте им да́ли** една́ кни́га.	*You've given them a book.*
Те **са й да́ли** една́ кни́га.	*They've given her a book.*

With **той**, **тя** and **то**, however, the short pronoun comes *before* the verb *to be*:

Той ми е дал едно́ писмо́.	*He's given me a letter.*
Тя му е да́ла едно́ писмо́.	*She's given him a letter.*

When the past participle is the first word in the sentence, these sequences are preserved. The verb *to be* is followed by the pronoun in the *I*, *you*, *we* and *they* forms, but in the *he*, *she*, *it* form the pronoun comes *before* the verb *to be*. Compare:

288

Да́ла съм му ло́ша ста́я.   *I've given him a bad room.*

and

Да́ла му е ло́ша ста́я.   *She's given him a bad room.*

7 Introducing a reason or cause: от *because of*

The preposition **от** corresponds to a number of expressions in English. You have already come across **от** meaning *from* referring to time and space as in:

Магази́нът е отво́рен   *The shop is open from 9 to 12.*
  от 9 до 12.

Самоле́тът от Ло́ндон   *The plane from London gets in*
  присти́га в о́сем часа́.   *at eight o'clock.*

И́ма шум от дискоте́ката.   *There is noise from the disco.*

От is also frequently used to express reason or cause. Note the possible English equivalents in these expressions taken from the dialogue:

Не съм **дово́лен от**   *I'm not happy with my room.*
  ста́ята си.

И дру́ги го́сти се   *Other hotel residents too*
  опла́кват **от шум**.   *complain of noise.*

Не мо́гат да спя́т **от шума́**   *They can't sleep because of the*
  на трамва́ите.   *noise from the trams.*

Exercises

1 If you were asked: **И́мате ли опла́квания?**, how would you answer if you were not happy with:

  a the price   **e** the food (use **храна́**)
  b the shop assistant   **f** the quality of the photos
  c the waiter   (use **ка́чество**)
  d the service station   **g** the service (use **обслу́жване**)?

Model: Не съм дово́лен/дово́лна от камерие́рката.

2 Nothing is right in the restaurant. Complete the sentences using the model provided by the dissatisfied businessman in the dialogue:

Ста́ята, коя́то сте ми да́ли, не ми харе́сва.

Don't forget to change to **кóйто, коя́то, коéто, кои́то** where necessary (cf. Unit 5).

a Кюфтéто, _____, не ми́ харéсва.
b Сýпата, _____, не ми́ харéсва.
c Ви́ното, _____, не ми́ харéсва.
d Сала́тите, _____, не ми́ харéсват.
e Сладолéдът, _____, не ми́ харéсва.

◄)) **CD 2, TR 48**

3 In this exercise, you can practise using two different tenses of (**да**) **дам** and also putting the pronouns in the right order. First, read out loud the short dialogue:

| **г-н и г-жа́ Ко́линс** | Не сте́ ни да́ли клю́човете. |
| **Портие́р** | Да́дох ви ги. Éто ги. |

Now, still reading out loud, complete the following dialogues, making sure you have chosen the correct short pronouns. If necessary, look them up in the Appendix:

a – Не сте́ ми да́ли паспóрта.
  • _____.
b – Не сте́ ни да́ли билéтите.
  • _____.
c – Не сте́ ни да́ли смéтката.
  • _____.
d – Не сте́ ни да́ли ключ.
  • _____.
e – Не сте́ ми да́ли визи́тна ка́ртичка*.
  • _____.

* визи́тка for short.

4 Read the following sentences in which you give several reasons why you cannot get off to sleep:

a Не мóга да спя от кафéто.
b Не мóга да спя от главобóлие.
c Не мóга да спя от горещина́.
d Не мóга да спя от кома́рите.
e Не мóга да спя от мýзиката в рестора́нта.

Now, giving the same reasons, say why you couldn't get off to sleep last night:

Снощи не можах да спя от шума на трамваите.

5 The story that follows tells of Michael Johnson's trip to Plovdiv which you first learnt about at the end of Unit 13. It consists of two parts – one told by Nikolai, who was there with Mr Johnson, and one told by Nadya, who was not. Read the story and try to work out who is talking first and where the first part finishes:

В Пловдив било много интересно. Майкъл ходил в най-интересните къщи, разгледал Римската стена и църквата «Свети Константин и Елена». Времето било много приятно. Имало много хора на панаира. Майкъл имаше възможност да бъде преводач на една група англичани. Той им помогна да намерят своя преводач. Той купи много картички от Пловдив, защото мислеше, че е загубил фотоапарата си.

храна	*food*
качество	*quality*
обслужване	*service*
визитна картичка	*business card*
горещина	*heat*
комар	*mosquito*
да се оженя, -ниш	*to get married*
празнувам, -ваш	*to celebrate*
родител	*parent*

QUICK VOCAB

🔊 **CD 2, TR 49**

6 Read aloud the following conversation at the reception desk. Eli and the young American Jim surprise Nevena with news of their marriage:

Ели	Невена, аз съм Ели. Ние с Джим се оженихме.
Невена	Каква изненада! Честито!
Ели и Джим	Благодарим.
Невена	Кога беше сватбата?
Ели	Вчера. Празнувахме в ресторант «Москва».
Невена	Отдавна ли се познавате?

Ёли	Запознахме се миналата зима в Банско. Джим беше там като турист. След това той дойде в София, за да се запознае с родителите ми.
Невена	Желая ви много щастие. Сега какво ще правите?
Ёли	Първо ще отидем на море. След това ще отидем на фолклорния фестивал в Копривщица.

The questions we are now going to ask are all in the special renarrated form, because we weren't in on the conversation. Answer using the same forms – you weren't there either!

a Кога била сватбата?
b В кой ресторант празнували?
c Къде се запознали Джим и Ёли?
d Защо дошъл Джим в София?
e Къде щели да отидат сега Джим и Ёли?

Another small step forward

◀) CD 2, TR 50–51

Dialogue 2 Грешката е моя *My mistake*

Nadya receives a misdirected phone complaint from an agitated customer.

Клиент	Ало? Добър ден. Искам да говоря с директора на фирма «Търговска реклама», моля.
Надя	Г-н Антонов разговаря с клиенти в момента. Да му предам ли нещо?
Клиент	Да, ако обичате. Обаждам се от фирма «ТрансПроект». Искам да се оплача. Предайте му, че не сме доволни от вашата работа.
Надя	От какво по-точно се оплаквате?
Клиент	Поръчахме 1 200 (хиляда и двеста) рекламни брошури, а получихме само 600 (шестстотин). Папките, който поръчахме, имат дефекти, а визитните картички са на лоша хартия.
Надя	Ще предам на директора оплакванията Ви. Ще Ви се обадя утре. Дочуване!

Надя	(*Later, to the director.*) Г-н Антонов, обади се един нервен клиент от фирма «ТрансПроект». Имаше цял куп оплаквания.
г-н Антонов	Какво е станало?
Надя	Поръчали 1 200 брошури, а получили само 600. Папките имали дефекти, а визитните картички били на лоша хартия.
г-н Антонов	Чакай, чакай! Тук има някаква грешка. Фирма «ТрансПроект» е поръчала 1 200 брошури и ние сме изпратили 1 200 – в два кашона по 600. Сигурно още не са получили втория кашон. Поръчка за папки и визитни картички от тях не сме имали. (*Telephone rings.*)
Клиент	Ало? Обаждам се пак от фирма «ТрансПроект». Искам да се извиня. Оказа се, че всичко е наред.
Надя	Г-н Антонов е тук. Искате ли да говорите с него?
Клиент	Няма нужда да го безпокойте. Получихме всички брошури. Както разбрах от секретарката, папките и визитните картички били поръчани на друго място, в друга фирма. Грешката е моя. Извинявайте още веднъж. Дочуване!
г-н Антонов	Нервният клиент ли беше?
Надя	Да, извини се. Бил направил грешка.
г-н Антонов	Нищо чудно. Казват, че в тази фирма ставали много грешки . . .

QUICK VOCAB

Търговска реклама	*Trade Publicity*
(да) предам, -дадеш	*to pass on/leave a message*
(да) се оплача, -чеш	*to make a complaint*
рекламен, -мна	*publicity* (adj)
има дефект	*has something wrong with it*
нервен, -вна	*agitated, stressed out*
цял куп	*a whole lot (of)*
хартия	*paper*
кашон	*cardboard box*
(да) се извиня, -ниш	*to apologize*
оказа се (*it* form)	*it turned out*
на друго място	*elsewhere*
още веднъж	*once again*

Test yourself

1 To see how well you have understood Dialogue 2 (and mastered the renarrated forms), answer the following questions:

    a Какво трябва да предаде Надя на директора?
    b От какво по-точно се оплаква клиентът?
    c Защо се обажда клиентът втори път?
    d Какво е разбрал клиентът от секретарката?
    e Какво казват за фирма «ТрансПроект»?

2 Complete the sentences:

    a _____ му, че не сме доволни от вашата работа.
    b Ще _____ на директора оплакванията Ви.
    c Имаше цял куп _____.
    d _____ се, че всичко е наред.
    e Папките _____ дефектни, а визитните картички _____ на лоша хартия.

3 How would you say:

    a Don't worry.
    b I want to make a complaint.
    c I want to apologize.
    d I'm not happy with the room.

Now can you:
- complain when things are not to your satisfaction?
- get things put right when they go wrong?
- recognize when events are not being reported first hand?
- use the Bulgarian preposition **от** to express reason or cause?

20

Бúхме úскали да дóйдем пак!
We would like to come again!

In this unit you will learn:

- How to take your leave of someone
- How to use some sentences with *if*
- How to express wishes and requests being especially polite
- How to agree to stay in touch

Dialogue 1

◄») CD 2, TR 52–53

At Sofia airport, Mrs Collins sees a young couple with a trolley.

г-жá Кóлинс	Извинéте, бúхте ли ми кáзали откъдé взéхте колúчка за багáж?
Милéна	О, но нúе се познáваме. Здравéйте! Видя́хме се в еднó кафé. Пóмните ли?
г-жá Кóлинс	Да, вя́рно – Вúе сте момúчето, коéто ни покáза Централна пóща, налú?
Милéна	Тóчно такá! Запознáйте се – товá е мóят колéга Николáй. Той заминáва за Áнглия.
г-жá Кóлинс	Знáчи ще пътýваме зáедно. (*Shaking hands.*) Приáтно ми е.
Милéна	Николáй, би ли взел колúчка за г-н и г-жá Кóлинс?
Николáй	Да, разбúра се. Едúн момéнт.
Милéна	Довóлни ли сте от престóя във Вáрна?
г-жá Кóлинс	Да, изкáрахме чудéсно. Мúсля, че видя́хме пóвечето забележúтелности óколо градá.

Миле́на	Ще до́йдете ли пак в Бълга́рия сле́дващата годи́на?
г-жа́ Ко́линс	Мно́го би́хме и́скали да до́йдем пак. Ако́ и́маме възмо́жност да до́йдем през зи́мата, би́хме оти́шли в Бо́ровец то́зи път.
Миле́на	Ако́ и́двате пак, обаде́те ми се непреме́нно! Е́то, Никола́й и́два с коли́чката.
г-н Ко́линс	Благодаря́, Никола́й. Викто́рия, тря́бва да бъ́рзаме. Дови́ждане, Миле́на! Ще Ви пи́шем от А́нглия.
Миле́на	Вси́чко ху́баво, г-н Ко́линс! Г-жа́ Ко́линс, и́мам една́ молба́ към Вас. Би́хте ли помо́гнали на Никола́й на Хи́йтроу? Той се безпоко́и, че не разби́ра англи́йски мно́го добре́.
г-жа́ Ко́линс	Ще му помо́гна с удово́лствие. Дови́ждане, Миле́на!
Миле́на	Прия́тен път! (*To Nikolai.*) Никола́й, ще ми пра́тиш ли и́мейл от Че́лмсфорд?
Никола́й	Зна́еш, че ще ти пра́тя . . . (*With a sigh.*) Ко́лко бих и́скал ти да пъту́ваш с ме́не!
Миле́на	Ха́йде, ха́йде, тръ́гвай! Ще закъсне́еш за самоле́та. Прия́тно изка́рване!
Никола́й	Благодаря́! До ско́ро!

Би́хте ли ми ка́зали?	*Could you please tell me?*
По́мните ли?	*Do you remember?*
Би ли взел коли́чка?	*Could you please take a trolley?*
Еди́н моме́нт.	*Just a moment.*
Изка́рахме чуде́сно.	*We had a marvellous time.*
Видя́хме по́вечето забележи́телности о́коло града́.	*We saw most of the sights around the town.*
Би́хме и́скали да до́йдем пак.	*We'd like to come again.*
би́хме оти́шли	*we would go*
обаде́те ми се непреме́нно	*don't fail to/do let me know*
Ще Ви пи́шем.	*We'll write to you.*
Вси́чко ху́баво.	*All the best.*
Би́хте ли помо́гнали?	*Could you please help?*
Ще ми пра́тиш ли и́мейл?	*Will you send me an email?*
Ко́лко бих и́скал ти да пъту́ваш с ме́не!	*How I wish you were going with me!*
Ха́йде, ха́йде, тръ́гвай.	*Come on/now, now, off you go.*
До ско́ро!	*See you soon/later.*

1 Questions

a Какво́ пока́за Миле́на на г-н и г-жа́ Ко́линс?

b Кога́ би́ха и́скали да до́йдат г-н и г-жа́ Ко́линс пак в Бълга́рия?

c Къде́ би́ха оти́шли те, ако́ и́маха възмо́жност?

d Каква́ молба́ и́ма Миле́на към г-жа́ Ко́линс?

e Какво́ би и́скал Никола́й?

2 True or false?

a Никола́й ня́ма да пъту́ва за́едно с г-н и г-жа́ Ко́линс.

b Г-н и г-жа́ Ко́линс са виде́ли вси́чки забележи́телности о́коло Ва́рна.

c Г-н и г-жа́ Ко́линс би́ха и́скали да до́йдат пак в Бълга́рия.

d Г-н и г-жа́ Ко́линс ня́ма да пи́шат на Миле́на от А́нглия.

e Никола́й ще пра́ти ка́ртичка на Миле́на от Че́лмсфорд.

How do you say it?

- Taking your leave

До ско́ро (ви́ждане)!	*See you soon/later.*
Прия́тен път!	*Have a pleasant journey.*

- Expressing a wish politely

Бих и́скал/а ...	*I would like ...*
(Мно́го) би́хме и́скали ...	*We would (very much) like ...*

- Intensifying a statement or a wish

Ела́те непреме́нно!	*Do come!*
Непреме́нно ще до́йда.	*I certainly will come.*

- Making a polite request for assistance

Би́хте ли ми ка́зали ... ?	*Would you be so kind as to tell me ...?*
Би ли взел коли́чка?	*Would you be so kind as to take a trolley?*
Би́хте ли ми помо́гнали?	*Could you please help me?*

- Asking someone to wait a moment

Еди́н моме́нт!	*Just a moment/hold on!*

- Saying you have enjoyed yourself very much

Изкáрахме чудéсно.   *We had a marvellous time.*

- Expressing eager expectation

Очáквам Николáй с   *I'm looking forward to*
   нетърпéние.   *Nikolai coming.*
С нетърпéние очáквам   *I'm looking forward to hearing*
   да се обáдите.   *from you.*

Grammar

1   Expressing wishes and requests more formally

Бих úскал да . . . *I would like to . . .*

In Unit 6, you learned that the Bulgarian equivalent of *I want to* is **Úскам да**, and you may have felt this way of expressing a wish rather rude. Although **úскам** in Bulgarian is socially more acceptable than *I want* in English – ('I want never gets', remember!) – Bulgarian does also have more formal polite alternatives. These are based on a special form of **съм** and come close to English polite expressions with *would* and *could*. Compare:

Úскам да сменя́ стáята си.   *I want to change my room.*
and
Бих úскал(а) да сменя́   *I would like to change my room.*
   стáята си.
Úскам да говóря с   *I want to speak to the director.*
   дирéктора.
and
Бих úскал(а) да говóря   *I would like to speak to the*
   с дирéктора.   *director.*

These ultra-polite forms, *would like to . . .*, and also the conditionals about which you will discover more shortly, consist of the special form of **съм** plus a past participle, usually from a verb of *wanting* or *wishing*:

(аз) бих úскал(а) да . . .	(нúе) бúхме úскали да . . .
(ти) би úскал(а) да . . .	(вúе) бúхте úскали да . . .
(той) би úскал да . . .	(те) бúха úскали да . . .
(тя) би úскала да . . .	
(то) би úскало да . . .	

Би́хте ли . . .? *Would you be so kind as to . . .? (Could you . . .?)*

You can use the same form of **съм** to make polite requests:

Би ли ми ка́зал(а) ко́лко е часъ́т?	*Could you tell me what the time is?*
Би́хте ли ми пока́зали пъ́тя за Ва́рна?	*Would you be so kind as to show me the way to Varna?*

These requests are a degree more formal than questions using **Мо́же ли . . .?** (see Unit 6).

2 Бих оти́шъл (ако́ . . .) *I would go (if . . .)*

The same forms are used to express willingness to do something if the circumstances permit or if certain conditions are fulfilled:

Би́хме оти́шли в Бо́ровец, ако́ до́йдем през зи́мата.	*We'd go to Borovets if we were to come in winter.*
Бих оти́шла в А́нглия (ако́ и́мам пари́)	*I'd go to England (if I were to have the money).*

Insight

Unlike constructions with **щях** in Unit 16, these are states of affairs that still can happen; they are 'open':

Би́хме дошли́ с вас, ако́ не сме́ зае́ти.	*We will come with you if we aren't busy.*

In this last example, the statement is more tentative and the Bulgarian expresses willingness and politeness as much as condition.

In all three examples, the Bulgarian polite form could be replaced by the normal future: **ще оти́дем, ще оти́да** and **ще до́йдем,** all of which are more assertive and definite – *I will* rather than *I would*.

3 Catching up with new verbs with 'ce'

In Unit 6, you learned that some Bulgarian verbs, called reflexive verbs, are accompanied by the 'satellite' word **ce**. Since then you have come across more reflexive verbs and they can now be summed up in three groups:

(a) when the object of the verb in English is *myself, yourself*, etc. (or such an object is implied) as in:

Момчето се облече.	*The boy got (himself) dressed.*
Той се чувства по́-добре́ сега́.	*He feels better now.*
Той се безпокои́.	*He is worried.*

These verbs can usually also appear without **ce** and with an object. Compare:

Невена облече момчето.	*Nevena got the boy dressed.*
Чувствам болка в кръста.	*I feel a pain in the back.*
Извиня́вай, че те безпокои́.	*Forgive me for troubling you.*

Other similar verbs include:

(да) въ́рна	*to return, give back*
(да) оже́ня	*to marry someone off*
(да) разваля́	*to break something*
(да) се въ́рна	*to return, go back*
(да) се оже́ня	*to get married*
(да) се разваля́	*to break down, go wrong*

(b) when the object of the verb in English is *each other* or *one another*. These verbs can also be used without **ce**:

Аз позна́вам Никола́й.	*I know Nikolai.*
but:	
Ни́е се позна́ваме.	*We know each other.*
Миле́на видя́ г-жа́ Ко́линс.	*Milena saw Mrs Collins.*
but:	
Те се видя́ха в едно́ кафе́.	*They saw one another in a café.*
Ще запозна́я Никола́й с те́зи англича́ни.	*I'll introduce Nikolai to these Englishmen.*
but:	
Те ще се запозна́ят на лети́щето.	*They'll get to know one another at the airport.*

(c) when the verb denotes feelings or emotions. These verbs never appear without **ce**:

гри́жа се	to look after	страху́вам се	to be afraid
наде́вам се	to hope	съмня́вам се	to be in doubt
ра́двам се	to be pleased	шегу́вам се	to joke
смея се	to laugh		

4 To be doing something and to begin doing something

The difference in meaning of 'twin' verbs like **ра́двам се** *to be glad* and (**да**) **се зара́двам** *to rejoice* or **смея се** *to be laughing* and **да се засмея** *to begin to laugh* is often difficult to render succinctly in English. One is imperfective, the other perfective (see Unit 12). When the prefix **за-** is added to a verb it often denotes the beginning of an action. Compare the beginning perceived as a moment in time A, with B, an action that is going on:

A Тя го видя́ и се засмя́.   *She saw him and began to laugh.*
Той я видя́ и веднага го   *He saw her and immediately got*
заболя́ глава́та.   *a headache.*

B Тя пак се смее.   *She's laughing again.*
Пак го боли глава́та.   *He's having a headache again.*

Also compare the verb **по́мня** *to remember* with the verb (**да**) **запо́мня**. The first verb can be paraphrased as '*to be keeping something in one's memory*' (that is why it is imperfective) and the second one as '*to get something fixed in one's memory*' (that is why it is perfective).

5 Keeping in touch

(**Да**) **се оба́дя** *to get in touch, to phone* does not fit into any of the three groups and literally means '*to let oneself be heard*' (see Unit 11). When you use it in the phrase **обади́ ми се!** you have to remember where to put the two little unstressed words. The indirect object pronoun (**ми**) always comes before **се**, no matter whether they both follow or precede the verb (see Appendix):

Обаде́те **ми се!**   *Give me a ring/call.*
Обади́ **ми се** с есеме́с.   *Text me.*
Тря́бва да **ми се** оба́диш.   *You must give me a ring/call/get in touch.*

Insight

To emphasize keeping or staying in touch, you need to use the imperfective 'twin':

Обáждай се!/Обáждайте се!   *Keep/stay in touch!*

Exercises

1 Following the model, respond to the following requests. Watch the word order!

Request: Обади́ се на г-н Антóнов, мóля те.
Responses: **a** Ще му се обáдя.
              b Обáдих му се вéче.
              c Вéче му се обáдих.

   i Обадéте се на секретáрката, мóля Ви.
   ii Обади́ се на Николáй, мóля те.
   iii Обади́ се на Джим и Éли, мóля те.
   iv Обадéте се на Невéна Петкóва, мóля Ви.

2 Make these requests, already quite decently civil, even more polite. The model may help:

Model: Покажéте ми, мóля Ви, тáзи вáза.
         Би́хте ли ми показáли тáзи вáза?

   a Мóля Ви, кажéте ми Вáшия адрéс.
   b Обадéте ми се пó-късно, мóля Ви.
   c Мóля Ви, помогнéте ни да намéрим пъ́тя за Вáрна.
   d Дáйте ми дрýга стáя, акó оби́чате.
   e Мóля Ви, порúчайте ми такси́ за дéсет часá.

Here are the past participles to choose from. You won't need them all!

казáл дал донéсъл порúчал помóгнал се обáдил спрял

◀) CD 2, TR 54

3 Answer these questions using the future form and, demonstrating your willingness to do what you are asked (provided certain conditions are met!), by using бих and the past participle:

302

Model: Ще оти́деш ли на мач (*match*)? Ще оти́да/бих оти́шъл, ако́ не вали́ дъжд.

a Ще ку́пите ли пода́ръци за жена́ Ви? (ако́ наме́ря не́що ху́баво)

b Ще се оба́диш ли от лети́щето? (ако́ и́мам вре́ме)

c Ще до́йдеш ли на те́нис? (ако́ се чу́вствам по́-добре́)

d Ще уча́ствате ли в конфере́нцията? (ако́ и́мам пари́)

Past participles to choose from (again, you won't need them all):

дошъ́л	ку́пил	уча́ствал	се оба́дил	разбра́л

4 If you have ever attended a conference in Bulgaria, you might find parts of the following brief address familiar. It contains several polite expressions that you yourself might have occasion to try out. Read the address out loud, then answer the questions in English:

Да́ми и господа́, скъ́пи прия́тели!

Бих и́скал(а) да ви поздравя́ с «Добре́ дошли́» в на́шата краси́ва сто́лица и да ви пожела́я успе́х в ра́ботата ви на та́зи конфере́нция. Мно́го се ра́дваме, че ви́ждаме тук то́лкова мно́го прия́тели на Бълга́рия от цял свят. Би́хме се ра́двали, ако́ та́зи конфере́нция е поле́зна за все́ки от вас.

О́ще веднъ́ж добре́ дошли́ в Бълга́рия! От все сърце́ ви пожела́вам прия́тна и плодотво́рна ра́бота и до но́ви тво́рчески и прия́телски сре́щи.

a On what occasion is this address given?

b At what point in the proceedings is the speech made?

c How does the speaker address his audience?

d Where do the conference participants come from?

e What else do they have in common?

f In what city is this particular conference taking place?

g What benefit does the speaker hope the participants will derive from the conference?

то́лкова мно́го	so *many/much*
от все сърце́	*with (lit. from) all my heart*
плодотво́рен, -рна	*fruitful*
тво́рчески	*creative*
мно́го по́здрави	*best wishes* (lit. *many greetings*)

QUICK VOCAB

5 Back in Britain, Michael Johnson is attending another conference. In the coffee break, he dashes off a postcard to his friends in Bulgaria. Read aloud what he says:

Скъпи приятели,

Пиша ви от Лóндон, къдéто съм на конферéнция. На конферéнцията има двáма бизнесмéни от Плóвдив, които добрé познáват г-жá Кóлинс. Кáзват, че говóря вéче не пó-лóшо от нéя . . . Бих искал да ви благодаря óще веднъ́ж за помощтá ви и за приятните дни в Бългáрия. Очáквам Николáй с нетърпéние. Надя́вам се да се видим скóро пак.
Всичко хýбаво и до скóро виждане!

Мнóго пóздрави,
Мáйкъл Джóнсън

Лóндон, 6.VI. 2011

Now you write a postcard, also in Bulgarian, to Nikolai and Nadya.

Another small step forward

🔊 **CD 2, TR 55–56**

Dialogue 2 На летището *At the airport*

Sofia airport is not large and, shortly before taking off for Heathrow, Mr and Mrs Collins bump into some more acquaintances.

г-н Кóлинс	Виктóрия, виж! Óще еднá познáта.
г-жá Кóлинс	А, да – момичето от рецéпцията в хотéла в Сóфия.
Невéна	Каквá изненáда! Здравéйте, г-н Кóлинс. Здравéйте, г-жá Кóлинс.
г-жá Кóлинс	Здравéйте, Невéна. И Вие ли ще пътýвате за Áнглия?
Невéна	Не, аз изпрáщам едни приятели – Марк Дéйвис и женá му. Пóмните ли, аз Ви кáзах за нéго.
г-жá Кóлинс	Да, пóмня. Америкáнският журналист, нали?
Невéна	Тóчно такá. Елáте да Ви запознáя с тях, те мнóго ще се зарáдват.
Марк	Приятно ми е. Невéна мнóго ми е разкáзвала за Вас. Щях да Ви изпрáтя съобщéние чрез нéя от Óлбани, за да Ви покáня на еднá конферéнция за Бългáрия. Бихте ли искали да учáствате?

г-жа́ Ко́линс	Бих уча́ствала с удово́лствие, ако́ не съм зае́та по съ́щото вре́ме.
Марк	Чуде́сно, ще Ви пра́тя пока́на и програ́мата. Би́хте ли ми да́ли и́мейла си, мо́ля.
г-жа́ Ко́линс	Заповя́дайте, това́ е визи́тната ми ка́ртичка. Ви́е в Аме́рика ли живе́ете?
Марк	Да, по́вечето вре́ме живе́ем в Аме́рика, но мно́го че́сто и́дваме в Бълга́рия.
г-жа́ Ко́линс	Нада́вам се да се ви́дим пак. Обаде́те се!

(*The public address system crackles into life.*) Мо́ля за внима́ние! Вси́чки пъ́тници, замина́ващи за Ло́ндон, да се явя́т на и́зход но́мер че́тири!

г-жа́ Ко́линс	Сега́ тря́бва да бъ́рзаме. Дови́ждане на вси́чки!
Неве́на	Дови́ждане и вси́чко ху́баво! Ела́те пак непреме́нно!
Вси́чки	НЕПРЕМЕ́ННО!

QUICK VOCAB

(да) се зара́двам, -ваш	*to be pleased*
разка́звам, -ваш	*to tell, relate*
през	*through, by means of*
(да) уча́ствам, -ваш	*to take part*
пъ́тник, (pl) -ици	*passenger, traveller*
замина́ващ за	*travelling to*
(да) се явя́, яви́ш	*to present oneself*
и́зход	*gate; exit*

Test yourself

1 To see how well you have understood Dialogue 2, answer the following questions:

   a Коя́ позна́та ви́ждат г-н и г-жа́ Ко́линс на лети́щето?
   b Защо́ е на лети́щето Неве́на?
   c За кого́ е разка́звала Неве́на на Марк?
   d За какво́ щял Марк да изпра́ти съобще́ние на г-жа́ Ко́линс?
   e В какъ́в слу́чай би уча́ствала г-жа́ Ко́линс в конфере́нцията?
   f Какво́ да́ва г-жа́ Ко́линс на Марк?

2 Complete the sentences:

a ____ искала да ви поздравя́ с «Добре́ дошли́».
b Би́хме ____ ра́двали, ако́ та́зи конфере́нция е поле́зна.
c Бих _____ да ви благодаря́ о́ще веднъ́ж.
d Би́хте ли и́скали ____ уча́ствате?

3 How would you say:

a What a surprise!
b Do you remember?
c This is my business card.
d Stay in touch!
e See you soon!
f Send me a text (message).

Now can you:
- take your leave of someone?
- be especially polite in expressing your wishes?
- use the different types of reflexive verb?
- arrange to stay in touch?

Taking it further

We hope you have found it fun working your way through *Complete Bulgarian*. We also hope you will wish to develop further your knowledge of the language, the country and its people. At present there is a sad lack of dedicated printed English language materials for intermediate learners of Bulgarian. We cannot direct you to any single book or course that takes you logically on from where you left off at the end of Unit 20. The only self-study course book we can confidently recommend to take you further is *Bulgarian: Beyond the First Steps*, also by Mira Kovatcheva, published in 2005 by Prosveta, Sofia. Other courses published in Sofia are primarily aimed at complete beginners. What you will have to do, therefore, is pick and mix from a variety of sources, combining limited printed materials with the expanding and ever-changing offerings of the internet. To help you on your way, in this section, we have listed a few books and other sources you might find useful.

Dictionaries and phrasebooks

Many of the bilingual dictionaries that have long been in service have recently been revised and reissued. You will also find an increasing number of new dictionaries, large and small, mostly targeted at Bulgarian learners of English, but nevertheless of value to English-language learners of Bulgarian. Few of them will be on the shelves of bookshops, so you need to ask for them by name, giving the author and publisher. Try the two-way pocket dictionary by Levkova and Pishtalova: *English–Bulgarian, Bulgarian–English Dictionary*, Colibri, Sofia (2001). Daniela Shurbanova and Krasimira Rangelova have compiled a number of useful new dictionaries all in the 21st Century Reference series published by Prozorets i Trud in Sofia. Ask for their *English–Bulgarian Dictionary* (2000 and 2008) and their *Bulgarian–English Dictionary* (2004). Or get the two in one in their single volume *English–Bulgarian, Bulgarian–English Dictionary*, Sofia (2005), which is excellent. The greatest variety of reference works has been produced by the German publisher Ernst Klett Verlag, operating in Bulgaria as 'PONS Bulgaria'. Look for the firm's distinctive light green bindings. We can particularly recommend the *Нов училищен речник* (*New Learner's Dictionary*), an up-to-date Bulgarian learner's dictionary, with maps, pictures, model letters, cultural explanations and a concise grammar of both English and Bulgarian. If you are looking for something really substantial, then go for the two big PONS dictionaries: the *Нов универсален българско–английски речник* and the *Нов универсален английско–български речник*. With 121,000 and 97,000 words respectively, they should have all you need. For further PONS publications, go to the website: **pons.bg**.

It is difficult to choose between the numerous phrasebooks currently on offer, but you won't go far wrong with either of the following: first, and top of the price range, the handsome, illustrated *Pons Bulgarian Travellers' Language Guide* (2004) by Edward Richards; second, the handy, very practical *Bulgarian Phrasebook*, published by Chambers (2007). This contains thematic vocabulary lists, related sentences, a mini grammar section and a 4000-word two-way dictionary. Phrasebooks are generally more available than dictionaries on the shelves of bookshops – especially in Bulgaria – so take a look and choose what best suits your needs.

Grammars, primers

For the intermediate learner, the most appropriate primer is *Intensive Bulgarian: a textbook and reference grammar* by Ronelle Alexander assisted by Olga Mladenova. Published by the University of Wisconsin Press (2000), it comes in two hefty volumes, combines grammar and exercises and will both help you revise and take you further. Grammars of Bulgarian produced in Bulgaria are traditionally on the turgid side and are intended for a largely academic readership. They are also, of course, mostly in Bulgarian and written in an appropriate style! For a relatively modern grammar of Bulgarian in English, try *A Short Grammar of Contemporary Bulgarian* by Kjetil Rå Hauge, published by Slavica in Bloomington, Indiana (1999).

Courses

A number of Bulgarian universities organize short courses in Bulgarian language and culture, usually in the summer, for keen and interested foreigners. Try the Sofia University Faculty of Slavic

Studies website: **slav.uni-sofia.bg** and click on Летен семинар (email: **summercourse@slav.uni-sofia.bg**), or the International Centre for Bulgarian Studies at the University of Veliko Turnovo: **uni-vt.bg** and click on International Summer Seminar in Bulgarian Language and Culture (email: **issbic@uni-vt.bg**. For short courses run at intervals throughout the year, go to **deo.uni-sofia.bg**.

Book buying

Most large internet booksellers can supply Bulgarian books if they are in print. In the UK, the specialist booksellers Grant and Cutler Ltd (55–57 Great Marlborough Street, London W1F 7AY) supply a variety of learning materials published in and outside Bulgaria. They have dictionaries, including technical dictionaries, phrasebooks, literature in Bulgarian, language-learning CD ROMs and even Bulgarian Scrabble. Try **grantandcutler.com** or email to **mail@grantandcutler. com** or phone 00 44 (0)20 7734 2012 and ask for the Slavonic Section.

Ypá! (*Hurrah!*) for the .bg internet address!

By far the most exciting source of authentic Bulgarian language material today is the internet. The .bg sites, and the information they provide, multiply by the minute. Here are just a few promising addresses for you to get started on.

An excellent site, in Bulgarian and English, with a multitude of links, is **online.bg.** Here you will find newspapers, literary journals, theatre and cinema programmes and much else besides. Also try the lively **dir.bg**, which even has a section titled 'FUN'. A more general site with good Bulgarian links is **digitaldialect.com/Bulgarian/links.htm**. Most Bulgarian newspapers have their own websites, so try **capital.bg**, **standartnews.bg** or **duma.bg** for a start. The Bulgarian National Radio has an excellent site: **bnr.bg** with news, culture and current affairs. Also try the site of Darik Radio: **darik.net** for similar fare. For online news go to **dnevnik.bg**, **dnes.bg** or simply **news.bg**. For access to authentic live language and native speakers, visit one of the social networks such as **MyLanguageExchange.com** or **Livemocha.com**. And if you are looking for authentic Bulgarian literature, try **liternet.bg**. There are lots of online language courses, almost exclusively for beginners, but they are still worth investigating. Google 'Bulgarian language online' or simply 'Bulgarian grammar' and you'll be on your way!

The **sofiaecho.com** site – all in English – is an excellent source of up-to-date information about Sofia and beyond. Finally, if you want to discover more about Bulgarian life and culture in hard copy, the most honest, entertaining and informative book, also in English, is *The Insider's Guide to Sofia and Beyond*, written by Christine Milner and Paromita Sanatani and published in Sofia by Inside and Out Ltd (2005). Order via the website: **insidesofia.com**.

Congratulations on successfully making it to the end of *Complete Bulgarian*!

We hope you have enjoyed working your way through the book. We are always keen to receive feedback from people who have used our courses, so why not contact us and let us know your reactions? We'll be particularly pleased to receive your praise, but we should also like to know if you think things could be improved. We always welcome comments and suggestions and we do our best to incorporate constructive suggestions into later editions.

You can contact us through the publishers at:

Teach Yourself Books, Hodder Headline Ltd, 338 Euston Road, London NW1 3BH.

So **приятен път! приятно изка́рване!** and **на добъ́р час!** (*farewell!*). And happy hunting!

Michael Holman and Mira Kovatcheva,
Tunbridge Wells and Sofia, 2011

Key to the exercises

Alphabet and pronunciation: trying out what you have learnt

1 Alaska, address, Estonia, espresso, Canada, credit, Milan, minute, Ottawa, omelette, Texas, telephone. **2** Berlin, bar, Glasgow, garage, Dakota, vodka, Geneva, jury, Zambezi, Arizona, Istanbul, India, York, Mallorca, London, Balkan, Panama, police, Frankfurt, Sofia, Zurich, Donetsk, Chad, Churchill, Sheffield, show business, Stuttgart, Budapest, Updike, Bulgaria, chauffeur, signora, Yukon, Leeds United, Yalta, Yankee. **3** Vienna, Vivian, Namibia, Varna, Richard, Yorkshire, Sinatra, Amsterdam, Hungary, Liverpool, Hyde Park, Sahara. **4** Address, espresso, telephone, credit, Ottawa, garage, minute, Donetsk, show business, Budapest, Vivian, Amsterdam.

Exercises 1 (a) iv, (b) xii, (c) v, (d) x, (e) xi, (f) iii, (g) i, (h) vi, (i) vii, (j) ii, (k) ix, (l) viii. **2** (a) v, (b) iii, (c) vii, (d) viii, (e) vi, (f) ix, (g) i, (h) x, (i) iv, (j) ii. **3** (a) viii, (b) xiv, (c) iii, (d) v, (e) vi, (f) xvi, (g) ix, (h) iv, (i) ii, (j) i, (k) xiii, (l) xv, (m) xi, (n) vii, (o) xii, (p) x. **4** 201 Business Club, 202 Restaurant, 203 Reception, 204 Fitness centre, 205 Bar, 206 Taxi, 207 Information, 166 Police.

Test yourself

1 (a) Milano (b) Moskva (c) Sheraton (d) Orient. **2** (a) 17.25, (b) 17.05, (c) 16.35, (d) 18.05, (e) 18.30, (f) 15.40, (g) 16.10.
3 Майкъл Джонсън   Майкъл Джонсън
   4, Маунт Драйв   апартамент 8
   Челмсфорд   хотел «Родина»
   Есекс   1000 София
   Англия   България
   CM2 7AE

Майкъл Джонсън
4, Маунт Драйв
Челмсфорд
Есекс CM2 7AЕ
Англия

Майкъл Джонсън
апартамент 8
хотел „Родина"
1000 София
България

Unit 1

1 Questions (a) Да, и́ма. (b) Не, ня́ма. (c) Ка́звам се . . . **2** (a) T
(b) F: Бизнесме́н съм. (c) T.

Exercises 1 (a) *agency* (f), (b) *address* (m), (c) *aspirin* (m), (d) *bank* (f),
(e) *business* (m), (f) *beer* (f) (g) *vodka* (f) (h) *computer* (m),
(i) *show* (n), (j) *music* (f), (k) *calendar* (m), (l) *problem* (m),
(m) *soda water* (f), (n) *sport* (m), (o) *tonic* (m), (p) *tourist* (m),
(q) *firm* (f), (r) *football* (m), (s) *chauffeur* (m), (t) *printer* (m),
(u) *office* (m), (v) *fax* (m), (w) *video* (n), (x) *xerox* (m). **2** (a) здраве́й
(b) здраве́йте (c) здраве́йте (d) здраве́йте (e) здраве́й (f)
здраве́й (g) здраве́йте. **3** (a) Добро́ у́тро. (b) До́бър ден.
(c) До́бър ден. (d) До́бър ве́чер. **4** i (f), ii (e), iii (a), iv (c), v (d),
vi (b). **5** (a) Да, и́ма. (b) Да, и́ма. (c) Не, ня́ма. (d) Не, ня́ма.
(e) Да, и́ма. (f) Не, ня́ма. **6** (a) И́ма ли уи́ски? (b) И́ма ли би́ра?
(c) И́ма ли лимона́да? (d) И́ма ли чай? **7** (a) Уи́ски, мо́ля. Джин,
мо́ля. (b) Би́ра, мо́ля. Ко́ка-Ко́ла, мо́ля. (c) Капучи́но, мо́ля.
Еспре́со, мо́ля. (d) Кафе́, мо́ля. Чай, мо́ля. **8** (a) a lovely hotel
(b) a good-looking man (c) a beautiful sea (d) lovely beer
(e) a beautiful name (f) a beautiful Bulgarian (female!) (g) Ху́бава
стая́! (h) Ху́бав апартаме́нт! (i) Ху́баво бъ́лгарско ви́но!

Test yourself

1 (a) Evening. (b) Yes. (c) Because there's no music. (d) No.
(e) Whisky and mineral water. **2** (a) И́ма ли во́дка? (b) Не, ня́ма.
(c) И́ма ли чай? (d) Запове́дайте! - Благодаря́! (e) Не е́ шофьо́р,

бизнесме́н е. (*f*) И́ма ли пробле́м? – Не, ня́ма. **3** (*a*) football
(*b*) golf (*c*) boxing (*d*) tennis (e) basketball (f) polo (g) hockey
(h) cricket (i) baseball.

Unit 2

1 Questions (*a*) Да, благодаря́. добре́ съм. (*b*) Не, ни́що. (*c*) Това́
е но́ва брошу́ра от господи́н Джо́нсън. (*d*) Самоле́т от Ло́ндон
и́ма в се́дем часа́. (*e*) Да, той присти́га днес. **2** (*a*) F: На́дя е
добре́. (*b*) Т (*c*) Т (*d*) F: Господи́н Анто́нов ня́ма вре́ме за кафе́.
(*e*) F: Господи́н Анто́нов и́ма мно́го ра́бота.

Exercises 1 (*a*) Къде́ е тя? (*b*) Той е добре́. (*c*) Как е той? (*d*) Къде́
са те? (*e*) Тя е в хоте́л «Роди́на». (*f*) Той и́ма ра́бота. (*g*) Тук ли
са те? **2** (*a*) Ка́звам се Джу́ли Джеймсън. (*b*) Ка́звам се То́ни.
(*c*) Ка́звам се Боя́н Анто́нов. (*d*) Ка́зваме се Ко́линс. **3** (*a*) Как
се ка́зваш? (*b*) Как се ка́звате? (*c*) Как се ка́звате? **4** Не, аз съм
г-жа́/г-н _____ (Try writing out your name in longhand and
in printed letters.) Не, аз съм в ста́я но́мер се́дем. **5** Трамва́й
но́мер две, пет, шест, о́сем. Троле́й но́мер едно́, че́тири, се́дем,
де́вет. **6** (*a*) Какво́ е това́? (*b*) Как е тя? (*c*) Как са те? (*d*) Какво́
е това́? (*e*) Как си? (*f*) Какво́ е това́ (*g*) Как сте? (*h*) Какво́ е
това́? **7** i (*b*), ii (*d*), iii (*a*), iv (*e*), v (*c*). **8** (*a*) Това́ ли е рестора́нт
«Криста́л»? Не, рестора́нт «Криста́л» е там. (*b*) Това́ ли е
булева́рд Ле́вски? Не, булева́рд Ле́вски е там. (*c*) Това́ ли е
Центра́лна по́ща? Не, Центра́лна по́ща е там. (*d*) Това́ ли е
хоте́л «Хе́мус»? Не, хоте́л «Хе́мус» е там. (*e*) Това́ ли е у́лица
Ра́ковски? Не, у́лица Ра́ковски е там. **9** (*a*) Не, ня́мам.(*b*) Да,
и́мам.(*c*) Не, ня́мам. (*d*) Да, и́мам. (*e*) Да, и́мам. **10** (*a*) Мо́ля,
къде́ и́ма рестора́нт? (*b*) Мо́ля, къде́ и́ма ба́нка? (*c*) Мо́ля, къде́
и́ма телефо́н? (*d*) Мо́ля, къде́ и́ма тоале́тна? (*e*) Мо́ля, къде́ и́ма
по́ща? (*f*) Мо́ля, къде́ и́ма фи́тнес це́нтър? **11** (*a*) съм, е (*b*) съм,
е (*c*) съм, е (*d*) сме, са (*e*) съм, е.

Test yourself

1 (*a*) F: Булева́рд Ви́тоша не е́ бли́зо. (*b*) F: Г-н Джо́нсън ня́ма
ка́рта на Со́фия. (*c*) Т (*d*) F: И́ма трамва́й до булева́рд Ви́тоша.

(*e*) T (*f*) T (*g*) F: Той пристига в Боровец в десет часа. **2** (*a*) съм . . .
е . . . (*b*) съм . . . е . . . (*c*) съм . . . е . . . (*d*) сме . . . са . . .
(*e*) съм . . . е . . . **3** (*a*) Това е всичко. (*b*) Имам още един въпрос.
(*c*) Довиждане! Лек ден!

Unit 3

1 Questions (*a*) Тя е от Манчестър. (*b*) Тя е преводачка. (*c*) Да,
омъжена е. (*d*) Да, има едно дете. (*e*) Той е учител. (*f*) Да, тя
познава България добре. **2** (*a*) F: Г-жа Колинс е от Манчестър.
(*b*) F: Г-жа Колинс има едно дете. (*c*) T (*d*) T (*e*) F: Г-жа Колинс
не е за първи път в България. (*f*) T.

Exercises 1 (*a*) Имам едно дете. (*b*) Омъжена ли сте? (*c*) Г-жа
Колинс е преводачка. (*d*) Каква е професията Ви, госпожо?
(*e*) За първи път ли е г-жа Колинс в България? (*f*) Откъде са
г-жа Колинс и г-н Колинс? (*g*) Познавам страната ви добре.
2 i (*d*), ii (*f*), iii (*a*), iv (*b*), v (*c*), vi (*g*), vii (*h*), viii (*e*). **3** (*a*) Не, не
съм лекарка. Каква сте? Секретарка/учителка съм. (*b*) Не, не
съм българка. Каква сте? Ирландка/англичанка/шотландка
съм. (*c*) Не, не съм сервитьор. Какъв сте? Преводач/лекар/
студент съм. (*d*) Не, не съм англичанин. Какъв сте? Ирландец/
шотландец/американец съм. **4** (*a*) Марк Дейвис е журналист.
Той е от Санта Барбара. Той е женен. (*b*) Милена е фотографка.
Тя е от София. Тя не е омъжена. (*c*) Андрю е студент. Той е
от Глазгоу. Той не е женен. (*d*) Г-жа Колинс е преводачка. Тя
е от Манчестър. Тя е омъжена. (*e*) Надя е секретарка. Тя е от
Пловдив. Тя не е омъжена. (*f*) Майкъл Джонсън е бизнесмен.
Той е от Челмсфорд. Той е женен. (*g*) Г-н Антонов е директор.
Той е от Бургас. Той е женен. (*h*) Николай е програмист. Той
е от Варна. Той не е женен. **5** (*a*) ът (*b*) та (*c*) ът (*d*) та (*e*) та
(*f*) ът (*g*) ът (*h*) ът. **6** (*a*) Лекарят е шотландец. (*b*) Учителят е
англичанин. (*c*) Чаят е хубав. Той е от Англия. **7** (*a*) Запознайте
се - мъжът ми! (*b*) Запознайте се - синът ми! (*c*) Запознайте се -
дъщеря ми! (*d*) Запознайте се - брат ми! (*e*) Запознайте се -
сестра ми! **8** (*a*) Синът ми се казва Андрю. (*b*) Детето ми се казва
Виктор. (*c*) Майка ми се казва Ирина. (*d*) Жена ми се казва Мария.
(*e*) Дъщеря ми се казва Силвия. (*f*) Баща ми се казва Пол.

9 (*a*) Но тя е студéна! (*b*) Но той е студéн! (*c*) Но тя е тóпла! (*d*) Но то е тóпло! (*e*) Но тя е тóпла! (*f*) Но той е тóпъл. **10** Заповя́дайте, товá е ви́зата ми. Заповя́дайте, товá е резервáцията ми. Заповя́дайте, товá е билéтът ми. **11** (*a*) кáрта(та) (*b*) Чéрно морé (*c*) Дýнав (*d*) Гъ́рция и Тýрция (*e*) Сóфия.

Test yourself

1 (*a*) T (*b*) F: Милéна е фотогрáфката на фи́рмата. (*c*) T (*d*) T (*e*) F: Николáй и Милéна и́мат врéме за кафé. **2** (*a*) Нáдя е секретáрката му. (*b*) Елéна е секретáрката ѝ.(*c*) Васи́л е преводáчът им. Васи́л е преводáчът ми. Елéна е секретáрката ми. **3** (*a*) Аз съ́що. (*b*) Разби́ра се. (*c*) Каквá сте по нарóдност? Какъ́в сте по нарóдност? (*d*) Прия́тно ми е.

Unit 4

1 Questions (*a*) Три писмá. (*b*) Не, той не разби́ра бъ́лгарски добрé. (*a*) Той и́ма срéща тóчно в дванáйсет часá. (*d*) Срéщата на г-н Джóнсън е в цéнтъра. (*e*) Той и́ма пет минýти врéме. (*f*) Той е в Бългáрия за две сéдмици. **2** (*a*) T (*b*) T (*c*) F: В хотéла и́ма англи́йски вéстници и списáния. (*d*) F: Невéна и́ма сáмо еди́н въпрóс. (*e*) F: Той е в Бългáрия за две сéдмици. (*d*) F: Часъ́т е дванáйсет без двáйсет и пет.

Exercises **1** Автобýсът за Мальóвица заминáва в шест (часá) и трийсет и пет (минýти) и присти́га в дéвет (часá) и петнáйсет (минýти)./Автобýсът за Бáнкя заминáва в дéсет (часá) и дéсет (минýти) и присти́га в дéсет (часá) и чети́рисет и пет (минýти)./ Автобýсът за Сáмоков заминáва в единáйсет (часá) и двáйсет (минýти) и присти́га в тринáйсет (часá) и трийсет (минýти)./ Автобýсът за Бóровец заминáва в тринáйсет (часá) и петдесéт (минýти) и присти́га в седемнáйсет (часá) и двáйсет и пет (минýти). **2** (*a*) Автобýсът за Сáмоков заминáва след пет минýти. (*b*) Автобýсът за Бóровец заминáва след двáйсет минýти. (*c*) Автобýсът за Мальóвица заминáва след дéсет минýти. **3** (*a*) Автобýсът за Плóвдив заминáва в единáйсет часá и двáйсет минýти. (*b*) Самолéтът от Лóндон присти́га в деветнáйсет часá и четѝрисет минѝти. (c) Ѝма самолѐт за Вѐрна в дѐсет часѐ и петнѐйсет минѝти. (d) Заминѐвам за Сѐфия в петнѐйсет часѐ и трѝйсет минѝти (три и половѝна). (e) Срѐщата на г-н Джѐнсън е тѐчно в дванѐйсет часѐ. **4** (a) Аз съм в Бългѐрия за дванѐйсет/петнѐйсет/двѐйсет дни. (b) Аз съм в хотѐла за три/тринѐйсет нѐщи. (c) Аз съм във Вѐрна за еднѐ сѐдмица/две сѐдмици. **5** от сѐдем часѐ до двѐйсет часѐ и трѝйсет минѝти; от дѐвет до двѐйсет и едѝн часѐ; от осемнѐйсет до двѐйсет и три часѐ; от ѐсем до дванѐйсет и от шестнѐйсет до двѐйсет часѐ; от дѐсет до тринѐйсет и от четиринѐйсет до деветнѐйсет часѐ. (a) Пѐщата рабѐти от сѐдем часѐ сутринтѐ до ѐсем и половѝна вечертѐ. (b) Аптѐката рабѐти от дѐвет часѐ сутринтѐ до дѐвет часѐ вечертѐ. (c) Ресторѐнтът рабѐти от шест до единѐйсет часѐ вечертѐ. (d) Сладкѐрницата рабѐти от дѐсет часѐ сутринтѐ до едѝн часѐ на ѐбед и от два часѐ следѐбед до сѐдем часѐ вечертѐ. **6** (a) Кѐлко американки ѝма в хотѐла? (b) За кѐлко сѐдмици е г-н Джѐнсън в Бългѐрия? (c) След кѐлко дни пристѝга брат ти? (d) От кѐлко дни са г-н и г-жѐ Кѐлинс в Сѐфия? (e) В кѐлко часѐ заминѐва автобѝсът? (f) Кѐлко писмѐ и кѐртички ѝмам днес? (g) Кѐлко децѐ ѝма г-н Джѐнсън? **7** (a) Нѐдя пѝе кафѐ с Николѐй и Милѐна. (b) Нѐдя пѝе кафѐто с мѐлко зѐхар. (c) Николѐй пѝе кафѐто с мнѐго зѐхар. (d) Милѐна ѝска кафѐ без зѐхар. (e) Те обѝчат кафѐто с мѐлко млякѐ. (f) Аз обѝчам кафѐ _____. **8** (a) В кафѐто ѝма зѐхар, налѝ? Да, ѝма мѐлко зѐхар. (b) В кафѐто ѝма млякѐ, налѝ? Да, ѝма мѐлко млякѐ. (c) В чѐя ѝма млякѐ, налѝ? Да, ѝма мѐлко млякѐ. **9** (a) В кафѐто нѐма млякѐ, налѝ? Не, нѐма/Да, нѐма. (b) В кафѐто нѐма зѐхар, налѝ? Не, нѐма/Да, нѐма. (c) В чѐя нѐма зѐхар, налѝ? Не, нѐма/Да, нѐма. **10** (a) две леглѐ (b) чужденцѝ (c) американци (d) бѐлгарски вѐстници (e) мнѐго въпрѐси (f) мнѐго езѝци (g) мнѐго продавѐчки (h) трамвѐи (i) мнѐго чужденкѝ. **11** (a) Ѐфисът е до ресторѐнта. (b) Ресторѐнтът е до ѐфиса. (c) Магазѝнът е до теѐтъра. (d) Теѐтърът е до магазѝна. (e) Музѐят е до пѐрка. (f) Пѐркът е до музѐя.

Test yourself

1 (a) F: Николѐй заминѐва за Ѐнглия. (b) F: Той не разбѝра англѝйски. (c) F: Едѝн англичѐнин от фѝрмата разбѝра мѐлко български. (d) F: Фирмата е в Чéлмсфорд. (e) Т (f) Т (g) F: Проéктът с фирмата в Áнглия е нов. (h) F: Той заминáва след три сéдмици. **2** (a) Чудéсно, налú? (b) Мнóго интерéсно. (c) Кóлко е часът? (d) Не разбúрам бългáрски мнóго добрé. (e) Извинéте! (f) Каквó прáвиш/-ите? **3** (m): часóвник, óфис, компютър, музéй, чужденéц, турúст, езúк, трамвáй, шотлáндец; (f): сéдмица, стáя, америкáнка, нощ, вéчер.

Unit 5

1 Questions (a) Англичáни úма в мнóго странú по светá. (b) Тя говóри мнóго добрé бългáрски езúк. (c) Г-жá Кóлинс е англичáнката в стáя нóмер дéсет. (d) Невéна говóри три езúка. (e) Тя знáе фрéнски, рýски и испáнски. (f) Той живéе в Чéлмсфорд. **2** (a) F: Не мнóго англичáни говóрят бългáрски. (b) F: Г-жá Кóлинс е анличáнката, коáто живéе в стáя нóмер дéсет. (c) Т (d) Т (e) F: Тя говóри фрéнски нáй-добрé. (f) F: Мнóго бългáри говóрят чýжди езúци.

Exercises 1 (a) Мнóго англичáни ли úма в хотéла? (b) Мнóго бългáри ли говóрят англúйски? (c) Бългáри ли са г-н Антóнов и Николáй? (d) Бългáри и англичáни ли рабóтят във фúрмата? (e) Англичáни ли са г-н и г-жá Кóлинс? **2** (a) дрýги (b) дрýго (c) дрýга (d) дрýги (e) друг (f) дрýги (g) друг (h) дрýго (i) дрýга (j) дрýги. **3** (i) (a) Тук на кáртата úма два ресторáнта. Кой (ресторáнт) е пó-блúзо? (b) Тук на кáртата úма два грáда. Кой (град) е пó-блúзо? (c) Тук на кáртата úма два курóрта. Кой (курóрт) е пó-блúзо? (d) Тук на кáртата úма два къмпинга. Кой (къмпинг) е пó-блúзо? (e) Тук на кáртата úма два мотéла. Кой (мотéл) е пó-блúзо? (ii) (a) На кáртата úма две аптéки. Коá (аптéка) е пó-блúзо? (b) На кáртата úма две бензиностáнции. Коá (бензиностáнция) е пó-блúзо? (c) На кáртата úма две спúрки. Коá (спúрка) е пó-блúзо? **4** (a) Кой (b) Кой (c) Коá (d) Кой (e) Коá (f) Кой. **5** (a) Кóлко чýжди езúка говóри Невéна? (b) Кóлко билéта úскат те? (c) Кóлко джúна сервúра сервитьóрът? (d) Кóлко чýжди езúка знáе Мáйкъл Джóнсън? **6** (a) **Турúст:** Извинéте, úма ли хотéли до гáрата? **Граждáнин:** Да, до гáрата úма нáколко хотéла. (b) **Турúст:** Извинéте, úма ли ресторáнти

до га́рата? **Граждани́н:** Да, до га́рата и́ма ня́колко рестора́нта.
(c) **Тури́ст:** Извине́те, и́ма ли музе́и до га́рата? Граждани́н: Да,
до га́рата и́ма ня́колко музе́я. (d) **Тури́ст** Извине́те, и́ма ли о́фиси
до га́рата? **Граждани́н** Да, до га́рата и́ма ня́колко о́фиса.
7 (a) мъжа́, ко́йто присти́га от Ло́ндон; жена́та, коя́то гово́ри
ху́баво бъ́лгарски; англича́ни, ко́йто живе́ят в Бъ́лгария;
семе́йството, кое́то живе́е в ста́я но́мер де́сет. (b) бъ́лгарина,
ко́йто замина́ва за А́нглия?; англича́ни, ко́йто са же́нени
за бъ́лгарки?/ко́йто не пи́ят уи́ски?; шотла́ндци, ко́йто не
пи́ят уи́ски?/ко́йто са же́нени за бъ́лгарки?; бъ́лгарката,
коя́то е омъ́жена за англича́нин? **8** (a) Е́то трамва́я. Е́то два
трамва́я. (b) Е́то троле́я. Е́то два троле́я. (c) Е́то автобу́са. Е́то
два автобу́са. (d) Е́то къ́мпинга. Е́то два къ́мпинга. (e) Е́то
компю́търа. Е́то два компю́търа. (f) Е́то банкома́та. Е́то два
банкома́та. **9** (a) Е́то биле́та ми. (b) Е́то паспо́рта ми. (c) Е́то
мъжа́ ми. (d) Е́то сина́ ми. (e) Е́то бага́жа ми. **10** Ну́ла, о́сем,
о́сем, о́сем, три, две, едно́, о́сем, де́вет, едно́ = ну́ла, о́сем, о́сем,
о́сем, три́йсет и две, осемна́йсет, деветдесе́т и едно́; ну́ла, о́сем,
де́вет, о́сем, едно́, пет, шест, се́дем, че́тири, две = ну́ла, о́сем,
де́вет, о́сем, петна́йсет, шейсе́т и се́дем, чети́рисет и две; се́дем,
о́сем, де́вет, ну́ла, две, шест, шест = се́дем, о́сем, де́вет, ну́ла, две,
шейсе́т и шест; де́вет, че́тири, се́дем, пет, че́тири, две, шест =
де́вет, че́тири, се́дем, петдесе́т и че́тири, два́йсет и шест.

Test yourself

1 (a) F: Никола́й у́чи англи́йски. (b) Т (c) F: Миле́на позна́ва
ня́колко учи́тели по англи́йски. (d) F: Миле́на и́ма два уче́бника
по англи́йски. (e) F: Никола́й и́ма ну́жда от уче́бници. (f) Т
(g) F: Никола́й е на два́йсет и шест годи́ни. **2** (a) Коя́ е На́дя?
(b) Кой е Васи́л? (c) Кои́ са Джон и Кен? **3** (a) Разби́рате ли
англи́йски? (b) Зна́ете ли фре́нски? (c) (Аз) гово́ря ма́лко
бъ́лгарски.

Unit 6

1 Questions (a) Ма́йкъл Джо́нсън и́ма сре́ща с г-н Анто́нов.
(b) Г-н Анто́нов ча́ка г-н Джо́нсън. (c) Не, той ня́ма пробле́ми

в София. (d) Той иска да отиде първо в банката. (e) Майкъл Джонсън трябва да обмени пари. (f) Той трябва да говори по-бавно. **2** (a) F: Г-н Джонсън е доволен от хотела. (b) T (c) F: Банката и ресторантът не са далече от офиса. (d) T (e) F: Г-н Антонов и г-н Джонсън нямат нужда от преводач. (f) T.

Exercises 1 Имате ли пинкод/парола/кредитна карта? Не. Трябва ли да имам пинкод/парола/кредитна карта? Да, трябва. **2** Искате ли да отидем: (a) на опера? (b) на концерт? (c) на сладкарница? (d) на дискотека? (e) на театър? (f) на екскурзия? (g) на ски? (h) на плаж? **3** Николай трябва да отиде в Челмсфорд след три седмици. **4** i (g, h), ii (d), iii (a), iv (f), v (c), vi (b), vii (e), viii (a), ix (a). **5** (a) нея (b) него (c) тях. **6** (a) него (b) него (c) нея (d) него (e) нея (f) него. **7** Казвам се (*your name*). Имате ли билети/писма/ покана/маса за мене? **8 Николай:** Искам да/може ли да говоря с Вас? **Г-н А:** Съжалявам, но сега нямам време за тебе. Имам среща с г-н Джонсън. **Надя:** Г-н Антонов, имате ли нужда от мене? **Г-н А:** Мисля, че нямаме нужда от преводач. Може ли да направиш кафе за нас? **Надя:** Нямам нищо против. **9** (a) ютия (b) чадър (c) количка (d) такси (e) носач (f) пари. **10** (a) се надявам (b) се радвам (c) се чувствам добре.

Test yourself

1 (a) Един клиент иска да говори с директора. (b) Не, не е свободен. (c) Той трябва да се обади по-късно следобед. (d) Той иска да отиде на тенис. (e) Да, Надя иска да отиде с тях. **2** (a) Може ли да обменя пари тук? (b) Г-н Антонов е зает в момента. (c) Милена, свободна ли си днес след работа? (d) Искаш ли да отидем на тенис? (e) Първо трябва да се обадя на брат ми. **3** (a) Може ли да говоря с г-н Джонсън? (b) Как се чувствате? (c) Може ли да седна?

Unit 7

1 Questions (a) Най-добре е да отидат на пазара. (b) Плодовете и зеленчуците на пазара не са евтини, но са най-пресни.

(c) Г-жа́ Ко́линс не оби́ча ти́квички. (d) Той и́ска еди́н килогра́м
дома́ти. (e) Тя прода́ва я́бълки, пра́скови и гро́зде. (f) Вси́чко
стру́ва двана́йсет ле́ва и осемдесе́т стоти́нки. 2 (a) F: Г-н и
г-жа́ Ко́линс и́скат Неве́на да им пока́же магази́н за плодове́ и
зеленчу́ци. (b) F: Г-н Ко́линс не и́ска да ку́пи ти́квички. (c) Т
(d) Т (e) F: Г-жа́ Ко́линс не и́ска пра́скови. (f) Т.

Exercises 1 (a) пли́кове (b) два пли́ка (c) два бана́на (d) бана́ни
(e) два пъ́пеша (f) пъ́пеши (g) ножо́ве (h) ня́колко но́жа
(i) ня́колко бъ́лгарски гра́да (j) градове́. **2** (a) Плате́те на
ка́сата! Не пи́пай! (b) Пазе́те чистота́! Не газе́те трева́та!
(c) Бутни́! Дръпни́! (d) Не пи́пай! **3** Мо́же ли да ми ка́жете:
(a) къде́ и́ма по́ща? (b) къде́ и́ма ба́нка? (c) къде́ и́ма апте́ка?
(d) къде́ и́ма павилио́н? **4** Мо́же ли да ми пока́жете: (a) то́зи
чадъ́р/крем? (b) та́зи ка́рта/ча́ша? (c) това́ списа́ние/лека́рство?
(d) те́зи ножо́ве/списа́ния/ кре́мове/ча́ши? **5** (a) Ко́лко
стру́ват кра́ставиците? Да́йте ми едно́ кило́ кра́ставици.
(b) Ко́лко стру́ват ти́квичките? Да́йте ми едно́ кило́ ти́квички.
(c) Ко́лко стру́ват я́бълките? Да́йте ми едно́ кило́ я́бълки. (d)
Ко́лко стру́ват пра́сковите? Да́йте ми едно́ кило́ пра́скови.
6 (a) Да, да оти́дем! (b) Да, да оти́дем! (c) Да, да плати́м! (d) Да,
да се оба́дим! **7** (a) Да, мно́го оби́чам да пъту́вам. (b) Не, не
оби́чам да игра́я на компю́тър. (c) Не, не оби́чам да пазару́вам.
(d) Да, мно́го оби́чам да ка́рам ски. (e) Да, мно́го оби́чам да
чета́. **8** (a) Купи́ мля́ко, мо́ля! (b) Ела́, мо́ля! (c) Седни́, мо́ля!
(d) Ви́ж, мо́ля! (e) Кажи́, мо́ля! (f) Да́й, мо́ля! **9** (a) Я́бълките
са по́-евтини от пра́сковите. (b) Дома́тите са по́-пре́сни от
ти́квичките. (c) Пъ́пешът е по́-сла́дък от гро́здето. (d) На́дя
е по́-зае́та от Неве́на. (e) Кра́ставиците са по́-голе́ми от
ти́квичките.

Test yourself

1 (a) Голе́мият буке́т ро́зи стру́ва осемна́йсет ле́ва. (b) Лале́тата
са по́-евтини. (c) Тя и́ска да ку́пи и не́що за пода́рък. (d) Ма́лки
пли́кчета от осемдесе́т стоти́нки и по́-голе́ми пли́кове
от лев и петдесе́т. (e) Тя тря́бва да плати́ осемна́йсет и
петдесе́т. **2** (a) Ко́лко стру́ва то́зи буке́т? (b) Покаже́те ми
по́-евтини буке́ти. (c) Лале́тата са по́-евтини. (d) Да Ви дам

ли плик? (e) Да́йте ми два пли́ка. **3** (a) Да Ви дам ли солта́?
(b) Мо́же ли да ни пока́жете ста́ята? (c) Да́йте ни клю́ча, мо́ля!
(d) Мо́ля, покаже́те ми това́ списа́ние! (e) Мо́же ли да ми даде́те
то́зи пъ́пеш?

Unit 8

1 Questions (a) Г-н Джо́нсън и́ска да ви́ди менюто. (b) Той
предла́га шо́пската сала́та. (c) Тарато́р е студе́на су́па от
ки́село мля́ко и кра́ставици. (d) Той предпочи́та то́пла су́па.
(e) За пи́ене г-н Джо́нсън и́ска пло́дов сок. (f) Г-н Анто́нов
и́ска да поръ́ча ча́ша ви́но. **2** (a) F: Шо́пската сала́та е с
дома́ти, кра́ставици и си́рене. (b) T (c) T (d) F: Г-н Анто́нов и
г-н Джо́нсън и́скат че́тири бе́ли хле́бчета. (e) T (f) F: На обе́д
г-н Анто́нов пи́е бя́ло ви́но.

Exercises 1 (a) Сервитьо́рката предла́га пи́лзенска би́ра, но
аз предпочи́там бъ́лгарска. Да поръ́чаме бъ́лгарска би́ра!
(b) Сервитьо́рката предла́га гро́здова раки́я, но аз
предпочи́там сли́вова. Да поръ́чаме сли́вова раки́я!
(c) Сервитьо́рката предла́га пи́лешка су́па, но аз предпочи́там
зеленчу́кова. Да поръ́чаме зеленчу́кова су́па! **2** В тарато́ра и́ма
ки́село мля́ко, кра́ставица, че́сън, сол, о́лио и о́рехи. **3** (a) И́ма
не́скафе и еспре́со. (b) И́ма че́рен чай, ме́нтов чай и би́лков
чай. (c) И́ма пло́дова то́рта, шокола́дова то́рта и о́рехова
то́рта. (d) И́ма портока́лов сок, гро́здов сок, я́бълков сок
и сок от я́годи. **4** (a) две, две (b) два, две (c) две (d) две
(e) два, две (f) два (g) два́ма (h) два (i) две (j) два́ма (k) две
(l) два. **5** Try the following menus – other combinations will
also do: (a) Една́ зеленчу́кова су́па и еди́н омле́т със си́рене;
(b) Две вегетариа́нски су́пи и два пъ́ти омле́т с шу́нка/
кюфте́та; (c) Че́тири зеленчу́кови су́пи и че́тири пъ́ти
кюфте́та/пи́ца с кашкава́л. **6** (a) бя́лото ви́но (b) сли́вовата
раки́я (c) вегетариа́нската су́па (d) шокола́довата то́рта
(e) бъ́лгарските специалите́ти (f) пи́лзенската би́ра. **7** Какви́
са́ндвичи и́мате?/Два са́ндвича с шу́нка и еди́н с кашкава́л,
мо́ля./Еди́н портока́лов сок, две ко́ли и три кафе́та, мо́ля.

8 (i) (*a*) две кебáпчета (*b*) кебáпчетата (ii) (*a*) две хлéбчета
(*b*) хлéбчетата (iii) (*a*) две кюфтéта (*b*) кюфтéтата.
9 (*a*) вегетериáнската сýпа (*b*) пълнените чýшки (*c*) бя́лото
грóзде (*d*) пи́лешката сýпа (*e*) червéните я́бълки (*f*) плóдовата
тóрта (*g*) бéлите хлéбчета (*h*) бългáрското ки́село мля́ко.

Test yourself

1 (*a*) Часът е óсем и половина. (*b*) Да, óще е рáно за рáбота.
(*c*) Не, кафéто е отвóрено. (*d*) За закýска и́ма сáндвичи,
ки́фли и бáнички. (*e*) За я́дене те и́скат два сáндвича и две
парчéта тóрта. (*f*) За пи́ене те и́скат две кафéта еспрéсо и два
я́бълкови сóка. **2** (*a*) Каквó и́ма за закýска? (*b*) За мéне еди́н
сáндвич. (*c*) Два я́бълкови сóка, акó оби́чате. (*d*) Éто, товá
е смéтката. **3** (*a*) предлáгате оr предпочи́тате (*b*) поръ́ча
(*c*) предпочи́тате (*d*) предлáга/предпочи́та (*e*) поръ́чаме
(*f*) предпочи́та (*g*) поръ́чате.

Unit 9

1 Questions (*a*) Виолéта и́ска да поръ́ча такси́ за лети́щето.
(*b*) Пи́колото ще помóгне с багáжа. (*c*) Във фоайéто и́ма
кýфари и чáнти на дрýги гóсти на хотéла. (*d*) Виолéта не
мóже да намéри чáнтата на Марк. (*e*) Марк нóси свóята чáнта.
(*f*) Чáнтата на Марк е голя́ма и чéрна. **2** (*a*) F: Виолéта и́ска
да поръ́ча такси́ за дéсет и петнáйсет. (*b*) Т (*c*) Т (*d*) F: Чéрният
кýфар и си́нята рáница са на Марк и Виолéта. (*e*) Т.

Exercises 1 Да, мóга да/Не, не мóга да: (*a*) игрáя тéнис (*b*) кáрам
ски (*c*) плýвам (*d*) кáрам колá (*e*) игрáя на кáрти. **2** Извинéте,
мóжете ли да ми покáжете: (*a*) къдé е аптéката? (*b*) къдé е
метрóто? (*c*) къдé е хотéл «Шéратон»? (no definite article
needed with names of hotels!) (*d*) къдé е спи́рката на тролéй
нóмер две? (*e*) къдé е Централна гáра? (no definite article
here either.) **3** i (*e*); ii (*d*); iii (*a*); iv (*b*); v (*c*). **4** (*a*) Твóят кýфар
ли е товá? Не, тóзи кýфар не é мой. Мóят кýфар е пó-голя́м.

(b) Твóето портмонé ли е товá? Не, товá портмонé не é мóе. Мóето портмонé е пó-голя́мо. (c) Твóят чадъ́р ли е товá? Не, тóзи чадъ́р не é мой. Мóят чадъ́р е пó-голя́м. (d) Твóята пáпка ли е товá? Не, тáзи пáпка не é моя́. Мóята пáпка е пó-голя́ма. (e) Твóят мобúлен телефóн ли е товá? Не, тóзи мобúлен телефóн не é мой. Мóят мобúлен телефóн е пó-голя́м. (f) Твóят молúв ли е товá? Не, тóзи молúв не é мой. Мóят молúв е пó-голя́м. (g) Твóят бележнúк ли е товá? Не, тóзи бележнúк не é мой. Мóят бележнúк е пó-голя́м. (h) Твóята химикáлка ли е товá? Не, тáзи химикáлка не é моя́. Мóята химикáлка е пó-голя́ма. **5** Портмонéто ми го ня́ма! or Чáнтата ми я ня́ма! Багáжът ми го ня́ма! Чадъ́рът ми го ня́ма! Бележнúкът ми го ня́ма! Пáпката ми я ня́ма! Парúте ми ги ня́ма! **6** (a) Турúстът не мóже да намéри свóя хотéл. (b) Не, турúстът не знáе úмето му/úмето на хотéла. (c) Хотéлът е блúзо до спúрката на тролéй нóмер еднó и тролéй нóмер пет. (d) До Университéта úма два хотéла. (e) Нéговият хотéл се кáзва «Сóфия Рáдисън». **Турúст** Извинéте, мóжете ли да ми помóгнете? Не мóга да намéря свóя хотéл. **Полицáй** Как се кáзва хотéлът Ви? **Турúст** За съжалéние, не знáя. Знáя сáмо, че е блúзо до спúрката на тролéй нóмер еднó и тролéй нóмер пет. **Полицáй** На коя́ ýлица е хотéлът? **Турúст** Не знáя на коя́ ýлица е, но е блúзо до Университéта. **Полицáй** Úма два хотéла блúзо до Университéта. Едúният се кáзва «Сóфия Рáдисън», дрýгият се кáзва хотéл «Бългáрия». **Турúст** Вéче знáя úмето на хотéла ми. Мóят хотéл се кáзва «Сóфия Рáдисън». **7** (a) F (b) F (c) Т (d) Т (e) F. **8** (a) Ня́ма я. (b) Ня́ма го. (c) Ня́ма го. (d) Ня́ма ги. (e) Ня́ма я. (f) Ня́ма го.

Test yourself

1 (a) F: До г-н и г-жá Кóлинс úма свобóдни местá. (b) Т (c) Т (d) F: Г-н и г-жá Кóлинс úмат мáлко рáбота в Сóфия. (e) Т (f) F: Едúн нéин колéга заминáва скóро за Áнглия. (g) F: Те не знáят къдé е Централна пóща. **2** (a) Извинéте, мóже ли да сéдна до вас? (b) Да, разбúра се, заповя́дайте! (c) Бългáрският езúк е мóята професúя. (d) Мóга ли да ви помóгна? (e) Мúсля, че мо́жете. (f) Пожела́вам Ви да оти́дете в А́нглия. **3** (a) С какво́ мо́га да Ви помо́гна? (b) Го́стите от Аме́рика и́мат ну́жда от такси́. (c) Виоле́та не мо́же да наме́ри ча́нтата на своя́ мъж. (d) Това́ не е́ мо́ят бага́ж. (e) Ма́лката си́ня ча́нта е на Марк/ Ма́лката ча́нта на Марк е си́ня.

Unit 10

1 Questions (a) Никола́й бъ́рза, защо́то тря́бва да поръ́ча такси́ и да запа́зи ма́са в рестора́нта за Ма́йкъл Джо́нсън и Боя́н Анто́нов. (b) Те мо́гат да чу́ят прогно́зата по ра́диото. (c) У́тре по висо́ките планини́ вре́мето ще бъ́де о́блачно. Възмо́жно е да вали́. (d) На́дя предла́га да оти́дат в Ме́лник. (e) В кра́я на се́дмицата вре́мето ще бъ́де ху́баво. (f) На́дя ще гово́ри с ше́фа. **2** (a) T (b) F: Никола́й тря́бва да поръ́ча такси́ и да запа́зи ма́са в рестора́нта. (c) T (d) F: У́тре вре́мето на Ви́тоша ня́ма да бъ́де мно́го ху́баво. (e) F: Г-н Джо́нсън си́гурно не но́си марато́нки. (f) F: Ше́фът ще се съгласи́ да оти́де в Ме́лник.

Exercises 1 (a) У́тре ще бъ́де ли о́блачно и мра́чно? Не, у́тре ня́ма да бъ́де о́блачно и мра́чно. (b) У́тре ще бъ́де ли мъгли́во? Не, у́тре ня́ма да бъ́де мъгли́во. (c) У́тре ще бъ́де ли то́пло и слъ́нчево? Не, у́тре ня́ма да бъ́де то́пло и слъ́нчево. (d) У́тре ще бъ́де ли студе́но и вла́жно? Не, у́тре ня́ма да бъ́де студе́но и вла́жно. (e) У́тре ще бъ́де ли дъждо́вно? Не, у́тре ня́ма да бъ́де дъждо́вно. **2** (a) Наи́стина, мно́го е горе́що. Не съм съгла́сен/ съгла́сна. Изо́бщо не е́ горе́що. (b) Наи́стина, мно́го е къ́сно. Не съм съгла́сен/съгла́сна. Изо́бщо не е́ къ́сно. (c) Наи́стина, мно́го е заба́вно. Не съм съгла́сен/съгла́сна. Изо́бщо не е́ заба́вно. (d) Наи́стина, мно́го е удо́бно. Не съм съгла́сен/съгла́сна. Изо́бщо не е́ удо́бно. (e) Наи́стина, мно́го е възмо́жно. Не съм съгла́сен/съгла́сна. Изо́бщо не е́ възмо́жно. **3** (a) Г-н Анто́нов ще се съгласи́ бъ́рзо/тру́дно. (b) Тру́дно/бъ́рзо ще наме́рим га́рата. (c) Шшш! Говори́ по́-ти́хо! (d) Бъ́рзо/тру́дно ще наме́рят бага́жа. **4** (a) Не, у́тре ще бъ́де я́сно и горе́що. (b) Не, вя́търът по Черномо́рието ще бъ́де слаб до уме́рен. (c) Ще бъ́де между́

двáйсет и óсем и трийсет и два грáдуса. (d) Температýрата
на морéто ще бъ́де óколо двáйсет и три грáдуса. 5 i (d); ii (e);
iii (a); iv (c); v (b). 6 Ня́ма да дóйда, защóто ня́мам врéме./
Ýтре./Предлáгам да отúдем на екскýрзия. Съглáсна ли си?/
Врéмето ще бъ́де слъ́нчево и тóпло. Добрé. И аз ще взéма
мóето я́ке.

Test yourself

1 (a) Т (b) F: На Вúтоша вúнаги е пó-студéно. (c) F: Мéлник е
на юг. (d) Т (e) F: Милéна не обúча да стáва рáно. (f) Т.
2 (a) Врéмето не изглéжда лóшо. (b) В Мéлник сúгурно ще бъ́де/е
тóпло. (c) Нáдя съ́що ще дóйде. (d) Ще бъ́де/е пó-интерéсно с
две хýбави момúчета. 3 (a) Жáлко! (b) Чудéсно е! (c) Къ́сно е.
(d) Възмóжно е. (e) Удóбно е.

Unit 11

1 Questions (a) Г-н Антóнов и г-н Джóнсън тря́бва да напрáвят
план за слéдващата сéдмица. (b) Г-н Джóнсън úска да отúде
в Бóровец, за да разглéда хотéлите. (c) Г-н Джóнсън и г-н
Антóнов са покáнени на излóжба във втóрник предú обéд.
(d) Те ще отúдат на панаúра на пъ́рвия ден, за да úмат врéме да
разглéдат всúчко. (e) Г-н Антóнов тря́бва да се въ́рне в Сóфия
на двáйсет и втóри май. 2 (a) F: Г-н Джóнсън úска да отúде
сам. (b) Т (c) F: Прéговорите ще бъ́дат на втóрия и трéтия ден.
(d) F: Г-н Антóнов ще посрéщне делегáция, коя́то пристúга от
Япóния. (e) Т.

Exercises 1 (a) На пáртера úма подáръци и козмéтика. (b) На
пъ́рвия етáж úма всúчко за детéто. (c) На втóрия етáж úма
обýвки. (d) На трéтия етáж úма телевúзори, компю́три,
мобúлни телефóни. (e) На четвъ́ртия етáж úма килúми. (f) На
пéтия етáж úма ресторáнт и тоалéтна. 2 (a) Маратóнки
продáват на втóрия етáж. (b) Парфю́ми продáват на пáртера.
(c) Компю́три продáват на трéтия етáж. (d) Шампоáни продáват
на пáртера. 3 (a) на нéго, го (b) на нéя, я (c) на нéго, го (d) на
тях, ги. 4 (a) съ́бота, за съ́бота (b) пéтък, в пéтък (c) сря́да, за

ýтре. **5** (*a*) Еди́н прия́тен уи́кенд. (*b*) Луксо́зен автобу́с.
(*c*) В хоте́л в це́нтъра на Бе́лград. (*d*) Два́йсет и о́сми апри́л;
вто́ри ю́ни; четвъ́рти а́вгуст; о́сми септе́мври; трина́йсети
окто́мври. (*e*) Екску́рзия до Но́ви Сад. (*f*) Бъ́лгарски ези́к.
(*g*) Не. Цена́та не включва биле́ти за музе́и. **6** (*a*) В понеде́лник
На́дя ще помо́гне на Никола́й с докуме́нтите. (*b*) Във вто́рник
На́дя ще ка́же на ше́фа за да́тата на изло́жбата. (*c*) В сря́да На́дя
ще отгово́ри на писмо́то на диза́йнера. (*d*) В четвъ́ртък На́дя
ще изпра́ти пока́ни на всички, кои́то рабо́тят във фи́рмата.
(*e*) В пе́тък На́дя ще се оба́ди на коле́гата в Пло́вдив. (*f*) В
съ́бота На́дя ще ку́пи пода́рък на сина́ на Анто́нови. (*g*) В
неде́ля На́дя ще пока́же на Миле́на но́вите плака́ти./Dates:
Какво́ ще пра́виш на осемна́йсети, деветна́йсети, два́йсети,
два́йсет и пъ́рви, два́йсет и вто́ри, два́йсет и тре́ти и два́йсет
и четвъ́рти май?

Test yourself

1 (*a*) T (*b*) F: Г-н и г-жа́ Ко́линс ще бъ́дат във Ва́рна до
четвъ́рти ю́ни. (*c*) T (*d*) F: Джим не мо́же да пъту́ва на два́йсет
и вто́ри ю́ли. (*e*) T (*f*) F: Джим тря́бва да оти́де в аге́нцията в
понеде́лник. **2** (*a*) Неве́на ще помо́гне на Джим. (*b*) Защо́то
и́ска да оти́де в Копри́вщица, за да ви́ди фолкло́рния
фестива́л. (*c*) сря́да (*d*) в понеде́лник. **3** (*a*) молба́
(*b*) четвъ́рти ю́ни (*c*) ня́ма (*d*) трина́йсети а́вгуст (*e*) прода́дени
(*f*) изка́рване.

Unit 12

1 Questions (*a*) На́дя не оби́ча да ча́ка. (*b*) Миле́на ка́зва на
На́дя да не поръ́чва о́ще, защо́то Никола́й ще до́йде след ма́лко.
(*c*) Спо́ред На́дя Никола́й ще до́йде, защо́то харе́сва Миле́на.
(*d*) Миле́на и́ска да се оба́ди на Никола́й, за да го попи́та защо́
не и́два. (*e*) Да, тя и́ма моби́лен телефо́н (джие́сём). (*f*) Никола́й
оби́ча да ся́да до ху́бави моми́чета. **2** (*a*) F: Никола́й тря́бва
да до́йде след ма́лко. (*b*) F: На́дя ка́зва, че Никола́й ви́наги
закъсня́ва. (*c*) T (*d*) F: Миле́на не оби́ча да ча́ка. (*e*) T.

Exercises 1 (a) Остави́ (b) оста́вя (c) оста́вяш (d) оста́вяйте (e) оставе́те. **2** (a) ii; (b) i; (c) v; (d) vi; (e) iii; (f) iv. **3** (a) пома́га (b) ста́ваме (c) и́два (d) поръ́чва. **4** И́скам да ви́дя; Ще до́йдеш; Ха́йде да вле́зем; Искам да се́днем; да избере́м; Мо́жеш ли да ги ви́диш; поръ́чаме; и́ска да се оба́ди; Ще напра́ви; Искам да оти́да; за да чу́я; ще запо́чна. **5** Ето, тя и́два, ви́жда, вли́за. Ето ви́жда, ся́да. Ето избира, поръ́чва. Ето но́си. Ето, не ча́ка. Ето, пла́ща, ста́ва и оти́ва. **6** (a) обича (b) харе́сва/обича (c) обича (d) харе́сва (e) оби́ча (f) харе́сате (g) харе́сват/оби́чат (h) оби́чам (i) оби́ча (j) харе́са (k) харе́сва.

Test yourself

1 (a) Г-н Джо́нсън не тря́бва да парки́ра до табе́лката, защо́то хоте́лът е в ремо́нт и поня́кога па́дат те́жки предме́ти. (b) Па́ркингът е зад хоте́ла. (c) Полица́ят предла́га ма́лкия рестора́нт, защо́то г-н Джо́нсън ня́ма да ча́ка дъ́лго там. (d) Г-н Джо́нсън не мо́же да се́дне на ма́сата в ъ́гъла, защо́то тя е запа́зена. (e) Г-н Джо́нсън ка́зва «Мо́ля, неде́йте да бъ́рзате». (f) Сервитьо́рката ще помо́гне на г-н Джо́нсън, защо́то той не разби́ра вси́чко в меню́то. **2** (a) парки́райте (b) ся́дайте (c) запа́зена (d) неде́йте да. **3 Perfective:** ха́йде да се́днем; ще харе́саш то́зи град; той тря́бва да до́йде; ще напра́вя кафе́; и́скам да помо́гна; мо́же ли да ви́дя?; какво́ ще ка́жеш? **Imperfective:** ни́е оби́чаме ди́ско; не поръ́чвай; надя́вам се; неде́й да и́дваш ра́но; отда́вна ли ча́кате?; ху́баво е да пома́гаме на прия́тели.

Unit 13

1 Questions (a) Присти́гнахме към се́дем часа́. (b) Пъту́ването ни бе́ше прия́тно. (c) И́махме пробле́ми, защо́то ня́махме ка́рта на града́. (d) Пробле́мите ни запо́чнаха, кога́то присти́гнахме в града́. (e) Не, кога́то присти́гнахме, бе́ше о́ще свѐтло. (f) Не сти́гнахме до площа́да с цъ́рквата, защо́то у́лицата бе́ше в ремо́нт. **2** (a) F: Г-н и г-жа́ Ко́линс ще ка́рат напра́во и ще сти́гнат еди́н площа́д, на кой́то и́ма цъ́рква. (b) F: Хоте́л

«Оде́са» е вдя́сно, срещу́ Мо́рската гради́на. (c) F: Г-н и г-жа́ Ко́линс присти́гнаха във Ва́рна към се́дем часа́. (d) Т (e) F: Рестора́нтът е на па́ртера вля́во.

Exercises 1 i (e); ii (f); iii (a); iv (c); v (d); vi (b). **2** (a) Кога́ запо́чна да вали́? (b) Защо́ загу́бихте пъ́тя? (c) Къде́ е ба́нката? (d) Кого́ пи́тахте къде́ е магистра́лата? (e) Кой ви помо́гна да наме́рите пъ́тя? (f) Къде́ зави́хте надя́сно? **3** (a) обя́двах (b) ку́пи (c) зами́наха (d) напра́ви (e) запо́чна (f) попи́тахме (g) поръ́чах (h) изпра́ти. **4** Въ́рнах се по съ́щата у́лица. Сти́гнах до еди́н булева́рд. Зави́х надя́сно и ка́рах напра́во. Като́ сти́гнах до площа́да, парки́рах на па́ркинга и попи́тах пак. Музе́ят не бе́ше дале́че от площа́да. **5** Върве́те напра́во по та́зи у́лица. На вто́рата у́лица зави́йте наля́во и по́сле ведна́га зави́йте надя́сно. Върве́те напра́во и ще сти́гнете до еди́н площа́д. На тре́тата у́лица вля́во зави́йте наля́во. Апте́ката е на о́коло два́йсет ме́тра вля́во. **6** Ка́рахме напра́во по та́зи у́лица. На вто́рата у́лица зави́хме наля́во и по́сле ведна́га зави́хме надя́сно. Ка́рахме напра́во и сти́гнахме до еди́н площа́д. На тре́тата у́лица вля́во зави́хме наля́во. Апте́ката бе́ше на о́коло два́йсет ме́тра вля́во.

Test yourself

1 (a) Т (b) F: Той и́маше вре́ме да разгле́да ста́рия град. (c) Т (d) F: На панаи́ра и́маше мно́го хо́ра. (e) F: Ма́йкъл напра́ви сни́мки. (f) Т. **2** (a) И́махте (b) бе́ше (c) присти́гнаха (d) и́мах (e) Напра́вихте (f) загу́бих (g) ку́пих. **3** (a) Върве́те напра́во. (b) Зави́йте наля́во/надя́сно. (c) Ня́мах предста́ва от бъ́лгарската исто́рия. (d) Разгле́дах ста́рия град. (e) Ня́маше мно́го хо́ра на у́лицата.

Unit 14

1 Questions (a) Кога́то се хо́ди на го́сти в Бълга́рия на домаки́нята се но́сят цветя́ или́ бонбо́ни. (b) Днес се празну́ва деня́т на бъ́лгарската култу́ра. (c) Ма́йкъл Джо́нсън не мо́же да ка́же

на Са́шко «Чести́т рожде́н ден», защо́то днес не é рожде́ният ден на Са́шко. (d) Са́шко благодари́ на Ма́йкъл Джо́нсън за шокола́да и моли́вите. (e) Пода́ръци се получа́ват на рожде́н ден. (f) Боя́н Анто́нов ще донесе́ ви́ното от ку́хнята.
2 (a) F: Мно́го хо́ра купу́ват цветя́ днес. (b) Т (c) Т
(d) F: Зла́тка ще пока́ни го́стите в хо́ла. (e) F: Са́шко оби́ча да пома́га. (f) Т.

Exercises 1 (a) Поздравя́вам Ви с но́вата ра́бота. Чести́то!
(b) Поздравя́вам Ви с но́вия апартаме́нт. Чести́то!
(c) Поздравя́вам Ви със сва́тбата. Чести́то! (d) Поздравя́вам Ви с успе́ха. Чести́то! (e) Поздравя́вам Ви с пра́зника. Чести́то!
(f) Поздравя́вам Ви с добри́я и́збор. Чести́то! **2** (a) Миле́на е пока́нена на о́пера. (b) Пока́нен(а) съм на сва́тба. (c) Ма́йкъл Джо́нсън е пока́нен на изло́жба. (d) Те са пока́нени на па́рти.
(e) Пока́нени ли сте на кокте́йла? **3** (a) Къде́ се обме́ня валу́та?
(b) Какво́ не сé прода́ва на малоле́тни? (c) Кога́ се пра́вят резерва́ции? (d) Къде́ се оти́ва с то́зи трамва́й? (e) Какво́ се ви́жда на та́зи ка́ртичка? (f) Какво́ се ви́жда отту́к? (Singular verb after **какво́**, remember?). **4** Видя́ ли катедра́лата «Свети́ Алекса́ндър Не́вски»? • Да, видя́х я. — Харе́са ли ти? • Мно́го ми харе́са. — Разгле́да ли кри́птата? • Да, разгле́дах и не́я. Пред кри́птата се прода́ваха ико́ни. Ку́пих една́ ма́лка ико́на. — Мо́же ли да я ви́дя? • Разби́ра се. Éто я. Харе́сва ли ти? — Аз не разби́рам от ико́ни, но та́зи ми харе́сва. **5** (a) Да, компа́ктдискът с бъ́лгарска му́зика мно́го ми харе́сва. (b) Да, тарато́рът мно́го ми харе́сва. (c) Да, ба́ницата мно́го ми харе́сва.
(d) Да, те́зи цветя́ мно́го ми харе́сват. (e) Да, бъ́лгарското ви́но мно́го ми харе́сва. (f) Да, пъ́лнените чу́шки мно́го ми харе́сват.
(g) Да, бонбо́ните мно́го ми харе́сват. (h) Да, шо́пската сала́та мно́го ми харе́сва. **6** (a) Вче́ра Ма́йкъл Джо́нсън и Никола́й доне́соха ро́зи за Зла́тка Анто́нова. (b) Вче́ра Миле́на доне́се еди́н уче́бник за Никола́й. (c) Вче́ра доне́сохме брошу́ри от панаи́ра в Пло́вдив. (d) Вче́ра доне́сохте ли пода́рък за сво́ите прия́тели? (e) Вче́ра Ма́йкъл Джо́нсън доне́се шокола́д за Са́шко. (f) Вче́ра г-н Анто́нов и синъ́т му доне́соха две буту́лки ви́но от ку́хнята.

Test yourself

1 (*a*) Г-н Джо́нсън и́ска да зна́е как се купу́ва къ́ща в Бълга́рия. (*b*) Съве́тът на бро́керката е Ма́йкъл да оти́де да ви́ди къ́щата с адвока́т. (*c*) Къ́щата, коя́то г-н Джо́нсън харе́сва, е бли́зо до Ба́нско. (*d*) Цветя́ се но́сят в цъ́рквата на пра́зника на Свети́ Ки́рил и Мето́дий. (*e*) Боя́н Анто́нов пожела́ва на г-н Джо́нсън ща́стливи дни и мно́го пра́зници в Бълга́рия. **2** (*a*) съве́т (*b*) да (*c*) купу́ва (*d*) ми (*e*) но́сят. **3** като́ избере́те – да избера́ – изби́рам; да я ви́дите – да ви́дя – ви́ждам; харе́сах – да харе́сам – харе́свам; доне́сох – да донеса́ – но́ся (дона́сям); ку́пих – да ку́пя – купу́вам; ще ви пока́ня – да пока́ня – ка́ня; дойдо́х – да до́йда – и́двам.

Unit 15

1 Questions (*a*) Миле́на не и́ска по́вече кекс, защо́то не й се яде́. (*b*) Тя не се́ чу́вства добре́. От вче́ра я боли́ стома́хът. (*c*) Пи́е й се вода́./На На́дя й се пи́е вода́. (*d*) Ми́налата годи́на по това́ вре́ме тя и́маше грип с висо́ка температу́ра. (*e*) Чове́к тря́бва да се грижи за здра́вето си. **2** (*a*) F: Миле́на не и́ска кекс, защо́то я боли́ стома́хът/и́ма бо́лки в стома́ха. (*b*) F: Ке́ксът мно́го й харе́са. (*c*) T (*d*) F: Тя ня́ма хре́ма и ка́шлица. (*e*) T.

Exercises 1 i (*c*); ii (*g*); iii (*e*); iv (*f*); v (*a*); vi (*b*), (*d*), (*e*); vii (*b*), (*d*), (*e*). **2** (*a*) (i) Не, не го́ боля́т очи́те. (ii) Не, не я́ боли́ зъб. (iii) Не, не ги́ боля́т крака́та. (iv) Не, не го́ боли́ коля́ното. (v) Не, не я́ боли́ ръка́та. (*b*) (i) Не ми́ се хо́ди на плаж. (ii) Не ми́ се пи́е чай. (iii) Не ми́ се гово́ри бъ́лгарски. (iv) Не ми́ се у́чи. (v) Не ми́ се рабо́ти на компю́тър. **3** Какво́ ти е?/Какво́ ти ка́за ле́карят?/Спи ли ти се?/Ску́чно ли ти е?/Не се́ безпоко́й! Ско́ро ще ти ми́не. **4** Ле́карят ми ка́за, че и́мам (*a*) грип (*b*) апендиси́т (*c*) висо́ка температу́ра (*d*) хре́ма (*e*) хепати́т. **5** (*a*) Не, не можа́ да оти́де, защо́то го боле́ше глава́та. (*b*) Не, не можа́х да я донеса́, защо́то ме боле́ше кръ́стът. (*c*) Не, не можа́ха да го разгле́дат, защо́то ги боля́ха крака́та. (*d*) Не, не можа́хме да го пра́тим, защо́то ня́махме ма́рки. (*e*) Не, не можа́х да ям от тях, защо́то и́мах бо́лки в стома́ха. **6** (*a*) Оти́дох да си ку́пя марато́нки. (b) Оти́дохме да си почи́нем. (c) Оти́дох да си ку́пя лека́рства. (d) Оти́дох да посре́щна дъщеря́ си. (e) Оти́дох на ле́кар. (f) Оти́дохме да пра́тим писмо́ на роди́телите си.

Test yourself

1 (a) Мъжъ́т на г-жа́ Ко́линс не се́ чу́вства добре́. (b) Той и́ма си́лно главобо́лие и все му е студе́но. (c) Ко́жата на г-н Ко́линс е черве́на, защо́то вче́ра цял ден бе́ше на пла́жа. (d) Г-н Ко́линс тря́бваше да сло́жи ша́пка. (e) Сега́ той тря́бва да стои́ на ся́нка ня́колко дни. **2** (a) F: Джордж се чу́вства зле. (b) F: Температу́рата на Джордж не е́ мно́го висо́ка. (c) F: Не го́ боли́ гъ́рлото. (d) Т (e) F: Джордж оби́ча да стои́ на слъ́нце. **3** (a) се чу́вства (b) му (c) ни́то (d) Страху́вам (e) Ви (f) мо́га.

Unit 16

1 Questions (a) После́дния ден в хоте́ла плати́хме сме́тката. (b) Той ѝ подари́ еди́н беле́жник. (c) За г-жа́ Джо́нсън избра́хме една́ сре́бърна гри́вна. (d) Да, да́дох го. (e) Той ще ми я пра́ти с и́мейл или́ с факс. (f) Це́лия ден гово́рих на англи́йски. **2** (a) Т (b) Т (c) F: Ма́йкъл Джо́нсън избра́ една́ сре́бърна гри́вна за жена́ си. (d) F: Той не му́ пока́за програ́мата. (e) F: Ако́ На́дя бе́ше на не́гово мя́сто, тя ня́маше да се безпокои́. (f) F: Боя́н Анто́нов разбра́ това́, кое́то и́скаше да зна́е.

Exercises 1 (a) . . . щя́хме да оти́дем на плаж. (b) . . . щях да оти́да на Ви́тоша. (c) . . . щя́хме да оти́дем на те́нис. (d) . . . щях да оти́да на го́сти. (e) . . . щях да оти́да на ски. **2** Ако́ и́сках да ку́пя пода́рък от Бълга́рия, щя́х да ку́пя кути́я бонбо́ни/календа́р/ плака́т/бути́лка ви́но/кни́га/ кути́я с луксо́зни пли́кове. **3** (a) Да, ако́ бях на тво́е мя́сто, щях да приема́ пока́ната./Не, ако́ бях на тво́е мя́сто, ня́маше да приема́ пока́ната. (b) Да, . . ., щях да ку́пя цветя́./Не, . . ., ня́маше да ку́пя цветя́. (c) Да, . . ., щях да изпра́тя моми́чето./Не, . . ., ня́маше да изпра́тя моми́чето. (d) Да, . . . щях да донеса́ пода́рък./Не, . . . ня́маше да донеса́ пода́рък. (e) Да, . . .

щях да посрещна американеца. /Не, . . . нямаше да посрещна американеца. **4** (*a*) Невена даде две картички от Рилския манастир на Марк и Виолета. Те искаха още, но тя нямаше повече. (*b*) Ние дадохме две картички от Рилския манастир на туристите. Те искаха още, но ние нямахме повече. (*c*) Г-н и г-жа Колинс дадоха две картички от Рилския манастир на своя приятел. Той искаше още, но те нямаха повече. **5** (*a*) още (*b*) още (*c*) повече (*d*) повече (*e*) още (*f*) повече (*g*) още. **6** *You*: Какво искаше да даде г-жа Антонова на Майкъл Джонсън? *Friend*: Г-жа Антонова искаше да даде на Майкъл Джонсън малък подарък. *You*: Какво разбра тя от него? *Friend*: Тя разбра от него, че жена му много обича кристални вази. *You*: Къде отиде тя вчера сутринта? *Friend*: Вчера сутринта тя отиде в магазин за подаръци. *You*: Какво искаше да избере? *Friend*: Искаше да избере най-красивата кристална ваза. *You*: Тя защо не купи кристална ваза? *Friend*: Тя не купи кристална ваза, защото кристалните вази бяха ужасно скъпи. *You*: Какво избра г-жа Антонова? *Friend*: Г-жа Антонова избра една красива икона. *You*: На кого тя после даде подаръка за г-жа Джонсън? *Friend*: После тя даде подаръка за г-жа Джонсън на Николай. **7** (*a*) Г-н и г-жа Колинс питаха къде има търговски център. (*b*) Невена попита г-н Джонсън дали има/ има ли/свободно време. (*c*) Боян Антонов попита кога Майкъл Джонсън ще изпрати програмата. (*d*) Милена каза, че има среща в два часа. (*e*) Джордж и Виктория казаха, че ще заминат за Варна на двайсет и осми май. (*f*) Шефът каза, че не иска повече кафе.

Test yourself

1 (*a*) Майкъл Джонсън ще изпрати още реклами. (*b*) Той може да даде рекламите на Николай. (*c*) Милена разбра за чудесната възможност от Надя. (*d*) Ако беше на мястото на Николай, Милена веднага щеше да приеме. (*e*) Тя щеше да му ги донесе. (*f*) Николай предпочита да изпрати Милена. **2** (*a*) Избрахме (*b*) даде (*c*) искаха (*d*) дадоха (*e*) избрах (*f*) искаше. **3** (*a*) Дадох му го/я. (*b*) Надя ми го/я показа. (*c*) Ще те/Ви изпратя. (*d*) Щях да забравя. (*e*) Благодаря, не искам повече.

Unit 17

1 Questions (*a*) Не, не é бóлна. (*b*) Учýден съм, защóто тáзи сýтрин я видя́х от трамвáя. (*c*) Когáто я видя́х, Нáдя оти́ваше на рáбота. (*d*) Нáдя не тря́бваше да парки́ра пред бóлницата. (*e*) Мотóрът спря́ пред бóлницата. (*f*) Кáзах му, че колáта и́ма повре́да. **2** (*a*) F: Полицáят покáзваше на Нáдя знáка «Спи́рането забранéно». (*b*) F: Нáдя ня́маше предстáва каквó му е на мотóра. (*c*) T (*d*) T (*e*) F: Нéйният познáт намéри повре́дата веднáга. (*f*) F: Колáта ня́маше бензи́н.

Exercises **1** не рабóтеше добрé, мотóра, на серви́з, да кáра колáта, с трамвáй, и́маше неприя́тности, пред бóлницата, повре́дата, тря́бваше, спи́рането е забранéно, глóба, и́ма, ЗАБРАНÉНО, познáт, колáта, ня́маше бензи́н.
2 (*a*) Каквó прáвеха те? (*b*) Каквó прáвеше той? (*c*) Каквó прáвеше тя? (*d*) Каквó прáвеше той? (*e*) Каквó прáвеха те? (*f*) Каквó прáвеха те? **3** Товá стáна преди петнáйсет минýти. Аз бях в хотéла. Чáках такси́. И́маше сáмо еди́н мъж. (Той) говорéше по телефóна. (Той) стоéше пред хотéла.
4 (*a*) Преди́ (аз) рабóтех в еди́н магази́н. (*b*) Преди́ две годи́ни (аз) рабóтех в музéя. (*c*) Преди́ (аз) рабóтех кáто сервитьóр. (сервитьóрка if you are a woman!) (*d*) Преди́ мнóго годи́ни (аз) рабóтех кáто учи́тел(ка). (*e*) Преди́ рабóтех в бáнката.
5 (*a*) (i) и́дваше (ii) дойдé (*b*) (i) кáзваше (ii) кáза (*c*) (i) кýпих. (ii) купýвах.

Test yourself

1 (*a*) Г-жá Кóлинс не мóже да спре дýша, защóто крáнът е повре́ден. (*b*) Той говорéше с еднá женá пред вхóда на Мóрската гради́на. (*c*) Пъ́рво крáнът на дýша се развали́. Пóсле мъжъ́т ѝ изчéзна. (*d*) Когáто го видя́ портиéрът, г-н Кóлинс купýваше нéщо. (е) Вси́чки знáеха къдé е г-н Кóлинс. **2** (*a*) развали́ (*b*) повре́да (*c*) рабóтеше **3** (*a*) Ня́мам предстáва. (*b*) Ни́що осóбено. (*c*) Каквó стáва/и́ма? (*d*) И́мам проблéми с колáта. (*e*) Каквó прáвеха те?

1 Questions (a) Миле́на о́ще не се́ е обля́кла. (b) Да, прия́телката на Миле́на си е оти́шла. (c) Никола́й предла́га да вечеря́т след представле́нието. (d) Представле́нието не е́ запо́чнало, защо́то е о́ще ра́но. (e) Никола́й е ста́нал мно́го разсе́ян. (f) Споре́д Миле́на Никола́й се е умори́л от мно́го у́чене. **2** (a) Т
(b) F: Ня́ма да закъсне́ят, защо́то Миле́на ве́че е реши́ла какво́ да облече́. (c) F: Никола́й о́ще не е́ вечеря́л. (d) Т (e) Т (f) Т
(g) F: На Никола́й ня́ма да му е ску́чно с Миле́на.

Exercises 1 (a) Запо́чнало ли е представле́нието? (b) О́ще не съм се обля́кла. (c) Ня́мам предста́ва как съм напра́вил така́ва гре́шка! (d) Какво́ се е слу́чило? (e) Ве́че съм реши́ла какво́ да облека́. **2** (a) Не е́ вя́рно, На́дя е дошла́! (b) Не е́ вя́рно, На́дя е доне́сла цветя́! (c) Не е́ вя́рно, На́дя е ку́пила бонбо́ни! (d) Не е́ вя́рно, На́дя е напра́вила кафе́! **3** (a) Хо́дила ли си в Бо́ровец? (b) Хо́дили ли сте в Бо́ровец? (c) Хо́дили ли сте в Бо́ровец? (d) Хо́дил ли си в Бо́ровец? **4** (a) Забра́вила съм да взе́ма чадъ́р. Ста́нала съм мно́го разсе́яна! (b) Забра́вил съм да взе́ма фо́тоапара́т. Ста́нал съм мно́го разсе́ян! (c) Забра́вили сме да взе́мем пари́. Ста́нали сме мно́го разсе́яни! **5** (a) Г-н Анто́нов бе́ше забра́вил да ку́пи би́ра. (b) Г-жа́ Анто́нова бе́ше забра́вила да ку́пи хляб. (c) Г-н и г-жа́ Ко́линс бя́ха забра́вили да ку́пят дома́ти. (d) (Аз) бях забра́вил/а да ку́пя газ́ирана вода́. **6** (a) Взех фо́тоапара́та, но сега́ го ня́ма. Си́гурно съм го загу́бил/а. (b) Взех ша́пката, но сега́ я ня́ма. Си́гурно съ я загу́бил/а. (c) Взех сни́мките, но сега́ ги ня́ма. Си́гурно съм ги загу́бил/а. (d) Взех беле́жника, но сега́ го ня́ма. Си́гурно съм го загу́бил/а. (e) Взех кни́гата, но сега́ я ня́ма. Си́гурно съм я загу́бил/а. (f) Взех ве́стника, но сега́ го ня́ма. Си́гурно съм го загу́бил/а.

Test yourself

1 (a) Джордж о́ще го боли́ глава́та. (b) На не́го му е ску́чно. (c) Тя не му́ е ка́зала досега́, че бли́зо до Балчи́к и́ма игри́ще за голф. (d) Джордж не е́ взел сти́ковете си. (e) Джордж

ще вземе стикове под наем. (*f*) Французинът от съседната
стая вече е играл голф на игрището. **2** (*a*) забравила
(*b*) облякла (*c*) поканила (*d*) отишла (*e*) вечерял (*f*) започнало
(*g*) направил (*h*) забравил (*i*) взел (*j*) решили. **3** (*a*) Вината е
моя. (*b*) Няма значение. (*c*) Вече съм решил(а). (d) Много се
съмнявам.

Unit 19

1 Questions (*a*) Бизнесменът иска да смени стаята си.
(*b*) Контактът за самобръсначка не работи, прозорецът е
счупен и вентилаторът в банята е развален. (*c*) Стаята му е
шумна, защото е точно над дискотеката. (*d*) Бизнесменът не
може да чака, защото има важна среща. (*e*) Другите гости на
хотела се оплакват от шума на трамваите. (*f*) Той предлага
да го сложат в стая на дванайсетия етаж. **2** (*a*) F: Бизнесменът
каза, че не бил доволен от стаята, която са му дали.
(*b*) F: Прозорецът бил счупен. (*c*) T (*d*) F: Той щял да се върне
към шест часа. (*e*) T.

Exercises 1 Не съм доволен/доволна от: (*a*) цената
(*b*) продавачката (*c*) сервитьора (*d*) сервиза (*e*) храната
(*f*) качеството на снимките (*g*) обслужването. **2** (*a*) Кюфтето,
което сте ми дали, не ми харесва. (*b*) Супата, която сте ми дали,
не ми харесва. (*c*) Виното, което сте ми дали, не ми харесва.
(*d*) Салатите, които сте ми дали, не ми харесват. (*e*) Сладоледът,
който сте ми дали, не ми харесва. **3** (*a*) Дадох Ви го. Ето го.
(*b*) Дадох ви ги. Ето ги. (*c*) Дадох ви я. Ето я. (*d*) Дадох ви
го. Ето го. (*e*) Дадох Ви я. Ето я. **4** (*a*) Снощи не можах да
спя от кафето. (*b*) Снощи не можах да спя от главоболие.
(*c*) Снощи не можах да спя от горещина. (*d*) Снощи не можах
да спя от комарите. (*e*) Снощи не можах да спя от музиката в
ресторанта. **5** Nadya is talking as far as «Имало много хора на
панаира». Then Nikolai takes over. **6** (*a*) Сватбата била вчера.
(*b*) Те празнували в ресторант «Москва». (*c*) Те се запознали в
Банско. (*d*) Той дошъл в София на гости на родителите на Ели.
(*e*) Сега щели да отидат на море.

Test yourself

1 (*a*) На́дя тря́бва да предаде́ на дире́ктора, че клие́нтите не били́ дово́лни от тя́хната ра́бота. (*b*) Поръ́чали 1 200 брошу́ри, а полу́чили са́мо 600. Па́пките и́мали дефе́кти, а визи́тните ка́ртички били́ на ло́ша харти́я. (*c*) Клие́нтът се оба́жда за вто́ри пъ́т, за да се извини́. (*d*) Па́пките и визи́тните ка́ртички били́ поръ́чани на дру́го мя́сто в дру́га фи́рма. (*e*) Ка́зват, че в та́зи фи́рма ста́вали мно́го гре́шки. **2** (*a*) Преда́йте (*b*) преда́м (*c*) опла́квания (*d*) Ока́за (*e*) и́мали; били́. **3** (*a*) Не се́ безпоко́й(те). (*b*) И́скам да се опла́ча. (*c*) И́скам да се извиня́. (*d*) Не съ́м дово́лен/дово́лна от ста́ята.

Unit 20

1 Questions (*a*) Миле́на пока́за Центра́лна по́ща на г-н и г-жа́ Ко́линс. (*b*) Г-н и г-жа́ Ко́линс би́ха и́скали да до́йдат в Бълга́рия през зи́мата. (*c*) Ако́ и́маха възмо́жност, те би́ха оти́шли в Бо́ровец. (*d*) Миле́на би и́скала г-жа́ Ко́линс да помо́гне на Никола́й на Хи́йтроу. (*e*) Никола́й би и́скал Миле́на да пъту́ва с не́го. **2** (*a*) F: Никола́й ще пъту́ва за́едно с г-н и г-жа́ Ко́линс. (*b*) F: Г-н и г-жа́ Ко́линс са виде́ли по́вечето забележи́телности о́коло Ва́рна. (*c*) T (*d*) F: Г-н и г-жа́ Ко́линс ще пи́шат на Миле́на от А́нглия. (*e*) F: Никола́й ще пра́ти и́мейл на Миле́на от Че́лмсфорд.

Exercises 1 (i) (*a*) Ще ѝ се оба́дя. (*b*) Оба́дих ѝ се ве́че. (*c*) Ве́че ѝ се оба́дих. (ii) (*a*) Ще му се оба́дя .(*b*) Оба́дих му се ве́че. (*c*) Ве́че му се оба́дих. (iii) (*a*) Ще им се оба́дя. (*b*) Оба́дих им се ве́че. (*c*) Ве́че им се оба́дих. (iv) (*a*) Ще ѝ се оба́дя. (*b*) Оба́дих ѝ се ве́че. (*c*) Ве́че ѝ се оба́дих. **2** (*a*) Би́хте ли ми ка́зали Ва́шия адре́с? (*b*) Би́хте ли ми се оба́дили по́-къ́сно? (*c*) Би́хте ли ни помо́гнали да наме́рим пъ́тя за Ва́рна? (*d*) Би́хте ли ми да́ли дру́га ста́я? (*e*) Би́хте ли ми поръ́чали такси́ за де́сет часа́? **3** (*a*) Ще ку́пя/Бих ку́пил, ако́ наме́ря не́що ху́баво. (*b*) Ще се оба́дя/Бих се оба́дил(а), ако́ и́мам вре́ме. (*c*) Ще до́йда/Бих дошъ́л (дошла́), ако́ се чу́вствам по́-добре́. (*d*) Ще уча́ствам/Бих уча́ствал(а), ако́ и́мам пари́. **4** (*a*) At a conference in Bulgaria. (*b*) At the beginning of the conference. (*c*) Ladies and Gentlemen, Dear Friends. (*d*) From all over the world. (*e*) They are all friends of Bulgaria. (*f*) Sofia. (*g*) He hopes their deliberations will be enjoyable and fruitful.

Test yourself

1 (*a*) На лети́щето г-н и г-жа́ Ко́линс ви́ждат Неве́на. (*b*) Неве́на е на лети́щето, защо́то тя изпра́ща Марк Де́йвис и жена́ му. (*c*) Неве́на е разка́звала на Марк за г-жа́ Ко́линс. (*d*) Марк щял да изпра́ти съобще́ние на г-жа́ Ко́линс за една́ конфере́нция за Бълга́рия. (*e*) Г-жа́ Ко́линс би уча́ствала в конфере́нцията, ако́ не е́ зае́та по съ́щото вре́ме. (*f*) Г-жа́ Ко́линс да́ва на Марк визи́тната си ка́ртичка. **2** (*a*) Бих (*b*) се (*c*) и́скал(а) (*d*) да. **3** (*a*) Каква́ изнена́да! (*b*) Спо́мняте ли си? (*c*) Това́ е визи́тната ми ка́ртичка/визи́тката ми. (*d*) Оба́ждайте се! (*e*) До ско́ро! (*f*) Прати́ ми есеме́с.

Appendix

Pronunciation and spelling

Bulgarian letters are, for the most part, constant and reliable. English letters can be very fickle. In English, one letter can have many sounds and the right sound depends on the letters that come before and after it. This makes English spelling and pronunciation very difficult. Compare, for example, *laughter* and *slaughter* or *bough*, *cough* and *enough*. Bulgarian letters are altogether more trustworthy and their pronunciation only rarely depends on the company they keep. One letter has basically one sound. So you can usually pronounce Bulgarian correctly by moving logically through the words and combining the sounds of the individual letters as you go. This also makes spelling relatively straightforward.

A few Bulgarian letters do, however, alter their pronunciation depending on the company they keep and also on their position in the word. This particularly affects certain consonants that we can conveniently group in pairs. In each pair one of the letters is 'voiced' (i.e. pronounced with your vocal chords vibrating) and the other is 'voiceless' (i.e. pronounced without using your vocal chords, almost as if whispering). Read these letters out loud, holding your Adam's apple between your thumb and forefinger and you'll see the difference!

Voiced	Voiceless
б	п
в	ф
г	к
д	т
ж	ш
з	с

(Additional pairs are **дж/ч** and **дз/ц**. The consonant **х**, which has no partner, is also voiceless.)

Remember particularly that:

(a) When a voiced consonant is the last letter in a word, you usually pronounce it as if it were its voiceless partner:

Written		Pronounced
хля**б**	*bread*	хля**п**
ху́ба**в**	*beautiful*	ху́ба**ф**
Бо**г**	*God*	Бо**к**
мла**д**	*young*	мла**т**
мъ**ж**	*man*	мъ**ш**
вле**з**!	*come in*	вле**с**!

(Did you notice ху́бав (ху́баф) and млад (млат) when you listened to the alphabet on the recording? And you will remember how Victoria Collins has to spell her name in Bulgarian: Ко́линс.) (See 'Writing Bulgarian' in the 'Alphabet and pronunciation' section at the front of the book.)

(b) When **б, в, г, д, ж** or **з** come before a voiceless consonant, they too become voiceless: авто**б**у́с (аф**т**обу́с) *bus*, в**к**ъ́щи (**ф**къ́щи) *at home*, коман**д**иро́вка (командиро́**ф**ка) *business trip*, ирла́н**дк**а (ирла́н**тк**а) *Irishwoman*, дъ**жд** (дъ**шт**) *rain*, и́**зх**од (и́**сх**от) *exit*.

(c) Bulgarian vowels are all single syllables and pure sounds, unlike the English vowels which begin on one sound and end on another (diphthongs). In Bulgarian, such sounds are formed by placing the vowels **а, е, и, о** or **у** before or after the letter **й**, which is itself not a vowel and fulfils the function of the English 'y' (as in *yes*, *soya* or *York*): ха́**й**де! *come on!*; здраве́**й**! *hello!*; **й**о́га *yoga*.

(d) The letter **ь** is only found after consonants and in combination with the letter **о**: шоф**ьо́**р *driver*.

(e) The diphthong **йо/йе** is only found after a vowel: фоа**йе́** *foyer* or at the beginning of a word: **Йо**рк *York*.

(f) Bulgarians do tend to speak quickly and the more quickly they speak the further they depart from 'standard' pronunciation.

Listen, for example, how the letter 'o', when unstressed, particularly when coming after a stressed syllable, is pronounced more like the letter 'y', as in Ви́тоша and бли́зо (pronounced Ви́туша and бли́зу). Similarly, the letter 'a', especially when coming after or before a stressed syllable, gets 'reduced' to 'ъ', as in ма́са, часо́вник and разби́ра се (pronounced чъсо́вник and ръзби́ръ се). You will also notice, even on TV and radio, a tendency to slur and swallow the beginning, middle and end of commonly used words, e. g. зе for взе, нес for днес, тва for това́, тури́с for тури́ст.

Finally, watch out for the Bulgarian letter л which in certain positions is increasingly being pronounced like the English letter 'w', e. g. а́уо for а́ло, уош for лош, муа́да for мла́да, пуан for план.

Numerals

Cardinals

0	ну́ла	19	деветна́йсет
1	едно́ (еди́н, една́)	20	два́йсет (два́десет)
2	две (два)	21	два́йсет и едно́
3	три	22	два́йсет и две
4	че́тири	23	два́йсет и три
5	пет	24	два́йсет и че́тири
6	шест	25	два́йсет и пет
7	се́дем	26	два́йсет и шест
8	о́сем	27	два́йсет и се́дем
9	де́вет	28	два́йсет и о́сем
10	де́сет	29	два́йсет и де́вет
11	едина́йсет	30	три́йсет (три́десет)
12	двана́йсет	40	чети́рисет (чети́ридесет)
13	трина́йсет	50	петдесе́т
14	четирина́йсет	60	шейсе́т (шестдесе́т)
15	петна́йсет	70	седемдесе́т
16	шестна́йсет	80	осемдесе́т
17	седемна́йсет	90	деветдесе́т
18	осемна́йсет	100	сто

101	сто и едно́ (еди́н, една́)	300	три́ста
110	сто и де́сет	400	че́тиристотин
123	сто два́йсет и три	500	пе́тстотин
200	две́ста		

Numbers of four digits and more are separated by a space where English (sometimes) uses a comma:

1 000	хиля́да	1 000 000	еди́н милио́н
2 000	две хи́ляди	2 000 000	два милио́на
3 000	три хи́ляди		

Ordinals

1st	пъ́рви	8th	о́сми
2nd	вто́ри	9th	деве́ти
3rd	тре́ти	10th	десе́ти
4th	четвъ́рти	11th	еди́найсети
5th	пе́ти	21st	два́йсет и пъ́рви
6th	ше́сти	22nd	два́йсет и вто́ри
7th	се́дми		

Grammatical terms

1 Prepositions

Spatial prepositions

Location (*Where?*)

в	*in*
върху́	*on top of*
до	*by, next to*
зад	*behind*
между́	*between*
на	*on, at*
над	*above*
под	*under*
пред	*in front of*
срещу́	*opposite*
у	*at, with*

Movement (*Where to/from?*, etc.)

към	*to(wards)*
о́коло	*(a)round*
от	*from; out of*
по	*on; along*
през	*through*
след	*after*

Bulgarian prepositions and their English equivalents

| без | *without* | без преводáч |
| | *to* | часъ́т е три без пет |

в (във)	*in*	в Плóвдив
	to	(отúвам) в бáнката, в Мéлник
	at	(рабóтя) във фúрма ТрáнсПроéкт, в дванáйсет часá, в момéнта
	on	в срядá

до	*by*	мáсата е до вратáта
	next to	хотéлът е до бáнката
	to	(стúгам) до площáда, ексýрзия до Вúтоша
	until	до четвъ́рти юни
	till	до къ́сно

за	*for*	писмó за Вас, магазúн за плодовé, за две сéдмици, (заминáвам) за Áнглия
	about	(говóря) за англичáнката
	to	пъ́тят за Вáрна
	—	(пúтам) за пъ́тя

към	*towards*	(отúвам) към Мóрската градúна
	around	към шест часá
	—	молбá към Вас

на	*on*	на кáртата, на пáртера, на почúвка, на ýлица Ракóвски, на Вúтоша, на петнáйсети май
	at	на мáсата, на летúщето, на светофáра
	of	кáрта на Сóфия, чáнтата на Марк
	in	на юг; на англúйски езúк
	to	(отúвам) на морé, на óпера
	for	(да кýпя) подáрък на синá на Антóнови

342

óколо	{	*around*	óколо града́
		about	óколо пет часа́
от	{	*from*	писмо́ от Ло́ндон
		(made) of	су́па от зеленчу́ци
		with	дово́лен съм от хоте́ла
		since	в Со́фия съм от четвъ́рти май
		—	и́мам ну́жда от прево́да́ч
по	{	*on*	по ра́диото, по телефо́на
		over	по висо́ките планини́
		along	по пъ́тя, по Черномо́рието
под	{	*under*	под ма́сата
		—	(да взе́ма) кола́ под на́ем
преди́	{	*before*	преди́ о́бед
		ago	преди́ две се́дмици
през	{	*through*	през града́
		in/during	през зи́мата,
			през ме́сец май
		at	през нощта́
проти́в		*against*	проти́в не́го
с (със)	{	*with*	сре́ща с не́го, с удово́лствие
		on	(поздравя́вам) с пра́зника
		—	(да запозна́я) с г-н Анто́нов
след	{	*after*	след те́бе, след ра́бота
		in	след две се́дмици
у	{	*at*	у нас
		with	кни́гата е у не́я
чрез	{	*through*	
		by means of	чрез не́я
		via	

2 Nouns

Gender	Indefinite singular	Indefinite plural	Definite singular	Definite plural
Masculine consonant	хотéл	хотéли	хотéлът	хотéлите
	вéстник	вéстници	вéстникът	вéстниците
	лéкар	лéкари	лéкарят	лéкарите
	учи́тел	учи́тели	учи́телят	учи́телите
-й	музéй	музéи	музéят	музéите
one syllable	ключ	ключове	клю́чът	клю́човете
	NB Plural after numbers: хотéла вéстника музéя ключа		NB Non-subject definite: хотéла вéстника лéкаря учи́теля музéя клю́ча	
Feminine -а	женá	жени́	женáта	жени́те
-я	стáя	стáи	стáята	стáите
consonant	вéчер	вéчери	вечертá	вéчерите
	нарóдност	нарóдности	народносттá	нарóдностите
	нощ	нóщи	нощтá	нóщите
	прóлет	прóлети	пролеттá	прóлетите
	су́трин	су́трини	сутринтá	су́трините
Neuter -о	писмó	писмá	писмóто	писмáта
-е	кафé	кафéта	кафéто	кафéтата
-ие	списáние	списáния	списáниетo	списáнията
-и	такси́	такси́та	такси́то	такси́тата
-ю	меню́	меню́та	меню́то	меню́тата

Some irregular plurals

Masculine	Feminine	Neuter
брат-брáтя		
бългáрин-бългáри	ръкá-ръцé	детé-децá
господи́н-господá		и́ме-именá
гост-гóсти		окó-очи́
ден-дни		ухó-уши́
крак-кракá		
мъж-мъжé		

3 Adjectives and adverbs

	Masculine	Feminine	Neuter	Plural
without loss of vowel **Indefinite** **Definite**	висóк син висóкият сѝният	висóка сѝня висóката сѝнята	висóко сѝньо висóкото сѝньото	висóки сѝни висóките сѝните
with loss of vowel **Indefinite** **Definite**	добър прия́тен добрия́т прия́тният	добра́ прия́тна добра́та прия́тната	добро́ прия́тно добро́то прия́тното	добри́ прия́тни добри́те прия́тните
ending in -ски **Indefinite** **Definite**	бъ́лгарски бъ́лгарският	бъ́лгарска бъ́лгарската	бъ́лгарско бъ́лгарското	бъ́лгарски бъ́лгарските

Comparison of adjectives

добър *good* пó-добър *better* нáй-добър *best*

Comparison of adverbs

бъ́рзо *quickly* пó-бъ́рзо *quicker* нáй-бъ́рзо *quickest*
добре́ *well* пó-добре́ *better* нáй-добре́ *best*
мáлко *little* пó-мáлко *less* нáй-мáлко *least*
мнóго *much* пóвече *more* нáй-мнóго *most*

4 Pronouns

Subject form	Object form		Indirect object form	
	Full	**Short**	**Full**	**Short**
аз	мéне	ме	на мéне	ми
ти	тéбе	те	на тéбе	ти
той	нéго	го	на нéго	му
тя	нея́	я	на нея́	й
то	нéго	го	на нéго	му
нѝе	нас	ни	на нас	ни
*вѝе	*вас	*ви	на *вас	*ви
те	тях	ги	на тях	им

(*When the polite form for *you* is used referring to a single person, then you must use a capital letter in writing. This also applies to the possessives.)

Subject form		Possessive adjectival forms			
		Masculine	Feminine	Neuter	Plural
аз	indefinite	мой	мо́я	мо́е	мо́и
	definite	мо́ят	мо́ята	мо́ето	мо́ите
ти	indefinite	твой	тво́я	тво́е	тво́и
	definite	тво́ят	тво́ята	тво́ето	тво́ите
той	indefinite	не́гов	не́гова	не́гово	не́гови
	definite	не́говият	не́говата	не́говото	не́говите
тя	indefinite	не́ин	не́йна	не́йно	не́йни
	definite	не́йният	не́йната	не́йното	не́йните
то	indefinite	не́гов	не́гова	не́гово	не́гови
	definite	не́говият	не́говата	не́говото	не́говите
ни́е	indefinite	наш	на́ша	на́ше	на́ши
	definite	на́шият	на́шата	на́шето	на́шите
ви́е	indefinite	ваш	ва́ша	ва́ше	ва́ши
	definite	ва́шият	ва́шата	ва́шето	ва́шите
те	indefinite	те́хен	тя́хна	тя́хно	те́хни
	definite	те́хният	тя́хната	тя́хното	те́хните
той тя то те		*own*			
	indefinite	свой	сво́я	сво́е	сво́и
	definite	сво́ят	сво́ята	сво́ето	сво́ите

Definiteness and possession

(*a*) Short forms (noun + definite article + short indirect object pronoun)

(*b*) Full forms (possessive adjective + definite article + noun)

Singular			Plural		
Short		Full	Short		full
ле́карят ми	=	мо́ят ле́кар	ку́фарите ми	=	мо́ите ку́фари
ста́ята ми	=	мо́ята ста́я	ча́нтите ми	=	мо́ите ча́нти
дете́то ми	=	мо́ето дете́	деца́та ми	=	мо́ите деца́

Other pronouns

	Persons					Things
	Subject form				Object form	
	Masc.	Fem.	Neuter	Plural		
Demonstrative pronouns	тóзи	тáзи	товá	тéзи		товá
Questions (interrogative pronouns)	кой	коя́	коé	кой	когó	каквó
	какъ́в	каквá	каквó	какви́		
Relative pronouns	кóйто	коя́то	коéто	кóйто	когóто	каквóто
	какъ́вто	каквáто	каквóто	какви́то		
Indefinite pronouns	ня́кой	ня́коя	ня́кое	ня́кои	ня́кого	нéщо
Negative pronouns	ни́кой	ни́коя	ни́кое	ни́кои	ни́кого	ни́що
Generalizing pronouns	всéки	вся́ка	вся́ко	вси́чки	всéкиго	вси́чко

Other question words and their relative equivalents

защó?	*why?*		защóто	*because*
как?	*how?*		кáкто	*as*
когá?	*when?*		когáто	(*the time*) *when*
къдé?	*where?*		къдéто	(*the place*) *where*

5 Verbs

съм *to be*

Present		Future	
		Positive	Negative
аз	съм	ще съм/бъ́да	ня́ма да съм/бъ́да
ти	си	ще си/бъ́деш	ня́ма да си/бъ́деш
той			
тя }	е	ще е/бъ́де	ня́ма да е/бъ́де
то			
ни́е	сме	ще сме/бъ́дем	ня́ма да сме/бъ́дем
ви́е	сте	ще сте/бъ́дете	ня́ма да сте/бъ́дете
те	са	ще са/бъ́дат	ня́ма да са/бъ́дат

Past		Present perfect
аз	бях	бил съм/била́ съм/било́ съм
ти	бе́ше	бил си/била́ си/било́ си
той		бил е
тя	бе́ше	била́ е
то		било́ е
ни́е	бя́хме	били́ сме
ви́е	бя́хте	били́ сте
те	бя́ха	били́ са

Future in the past

	Positive	Negative
аз	щях да съм/бъ̀да	ня́маше да съм/бъ̀да
ти	ще́ше да си/бъ̀деш	ня́маше да си/бъ̀деш
той		
тя	ще́ше да е/бъ̀де	ня́маше да е/бъ̀де
то		
ни́е	щя́хме да сме/бъ̀дем	ня́маше да сме/бъ̀дем
ви́е	шя́хте да сте/бъ̀дете	ня́маше да сте/бъ̀дете
те	щя́ха да са/бъ̀дат	ня́маше да са/бъ̀дат

Present tense

	e-pattern (Conjugation 1)	и-pattern (Conjugation 2)	a-pattern (Conjugation 3)
аз	пи́ша	рабо́тя	и́мам
ти	пи́шеш	рабо́тиш	и́маш
той			
тя	пи́ше	рабо́ти	и́ма
то			
ни́е	пи́шем	рабо́тим	и́маме
ви́е	пи́шете	рабо́тите	и́мате
те	пи́шат	рабо́тят	и́мат

348

Imperative (commands)

	Positive (Perfective and imperfective)		Negative (Imperfective)	
	Singular	**Plural**	**Singular**	**Plural**
e-pattern			**a-pattern**	
(да) сéдна	седни! *sit down*	седнéте!	не ся́дай! недéй да ся́даш	не ся́дайте! недéйте да ся́дате
и-pattern				
платя́	плати! *pay*	платéте!	не плáщай! недéй да плáщаш	не плáщайте! недéйте да плáщате
a-pattern				
чáкам	чáкай! *wait*	чáкайте!	не чáкай! недéй да чáкаш	не чáкайте! недéйте да чáкате
Verbs with two vowels				
пия	пий! *drink*	пийте!	не пий! недéй да пиеш	не пийте! недéйте да пиете
Irregular				
(да) вѝдя	виж! *look*	вѝжте!	не глéдай! недéй да глéдаш	не глéдайте! недéйте да глéдате
(да) вля́за	влез! *go/come in*	влéзте!	не влѝзай! недéй да влѝзаш	не влѝзайте! недéйте да влѝзате
(да) дóйда	елá! *come*	елáте!	не ѝдвай! недéй да ѝдваш	не ѝдвайте! недéйте да ѝдвате
(да) държá	дрьж! *hold*	дрьжте!	не дрьж! недéй да държѝш	не дрьжте! недéйте да държѝте
(да) изля́за	излéз! *go out*	излéзте!	не излѝзай! недéй да излѝзаш	не излѝзайте! недéйте да излѝзате
(да) (от)ѝда	(от)идѝ! *go*	(от)идéте!	не отѝвай! недéй да отѝваш	не отѝвайте! недéйте да отѝвате

(да) ям	яж!	я́жте!	не яж!	не я́жте!
	eat		неде́й да яде́ш	неде́йте да яде́те

Past tense (personal endings*)

Past					Past imperfect			
аз	-ах	-ях**	-их	-ох	-ех	-ах	-ях	-я́х
ти	-а	-я	-и	-е	-еше	-аше	-яше	-е́ше
той тя то	-а	-я	-и	-е	-еше	-аше	-яше	-е́ше
ни́е	-ахме	-яхме	-ихме	-охме	-ехме	-ахме	-яхме	-я́хме
ви́е	-ахте	-яхте	-ихте	-охте	-ехте	-ахте	-яхте	-я́хте
те	-аха	-яха	-иха	-оха	-еха	-аха	-яха	-я́ха

(*For the main conjugation patterns in the past see Verb tables 1 and 2.)
(**With and without stress.)

Table 1 Ordinary past tense

Here are the main verb patterns of the ordinary past tense (+ past participles derived from them), arranged according to features 1–8. The verbs are mostly perfective. Imperfective verbs in the table are indicated with*.

1 Verbs ending in two vowels.
2 Verbs with **д/т, з/с** and **к** before the ending.
3 Verbs with **-на** before the ending.
4 Verbs with **ш** or **ж** before the ending change them to **с** and **з** in the past.
5 Verbs with **-бер-/-пер-** lose the е in the past.
6 Irregular verbs.
7 Verbs *without* stress on the final syllable in the past.
8 Verbs *with* stress on the final syllable in the past.

Present	Past	Past participle			
		Masculine	Feminine	Neuter	Plural
е-pattern 1 *живе́я *live* *пи́я *drink*	живя́х пих	живя́л пил	живя́ла пи́ла	живя́ло пи́ло	живе́ли пи́ли

Present	Past	Past participle			
		Masculine	Feminine	Neuter	Plural
2 вля́за *go in* дам *give* донеса́ *bring* оти́да *go* облека́ *get dressed*	вля́зох да́дох доне́сох оти́дох обля́кох	вля́зъл дал доне́съл оти́шъл обля́къл	вля́зла да́ла доне́сла оти́шла обля́кла	вля́зло да́ло доне́сла оти́шло обля́кло	вля́зло да́ли доне́сли оти́шло обле́кли
3 запо́чна *begin*	запо́чнах	запо́чнал	запо́чнала	запо́чнало	запо́чнали
4 *пи́ша *write* ка́жа *say*	писа́х ка́зах	писа́л ка́зал	писа́ла ка́зала	писа́ло ка́зало	писа́ли ка́зали
5 разбера́ *understand*	разбра́х	разбра́л	разбра́ла	разбра́ло	разбра́ли
6 взе́ма *take* *мо́га *can* спра *stop*	взех можа́х спрях	взел мо́гъл спрял	взе́ла могла́ спря́ла	взе́ло могло́ спря́ло	взе́ли могли́ спре́ли
и-pattern **7** *рабо́тя *work* *у́ча *study*	рабо́тих у́чих	рабо́тил у́чил	рабо́тила у́чила	рабо́тило у́чило	рабо́тили у́чили
8 ви́дя *see* *стоя́ *stand*	видя́х стоя́х	видя́л стоя́л	видя́ла стоя́ла	видя́ло стоя́ло	виде́ли стое́ли
a-pattern *вечеря́м *have supper* *ка́звам *say*	вечеря́х ка́звах	вечеря́л ка́звал	вечеря́ла ка́звала	вечеря́ло ка́звало	вечеря́ли ка́звали

Table 2 Past imperfect

Main patterns of past imperfect + past participles derived from them.

The past imperfect endings depend on stress and not on the conjugation pattern (see past endings given earlier). Table 2 contains all the imperfective (starred) verbs from Table 1 together with the imperfective twins of the perfective verbs found there. Here the verbs are organized differently, for the conjugation patterns of the perfective and imperfective twins are often not the same. Most imperfectives, you will see, are Conjugation 3.

Present	Past imperfect	Past participle			
		Masculine	Feminine	Neuter	Plural
e-pattern					
живѐя *live*	живѐех	живѐел	живѐела	живѐело	живѐели
пѝша *write*	пѝшех	пѝшел	пѝшела	пѝшело	пѝшели
пѝя *drink*	пѝех	пѝел	пѝела	пѝело	пѝли
мо́га *can*	мо́жех	мо́жел	мо́жела	мо́жело	мо́жели
и-pattern					
но́ся *carry*	но́сех	но́сел	но́села	но́село	но́сели
рабо́тя *work*	рабо́тех	рабо́тел	рабо́тела	рабо́тело	рабо́тели
у́ча *study*	у́чех	у́чел	у́чела	у́чело	у́чели
стоя́ *stand*	стоя́х	стоя́л	стоя́ла	стоя́ло	стоѐли
a-pattern					
взѝмам *take*	взѝмах	взѝмал	взѝмала	взѝмало	взѝмали
вѝждам *see*	вѝждах	вѝждал	вѝждала	вѝждало	вѝждали
влѝзам *go in*	влѝзах	влѝзал	влѝзала	влѝзало	влѝзали
да́вам *give*	да́вах	да́вал	да́вала	да́вало	да́вали
запо́чвам *begin*	запо́чвах	запо́чвал	запо́чвала	запо́чвало	запо́чвали
ѝмам *have*	ѝмах	ѝмал	ѝмала	ѝмало	ѝмали
ка́звам *say*	ка́звах	ка́звал	ка́звала	ка́звало	ка́звали
облѝчам *get dressed*	облѝчах	облѝчал	облѝчала	облѝчало	облѝчали
отѝвам *go*	отѝвах	отѝвал	отѝвала	отѝвало	отѝвали
разбѝрам *understand*	разбѝрах	разбѝрал	разбѝрала	разбѝрало	разбѝрали
спѝрам *stop*	спѝрах	спѝрал	спѝрала	спѝрало	спѝрали
вечѐрям *have supper*	вечѐрях	вечѐрял	вечѐряла	вечѐряло	вечѐряли

Table 3 Tense forms with the past participle

Present perfect (*I have had supper*)	Past perfect (*I had had supper*)	Conditional (*I would have had supper, if . . .*)
аз съм вечѐрял(а)	бях вечѐрял(а)	бих вечѐрял(а), ако́ . . .
ти си вечѐрял(а)	бѐше вечѐрял(а)	би вечѐрял(а), ако́ . . .
той е вечѐрял	бѐше вечѐрял	би вечѐрял, ако́ . . .
тя е вечѐряла	бѐше вечѐряла	би вечѐряла, ако́ . . .
то е вечѐряло	бѐше вечѐряло	би вечѐряло, ако́ . . .
нѝе сме вечѐряли	бя́хме вечѐряли	бѝхме вечѐряли, ако́ . . .
вѝе сте вечѐряли	бя́хте вечѐряли	бѝхте вечѐряли, ако́ . . .
те са вечѐряли	бя́ха вечѐряли	бѝха вечѐряли, ако́ . . .

Table 4 Renarrated forms (3rd person only)

Tenses	Statements	Renarrated forms Ка́зват, че... *(They say that...)*
Present	той пи́ше тя пи́ше то пи́ше те пи́шат	той пи́шел* тя пи́шела
Past Imper-fect	той пи́шеше тя пи́шеше то пи́шеше те пи́шеха	то пи́шело те пи́шели
Past	той пи́са тя пи́са то пи́са те пи́саха	той пи́сал** тя пи́сала то пи́сало те пи́сали
Future	той ще пи́ше тя ще пи́ше то ще пи́ше те ще пи́шат	той щял да пи́ше (ня́мало да пи́ше) тя щя́ла да пи́ше (ня́мало да пи́ше) то щя́ло да пи́ше (ня́мало да пи́ше) те ще́ли да пи́шат) (ня́мало да пи́шат)

(* See Table 2 for past participles (mainly imperfective).)
(**See Table 1 for past participles (mainly perfective).)

Table 5 Passive participles

Endings and verb group (Present)	Past form	Passive participle			
		Masculine	Feminine	Neuter	Plural

-ен
  и-pattern
  е-pattern
verbs with:
	затво́рих	затво́рен
		(*closed*)
			затво́рена	затво́рено	затво́рени

т/д	да́дох	да́ден (*given*)	да́дена	да́дено	да́дени
с/з	доне́сох	доне́сен (*brought*)	доне́сена	доне́сено	доне́сени
к	обля́кох*	обле́чен (*dressed*)	обле́чена	обле́чено	обле́чени

Endings and verb group (Present)	Past form	Passive participle			
		Masculine	Feminine	Neuter	Plural
-ан **a**-pattern **e**-pattern verbs with:	заплану́вах	заплану́ван (*planned*)	заплану́вана	заплану́вано	заплану́вани
-ая	игра́х	игра́н (*played*)	игра́на	игра́но	игра́ни
ш/ж	пи́сах	пи́сан (*written*)	пи́сана	пи́сано	пи́сани
	ка́зах	ка́зан (*said*)	ка́зана	ка́зано	ка́зани
-бер/пер	разбра́х	разбра́н (*understood*)	разбра́на	разбра́но	разбра́ни
-ян **e**-pattern verbs with: **-ея** **и**-pattern verbs with: stressed ending	живя́х	живя́н (*lived*)	живя́на	живя́но	живе́ни
	видя́х	видя́н (*seen*)	видя́на	видя́но	виде́ни
-т **e**-pattern verbs in: **-ия, -ея**	изпи́х	изпи́т (*drunk*)	изпи́та	изпи́то	изпи́ти
	изпя́х	изпя́т (*sung*)	изпя́та	изпя́то	изпя́ти
-на-	запо́чнах	запо́чнат (*begun*)	запо́чната	запо́чнато	запо́чнати
-ема	взех	взет (*taken*)	взе́та	взе́то	взе́ти

(*2nd person **ти обле́че**).

Passive forms
Reflexive

Вентила́торът се развали́.   *The fan broke down.*
Тарато́рът се серви́ра студе́н.   *Tarator is served cold.*
Биле́тите се прода́доха бъ́рзо.   *The tickets sold out quickly.*

Bulgarian–English vocabulary

In this Vocabulary, you should be able to find all the words used in this book with the meanings they have in the book. Occasionally, when a word has another very common meaning not used in the book, you will find the additional meaning.

The words are listed in a way that will be useful to you. The verbs, for example, show the *I* form followed by the final three letters of the *you* singular form. (Occasionally, with very short verbs, we have given the full *you* singular form.) All perfective verbs are preceded by (да). Where nouns have awkward plurals, the abbreviation (pl) is used and you will find either the last few letters — usually the last three — or the full plural form. The adjectives are listed in the masculine singular, but where the feminine, neuter and plural forms lose the letter е, we give you the last three letters of the feminine form too. Where a word has an odd gender, feminine nouns ending in consonants, for example, we give you the gender. The letter (f) means the word is feminine; the letter (n) that it is neuter.

Phrases are shown either under the most important word or according to the first word in the phrase.

Some words you will find in the Appendix rather than in the Vocabulary. You should look for most of the numerals, for example, and the different verb and pronoun forms, in the Appendix. The Appendix is really an addition to the Vocabulary, so use the two together.

a *but*
áвгуст *August*
áвиокомпáния *airline*
автобýс *bus*
агéнция *agency*
адвокáт *lawyer, attorney*
администрáтор(ка) *receptionist*
адрéс *address*

аз *I*
акó *if*
алéргия *allergy*
алкохóл *alcohol*
áло(?) *hello* (on the phone)
Амéрика *America*
америкáнец (pl) **-нци** *an American*

американка *American woman*

американски *American*

ами сега? *and now what?*

амфитеатър *amphitheatre*

английски *English*

англичанин (pl) **-ани** *Englishman*

англичанка *English woman*

Áнглия *England*

антибиотик *an antibiotic*

апартамент *flat, apartment*

апендисит *appendicitis*

април *April*

аптека *chemist's, pharmacy*

асансьор *lift, elevator*

аспирин *aspirin*

а-ха *a-ha*

баба *grandmother*

бавно *slowly*

багаж *luggage, baggage*

багажник (pl) **-ици** *boot/trunk*

балкански *Balkan* (adj)

банан *banana*

баница *(cheese) pasty*

баничка *(cheese) roll*

банка *bank*

банкнота *banknote*

банкомат *cashpoint, ATM*

баня *bathroom*

бар *bar*

баскетбол *basketball*

баща *father*

без *without; less; to* (telling time)

безпокоя, -оиш *to worry, trouble*

безпокоя, -оиш се *be anxious, to worry*

бейзбол *baseball*

бележник (pl) **-ици** *diary, notebook*

бензин *petrol, gas*

бензиностанция *petrol/gas station*

бидонче *small (petrol, gas) can*

бизнес *business*

бизнесмен *businessman*

билет *ticket*

билка *herb*

билков (made with) *herb(s)*

бира *beer*

благодаря *thank you*

благодаря, -риш *to thank*

близо *near*

блок *block*

блуза *blouse*

Бог *God*

(слава) Богу! *thank heavens!*

бокс *boxing*

болен, -лна *ill, sick*

боли (*it* form) *it hurts*

болка *pain*

болница *hospital*

бонбон *chocolate, sweet, candy*

брат (pl) **братя** *brother*

братовчед(ка) *cousin*

брой (pl) **броеве** *number; copy*

брокер(ка) *(real) estate agent*

брошура *brochure*

букет *bunch*

булевард *boulevard*

бутилка *bottle*

бутни! *push!*
бъдеще *future*
българин (pl) **българи** *a Bulgarian*
България *Bulgaria*
българка *Bulgarian woman*
български *Bulgarian*
бързам, -заш *to be in a hurry*
бързо *quickly, fast*
бюро *agency, office*
бял (pl) **бели** *white*

в/във *in; at; to; on*
в ремонт *under repair, reconstruction*
в такъв случай *in that case*
важен, -жна *important*
важно (**е**) *(it's) important*
ваза *vase*
вали *it's raining*
валута *(hard) currency*
варненски *Varna* (adj)
ваш, Ваш *your(s)*
вдясно *on the right*
вегетариански *vegetarian*
веднага *immediately*
веднъж *once*
Великден *Easter*
вентилатор *extractor fan*
весел *merry, happy*
вестник (pl) **-ици** *newspaper*
ветровито *windy*
вече *already*
вечер (f) *evening*
вечерта *in the evening*
вечеря *dinner, supper*
вечерям, -ряш *to have supper/dinner*

(да) взема, -меш *to take*
взимам, -маш *to take*
видео *video*
(да) видя, -диш *to see*
вие or **Вие** *you*
виждам, -даш *to see*
виза *visa*
визитка *business card*
визитна картичка *business card*
вилица *fork*
вина *fault*
винаги *always*
вино *wine*
висок *high, tall*
включвам, -ваш *to include*
вкусен, -сна *nice* (to eat), *delicious*
вкъщи *at home/(go) home*
влажен, -жна *damp*
влизам, -заш *to go in*
вляво *on the left*
(да) вляза, влезеш *to go in*
вместо *instead of*
внимавам, -ваш *to watch out*
внимание! *danger! watch out! attention!*
вода *water*
водка *vodka*
врата *door*
време (pl) **времена** *time*
време *weather*
все *all the time*
все едно/пак *all the same*
всеки, всяка *each*
всички *everybody*
всичко *all*

вто́рник *Tuesday*
вход *entrance*
вче́ра *yesterday*
въ́здух *air*
възмо́жно (**е**) *(it's) possible, likely*
възмо́жност (f) *possibility, opportunity*
въпро́с *question*
вървя́, -ви́ш *to walk*
(да) въ́рна, -неш *to return, give back*
(да) се въ́рна, -неш *to return, go back*
върху́ *on top of*
вя́рвам, -ваш *to believe*
вя́рно (**е**) *(it's) true*
вя́тър (pl) **ветрове́** *wind*

гази́ран *fizzy, sparkling*
гази́рана вода́ *soda water*
гале́рия *gallery*
га́ра *railway station*
гара́ж *garage*
г-жа́ = госпожа́ *Mrs*
глава́ *head*
главобо́лие *headache*
гла́ден, -дна *hungry*
гла́сова по́ща *voicemail*
гле́дам, -даш *to look*
гло́ба *fine*
г-н = господи́н *Mr*
гово́ря, -риш *to speak, talk*
годи́на *year*
големина́ *size*
голф *golf*
голя́м (pl) **голе́ми** *big*
го́ре-до́лу *so-so (lit. up and down)*

горещина́ *heat*
горе́що (**е**) *(it's) hot*
господи́н (pl) **-да́** *Mr*
госпожа́ *Mrs*
госпо́жица *Miss*
гост (pl) **го́сти** *guest, resident*
гото́в *ready*
гото́во (**е**) *(it's) ready, done, there you go!*
град (pl) **градове́** *town, city*
гради́на *garden, park*
гра́дус *degree*
градче́ *little town*
гра́жданин (pl) **-ани** *citizen*
грам *gram*
гра́ница *border*
гре́шка *mistake*
гри́вна *bracelet*
гри́жа, -жиш се *to look after, worry about*
грип *flu*
гро́зде *grapes*
гро́здов (made with) *grapes*
гру́па *group*
гъ́рло *throat*
Гъ́рция *Greece*

да *yes; to*
да́вам, -ваш *to give*
да́же *even*
дале́че *far*
дали́ *whether, if*
(да) дам, даде́ш *to give*
да́ми и господа́ *ladies and gentlemen*
да́мски *women's*
да́та *date*
два́ма (**ду́ши**) *two (people)*
дво́ен, дво́йна *double*

360

дворе́ц (pl) дворци́ *palace*
деке́мври *December*
делега́ция *delegation*
ден, деня́т (pl) дни *day*
дете́ (pl) деца́ *child*
дефе́кт *defect, flaw*
джи́есе́м *mobile phone*
джин *gin*
джоб *pocket*
ди́види́ *DVD*
дие́та *diet*
диза́йнер *designer*
дире́ктор *director*
дискоте́ка *disco*
дне́вник *diary*
днес *today*
до *next to; until, till; to*
добре́ *well; OK, fine*
добре́ дошъ́л, -шла́, -шли́!
  welcome!
добре́ зава́рил! lit. *well met!*
  (response to добре́ дошъ́л!)
добъ́р, -бра́ *good*
до́бър ден! *good morning/*
  afternoon!
добъ́р път! *have a good/safe*
  journey!
дови́ждане! *goodbye!*
дово́лен, -лна (от) *happy*
  (with)
(да) до́йда, -деш *to come*
докато́ *while*
до́ктор *doctor*
докуме́нт *document; paper*
до́лар *dollar*
домаки́н *host*
домаки́ня *hostess, lady of*
  the house

дома́т *tomato*
(да) донеса́, -се́ш *to bring*
дори́ *even*
досега́ *until now*
до́ста *quite, very*
дочу́ване *goodbye* (on the
  phone)
дошъ́л: добре́ дошъ́л!
  welcome!
друг *another; other*
дру́го? *anything else?*
дръ́пни! *pull!*
ду́ма *word*
Ду́нав *Danube*
(два́ма) ду́ши *two people*
душ *shower*
дъжд (pl) дъждове́ *rain*
дъждо́вно (е) (*it's*) *rainy*
дъ́лъг, дъ́лга *long*
дъ́нки *jeans*
държа́, -жи́ш *to hold*
дъщеря́ *daughter*
дя́до *grandfather*

е! *well!; really!*
е́вро *euro*
Евро́па *Europe*
е́втин *cheap*
ези́к (pl) ези́ци *language,*
  tongue
екску́рзия *outing,*
  excursion
екскурзово́д *guide*
е́семе́с *text (message)*
е́сен (f) *autumn, fall*
еспре́со *espresso*
ета́ж *floor*
е́то *here is*

Ж *ladies (toilet)*
жа́лко *it's a pity*
жена́ *woman; wife*
же́нен *married*
живе́я, -е́еш *to live*
живо́т *life*
жу́ри *jury*
журнали́ст *journalist*

за *for; to; at; about*
за да *(in order) to*
заба́вен, -вна *amusing*
заба́вно (е) *(it's) fun, amusing*
забележи́телност (f) *sight, tourist attraction*
(да) заболи́ (*it* form) *begins to hurt*
(да) забра́вя, -виш *to forget*
забране́но *prohibited*
(да) зави́я, -и́еш *to turn*
загу́бен *lost*
(да) загу́бя, -биш *to lose*
зад *behind*
за́едно *together*
зае́т *busy, engaged*
заку́ска *breakfast, snack*
закъсне́ние *delay*
(да) закъсне́я, -е́еш *to be late*
закъсня́вам, -ваш *to be late*
за́ла *hall*
(да) зами́на, -неш *to leave*
замина́вам, -ваш *to leave*
замина́ване *departure*
замина́ващ за *leaving for, travelling to*
(на) за́пад *(to the) west*

запа́зен *reserved; preserved*
(да) запа́зя, -зиш *to reserve, book*
(да) запа́ли (*it* form) *to start (car)*
(да) заплану́вам, -ваш *to plan*
заплану́ван *planned*
запов́я́дай(те)! *here you are, there you go; welcome; go ahead!*
запозна́вам, -ваш се *to get to know one another*
запозна́йте се! *meet . . .*
(да) запозна́я, -а́еш *to introduce*
(да) се запозна́я, -а́еш *to get to know one another*
(да) запо́мня, -ниш *to remember*
запо́чвам, -ваш *to begin*
(да) запо́чна, -неш *to begin*
(да) се зара́двам, -ваш *to be pleased*
засега́ *for now*
(да) се засме́я, -е́еш *to begin to laugh*
затва́рям, -ряш *to close*
затво́рен *closed*
(да) затво́ря, -риш *to close*
затова́ *that's why*
за́хар (f) *sugar*
защо́ *why*
защо́то *because*
здра́ве *health*
здраве́й(те)! *hello! hi!*
зеленчу́к (pl) **-у́ци** *vegetable*
зеленчу́ков (made with) *vegetable(s)*

зи́ма *winter*
Зла́тни пя́съци *Golden Sands*
зле *poorly*
знак (pl) зна́ци *sign*
зна́ние *knowledge, learning*
значе́ние *significance, meaning*
зна́чи *so, that means, that is to say*
зна́я, -а́еш *to know*
зъб (pl) зъ́би *tooth*
зъболе́кар(ка) *dentist*

и *and, too, as well*
игра́я, -а́еш *to play*
игри́ще за голф *golf course*
(да) и́да see (да) оти́да
и́двам, -ваш *to come*
иде́я *idea*
(да) избера́, -ре́ш *to choose*
изби́рам, -раш *to choose*
извине́те! *excuse/pardon me!*
(да) се извиня́, -ни́ш *to apologize*
извиня́вай(те)! *excuse/forgive me!*
извиня́вам, -даш се *to apologize*
извъ́н *outside*
и́зглед *view*
изгле́ждам, -даш *to look*
изго́ден, -дна *favourable*
(да) изка́рам, -раш *to spend (time)*
изка́рвам, -ваш *to spend (time)*
изка́рване, прия́тно *have a pleasant stay*

изключи́телен, -лна *exceptional*
изли́зам, -заш *to go out, leave*
изло́жба *exhibition*
(да) изля́за, -ле́зеш *to go out, leave*
изнена́да *surprise*
изо́бщо *at all*
изо́бщо не е . . . *it's not at all . . .*
(да) изпе́я, -е́еш *to sing*
(да) изпи́я, -и́еш *to drink*
(да) изпра́тя, -тиш *to accompany, to see off; to send*
изпра́щам, -щаш *to accompany, to see off; to send*
(на) и́сток *(to the) east*
и́сточен, -чна *(from/to the) east*
и́зход *exit; gate*
(да) изче́зна, -неш *to disappear*
ико́на *icon*
или *or*
и́ма *(it form) there is, are*
и́мам, -маш *to have*
и́ме (pl) имена́ *name*
и́мейл *email*
интервю́ *interview*
интере́сен, -сна *interesting*
и́нтернет *internet*
информа́ция *information (desk)*
ирла́ндец (pl) -дци *Irishman*
Ирла́ндия *Ireland*
ирла́ндка *Irishwoman*
и́скам, -каш *to want*

испа́нец (pl) -нци *Spaniard*
испа́нка *Spanish woman*
испа́нски *Spanish*
исто́рия *history*
италиа́нец (pl) -нци *an Italian*
италиа́нка *Italian woman*
италиа́нски *Italian*

(да) ка́жа, -жеш *to say*
ка́звам, -ваш *to say*
ка́звам, -ваш се *my (your) name is*
кажѐте! *can I help you?* (lit. *say!*)
как *how*
какво́ *what*
ка́кто *as*
какъ́в, каква́ *what (kind of)*
календа́р *calendar, diary*
камериѐрка *chambermaid*
капучи́но *capuccino*
ка́рам, -раш *to drive*
ка́рам, -раш ски *to ski*
ка́рта *map; card*
(крѐдитна) ка́рта *credit card*
(бо́рдна) ка́рта *boarding card/pass*
ка́ртичка (*post*) *card*
ка́са *checkout; ticket office; till*
касиѐрка *cashier, checkout operator*
катедра́ла *cathedral*
като́ *as; when; like*
кафѐ *coffee; café*
ка́чество *quality*
кашкава́л (*yellow*) *cheese*

ка́шлица *cough*
кашо́н *cardboard box*
кеба́пче *'kebapche' sausage*
кекс (*sponge*) *cake*
кили́м *carpet, rug*
килогра́м *kilogram*
ки́село мля́ко *yoghurt*
кита́йски (adj) *Chinese*
ки́фла *bun*
класи́чески *classical*
клиѐнт(ка) *customer*
климати́к *air conditioner*
клуб *club*
ключ *key*
кни́га *book*
кога́(то) *when*
ко́жа *skin*
козмѐтика *cosmetics*
кой, коя́, коѐ, кои́ *who*
ко́йто, коя́то, коѐто, кои́то (the one) *who*
коктѐйл *cocktail party*
(ко́ка-)ко́ла *coke*
кола́ *car*
колѐга *colleague*
Ко́леда *Christmas*
коли́чка *trolley, shopping cart*
ко́лко *how many, how much*
коля́но (pl) колена́ *knee*
командиро́вка *business trip*
кома́р *mosquito*
комбина́ция *combination*
компа́ктдиск (pl) -кове *CD*
компю́тър (pl) -три *computer*
конта́кт *contact; socket*
конфѐкция *ready-made clothes*
конферѐнция *conference*

концерт *concert*
коняк *brandy*
кораб(че) *(small) boat*
коридор *corridor*
край (pl) краища *end*
крак (pl) крака *foot; leg*
кран *tap*
красив *beautiful*
краставица *cucumber*
кредит *loan, credit*
кредитна карта *credit card*
крем *cream*
крепостен, -тна *fortification*
(adj)
крикет *cricket*
крипта *crypt*
кристален, -лна *crystal*
кроасан *croissant*
кръст *(small of the) back;*
cross
ксерокс *photocopier, xerox*
култура *culture*
купувам, -ваш *to buy*
(да) купя, -пиш *to buy*
курорт *resort, spa*
кутия *box*
куфар *suitcase*
кухня *kitchen*
къде(то) *where*
към *about; around; towards;*
to
къмпинг *campsite*
късно *late*
къща *house*
кюфте *meatball*

лале *tulip*
лаптоп *laptop*

лев(че) *lev*
легло *bed*
лек *light* (adj)
лека нощ! *good night!*
лекар(ка) *doctor*
лекарство *medicine*
летище *airport*
ли (question word)
лимон *lemon*
лимонада *lemonade*
лимонов (made with) *lemon*
(английска) лира *pound*
sterling
литература *literature*
литър (pl) литри *litre*
лифт *(ski/chair) lift*
лондонски *London* (adj)
лондончанин (pl) -ани
Londoner
лош *bad*
луксозен, -зна *deluxe*
лято *summer*

М *gents (toilet, washroom)*
магазин *shop, store*
магистрала *motorway,*
freeway
май *May*
майка *mother*
майстор *workman*
Македония *Macedonia*
малко *few, a little, not many,*
not much
малолетен, -тна *juvenile,*
young
малък, малка *small*
мама *mum, mother*
манастир *monastery*

марато́нки *trainers, athletic shoes*

ма́рка *(postage) stamp*

март *March*

маршру́тка *minibus (taxi)*

ма́са *table*

материа́ли *materials*

мач *match*

маши́на *machine*

между́ *between*

междунаро́ден, -дна *international*

ме́нта *(pepper)mint*

ме́нтов (made with) *mint*

меню́ *menu*

мерси́ *thank you*

ме́сец *month*

метро́ *metro, underground, subway*

ме́тър (pl) **ме́три** *metre*

механа́ *tavern*

мил *dear, sweet, kind*

(да) ми́на, -неш *to go, pass (of time)*

(ще ми) ми́не *I'll be OK*

ми́нал *past*

минера́лна вода́ *mineral water*

мину́та *minute*

ми́сля, -лиш *to think*

млад *young*

мля́ко *milk*

мно́го *a lot, much, many; very, very much*

мо́га, мо́жеш *I can, am able*

моде́рен, -рна *modern, fashionable, up-to-date*

мо́же *it is possible*

мо́же би *maybe*

мо́же ли? *may I?, could you?*

мой *my, mine*

молба́ *request*

моли́в *pencil*

мо́ля *please; I beg your pardon; don't mention it*

моме́нт *moment*

моне́та *coin*

моми́че (n) *girl*

момче́ (n) *boy*

море́ *sea*

мо́рски (of the) *sea, marine*

моте́л *motel*

мото́р *engine*

мра́чен, -чна *dull*

музе́й *museum*

му́зика *music*

музика́нт *musician*

мъгли́во *foggy*

мъж (pl) **мъже́** *man; husband*

мъжки *man's*

мя́сто (pl) **места́** *place*

на *on; of; at; in; to; for*

набли́зо *nearby*

навре́ме *in/on time*

нався́къде *everywhere*

навъ́н *outside*

над *above*

надя́вам, -ваш се *to hope*

надя́сно *to the right*

наздра́ве! *cheers!*

(под) на́ем *hired*

(да) нае́ма, -меш *to rent, hire*

наи́стина *really, indeed*

най-по́сле *at last*

(да) накáрам, -раш *to make* (someone do something)

налú? *isn't that so?*

наля́во *to the left*

(да) намéря, -риш *to find*

наóколо *nearby*

напúтка *drink*

напрáво *straight ahead*

(да) напрáвя, -виш *to make; to do*

напрéдвам, -ваш *to make progress*

нарéд *in order*

нередéн *arranged*

(да) наредя́, -дúш *to arrange*

нарóден, -дна *national*

нарóдност (f) *nationality*

натурáлен, -лна *natural, pure*

(да) наýча, -чиш *to learn*

национáлен, -лна *national*

нáция *nation*

начáло *beginning*

наш *our(s)*

не *no, not*

невя́рно *false*

нéгов *his*

недéй! *don't!*

недéля *Sunday*

нéин *her(s)*

нéмец (pl) **нéмци** *a German*

немкúня *German woman*

нéмски *German*

непрекъ́снато *all the time*

непремéнно *certainly; don't fail to*

неприя́тно *unpleasant*

неприя́тност (f) *unpleasantness, trouble*

непушáч *non-smoker*

нéрвен, нéрвна *agitated, stressed out*

нервóзни кюфтéта *spicy meatballs*

нéс(кафé) *instant (coffee)*

с нетърпéние *eagerly*

нéщо *something*

нéщо дрýго *some/anything else*

нéщо за пúене *something to drink*

нéщо за я́дене *something to eat*

нúе *we*

нúкой *nobody*

нúсък, -ска *short* (stature)

нúто . . ., нúто . . . *neither, nor . . .*

нúщо *nothing; no matter; never mind*

нúщо чýдно *(that's) hardly surprising*

но *but*

нов *new*

Нóва годúна *New Year*

новинá *news (item)*

нож (pl) **ножóве** *knife*

ноéмври *November*

нóмер *number*

нормáлно *normally; OK*

носáч *porter*

нóся, -сиш *to carry, have with one, bring, take*

нощ (f) *night*

(лéка) нощ! *good night!*

нýжда *need*

нýла *zero, nought*

ня́как *somehow*

ня́какъв, ня́каква *some kind of*

ня́кога *sometime*

ня́кой *somebody, some*

ня́колко *some, a few*

ня́къде *somewhere*

ня́ма *there isn't*

ня́ма защо́ *you're welcome, don't mention it*

ня́ма ни́що *it's nothing, don't mention it*

ня́мам, -маш *not to have*

(да) се оба́дя, -диш *to ring, phone, call*

оба́ждам, -даш се *to ring, phone, call*

о́бед and **обя́д** *lunch (time), noon*

обикнове́но *usually*

оби́чам, -чаш *to love, like*

о́блачно *cloudy*

(да) се облека́, -че́ш *to get dressed*

обме́нно бюро́ *bureau de change, currency exchange office*

(да) обменя́, -ни́ш *to change*

обмя́на на валу́та *currency exchange*

обра́тен, -тна *opposite; reverse*

обслу́жване *service (e.g. in a restaurant)*

обу́вки *shoes, footwear*

обя́д see **о́бед**

обя́двам, -ваш *to have lunch*

(да) обясня́, -ни́ш *to explain*

огледа́ло *mirror*

(да) оже́ня, -ниш *to marry off*

(да) се оже́ня, -ниш *to get married*

ока́за се *it turned out*

око́ (pl) **очи́** *eye*

о́коло *about, around*

окто́мври *October*

о́леле! *oh dear me!*

о́лио *vegetable oil*

омле́т *omelette*

омъ́жена *married* (for a woman)

о́нзи *that*

опа́сен, -сна *dangerous*

о́пера *opera*

(да) опи́там, -таш *to try*

опи́твам, -ваш *to try*

о́питен, -тна *experienced*

опла́квам, -ваш се *to complain*

опла́кване (pl) **-ния** *complaint*

(да) се опла́ча, -чеш *to complain*

(да) се опра́вя, -виш *to get better*

организи́ра се (*it* form) *is organized*

организи́рам, -раш *to organize*

о́рех(ов) (made with) *walnut(s)*

ориента́лски *oriental*

осве́н *apart from, besides*

осо́бено *especially*

(ни́що) осо́бено *nothing special*

оста́ва(т) is/are left
(да) оста́вя, -виш to leave
оста́вям, -вяш to leave
от from; (because) of; than;
    made of; with; since; out of
от ня́колко дни (for) the
    past few days
отво́рен open
отгова́рям, -ряш to answer
(да) отгово́ря, -риш to
    answer
отда́вна long since, long ago
отдале́че from afar
оти́вам, -ваш to go
(да) оти́да, -деш to go
    (there)
отклоне́ние diversion
отко́лкото than
откъде́ where from
отли́чно! excellent!
отпа́дък (pl) отпа́дъци
    litter, rubbish
отту́к from here
о́фис office
о́ще more; still; even; yet
о́ще веднъ́ж once again
о́ще не not yet

павилио́н kiosk
па́дам, -даш to fall
па́дащи предме́ти falling
    objects
(да) па́дна, -неш to fall
паза́р market
пазару́вам, -ваш to do the
    shopping
па́зя, -зиш to keep, preserve
пак again

панаи́р fair
па́пка folder, file
пари́ (pl) money
парк park; garden
па́ркинг car park, parking
    lot
парки́рам, -раш to park
Парла́ме́нт Parliament
паро́ла password
па́ртер ground floor
па́рти party
парфю́м perfume
парче́ piece
паспо́рт passport
(брита́нски) па́унд pound
    sterling
пе́тък Friday
(не́що за) пи́ене something
    to drink
пи́во beer, ale
пи́коло bellboy
пи́лзенска би́ра Pilsner
    (beer)
пи́лешки (made with) chicken
пи́нкод PIN (code)
пи́пам, -паш to touch
писа́лка pen
писмо́ letter
пи́там, -таш to ask
пи́ца pizza
пицари́я pizzeria
пи́ша, -шеш to write
пи́я, пи́еш to drink
плаж beach
плака́т poster, placard
план plan
планина́ mountain(s)
(да) платя́, -ти́ш to pay

пла́щам, -щаш *to pay*
плик *envelope; (plastic) bag*
пли́кче *small (plastic) bag,*
  envelope
плод (pl) плодове́ *fruit*
пло́дов (made of) *fruit*
плодотво́рен, -рна *fruitful*
площа́д *square*
плу́вам, -ваш *to swim*
по *along; over; on*
по́вече *more*
по́вечето *most of*
повре́да *fault*
повре́ден *out of order,*
  damaged
повторе́ние *repetition*
под *under*
пода́рък (pl) -ъци *present*
(да) подаря́, -ри́ш *to give*
подходя́щ *suitable*
пожела́вам, -ваш *to wish*
(да) пожела́я, -а́еш *to wish*
по́здрав *greeting*
(мно́го) по́здрави *best wishes*
поздравле́ния!
  congratulations!
(да) поздравя́, -ви́ш *to*
  welcome, greet; congratulate
поздравя́вам, -ваш *to*
  welcome, greet; congratulate
позна́вам, -ваш *to know*
  (someone, one another)
позна́т(а) *acquaintance*
(да) пока́жа, -жеш *to show,*
  point
пока́звам, -ваш *to show,*
  point
пока́на *invitation*

пока́нен *invited*
(да) пока́ня, -ниш *to invite*
поле́зен, -зна *useful*
по́лет *flight*
полица́й *policeman*
поли́ция *police*
по́ло *polo*
полови́н *half*
полови́на *a half*
(да) получа́, -чиш *to receive*
получа́вам, -ваш *to receive*
пома́гам, -гаш *to help*
(да) поми́сля, -лиш *to think*
  over
(да) помо́гна, -неш *to help*
по́мня, -ниш *to remember*
по́мощ (f) *help, assistance*
понеде́лник *Monday*
поня́кога *sometimes*
(да) попи́там, -таш *to ask*
(да) попра́вя, -виш *to mend*
портие́р *doorman*
портмоне́ *purse, (hand)bag*
портока́л(ов) (made with)
  orange(s)
(да) поре́чам, -чаш *to order*
поръ́чвам, -ваш *to order*
поръ́чка *order*
по́сле *after that, then*
после́ден, -дна *final, last*
посо́ка *direction*
(да) посре́щна, -неш
  to meet
по́стер *poster*
(да) поча́кам, -каш *to wait*
  a little
почи́вам, -ваш си *to be*
  resting

почи́вка *rest, break, holiday, vacation*
(да) си почи́на, -неш *to have a rest*
почти́ *almost*
по́ща *post office*
(гла́сова) по́ща *voicemail*
прав *right*
пра́вя, -виш *to do; to make*
пра́зник (pl) **-ици** *festival, holiday*
празну́вам, -ваш *to celebrate*
пра́скова *peach*
(да) пра́тя, -тиш *to send*
(да) преведа́, -де́ш *to translate*
пре́вод *translation*
преводáч(ка) *translator; interpreter*
пре́говори (pl) *negotiations; talks*
пред *in front of*
(да) преда́м, -даде́ш *to leave/pass on/a message*
преди́ *before; ago*
предла́гам, -гаш *to suggest, make an offer, propose*
(да) предло́жа, -жиш *to suggest; make an offer*
предпола́гам, -гаш *to suppose*
предпочи́там, -таш *to prefer*
предста́ва *idea*
представле́ние *performance*
през *during; through; in; at*
(да) пренеса́, -се́ш *to take (somewhere)*

препоръ́чвам, -ваш *to recommend*
(да) пресека́, -ече́ш *to cross*
пре́сен, пря́сна, пре́сни *fresh*
престо́й (duration of) *stay*
(да) придружа́, -жи́ш *to accompany*
(да) прие́ма, -меш *to accept*
при́нтер *printer*
присти́гам, -гаш *to arrive*
присти́гащ *arriving*
(да) присти́гна, -неш *to arrive*
прия́тел(ка) *friend*
прия́телски *friendly*
прия́тен, -тна *pleasant*
прия́тен пъ́т! *have a pleasant journey!*
прия́тно изка́рване! *have a nice time!/pleasant stay*
пробле́м *problem*
прови́нция *the country outside the capital*
прогно́за *forecast*
програ́ма *program(me)*
програми́ст (computer) *programmer*
прогре́с *progress*
прода́вам, -ваш *to sell*
продава́ч(ка) *shop assistant, sales person*
прода́ден *sold*
проду́кт *product*
продължа́вам, -ваш *to continue*
прозо́рец (pl) **-рци** *window*
прое́кт *project*
про́лет (f) *spring*

про́сто *simply*
проти́в *against*
профе́сия *occupation*
прови́нция *the country
(outside) the capital*
пу́ша, -шиш *to smoke*
пуша́ч *smoker*
пу́шене *smoking*
пъ́лен, -лна с *full of*
пъ́лнени чу́шки *stuffed
peppers*
пъ́пеш *melon*
пъ́рво *firstly*
път (pl) **пъ́ти** *time*
път (pl) **пъ́тища** *road, way*
пъ́тник (pl) **-ици** *passenger,
traveller*
пъту́вам, -ваш *to travel*
пъту́ване *journey*

ра́бота *work*
рабо́тник (pl) **-ици** *worker*
рабо́тно вре́ме *opening
hours*
рабо́тя, -тиш *to work*
ра́двам, -ваш се *to enjoy, be
glad*
ра́дио *radio*
ра́достен, -тна *joyous, glad*
(да) **разбера́, -ре́ш** *to
understand*
разби́ра се *of course*
разби́рам, -раш *to
understand*
развале́н *broken, not
working*
(да) **разваля́, -ли́ш** *to break
(something)*

(да) **се разваля́, -ли́ш** *to go
wrong; to break down*
разве́ден *divorced*
(да) **разгле́дам, -даш** *to
look at/around*
разгле́ждам, -даш *to look
at/round*
ра́зговор *conversation*
разка́звам, -ваш *to tell*
разписа́ние *timetable*
разсе́ян *absent-minded*
разхо́дка *trip, walk*
(да) **се разхо́дя, -диш** *to
have a walk*
раки́я *rakiya, brandy*
ра́ница *rucksack, backpack*
ра́но *early*
резерва́ция *reservation*
река́ *river*
рекла́ма *publicity* (adj)
рекла́мен, -мна *publicity,
advertisement*
рели́гия *religion*
(в) **ремо́нт** (*under*) *repair*
рестора́нт *restaurant*
реце́пция *reception*
ре́чник (pl) **-ици** *vocabulary,
dictionary*
(да) **реша́, -ши́ш** *to decide*
Ри́ла планина́ *the Rila
Mountains*
ри́мски *Roman* (adj)
роде́н(а) съм *I was born*
роди́на *fatherland,
motherland*
роди́тел *parent*
рожде́н ден *birthday*
ро́за *rose*

рокля *dress*
романтичен, -чна *romantic*
Румъния *Romania*
руски *Russian* (adj)
ръка (pl) ръце *hand; arm*
рядко *rarely*

с/със *with; on*
сайт *(internet) site*
салата *salad*
салфетка *serviette, napkin*
сам *alone*
само *only, just*
самобръсначка *razor, shaver*
самолет *airplane*
сандвич *sandwich*
сватба *wedding*
(по) света *around the world*
свети, света *Saint, holy*
светло *light*
светло пиво *lager*
светофар *traffic light*
свободен, -дна *free*
свой *one's own*
свят *world*
(на) север *(to the) north*
се (reflexive particle) *-self*
сега *now*
седмица *week*
(да) седна, -неш *to sit*
секретар(ка) *secretary*
село *village*
семейство *family*
септември *September*
сервиз *garage, service station*
сервитьор(ка) *waiter, waitress*
сервирам, -раш *to serve*
сериозно *seriously*

сестра *sister*
сигнал *beep, signal*
сигурен, -рна, ~ съм *I am sure; surely*
сигурно *most probably; certainly*
силен, -лна *strong*
симпатичен, -чна *nice*
син, (pl) синове *son*
син, синя, синьо, сини *blue*
сирене *white cheese, feta*
скара *grill*
ски (pl) *skis*
на ски *skiing*
скоро *soon*
скучно *boring*
скъп *dear; expensive*
слаб *light; weak*
слава Богу! *thank heavens!*
славянски *Slavic, Slavonic*
сладкарница *café, cakeshop, patisserie*
сладолед *icecream*
сладък, сладка *sweet*
след (като) *after; in*
следващ *(up)coming, following*
следващия(т) път *next time*
следобед *(in the) afternoon*
слива *plum*
сливов (made of) *plum*
(да) сложа, -жиш *to put*
служебен, -бна *official; for staff only*
служител(ка) *counter assistant, clerk*
(по) случай *(on the) occasion (of)*

случва се *it happens*
(да) се случи (*it* form) *happen*
слънце *sun*
Слънчев бряг *Sunny Beach*
слънчево *sunny*
(да) сменя, -ниш *to change*
сметана *cream*
сметка *bill*
смея, -ееш се *to laugh*
смешен, -шна *funny*
снимане *taking pictures*
снимка *photo, picture*
снощи *last night*
сняг *snow*
сода *soda water*
сок *juice*
сол (f) *salt*
софийски *Sofia* (adj)
спалня *bedroom*
специалист *specialist*
специалитет *speciality*
специално *specially*
спирам, -раш *to stop*
спиране *stopping*
спирка *(bus) stop*
списание *magazine*
спокойно *calmly*
спомен *memento*
спомням, -няш си *to remember*
според *according to*
спорт *sport*
(да) спра, спреш *to stop*
спя, спиш *to sleep*
сребърен, -рна (made of) *silver*
среща *appointment, meeting, get-together*

срещу *opposite*
сряда *Wednesday*
ставам, -ваш *to stand/get up; to happen; become*
(да) стана, -неш *to stand/get up; to happen; become*
стар *old*
старт *start*
стая *room*
стена *wall*
стига! *stop it! enough!*
(да) стигна, -неш *to reach*
стик *golf club* (instrument)
сто *hundred*
столица *capital*
стомах (pl) стомаси *stomach*
стотинка *stotinka*
стоя, стойш *to stand; stay*
страна *country*
страхувам, -ваш се *to be afraid*
страшен, -шна *awesome, terrific; terrible*
(колко) струва? *how much does it cost?*
студен *cold*
студент(ка) *student*
стъкло *glass*
супа *soup*
супер *super, ace*
супермаркет *supermarket*
сутрин (f) *morning*
сутринта *in the morning*
счупен *broken, not working*
(да) счупя, -пиш *to break*
(да) събера, -реш *to gather*
събота *Saturday*
съвет *advice*

374

съгла́сен, -сна съм *I agree*
(да) се съглася́, -си́ш *to agree*
(за) съжале́ние *unfortunately*
съжаля́вам, -ваш *to be sorry, regret*
(да) създа́м, -даде́ш *to create*
съм *I am* (to be)
съмня́вам, -ваш се *to doubt*
съобще́ние *message*
Сърбия *Serbia*
(от все) сърце́ *with all my heart*
съсе́ден, -дна *next door, neighbouring*
същ, съща *same*
също *also*
ся́дам, -даш *to sit down*
ся́нка *shade, shadow*

табе́лка *notice*
та́зи (f) *this*
така́ *right, so, likewise*
така́ ли? *really?, is that so?*
та́кса *fee*
така́ е *that is so*
такси́ (n) *taxi*
такъ́в, така́ва *such*
тало́ни *tickets in a booklet*
там *there*
танц *dance*
тарато́р *tarator* (Bulgarian cold summer soup)
твой *your(s)*
тво́рчески *creative*
те *they*
теа́тър (pl) -три *theatre*

те́жък, -жка *heavy*
те́зи (pl) *these*
телеви́зор *television*
телефо́н *telephone*
телефо́нен секрета́р *answerphone*
температу́ра *temperature*
те́нис *tennis*
те́хен, тя́хна *their(s)*
те́хника *equipment, technology*
ти *you*
ти́квичка *courgette, zucchini*
типи́чно *typically*
ти́хо *quietly*
то *it*
тоале́тна *toilet, bathroom, restroom*
това́ (n) *this*
тога́ва *then*
то́зи (m) *this*
той *he*
то́лкова *so*
то́ник *tonic water*
то́пъл, -пла *warm, hot*
то́рта *gateau, cake*
то́чен, -чна *punctual*
то́чно *exact(ly), precise(ly)*
трамва́й *tram*
транспо́рт *transport(ation)*
трева́ *grass*
три́ма (ду́ши) *three people*
троле́й *trolleybus*
тру́ден, -дна *difficult*
тръ́гвам, -ваш *to set off*
тря́бва *have to; must*
тря́бва да и́ма *there should be*
тук *here*

турист(ка) *tourist*
ту́рски *Turkish*
Ту́рция *Turkey*
тъ́мно *dark*
търго́вски *trade* (adj)
търго́вски це́нтър *shopping mall*
тъ́рся, -сиш *to look (ask) for*
тя *she*

у *at, with*
удо́бен, -бна *convenient, comfortable*
удово́лствие *pleasure*
ужа́сен, -сна *awful, terrible*
ужа́сно *terribly*
уике́нд *weekend*
уи́ски (n) *whisky*
у́лица *street*
уме́рен *moderate*
уми́рам *to die,* **-раш за** *to be dying for*
уморе́н *tired*
(да) се уморя́, -ри́ш *to get tired*
университе́т *university*
упра́вител *manager, director*
уро́к (pl) **уро́ци** *lesson*
успе́х *success*
у́тре *tomorrow*
у́тро *morning*
ухо́ (pl) **уши́** *ear*
у́ча, -чиш *to study, learn*
уча́ствам, -ваш *to take part*
уче́бник (pl) **-ници** *textbook*
у́чене *studying*
учени́к (pl) **и́ци** *pupil, student*

учи́тел(ка) *teacher*
учу́ден *surprised*

факс *fax*
(не е́) фата́лно *(it's not) fatal*
февруа́ри *February*
филм *film*
фина́л *finish*
фи́рма *firm*
фи́тнес це́нтър/клуб *fitness centre*
фоайе́ *foyer; lounge*
фолкло́р *folklore*
фолкло́рен фестива́л *folklore festival*
фо́рма *shape*
фо́тоапара́т *camera*
фото́граф *photographer*
францу́зин (pl) **-зи** *Frenchman*
французо́йка *Frenchwoman*
фре́нски *French*
фу́тбол *football*

ха́йде! *come on!*
ха́йде, ха́йде! *now, now!*
(да) харе́сам, -саш *to like*
харе́свам, -ваш *to like*
харти́я *paper*
ха-ха! *ha-ha!*
хвъ́рлям, -ляш *to throw*
хепати́т *hepatitis*
хиля́да (pl) **хи́ляди** *thousand*
Хи́йтроу *Heathrow*
химика́лка *(ballpoint) pen, biro*
хле́бче *bread roll*
хля́б *bread*

хо́дя, -диш to go, walk
хо́кей hockey
хол sitting/living room
хо́ра (pl) people
хоте́л hotel
храна́ food
хре́ма (head) cold
христия́нски Christian
ху́бав nice, beautiful,
   handsome
худо́жник (pl) -ици artist
худо́жничка artist (woman)
ху́мор humour
хълм hill

цве́те (pl) цветя́ flower
цел (f) aim, purpose
целодне́вен, -вна whole day
цена́ price
це́нност (f) (something)
   valuable
це́нтър (pl) це́нтрове centre,
   downtown
цига́ра cigarette
цъ́рква church
цял (pl) це́ли all; whole
цял куп a whole lot of

чадъ́р umbrella
чай tea
ча́кам, -каш to wait, expect
ча́нта bag, purse
час hour
часа́ o'clock
часо́вник (pl) -ици watch;
   clock
част (f) part
ча́ша cup; glass

че that
черве́н red
че́рен, -рна black
Черномо́рието the Black Sea
   coast
че́сън garlic
чести́т рожде́н ден! happy
   birthday!
чести́то! congratulations!
че́сто often
чета́, -те́ш to read
че́твърт (f) quarter
четвъ́ртък Thursday
чистота́ cleanliness
чове́к (pl) хо́ра person,
   human being
чрез through, by means of, via
чу́вам, -ваш to hear
чу́вствам, -ваш (се) to feel
чу́вство feeling, sense
чуде́сен, -сна wonderful,
   marvellous
чужд foreign
чуждене́ц (pl) -нци́ foreigner
чужденка́ foreigner (woman)
чу́шка bell pepper, capsicum
(да) чу́я, чу́еш to hear

шампа́нско champagne
шампоа́н shampoo
ша́пка hat
шегу́вам, -ваш се to joke
шеф boss
шокола́д bar of chocolate
шокола́дов (made of)
   chocolate
шо́пска сала́та 'shopska'
   salad

шотла́ндец *Scot*
Шотла́ндия *Scotland*
шотла́ндка *Scotswoman*
шотла́ндски *Scottish*
шо́у *show*
шофьо́р *driver*
шум *noise*
шу́мен, -мна *noisy*
шу́нка *ham*
шшш! *sh-sh-sh!*

ща́стие *happiness*
(за) ща́стие *fortunately,*
  luckily
щастли́в *happy*
щом *since, seeing that*

ъ́гъл (pl) ъ́гли *corner*

(на) юг *(to the) south*
юли *July*

юни *June*
юти́я *iron*

я́бълка *apple*
я́бълков (made with) *apple*
(да) се явя́, -ви́ш *to present*
  oneself
я́года *strawberry*
я́годов (made with)
  strawberry
(не́що за) я́дене *something*
  to eat
я́ке *jacket*
ям, яде́ш *to eat*
януа́ри *January*
Япо́ния *Japan*
я́сен, я́сна *clear, obvious*
я́сно защо́ *it's obvious why;*
  now I see why

English–Bulgarian vocabulary

This is a 'survival' vocabulary and you should use it in conjunction with the Appendix and the Bulgarian–English vocabulary. It includes most of the Bulgarian words you come across in the course – and a good few more besides. You'll be pleased to see that we have given most verbs in both imperfective and perfective forms. All other words we have listed in their basic form only, so for irregularities of form in nouns and adjectives, for example, or, indeed, for verb patterns, you'll have to turn to the Bulgarian–English vocabulary. If an English word has more than one equivalent in Bulgarian, we have attempted to list the more common word first. Where you might confuse forms, we have listed nouns before adjectives and verbs.

Although we trust that the Bulgarian equivalents of the 900 or so English words listed here will ensure your linguistic survival in a Bulgarian environment, do not expect it to replace a good English–Bulgarian dictionary.

Some words you will find in the Appendix rather than in the Vocabulary. You should look for most of the numerals, for example, and the different verb and pronoun forms, in the Appendix. The Appendix is really an addition to the Vocabulary, so use the two together.

able, be ~ мо́га
about о́коло, към
above над
accept прие́мам, (да) прие́ма
accompany изпра́щам, (да) изпра́тя; придружа́вам, (да) придружа́
according to спо́ред
acquaintance позна́т
address адре́с
advertisement рекла́ма
advice съве́т

afraid, be ~ страху́вам се
after след
afternoon следо́бед; in the ~ следо́бед
again пак
against срещу́
agency аге́нция
agitated не́рвен
ago преди́
agree, I ~ съгла́сен съм
air въ́здух
airline а́виокомпа́ния

airplane самолѐт

airport летѝще, аерогара

alcohol алкохол

all всѝчко; ~ of us всѝчки

allergy алѐргия

almost почтѝ

alone сам

along по, покрай

already вѐче

also също

always вѝнаги

America Амѐрика

American американец;
  американски

amusing забавен

and и, а

another друг

answer отговор; отговарям,
  (да) отговоря

answerphone телефонен
  секретар

anxious, be ~ безпокоя се

anybody някой

anything нещо

apart from освѐн

apartment апартамент

apologize извинявам се, (да)
  се извиня

appendicitis апендисѝт

apple ябълка

appointment срѐща

arm ръка

around около, към

arrival пристѝгане

arrive пристѝгам, (да)
  пристѝгна

artist художник

as както, като

ask пѝтам, (да) попѝтам

assistance помощ

(counter) assistant (f)
  служѝтелка

at на, у, в, през

ATM банкомат

attention внимание

attorney адвокат

attraction (tourist)
  забележѝтелност

Australia Австралия

Australian австралиец;
  австралийски

autumn ѐсен

awful ужасен

back гръб; small of the ~
  кръст; go ~ върнѐте се
  обратно!

bad лош

bag чанта

(plastic) bag плик(че)

baggage багаж

banana банан

bank банка

bar бар; ~ of chocolate
  шоколад

basketball баскетбол

bathroom баня, тоалѐтна

be съм

beach плаж

beard брада

beautiful красѝв, хубав

because защото

become ставам, (да) стана

bed легло

bedroom спалня

beer бѝра, пѝво

380

before преди
begin започвам, (да) започна
beginning начало
behind зад
beside до
besides освен
between между
big голям
bill сметка
birth раждане
birthday рожден ден; happy
  ~! честит ~!
black черен
block блок
blond рус
blue син
book книга; запазвам, (да)
  запазя
boot, car-~ багажник
border граница
boring скучен
born, I was ~ роден съм
boss шеф
bottle бутилка
boulevard булевард
box кутия
boxing бокс
boy момче
brandy коняк; Bulgarian ~
  ракия
bread хляб; ~ roll хлебче
break (something) чупя, (да)
  счупя; почивка, ваканция
break down развалям се,
  (да) се разваля
breakfast закуска
bring нося, (да) донеса
Britain Великобритания

British британски; the ~
  британците
broken счупен, развален
brother брат
Bulgaria България
Bulgarian българин;
  български
bun кифла
bunch букет
bus автобус
business бизнес; ~ card
  визитна картичка/визитка;
  ~ man бизнесмен
busy зает
but но, а, обаче
butter масло
buy купувам, (да) купя

café кафе, кафене,
  сладкарница
cake торта, кекс
calendar календар
call обаждам се, (да) се
  обадя
calmly спокойно
camera фотоапарат
campsite къмпинг
can мога; може; (petrol, gas) ~
  бидонче
Canada Канада
Canadian канадец; канадски
candy бонбон
capsicum чушка
car кола, автомобил; ~ park
  паркинг
card карта; credit ~ кредитна
  ~, post ~ картичка
carry нося, (да) донеса

case слу́чай; ку́фар
cashpoint банкома́т
CD компа́ктдиск
celebrate празну́вам, (да)
  отпразну́вам
central центра́лен
centre це́нтър
certainly си́гурно; разби́ра
  се; непреме́нно
chambermaid камерие́рка
champagne шампа́нско
change обме́ням, (да)
  обменя́; проме́ням, (да)
  променя́
cheap е́втин
checkout ка́са
cheers! наздра́ве!
cheese (white, feta) си́рене,
  (yellow) кашкава́л
chemist's апте́ка
chicken пи́ле; grilled ~ пи́ле
  на грил
child дете́
China Кита́й
Chinese кита́ец; кита́йски
chocolate бонбо́н; bar of ~
  шокола́д
choose избира́м, (да) избера́
Christmas Ко́леда; merry ~!
  чести́та ~!
church цъ́рква
cinema ки́но
cigarette цига́ра
citizen гра́жданин
city град
clean чист
clear я́сен
clock часо́вник

close затва́рям, (да) затво́ря;
  ~d затво́рен
clothes дре́хи
cloud о́блак; it's ~y облачно е
coffee кафе́; instant ~
  нес(кафе́)
coke ко́ла
cold студе́н; head ~ хре́ма
colleague коле́га
come и́двам, (да) до́йда; ~
  on! ха́йде!
come in вли́зам, (да) вля́за
come out излизам, (да)
  изля́за
comfortable удо́бен
complain опла́квам се, (да)
  се опла́ча
computer компю́тър
concert конце́рт
conference конфере́нция
congratulate поздравя́вам,
  (да) поздравя́
congratulations!
  поздравле́ния! чести́то!
continue продължа́вам, (да)
  продължа́
continuously непре́къснато
convenient удо́бен
conversation ра́зговор
corner ъ́гъл
cost, how much does it ~?
  ко́лко стру́ва?
cough ка́шлица
cousin братовче́д
country страна́
cream крем; смета́на
create създа́вам, (да) създа́м
creative тво́рчески

credit card кре́дитна ка́рта
cricket кри́кет
cross кръст; преси́чам, (да)
    пресека́
cucumber кра́ставица
culture култу́ра
cup ча́ша
currency валу́та; ~ exchange
    office обме́нно бюро́
customer клие́нт

damp вла́жен
dance танцу́вам
danger опа́сност; внима́ние!
dangerous опа́сен
dark тъ́мен
date да́та
daughter дъщеря́
day ден
dear скъп
decide реша́вам, (да) реша́
degree гра́дус
delay закъсне́ние
delegation делега́ция
delicious вку́сен
dentist зъболе́кар
departure замина́ване
dialogue ра́зговор, диало́г
diary дне́вник, беле́жник
dictionary ре́чник
die уми́рам, (да) умра́
diet дие́та, режи́м
different разли́чен
difficult тру́ден
dinner вече́ря
direction посо́ка
director дире́ктор
disappear изче́звам, (да)
    изче́зна

disco дискоте́ка
distance разстоя́ние
diversion отклоне́ние
do пра́вя, (да) напра́вя
doctor ле́кар
document докуме́нт
don't! неде́й!
door врата́; ~man портие́р
doubt съмня́вам се
downtown це́нтър
dress (oneself) обли́чам се,
    (да) се облека́
drink напи́тка, не́що за
    пи́ене; пи́я, (да) изпи́я
drive ка́рам; ~r шофьо́р
dull мра́чен
during през
DVD диви́ди́

each все́ки
ear ухо́
early ра́но
east и́зток; in/to the ~ на
    и́зток
eat ям, (да) изя́м; something
    to ~ не́що за я́дене
elevator асансьо́р
email и́мейл, електро́нна
    по́ща
end край
engaged зае́т
engine мото́р
England А́нглия
English англи́йски
Englishman англича́нин
enough доста́тъчно; сти́га!
entrance вход
envelope плик
especially специа́лно, осо́бено

estate agent бро́кер

even дори́, да́же; ра́вен

evening ве́чер; in the ~ вечерта́

every все́ки; ~ body все́ки; ~ thing вси́чко; ~ where нався́къде

exact то́чен; ~ly! то́чно така́!

excellent отли́чен

except осве́н

exceptional изключи́телен

excursion екску́рзия

excuse извине́ние; ~ me! извине́те! извиня́вайте!

exhibition изло́жба

exit и́зход

expensive скъп

explain обясня́вам, (да) обясня́

eye око́

fall па́дам, (да) па́дна; е́сен

false невя́рно

far дале́че

family семе́йство

fast бърз

fat мазнина́; (adj) дебе́л

father баща́

fault дефе́кт, повре́да; вина́

favour услу́га

fax факс

feel чу́вствам; ~ing чу́вство

festival пра́зник, фестива́л

few ма́лко a ~ ня́колко

file па́пка, файл

final после́ден; ~ly на́й-накра́я

find нами́рам, (да) наме́ря

fine гло́ба; ~! добре́!

finish свъ́ршвам, (да) свъ́рша

firm фи́рма

fish ри́ба

fizzy гази́ран

flat апартаме́нт; (adj) ра́вен

floor ета́ж

flower цве́те

flu грип

fly муха́; (vb) летя́

fog мъгла́

folklore фолкло́р; (adj) фолкло́рен

food храна́

foot крак

football фу́тбол

for за

forbidden забране́н

forecast прогно́за

foreign чужд; ~er чужде́нец

forget забра́вям, (да) забра́вя

forgive проща́вам, (да) простя́; ~ me извине́те! извиня́вайте!

fork ви́лица

fortunately за ща́стие

free свобо́ден; безпла́тен

freeway магистра́ла

France Фра́нция

French фре́нски

Frenchman францу́зин

frequent чест

fresh свеж, пре́сен

friend прия́тел; ~ly прия́телски

from от

front: in ~ of пред

fruit плод; ~ful плодотво́рен

full of пъ́лен с

fun, it's ~ заба́вно е
funny сме́шен
future бъ́деще

game игра́
garage гара́ж; серви́з
garden гради́на
garlic че́сън
gas бензи́н; газ
gas station бензиноста́нция
German герма́нец, не́мец;
    герма́нски, не́мски
Germany Герма́ния
get получа́вам, (да) получа́
get to know one another
    запозна́вам се, (да) се
    запозна́я
get up ста́вам, (да) ста́на
girl моми́че
give да́вам, (да) дам
give back връ́щам, (да)
    въ́рна
glad дово́лен; be ~ ра́двам се
gladly с удово́лствие
glass ча́ша
go хо́дя; (somewhere)
    оти́вам, (да) оти́да
go back връ́щам се, (да) се
    въ́рна
go in вли́зам, (да) вля́за
go out изли́зам, (да) изля́за
God Бог
golf голф; ~club (instrument)
    стик
good добъ́р
goodbye дови́ждане; (on the
    phone) дочу́ване
gram грам
grandmother ба́ба

grapes гро́зде
grass трева́
great голя́м; ~! чуде́сно!
green зеле́н
Greece Гъ́рция
Greek гръ́к; гръ́цки
greet поздравя́вам, (да)
    поздравя́; ~ing по́здрав
grey сив
grill ска́ра; грил
ground floor па́ртер
group гру́па
guest гост
guide екскурзово́д

hair коса́; ко́съм
half полови́н; a ~ полови́на
hall за́ла
ham шу́нка
hand ръка́
handsome ху́бав, краси́в
happen, it ~s ста́ва, (да)
    ста́не
happiness ща́стие
happy щастли́в, ве́сел; ~
    with дово́лен от; ~ . . . !
    чести́т . . . !
hard твърд, тру́ден
hat ша́пка
have и́мам; not to ~ ня́мам; ~
    to тря́бва
he той
head глава́
headache главобо́лие
health здра́ве
hear чу́вам, (да), чу́я
heart сърце́; with all my ~ от
    все сърце́
heat топлина́; горещина́

heavy тéжък

hello! здравéй(те)!; (on the phone) áло(?)

help пóмощ; помáгам, (да) помóгна

her(s) нéин

here тук; ~ is éто; ~ you are заповя́дай(те)

high висóк; ~way магистрáла

hill хълм

his нéгов

history истóрия

hockey хóкей

hold държá (се), (да) се хвáна

holiday прáзник, почи́вка

home дом; (go) ~/at ~ вкъ́щи

hope надéжда; надя́вам се

hospital бóлница

host домаки́н

hot горéщо

hotel хотéл

hour час

house къ́ща

how как; ~ many/much кóлко

however обáче

hungry глáден

hurry, be in a~ бъ́рзам

hurt, it ~s боли́

husband мъж, съпру́г

I аз

icecream сладолéд

icon икóна

idea идéя, предстáва

if акó

ill бóлен

immediately веднáга

important вáжен; it's ~ вáжно е

impossible невъзмóжен; it's ~ невъзмóжно е

in в/във, на, през, след; ~ front of пред

indeed наи́стина

information информáция

instead of вмéсто

interesting интерéсен

international междунарóден

interpreter превода́ч

introduce see get to know

invitation покáна

invite кáня, (да) покáня ~d покáнен

Ireland Ирлáндия

Irish ирлáндски ~man ирлáндец

iron юти́я

it то

Italian италиáнец; италиáнски

Italy Итáлия

its нéгов

jacket сакó, я́ке

jeans дъ́нки

job рáбота

joke шегу́вам се

journalist журнали́ст

journey пъту́ване

juice сок

just сáмо

juvenile малолéтен

keep пáзя, (да) запáзя

key ключ

kilogram килогра́м

kind добъ́р, любе́зен, мил;
  вид, род

kiosk павилио́н

kitchen ку́хня

knee коля́но

knife нож

know зна́я, позна́вам; get
  to ~ one another (да) се
  запозна́я

knowledge зна́ние

lady да́ма; ~ of the house
  домаки́ня

land земя́

language ези́к

laptop ла́птоп

last после́ден; at ~ на́й-по́сле

late къ́сно; to be ~
  закъсня́вам, (да) закъсне́я

laugh сме́я се

lawyer адвока́т

learn у́ча, (да) нау́ча

learning зна́ние

leave (go out) изли́зам,
  (да) изля́за; тръ́гвам, (да)
  тръ́гна; замина́вам, (да)
  зами́на

leave (behind) оста́вям, (да)
  оста́вя

left ляв; on/to the ~ наля́во

leg крак

lemon лимо́н; ~ade
  лимона́да

lesson уро́к

let's! (ха́йде) да!

letter писмо́, бу́ква

lie (nn) лъжа́; (vb) лъ́жа, (да)
  излъ́жа

lie (vb) лежа́

lie down ля́гам, (да) ле́гна

life живо́т

lift асансьо́р; ski/chair ~ лифт

light светлина́; (adj) све́тъл,
  лек, слаб

like като́

like харе́свам, (да) харе́сам,
  оби́чам

likewise така́

line ли́ния

lion лъв

listen слу́шам

litre ли́тър

little ма́лък; a ~ ма́лко

live живе́я

long дъ́лъг; ~ ago отда́вна

look гле́дам; разгле́ждам,
  (да) разгле́дам

look after гри́жа се (за)

look at/round разгле́ждам,
  (да) разгле́дам

look for тъ́рся

lose гу́бя, (да) загу́бя

lot, a ~ of мно́го

love любо́в; оби́чам

luckily за ща́стие

luggage бага́ж

lunch обя́д, о́бед; have ~
  обя́двам

machine маши́на

make пра́вя, (да) напра́вя;
  ка́рам, (да) нака́рам

man мъж; чове́к

manager дире́ктор,
  ме́ниджър, упра́вител

many мно́го

map ка́рта

market пазáр
married жéнен/омъ́жена
marry (да) се ожéня/омъ́жа
may I? мóже ли?
maybe мóже би
meaning значéние
mean, I ~ и́скам да кáжа
meat месó
medicine лекáрство
meet срéщам, (да) срéщна;
  посрéщам, (да) посрéщна
meeting срéща
melon пъ́пеш
memory пáмет
mend попрáвям, (да) попрáвя
mention споменáвам, (да)
  споменá
(don't) mention it нáма
  ни́що/защó
menu меню́
merry вéсел
message съобщéние
metre мéтър
mile ми́ля
milk мля́ко
mine мой
minute мину́та
mirror огледáло
Miss госпóжица
mistake грéшка
mobile (phone) моби́лен
  телефóн, GSM (джи́есéм)
modern модéрен
monastery манасти́р
money пари́
month мéсец
more пóвече, óще
morning су́трин, у́тро;
  in the ~ сутринтá

mosquito комáр
most нáй-мнóго; ~ of
  пóвечето
motel мотéл
mother мáйка
motorway магистрáла
mountain(s) планинá
mouth устá
Mr господи́н
Mrs госпожá
much мнóго
museum музéй
music му́зика
must тря́бва
my мой

name и́ме
napkin салфéтка
nation нáция
national национáлен,
  нарóден; ~ity нарóдност
natural натурáлен,
  естéствен; ~ly естéствено
near бли́зо; ~by наблизо
need ну́жда
neither . . . , nor . . . ни́то . . .
  ни́то
nervous нéрвен, притеснéн
never ни́кога
new нов
news (item) новинá; ~ paper
  вéстник
next слéдващ; ~ to до
nice ху́бав; симпати́чен
night нощ; last ~ снóщи
no не
nobody ни́кой
noise шум
noisy шу́мен

none нѝкакъв
non-smoker непушàч
nose нос
normally нормàлно, обикновèно
north сèвер; in/to the ~ на сèвер
not не; ~ yet òще не
note белèжка; ~book белèжник
notice табèлка
nothing нѝщо
(it's) nothing нѝма нѝщо
nought нỳла
now сегà
number нòмер, брой
nurse сестрà

object предмèт
obvious ѝвен, ѝсен
occasion слỳчай
occupation профèсия
of на; ~ course разбѝра се
offer предложèние; предлàгам, (да) предлòжа
office òфис, бюрò
official служèбен
often чèсто
OK добрè, мòже
old стар
on на, вѝрху, по, в
once веднѝж; ~ again òще веднѝж
only сàмо
open отвòрен; отвàрям, (да) отвòря; ~ing hours рàботно врèме
opposite срещỳ
or илѝ

orange (nn) портокàл
order ред; out of ~ поврèден; порѝчка; порѝчвам, (да) порѝчам
ordinary обикновèн
organize организѝрам; ~d организѝран
other (pl) дрỳги
our(s) наш
outside навѝн
over над
own свой

pain бòлка
paper хартѝя, докумèнт
pardon? мòля?
parent родѝтел
park парк; паркѝрам
parking lot пàркинг
Parliament Парламèнт
part част
party пàрти
pass минàвам, (да) мѝна
passenger пѝтник
passport паспòрт
password парòла
pay плàщам, (да) платѝ
peach прàскова
pen писàлка, химикàлка
pencil молѝв
people хòра
pepper чỳшка; чèрен пипèр
performance представлèние
petrol бензѝн; ~ station бензиностàнция; ~ can бидòнче
pharmacy аптèка
phone обàждам се, (да) се обàдя

photo *снимка;* ~ grapher
  фотограф
picture *снимка*
piece *парче́*
PIN (code) *пи́нкод*
pity, it's a ~ *жа́лко*
pizzeria *пицари́я*
place *мя́сто*
plate *чини́я*
pleasant *прия́тен*
please *мо́ля*
pleased *дово́лен;* be ~
  ра́двам се
pleasure *удово́лствие*
plum *сли́ва*
pocket *джоб*
point *пока́звам,* (да) *пока́жа*
police *поли́ция;* ~ man
  полица́й
polo *по́ло*
possible *възмо́жен;* it's ~
  възмо́жно е, мо́же
post (office) *по́ща;* ~card
  ка́ртичка
prefer *предпочи́там,* (да)
  предпочета́
present *пода́рък*
price *цена́*
private *ча́стен*
probably *вероя́тно*
problem *пробле́м*
program(me) *програ́ма*
punctual *то́чен*
pupil *учени́к*
purpose *цел*
purse *портмоне́, ча́нта*
put *сла́гам,* (да) *сло́жа*

quality *ка́чество*
quarter *че́твърт*
question *въпро́с*
quick *бърз*
quiet *тих*
quite *до́ста*

railway station *га́ра*
rain *дъжд;* it's ~ing *вали́*
rarely *ря́дко*
reach *сти́гам,* (да) *сти́гна*
read *чета́,* (да) *прочета́*
ready *гото́в*
real estate agent *бро́кер*
really *наи́стина;* ~? така́ ли?
receive *получа́вам,* (да)
  полу́ча
reception *реце́пция, при́ем*
receptionist *администра́тор*
recommend *препоръ́чвам,*
  (да) *препоръ́чам*
red *черве́н*
regret *съжаля́вам,* (да)
  съжаля́
religion *рели́гия*
remember *по́мня,* (да)
  запо́мня; спо́мням си, (да)
  си спо́мня
rent *на́ем; нае́мам,* (да)
  нае́ма; ~ed *под на́ем*
repair *ремо́нт*
repeat *повта́рям,* (да)
  повто́ря
request *молба́*
reserve *запа́звам,* (да)
  запа́зя; ~d *запа́зен,*
  резерви́ран

rest почивам си, (да) си
   почина; ~ room тоалетна
restaurant ресторант
return връщам (се), (да) (се)
   върна
right прав, десен; on/to the ~
   надясно
river река
road път
room стая
rose роза
route маршрут, път
Russia Русия
Russian руснак, (f) рускиня;
   руски

salad салата
sales person продавач
salt сол
same, the ~ същият
sandwich сандвич
say казвам, (да) кажа
school училище
Scot шотландец
Scotland Шотландия
Scottish шотландски
sea море
see виждам, (да) видя
sell продавам, (да) продам
send пращам, (да) пратя;
   изпращам, (да) изпратя
serious сериозен
service (in a
   restaurant) обслужване
service station сервиз
serviette салфетка
several няколко

shape форма
shaver самобръсначка
she тя
shoe обувка
shop магазин
shop assistant продавач
shopping, do the ~ пазарувам
short (stature) нисък, (time)
   кратък
show показвам, (да) покажа
shower душ
sick болен
side страна
sight, tourist ~
   забележителност
sign знак, табелка
simply просто
since тъй като, щом; (time)
   от
sing пея, (да) изпея
single единичен; неженен/
   неомъжена
sister сестра
sit седя
sit down сядам, (да) седна
size големина, размер
ski карам ски; ~ run писта
skiing на ски
skin кожа
Slavic (Slavonic) славянски
sleep спя
slow бавен
small малък
smoke (vb) пуша
smoker пушач
smoking пушене
snack закуска

snow сняг

so така́; то́лкова

sock чора́п

soda water гази́рана вода́,
  со́да

soft мек; ~ drink
  безалкохо́лна напи́тка

some ня́кои, ня́колко;
  ня́какъв; ~body ня́кой; ~
  how ня́как; ~thing не́що;
  ~time ня́кога, ~times
  поня́кога
  ~where ня́къде

son син

soon ско́ро

sorry, to be ~ съжаля́вам, (да)
  съжаля́

soup су́па

south юг; in/to the ~ на юг

Spain Испа́ния

Spaniard испа́нец

Spanish испа́нски

speak гово́ря

special специа́лен, осо́бен

spend (time) изка́рвам, (да)
  изка́рам; (money) ха́рча, (да)
  поха́рча

spoon лъжи́ца

spring про́лет

square площа́д

stamp (postage) ма́рка

stand стоя́

stand up ста́вам, (да) ста́на

stomach стома́х, коре́м

stop спи́рам, (да) спра; bus ~
  спи́рка

straight прав

strawberry я́года

street у́лица

strong си́лен

student студе́нт, учени́к

study (vb) у́ча

subway метро́

success успе́х

such такъ́в

sugar за́хар

suggest предла́гам, (да)
  предло́жа

suit костю́м

suitcase ку́фар

summer ля́то

sun слъ́нце

supermarket су́пермаркет

supper вече́ря; have ~ вече́рям

suppose предпола́гам, (да)
  предполо́жа

sure си́гурен

surprise изнена́да

sweet бонбо́н; (adj) сла́дък,
  мил

swim плу́вам

table ма́са

take взи́мам, (да) взе́ма; ~
  part уча́ствам; ~ pictures
  пра́вя сни́мки

take away (nn) (храна́) за
  вкъ́щи

talk гово́ря

tall висо́к

taxi такси́

tea чай

teacher учи́тел

telephone телефо́н; mobile ~
  моби́лен телефо́н, джи́есе́м

television телеви́зор

tell *ка́звам, (да) ка́жа*
temperature *температу́ра*
terrific *стра́шен*
text (message) *е́семе́с*
than *от, отко́лкото*
thank *благодаря́;* ~ you
  благодаря́, мерси́
that *това́; онова́; че*
theatre *теа́тър*
their(s) *те́хен*
then *тога́ва*
there *там;* ~ is/are *и́ма;* ~ isn't/
  aren't *ня́ма*
these *те́зи*
they *те*
thin *тъ́нък, слаб*
think *ми́сля*
this *това́*
throat *гъ́рло*
through *през*
ticket *биле́т;* ~ -office *ка́са*
till *ка́са*
time *вре́ме;* in ~ *навре́ме;*
  two ~s *два пъ́ти*
timetable *разписа́ние*
tired *уморе́н*
to *до, към;* in order ~ *за да*
today *днес*
together *за́едно*
toilet *тоале́тна*
tomato *дома́т*
tomorrow *у́тре*
tongue *ези́к*
too *съ́що, и; прекале́но*
tooth *зъб*
touch *пи́пам, (да) пи́пна*
tourist *тури́ст*
toward(s) *към*

town *град*
tram *трамва́й*
translate *преве́ждам, (да)*
  преведа́
translator *преводач*
travel *пъту́вам*
tree *дърво́*
trip *екску́рзня*
trolleybus *троле́й*
trouble *неприя́тност*
trousers *панталон*
true, it's ~ *вя́рно (е)*
trunk (car) *бага́жник*
try *опи́твам, (да) опи́там*
tulip *лале́*
Turk *ту́рчин*
Turkey *Ту́рция*
Turkish *ту́рски*
turn *зави́вам, (да) завия́*

umbrella *чадъ́р*
under *под*
underground *метро́*
understand *разби́рам, (да)*
  разбера́
unfortunately *за съжале́ние*
university *университе́т*
unpleasant *неприя́тен*
until *до, докато́;* ~ now *досега́*
up-to-date *моде́рен*
useful *поле́зен*
usually *обикнове́но*

vacation *почи́вка*
vase *ва́за*
vegetable *зеленчу́к*
vegetarian *вегетариа́нец;*
  вегетариа́нски

very   мно́го, тврьде, до́ста
village   село́
visit (stay)   престо́й
voicemail   гла́сова по́ща

wait   ча́кам
waiter   сервитьо́р
Wales   Уе́лс
walk   разхо́дка; вървя́, хо́дя
wall   стена́
want   и́скам
war   война́
warm   то́пъл
wash   ми́я (се), (да) (се) изми́я
washroom   тоале́тна
watch   часо́вник
watch out!   внима́ние!
water   вода́; mineral ~ минера́лна вода́
way   пъ́т
we   ни́е
weak   слаб, лек
wear   но́ся
weather   вре́ме
wedding   сва́тба
week   се́дмица
welcome!   добре́ дошъ́л! запова́дай(те)!
(you're) welcome   ня́ма защо́
well   добре́
Welsh   уе́лсец; уе́лски
west   за́пад; in/to the ~ на за́пад
what   какво́, какво́то; ~ kind of какъ́в
when   кога́; кога́то

where   къде́; къде́то; ~ from отку́де́
whether   дали́
which   кой; ко́йто
while   докато́
white   бял
who   кой; ко́йто
whole   цял
why   защо́
wife   жена́, съпру́га
wind   вя́тър
window   прозо́рец
wine   ви́но
winter   зи́ма
wish   жела́ние; жела́я; пожела́вам, (да) пожела́я
(best) wishes   мно́го по́здрави
with   с/със
without   без
woman   жена́
wonderful   чуде́сен
word   ду́ма
work   ра́бота; рабо́тя
world   свят
worry   гри́жа; безпокоя́ се
write   пи́ша, (да) напи́ша

year   годи́на
yellow   жълт
yes   да
yesterday   вче́ра
yet   о́ще; все пак
yoghurt   ки́село мля́ко
you   ти; ви́е
young   млад
your(s)   твой; ваш

zero   ну́ла

Index to grammar and usage

Although the grammatical explanations in this course are based on a pragmatic, need-to-know basis and we try to avoid grammatical jargon, grammatical categories are a very useful aid to learning. We hope, therefore, that this index, arranged according to grammatical features, will be a handy additional aid to finding your way around the book and the Bulgarian language.

The numbers refer you to the units. An asterisk indicates that you will find further material in the Appendix.